CW01391737

About the Author

Dr Joe Kenogbon was born into a large family in Shabomi, a Nigerian costal town, where he spent most of his early life.

Like most children where he grew up, he was expected to take the path of becoming a farmer, fisherman or a timber magnate. Instead of tilling and planting, Joe decided he would rather look after people by becoming a medical doctor. Much of his life is an example of triumphs against all odds. It is a life that is largely impacted by his faith in God on whom he always places his trust.

After graduating from University of Ibadan, Nigeria's premier university and the premier medical school, Dr Kenogbon worked briefly in a number of hospitals in preparation for his specialist surgical training in the United Kingdom. Faced with so many challenges, Dr Kenogbon trusted God to provide His angels. And by God's grace, he attained his dream – becoming a consultant surgeon.

Angels Along My Path provides an inspirational account of his journey from humble beginnings in the tiny Nigerian town where children were not expected to advance beyond a primary education, to the very top of his profession as a celebrated surgical consultant in the UK.

He worked incredibly hard, made sacrifices and endured hardships to realise this life dream, but his story goes beyond his own efforts. Every step of the way, he was guided and supported: obstacles were removed, the right people appeared, he was given everything that he needed, and more than once, his life was saved in the most spectacular way. At times, even he struggled to believe how blessed he has been, but his faith has always remained strong, and this is the message that he would like to share – that you can achieve anything in life with resilience, determination and faith.

Dr Kenogbon now lives with his family in the beautiful Yorkshire countryside. He takes regular walks and enjoys photography and farming.

Angels Along My Path
Autobiography of an African Surgeon

Joe Kenogbon

Angels Along My Path
Autobiography of an African Surgeon

Olympia Publishers
London

www.olympiapublishers.com
OLYMPIA PAPERBACK EDITION

Copyright © Joe Kenogbon 2021

The right of Joe Kenogbon to be identified as author of
this work has been asserted in accordance with sections 77 and 78 of the
Copyright, Designs and Patents Act 1988.

All Rights Reserved

No reproduction, copy or transmission of this publication
may be made without written permission.
No paragraph of this publication may be reproduced,
copied or transmitted save with the written permission of the publisher, or in
accordance with the provisions
of the Copyright Act 1956 (as amended).

Any person who commits any unauthorised act in relation to
this publication may be liable to criminal
prosecution and civil claims for damage.

A CIP catalogue record for this title is
available from the British Library.

ISBN: 978-1-78830-975-2

The events portrayed in this book are to the best of the author's memory. While
all the stories are true, some names and identifying details have been changed
to protect the privacy of the people involved.

First Published in 2021

Olympia Publishers
Tallis House
2 Tallis Street
London
EC4Y 0AB

Printed in Great Britain

Dedication

To my parents, the first angels that God provided. They did everything they could to ensure that their beloved son didn't leave his talent on the shelf. God had reassured them to do their best, and he would provide other angels to take the baton as I continued on destiny's journey.

To my father, from whom I learnt about perseverance and determination. He taught me humility, respect for other people's values and to be a good team player. From my early life, my father taught me to face challenges with resilience and perseverance. I learnt from my father wisdom and courage, and to recognise the value of friendship.

To my mother, for benevolence and belief in the wonderful power of God. I grew up to put my trust in the supreme power of the Lord. My mother taught me to stay away from bad companies and evil deeds; to believe in myself and do everything to the best of my ability. She taught me to be honest and truthful, to speak out my mind and stand up to bullies.

To my uncle, for recognising my talent and encouraging me to be among the best. He taught me to use every mistake or failure as a learning experience. Every bad can be turned into good and every good can be made better.

To my grandmother, who taught me to have a good heart and to be caring and generous. At an early age, I learnt to be brave and to not let fear rob me of life's opportunities.

To my beautiful wife, whom God has provided me by His special grace. She has been my rock throughout my struggles. I am lucky to have such a wonderful wife.

To my children, the wonderful gifts from God. I couldn't have had a better life than the life that I have spent with them. Their smiles have sustained me in times of despair, and their prayers and my wife's, no doubt, touched God's heart.

To all the teachers of knowledge; to all my good friends who have shown up at various stages of my life; and to all those special angels that have appeared at my times of need and whom God has used to fulfil His plans for my life.

PREFACE

This has always been my ambition: that someday, before departing this world, I would put pen and paper together to share my life experiences with my fellow human beings. Life is like any road, with bends and curves. Sometimes the road is bumpy. Other times, it is muddy and with puddles along the way. It has been a long journey. I have rounded crooked bends and climbed up steep mountains. I have also fallen into valleys, of which I still wonder how I clawed my way out. My path, to me, was uncharted, and with no one to show me the way, no one to show me the short course, my voyage was at the mercy of the wind, forcing me to drift into a destination that I was not destined for.

As I travelled the winding decades in my mind, the wonderful gift of the formidable organ called the brain, that nature has provided every one of us, never ceased to amaze me. Firstly, I tried to see how far my brain could travel to unlock those experiences that I had tucked into various nooks and corners of my mind. As my brain travelled, there were memories I wished I didn't remember. But my brain kept them in the memory library with bookmarks in certain pages and lines and paragraphs bearing strong highlights. They say that time heals. Of course, it does. Forgiving the people who have hurt me has healed my wounds. But time has not removed the scars. Nothing can remove scars. The scars are a reminder of the hurts in the past. Even when you ignore the scars, the brain brings those memories up at your most vulnerable times – when you are asleep. They manifest as dreams that bring tears to your eyes when you wake up.

But my brain also reminds me of breakthroughs in my life: wonderful achievements, narrow escapes, some of which are against all odds. Statistically, I was not expected to reach school age, given that one in three newborns in my place at the time of my birth died before their first birthday. I wasn't expected to go to school, let alone to one of the best universities to study medicine. The tiny village where I was born and grew up wasn't even on major maps at the time of my birth. I wouldn't be expected to reach the top of the professional ladder, let alone become a meritorious consultant surgeon.

Mine has been a long and difficult journey. I have been beaten numerous times. I have been pushed into valleys that seemed too deep for me to re-emerge. I have been left in the wilderness with no definitive path to escape. There have been times when I felt like I had had enough. But just at that moment when I felt hopeless, someone would come my way. Whilst I am eternally grateful to these people, I haven't used their real names in this book. Some of them have passed away, and I remember them with good memories, fondness and gratitude. Some of those who are still alive have preferred to remain anonymous. So, for confidentiality reasons, I have given them fictitious names. I hope they will know that I appreciate the contributions that they have made towards making me what I am today.

I do not believe in luck. But I believe in one true God. What people call luck is what I call miracles – little ones as well as big ones. His divine intervention brings miracles. And there have been many miracles in my life. I have shared many of these with my close friends and family. But the rest remains in my heart for my personal reflection and gratitude to God.

The journey has not finished. I don't know how many pieces are waiting in God's good hands to be put in their places to complete the plans that He has made for my life. I don't know how many more bends lie ahead. And I don't know how many angels are waiting to deliver their endowed errands. I pray that God will give me the grace to recognise them and appreciate His goodness through these angels. Good people continue to show up on my life path. I guess when my life journey has ended, it will be someone else who will be writing about me. Until then, I invite you to come with me as I take you through my incredible journey.

Chapter One
THE HUMBLE BEGINNINGS

Besides God, there is no glory above coming from humble beginnings,
from sleeping under a porous grass thatched mud hut to rising above
and beyond tabernacles of greatness.
Thabo Katlholo, The Mud Hut I Grew Up In

The Village Boy

When my mother heard the cry of a baby that she had just given birth to
and they told her, "It's a baby boy," she must have felt on top of the
world. Of course, she was happy that she had had two daughters before
me, but her first child was a boy, and he had died in infancy. She then
had two daughters, one after the other. In those days in Shabomi, a tiny
Nigerian costal village, male babies were more valued and every mother
prayed to bear sons. That was what gave them pride as a wife. Like many
babies born in those days, the birth took place at home and the delivery
was by a native midwife. This was usually an older, more experienced
mother in the family. Sometimes she was a female herbalist, unrelated to
the woman in labour. There was no suction machine. To clear fluid from
a baby's airways, the midwife would seal the baby's nose with her mouth.
She would suck the fluid with her mouth and spit it out. There were no
trained midwives, and no gynaecologists to provide antenatal care.
Women had no obstetric facilities, such as forceps deliveries and
Caesarean sections for complicated labour. And there were no health
visitors to provide postnatal care for both mother and baby. The nearest
hospital was more than two hours away, and you would be lucky to find
transportation. There was no ambulance service. At best, you would go
on a motorbike or bicycle. Otherwise, you would have to trek. Imagine a
woman in labour in my place! Those were the condition that I was born
into.

The cock would have crowed the second time. My father's

pendulum clock would have struck five times, confirming the time to be five o'clock on this Eke Market Monday morning. At that time, people would have risen to fetch water. The ringing sounds of their empty buckets, and their chats and laughter as they trekked to the river, would have helped to announce the beginning of a new day. Family and neighbours would have gathered, with both my grandmothers smiling with pride, to welcome a new baby to the family. The market women would have stopped over to wish my mother well. And within minutes, our house would have been full of family members and friends, all to welcome me, as I cried to announce my arrival and opened my eyes to the wonders of life.

Daddy wasn't present at my birth. I have no doubt in my mind that he would have loved to support my mother, whom he loved so much, but, like most men in Shabomi, he was hundreds of miles away in the jungle, logging trees under the most difficult circumstances, to provide a living for his family. The only means of communication with Daddy was through someone who would run the errands. This person would paddle a canoe in the treacherous tributaries of the Atlantic Ocean just to take or deliver messages, a journey of three days of continuous paddling.

In Shabomi, as is customary among the Yorubas, the naming ceremony is symbolic in the life of a baby. It takes place eight days after the birth. Until a baby undergoes this ceremony, he or she has no name. He or she is simply called 'Boy,' 'Titi' or 'Baby.' The baby's mother remains indoors to be cared for by the family members. She is not allowed to cook or do any house cleaning. Even tasks such as washing and cleaning the baby are undertaken by her relatives. The native midwife attends once daily to massage the mother's abdomen. This helps to relieve the afterbirth pains. It also helps to reduce the amount of blood loss. On the eighth day, the new mother is taken to the river where she has a good wash, ready for the ceremony. It is essentially a family affair but widely a community event. People rally around to support one another in times of joy, just as they do in times of sadness, so when you plan an event like this, you have to make allowances for uninvited guests. You have to make provision for just anyone and everyone.

During the ceremony, there is a bowl of palm oil, which signifies peace, a bowl of water, which signifies good health, a bowl of kola nuts, which signifies victory in life, and a bowl of bitter kola, signifying long life. Also present are salt, signifying happiness, and honey, signifying happiness and prosperity. The family elder puts a little bit of the ingredients on the baby's lips as he prays, wishing him a good and long life, happiness, good fortune and prosperity. He declares the name by which the baby will be called and puts a coin in the bowl of water. Each family adult throws a coin in the bowl of water as he announces the name he gives the baby. After that, it is a time for celebration, with plenty to eat and drink. From then on, the mother can go out with her baby whenever she likes, and she gradually gets back into her daily routine as she feels strong enough to do so.

My naming ceremony had to take place on the eighth day, as was customary, so my father was absent. But his uncle, whom we referred to as Baba Agba, meaning 'Senior Dad', presided over the ceremony. Baba Agba gave me the name Joseph, in memory of my late grandfather, whom they believed had reincarnated as me, as I was conceived shortly after his death. Although Dad later brought his own chosen name, it only became my second name, as the name that his uncle had given me was accepted by everyone and superseded his.

My father arrived more than two weeks after my birth. He carried the bouncing baby with a head fully covered with hair. As I yawned, wriggling in his tender hands, I sprayed his chest with warm urine. He smiled with pride that his wife had given him a son. Then, stroking his wife on her forehead, he said, "Well done!" And he really meant it. They slaughtered a goat and celebrated the beginning of my life, praying to God to keep me safe, prosper me and send His angels to watch over me in the journey that I had just begun. He was determined to give me a good life, to teach me to become a man and a good person. He would make every sacrifice to give me the best, and he would try at all times to protect me.

We didn't have much money, but we never starved. My paternal grandmother lived in the same house. My maternal grandmother was only a stone's throw from our house. We had the liberty to eat in grandmother's house. We were often overfed, with cousins and uncle's wives offering food. But, of course, my mother ensured that we all had meals together. We had no dining room or dining table, and no cutlery.

We ate with our bare hands. During dinner, we all sat down in groups of six around the bowl of food according to our ages. We ate as if the food wouldn't be enough, yet we always had leftovers. Mother always made sure that we had more than enough to eat.

I had one pair of sandals that I wore only to church on Sundays and during harvest, Christmas and New Year. After each use, I cleaned them and put them away in their original box. I also had a pair of slippers made from an old tyre that I wore daily.

Growing up in a polygamous family meant that we had to be looked after by other mothers, just like our mother had to care for other women's children. It was a normal practice with no formality to it. My father had two wives. We all lived together with my uncles' wives and my cousins. As the senior wife, my mother had her own apartment, a tiny room with an equally small sitting room, behind the main building. Mama had her own bed, but my sisters would join her. My stepmother, my father's second wife, accompanied him in his station far from home, leaving my half siblings for Mama to look after. In addition to my siblings, we had a number of cousins living with us. We had a wooden double bed in the living room. My older sisters slept on this when they weren't with Mama or when they didn't sleep over at Grandma's or our aunt's. The rest of us slept on a mat spread on the floor of the sitting room. Although we arranged ourselves orderly when we slept, the scene looked chaotic in the morning, with a tangle of heads and feet in places they were not intended. If you were unfortunate enough to lie next to a bedwetter, you would find yourself wet in the morning and would have to try hard to convince Mama that it wasn't you that had wet the bed.

Like most boys, I didn't have many clothes, but my parents didn't have to buy many clothes. My uncles passed down clothes to me – oversized white vests with multiple holes that had turned brown, in which I ran about with other bare-footed boys and girls.

It wasn't hard to find something to eat. God blessed our small community with a river teaming with fish. I didn't have to have any special training to fish. All you needed was to find bait, a hook and you were ready to fish. I knew exactly where to find the bait. Just lift any stone or wood that had been left outside, and you would find earthworms. Another ready source of worms was the palm oil makers' camp. After extracting the oil, they would throw the waste materials into the swamp. The dumps became habitats for baiting worms. They usually deposited the waste close to the stream.

One day, when I was about eight years old, I went with my friends to one of the camps to pick worms. We collected a full calabash of worms. I was covered with mud up to my thighs, so I decided to have a wash in the stream. As you would expect, my friends joined in.

"You boys, better be careful. There are alligators in the stream," one of the palm oil workers warned.

It was then I noticed that I was only an arm's length from a giant alligator. I couldn't explain why the man decided to warn us at that moment, but I found my energy from nowhere and flew out of the hungry jaws of the monster.

As a young boy growing up in my village, life was so easy that one could live without ambition. My people were farmers and fishermen. The men were predominantly timber magnates. It was every father's wish to raise sons who would take over the trade when he retired. Very few people had post-primary education. Those who managed to go beyond primary school got to modern school, which provided them with the opportunity to progress to teacher training college. But they could teach only in village schools.

We had no television and our only source of information was my father's old Philips radio. We were not allowed to touch the radio. Only my father could switch it on and off, and it was permanently tuned to WNBS (Western Nigeria Broadcasting Service), the station that the seller tuned into when my father bought it.

We also had an old gramophone that we only played when my father was home, which was four times in a year: Christmas and New Year, Easter and Harvest. During those periods, my father would spend several weeks with us before returning to his station. I had the opportunity to be close to my father when he was home. He was a true family man, always doing the best for all of us. With the little that he had, he made sure that we were happy.

Owning a gramophone was a big thing in my village. There were only three homes that had one. During Christmas and New Year, Daddy would buy the latest *Juju* records. Boys and girls, and even adults, used to gather in our house to dance to the latest IK Dairo, Sunny Ade and Ebenezer Obe. And we often had dancing competitions. I was a great dancer, and I won the competitions a number of times, with the prize of a shilling or sometimes a piece of meat or fish, a lolly or a *goody-goody*.

We didn't have robust toys, only wooden toys and cars. On one of the Christmases, Daddy bought a toy called Alapansapa. This toy, made from cardboard, was a caricature of a clown. When you pulled on the string, the toy would dance, moving all the limbs. My younger brother, Nuga, was fond of this toy. He would never leave it alone. Although, one Saturday morning, his life was saved by doing just that.

We had just woken up and hadn't even packed away our mat. Hung on the wall just below the window, Alapansapa was within reach of my toddler brother. He went straight for it, pulled on the string and looked back, expecting us to laugh as the toy danced. The more we laughed, the more he pulled on the string.

"This child will not let Alapansapa rest. And you are all laughing there when you have not done your morning duties," Mama shouted from her room.

Normally, you would have to physically carry Nuga away from there or command him several times, or even threaten him before he would stop doing something or being silly. But on that day, he replied, "Yes, Ma," and moved away to join the rest of us on my sisters' bed, just as I was about to go and pull him out of the place. He put one foot on the bed, all the while looking back at Alapansapa. And as he lifted his other foot from the floor, the wall on which Alapansapa was hanging collapsed. All we could do was look on the debris that scattered all over our mat and the dust that engulfed the room. Had my brother refused to move away, like he would normally do, I would have tried to force him out of the place. And the wall would have crushed us both.

I was very close to my grandparents, particularly my maternal grandmother. She used to refer to me as 'Ologun Joe,' meaning 'Brave Joe'. Grandma was the epitome of love. Love radiated through and around her. As a princess, she lived in one of the apartments in the old Kalashuwe Palace. My great grandfather, the powerful Kalashuwe of Apoiland, ruled the riverine area for decades. The large palace overlooked the sandy beach. At night, all the children would sit beside my grandmother as she told us folk tales. She once told us the story of a greedy boy. His mother had warned him not to take another person's things, and not to eat what his mother had not approved of. One day, the boy found an egg at one corner of their house. As no one was watching, he took the egg and ran into the kitchen. He hid behind the door and ate it all. At night, his stomach started to churn and rumble. His stomach started to ache, and it was getting bigger. His mother asked him what was wrong with him, but he said nothing. Then he felt something moving inside him. He felt like he needed to open his bowels. As he bent down in the toilet, a large snake crawled out of his back passage. That was when he realised that the egg he had eaten was a snake's egg. "This story teaches us not to steal, even when no one is watching you," grandmother concluded.

My grandmother was a very kind and generous person. If you visited her, you would be guaranteed a good meal, and you would also have takeaways. Her sister, with slight learning disability, whom she had looked after since childhood, lived with her.

Grandma never locked her door. When I asked her why she always left it open, she replied that her door was open to everyone. That was true. My grandmother drew no line between people. She loved everyone the same. Anyone could walk into her house and she would feed him or her. She even fed animals. Neighbours' chickens and goats would enter her yard, and she would feed them like hers. I learnt from my grandmother the principle of giving and sharing. Even when she had very little, she would share it out. She never held anything to herself.

"Your heart is at peace when you give," she used to say. "The closet of a giver will never be empty."

Grandmother believed in the supernatural. "If you are kind to people, God will be kind to you," she often said. "Give and you will be given. It is the secret magic in living. The more you give, the more you receive." I struggled with this philosophy for most of my early life. How could you give part of or all you have and receive more? I wondered. It just didn't make any sense to me. I tried reluctantly to share my piece of yam or corn with anyone, but I only did it if an adult was watching.

One day, one of my uncles had just arrived from Lagos. He was one of my favourite uncles. He always brought lots of gifts whenever he visited. I was the first child to receive my gift of bread. We treasured city bread, especially from Lagos. I knew I had to show it to Mama before eating it. That was the rule. You must show anything you received from people to Mama before eating it. It didn't matter whether the person was known to the family. And, of course, we must first thank the person. Unfortunately, my uncle hadn't expected that my friends would be there, so he hadn't brought any bread for them. I broke my bread into four unequal parts, with me taking the smallest share. Wasting no time, we ate and were soon out playing football and hunting birds.

When I returned home, my uncle called me. I thought I was in trouble. But the smiles on his face were reassuring.

"Joe," he called. "You have been a good boy."

I had totally forgotten about sharing my bread with my friends.

"I kept this for you," he said, pointing to a bowl of rice on the table.

"Wow!" I exclaimed, as I took off the lid, revealing two large pieces of fish.

"You impressed me by sharing your bread with your friends," he said. "And I am sharing mine with you."

It didn't sink in at first. All I wanted to do was devour it quickly. It was after I had finished that I reflected on this principle of giving that my grandmother had taught me: "Give and you shall receive."

Mummy often left us on our own on market days, and sometimes for several days, when she took goods to Lagos for sale. She always took farm produce in canoes to sell to the dwellers in islands further from the hinterland. So my eldest sister, Aunty Ileola, had to mature quickly. Although we had adults in our house and in the neighbourhood, Aunty Ileola was primarily responsible for preparing our meals, ensuring that we were clean and that we were well-behaved. But one Saturday, it was us who would have to look after her, with near-fatal consequences.

Left on our own, all eyes turned to Aunty Ileola as she started to cough. It soon became clear that she had a tilapia bone stuck in her throat. She coughed and almost coughed up her lungs, and we flew around her, trying all the tricks that we had learnt from the adults. My sister drank several cups of water and swallowed an egg-size hard bolus of *Eba*, the cassava pudding, but she couldn't dislodge the fish bone. Nothing we tried helped, and we knew that my sister was in great trouble. Yet we chose not to call the adults, fearing that they would blame her for being too greedy. She should have known that fish had bones or that a girl of her age should be sensible enough to pick out the bones.

I had heard that if you have a bone stuck in your throat, you should carry a heavy stone on your head to make it go. So we got the stone that we used for grinding pepper, and all of us carried it and placed it on my sister's head. Her head moved forward and backward like the top of a coconut tree in a whirlwind, as she tried to steady her neck. In spite of almost breaking her neck carrying the heavy stone, the bone remained stuck.

We tried everything that we could think of. Then my sister started to cough up blood. She could no longer swallow her saliva. We knew that her condition was serious, so we knelt down, with our eyes closed, and prayed from our hearts to God to take away the bone. She started to sweat and looked desperate. Then a thought came to me. I wondered if the bone was visible, and since I had a small hand, I could try to pick it or dislodge it. My sister opened her mouth wide without questioning my suggestion. The bone was large enough to be visible sitting to the left of her throat. My sister opened her mouth as wide as possible, but when I tried to remove the bone with my fingers, I ended up making her wretch and vomit. I contemplated using a stick. "What about that thing Mama uses to cut cloth?" I couldn't believe this, coming from my brother. Deji was the youngest, but in my sister's condition, we welcomed any suggestion, anything that would make her better.

Deji knew exactly where the scissors were. He had played with them the previous night, when sister had told him to put them away. He toddled away, and within seconds, he was back with them. With my sister's mouth wide open, and tears rolling down her cheeks, I thrust the scissors into her throat. And with a determined effort, I opened the blades, careful not to catch any tissue within them. The bone was clearly visible, looking like a vicious hook, as it stuck to the left of my sister's throat. After ensuring that it was fully between the scissors' blades, I carefully closed the blades round it, dislodged and retrieved it. A stream of heavily blood-stained saliva followed. It soon stopped when my sister rinsed her mouth. She heaved a sigh of relief, as tears of joy streamed down her cheeks. We all felt relieved, but none of us could continue with our meal. As smiles of relief and joy returned to my sister's face, I could not but remember my experience in the hospital when the doctor operated on my infected hand. I felt like I, too, had performed an operation to remove a fish bone from my sister's throat. This experience helped to strengthen my ambition to become a doctor.

The saying that it takes a community to raise a child is truer for a child brought up in Shabomi. As a closely knitted community, every adult watches over every child, even when not related by blood. This reciprocal protection keeps the children safe. An adult could chastise and discipline you if you were naughty, and he would only simply inform your parents with such statements as, "I caught him throwing stones at someone's goat. I have disciplined him. Please don't punish him." This would be enough for most parents, but it wasn't good enough for my parents. As far as they were concerned, there was no room for misbehaviour. You would receive further punishment to teach you a lesson. But this didn't mean that we lacked freedom. My parents never denied us the opportunity to enjoy our childhood. All that they tried to inculcate in us were the principles of integrity, responsibility, honesty and respect for law and order.

One sunny afternoon, my cousin came to play with me. He had just made a rat trap. Hunting rats was fun. We would set the traps, made from empty tins, and place them strategically on the burrows in the forest. We baited the rat with ripe palm fruits. When the rat entered the tin to eat the fruit, it would be trapped. We would take it home trapped in the tin. We would roast the rat and eat it with gari soaked in water. We also hunted squirrels, birds and bats. We used another type of trap. This was made with metal by the local welder, and we bought it from the market. The vicious trap was designed for larger animals, such as grasscutters, rabbits, porcupines and squirrels.

We set out to go into the forest to lay the traps. Normally, we would sneak out through the back of the house. On that day, we decided to go through the main house, thinking that the adults had all gone out, and there would be no one to stop us. As we stepped into the corridor, a cobra coiled up in the middle of the room. I don't know what got into our heads, but my cousin suggested that we catch it alive. Oh, I loved the challenge. Exciting, I thought. So my cousin took the back door to reach the front entrance to the corridor. We chased the snake forwards and backwards, laughing whenever the snake turned around. Then it stopped in the middle, seemingly exhausted. And then we realised that we were not alone.

"Who are the children there? You won't let me rest this afternoon." My aunt's alarm forced us to stop. But before we could escape, she was standing behind my cousin. "Snake!" she screamed. "Oh, my God!"

Two men came out from the opposite house and struck the tired snake to death. At first, my aunt was only after our safety and that the snake did not escape. However, knowing that she was a disciplinarian, I had no doubt that she would not let the matter rest. She had always warned against doing silly things. How could I justify wanting to catch a poisonous snake? I tiptoed to take a position behind her, but before I could escape, she grabbed me by my wrist and twisted my ear so much that I thought she had pulled it off. Throughout that day and the following days, I had expected her to tell my mother about this incident, but she never did, or if she did, she must have begged my mother not to punish me. That week, I made sure that I was in my best behaviour to avoid doing something to remind my aunt or my mother of my foolishness, but my ear was sore for nearly a week. That alone had taught me a good lesson.

As a coastal dweller, we had the luxury of a clean river with a sandy beach. Children and adults swam day and night in a safe environment. We didn't have to be taught how to swim. It was just natural. You see people swimming, you join them, and someday you see yourself swimming too. It was great fun competing with one another to swim across the river and back to the shore, but it was not without danger.

One day, my younger cousin, Tola, joined me in one of those competitions. Though I was older, I was only a little bigger than him. I mounted him on my back and started to swim across the river. We were right in the middle of the river and the tide began to rise. The rising tide frightened my cousin, and he tightened his grip on my shoulders. I was meant to be a support for him to do his own swimming, but I now became an object for him to hold onto in desperation. I tried to free myself from his grip, but he gripped my neck instead. I gulped gallons of water. We were both drowning and drifting away in the tide. Thankfully, an adult swimmer spotted us. He shouted for help as he jumped into the water and swam with all his strength. He grasped Tola and freed me from his grip. I was exhausted, but with my cousin freed, I was able to swim back to the shore.

The village had two main divisions. The people closer to the beach were referred to as the 'Odobutes', whilst those living closer to the hinterland were called the 'Okeles'. My mother was from Odobute. Although my father belonged to the Gbabijo clan of the Okele division, we lived among the Odobute families. Being related to two major families in Shabomi gave me a great advantage. But it also caused my parents a lot of stress, as it was often hard for them to find me. I could be with Okele or Odobute boys, which was a good way for me to escape from running errands. Since my meals were guaranteed in my cousins' houses, I didn't have to be home to eat. Of course, I knew I would be in trouble with Mama for not doing what I was supposed to do. One of those situations arose one day that I will never forget. Mother had just come back from the market. She was tired, but still had to prepare the meal for the family. She gave me six pence to go and buy tinned tomato from the grocery.

"I've spat on the floor. My sputum must not dry up before you come back," she warned. This was her way of telling me to be quick.

"Yes, Mum," I responded, as I flew out of the house.

No sooner had I left my mum than I got to our football playing ground. It was an open, unused ground with no grass but level with red soil. We had planned to play a match between Okele and Odobute. That was one of the reasons I wanted to do all my errands in time so I could join my friends.

It was always a problem for me to choose which side to play for, since I belonged to both communities, but it was more of a problem for my friends. I was a good scorer and so each side wanted me to play for them. Sometimes they made me choose my preferred side. Other times, it was by ballot. In that case, I would put a pebble or a palm nut in my fist and then ask them to identify which hand it was in. Whichever side got it right would have me for that match.

As I approached my friends, they all streamed to me. And as it so happened, I was to play for Okele that day. Odobute had beaten them in the previous three matches. My Okele cousins had reminded me that my father was from Okele. So if I was the true son of my father, I shouldn't let Odobute beat them again. I told them that I was on an errand for my mother and would join them as soon as possible, but my friends wouldn't accept that. Trusting that I would score within minutes, I kept my mother's six pence under my slippers and hid it behind the goalpost. As expected, I scored within minutes, but soon afterwards, my cousin, Martin from Odobute, scored. Martin was the smallest among us, though the oldest. He was a great dribbler and a fantastic scorer. Now we were one all. And it became a personal challenge. I totally forgot that I was running an errand for my mother.

The match carried on and ended four-three in favour of the Okele team. I couldn't believe I had spent over half an hour playing, and flew to the grocery store. The woman knew exactly what had happened. Unknown to me, my mother had sent one of my cousins to the grocery store. She had sensed that I must be playing football for me not to return sooner. Normally, it would take me less than ten minutes. My cousin had confirmed to my mother that she saw me playing football. When I got to the grocery woman, she acted as if she didn't know that I had been playing football. She smiled and said, "Send my regards to your mother," as she handed me the tomato tin.

My mother had finished cooking when I got home. As she dished out our meal, she showed no inkling that she knew I had been playing football, even though I was covered with red soil. I was the first person to sit behind the pounded yam that looked like a mountain. My siblings and cousins taunted me that I was eating like a horse, despite the fact that I didn't take part in its preparation. I ignored their taunts and ate as if there would be no food another day.

The last person to finish his or her meal would normally wash the plates. I wasn't prepared to wash the plates, so I finished before the rest of them. I didn't even care to drink water. In a flash, I was out of the house, playing with my friends.

In my childhood, it always felt like there were not enough hours in a day for me to do all that I liked to do. I dreamed about so many things. All the events of the day that had crept into my subconscious revealed themselves in the dreamland. Some of them caused me to smile. Some brought tears into my eyes. But some caused my heart to beat fast. That was what happened to me on that day. After her usual bedside stories, mother prayed for us, and within minutes, I was snoring away in my own world. I had just finished a football match. My friends and I gathered around, chatting and laughing. I heard my mother calling me, so I decided to leave my friends. As I turned around to pick up my slippers, a gorilla appeared. The monster was about to grab me by the neck when I woke up, sweating and panting, with my heart racing. My mother raced out of her room. I told her about the gorilla, and she reassured me that it was just a nightmare, but I couldn't go back to sleep. I lay down, still trembling, with my eyes wide open, despite my mother's reassurance. Soon, the cock crowed. We had to get up before the second cockcrow. My siblings and cousins got up one by one, and it was the beginning of another day. We had our morning prayer. After that, we set out to go about our morning duties.

"Joseph!" Mother called from her room. "Come and have this money for being a good boy." I should have wondered why mother wanted to reward me. How could I have been a good boy after my bad behaviour the previous day? But judged by her demeanour, I thought that maybe I had done something good that I hadn't realised. Mother had a habit of rewarding us whenever we did well.

I entered her room, smiling. Mother stretched out her hand, and as I stretched out mine to receive the gift, she grabbed me by the wrist and bolted the door behind me.

"Joseph!" she shouted. "I sent you on an errand yesterday, but you sent yourself on a different errand."

In retrospect, I should have anticipated that, because mother only called me Joseph when I was in trouble. Normally, she called me Joe. Everyone did. People rarely called me Joseph. Unknown to me, Mother had hidden a cane in the leaf of her wrapper. She landed this on me as she shouted: "I have warned you several times. You are too playful. You are moving with irresponsible boys." Mother had carefully planned and orchestrated her strategy. She knew, of course, that if she had tried to deal with my naughtiness in the afternoon I would have flown into refuge in my grandma's house. And, of course, Grandma would have come to my rescue, preventing her from disciplining me the way she had wanted.

Moreover, she could overreact in the heat of her anger. This is something that I have learnt from my mother: to take a break and not react in the heat of your anger, to take measured and appropriate action.

My grandmother rushed in from her room and pleaded to her. I was grounded the whole day. That was the last time, as far as I could remember, that mother caned me. But that was a good lesson. Although I still played football and did other things with my friends, I made sure that I did everything that I needed to do first. Mother inculcated in me the principle of work before pleasure. I learnt to prioritise things and to give my best shot to whatever I did.

My mother was a tough woman. She had to be in a male-dominant culture. Women's voices were not heard. Moreover, with over twenty children, including ten of her own, under her care, she needed to be tough. Women would spend time and energy to prepare the meals. They would break the firewood, set the fire and blow hard until it was ready for cooking. The only thing that men did was slaughter the animal. Then they would retract into leisure whilst the women did the cooking. The women would also pound the yam. I didn't appreciate how tedious it was to pound yam until I did it. Even after going through the pain, the women would obediently dish out the best part of the meal and kneel down to serve the men. They wouldn't eat until the men had finished. I struggled with this throughout my childhood, and I promised myself that if God ever gave me a daughter, she would have an equal voice as my son. No one deserves to be second-rated. Everyone's opinion matters. And we are all equal before God.

Mummy was strict, making sure that we behaved properly – she was a lioness protecting her cubs, and she had the eyes of a hawk watching over us – but she never overprotected us. She made sure that we understood that she expected us to behave ourselves wherever we went. She also encouraged us to stand up to bullies that came across our path.

One day, one of my cousins, who had bullied me, confronted me and wanted me to fight. Normally, I wouldn't engage in a fight. I knew I would get into trouble with Mummy if I fought outside, but I had had enough of my cousin's taunts, and he just wouldn't leave me alone. He hit me on the head with a stick, and I warned him that I would fight back if he continued. But, because he was bigger than me, he thought he could carry on taunting me. I kept going, but he followed me and hit me harder. He didn't expect what came next, though, as I powered a punch into his face, pushed him over and hit him hard with the stick, thoroughly beating him.

That evening, he came with his mum, my aunt, to see my mum. His mum complained that I had hurt her son. But my mum told her that he was the first person to hit me, and I had the right to hit back. Both mothers agreed to settle the problem, but from that day, I earned respect from my cousin, and we became great friends afterwards. I learnt a very important lesson from this unforgettable experience: Sometimes you've got to stand up to bullies that come across your path for you to have your respect and freedom.

In our family, we would pray for every occasion. We prayed before eating, thanking God for providing the food, to make the food go to the right place in our body, to have our daily meals and to provide for people who had nothing to eat. We prayed before going to bed and when we woke up in the morning. During the evening and morning prayers, Mama would first read the bible to us and explain the passages. By the age of four, I had learnt that God created the heaven and earth. I learnt about the Garden of Eden and Adam and Eve. I could recite the Lord's Prayer, and I knew about the Good Samaritan. I always wished I could be like the Good Samaritan. I wanted to lend people a helping hand. I also learnt to forgive people and to trust God to help in time of difficulties.

As I grew older, my siblings and I took the bible readings in turn. We always woke up by five o'clock in the morning and started the day with an hour of morning devotion before going about our morning duties. Mama also taught us to take our church worships seriously. We had to go to church in clean clothes and not be late. She encouraged us to always do the best for the Lord and to give the best to Him. Even the money we gave for the offering had to be clean and the notes unrumpled. As she used to say to us, "Cleanliness is next to godliness."

Daddy was a keen hunter and a great fisherman. I often accompanied him to hunt, and I learnt a great deal from him. We used to wake up several times at night to check fish nets and hooks. Fishing for shark was exciting. During the fishing trips, we often came in contact with alligators. One day, we went hunting in the middle of the night. I was on the back seat of the canoe. We paddled slowly and gently in the stillness of the night. We had to be careful not to disturb the fish and make sure that we had a good catch. I looked to my left and saw two glowing lights. I didn't know what to make of them. They were like torchlights shooting out from the edge of the river. I didn't want to cause a disturbance. I thought I would check it with my paddle to see whether somebody had left their torchlights. Just then, my father looked in my direction and whispered to me not to do that. Within seconds, the lights seemed to be going out. Without saying a word, Daddy shot his arrow. A heavy, chaotic ripple appeared on the water. It was then I realised that just a few metres away from me, a giant alligator had charged towards me. What I had thought were torchlights were the rapacious eyes of the alligator scanning for a prey. Father fired more arrows, and it wriggled in agony. Then it settled as its life was extinct. The animal was so large that we couldn't lift it into the boat. We tied it to the back and paddled to the shore. My uncles came and carried the animal to our house. It was a great night, and after slaughtering the animal, Daddy shared it among the members of the family.

Daddy was a hardworking man and he taught me the dignity of labour. He also had a great foresight. He used to say:

"God has a shelf full of talents. Don't leave yours on the shelf. Work hard and persevere. No matter how hard, you can achieve what you want to be. We cannot all be doctors, lawyers, etc. But whatever you choose to become, be the best. If you want to be a driver, be the best, and so on."

When my mother was expecting again and her pregnancy was advanced, she couldn't go to the market. Although we were never short of cassava, yams, plantains and beans, I knew that we would need fish and plenty of it. I knew, of course, that we would be busy entertaining guests when my mother delivered, so I thought of catching as many fish as possible and keeping them alive. I dug out the soil by the side garden of our house to make a fish pond. I then made fish traps with raffia branches. I went in the canoe every morning to check my traps. It was as if my traps attracted all the fish in the world. Each trap (*iyanma* and fish net) teamed with fish of various kinds: tilapia, catfish, mudfish and electric fish. I put the live fish in the pond and fed them with leftover cassava and worms.

One Saturday, I went fishing with both my elder sisters and cousins. It was a beautiful day with good sunshine. The river was calm with only a few engine boats to disturb our fishing. And the water was so clear you could see the fish when they bit your bait. The day ticked all the boxes for perfect fishing. Everyone was in her or his own boat. Whenever I threw my hook into the river, I caught a tilapia within seconds. After each catch, I shouted about the size, and then I started to sing and dance. Soon I exhausted my worms and had to get more. I caught so many fish that I had to be careful not to step on them as they swam freely in my boat.

As I pulled a massive catfish into my boat, I announced with excitement, "I have caught my hundredth fish. It is the biggest catfish in the entire world." Then I started to sing and dance. But I slipped and fell, landing with my outstretched right hand on a catfish. Its vicious fin stabbed my palm, and my whole body felt the pain.

Hearing my scream, my sisters and cousins paddled fast to help me pull out the fin. I shook all over. As I tried to sit down, I missed the seat and sat on the edge of the canoe. With the fin of a live catfish stuck to my palm, the boat capsized and was going down over me with no way of swimming away from underneath it. But before the boat could completely trap me, my sisters and cousins lifted it out so I could free myself. They pulled me into one of the other boats and my sister pulled the fin out of my palm. I shook all over, watching the monster disappear into freedom in the depths of the river, as agonising drops of my blood dispersed on the surface of the river.

We had to terminate our fishing after this, and I was still bleeding when we arrived home. I felt as though the fish was still in my hand, burrowing viciously into the highest centre of my brain. My whole body felt it. Every organ and every cell felt it, even my lacrimal glands. My sister thought it was unlike me to cry like a baby. She wondered if it was a marine snake and not a fish that stuck me, as my hand swelled by the minute. But we all saw the fish. It wasn't a snake.

My mother wasn't at home, so my cousin took a close look.

"I think I can see part of the fin deep in the wound," she announced. She then got a piece of bamboo stick and sharpened it to make a needle. I covered my eyes with my other hand and puffed several times. All my muscles twitched, my teeth clenched, and I almost bit my tongue as my cousin probed into the wound. After wiggling it several times, she chiselled the stump of the fin out of my wound and blood shot directly onto my face. It was as though the main artery of my body was right in the middle of my palm, and the fish fin had struck straight into it.

I had seen people spit into their wound to stop bleeding, so I tried it, but that didn't stop the bleeding. I also knew that you could cover a wound with mud, so I did just that, but it didn't stop the rage of my blood. And then I began to cry again. Not because of pain, which wasn't too bad, but I thought I was going to die. We all started to panic. My sister held her head in her hands, as the bleeding continued.

But we couldn't give up. We plucked several leaves of *Eranpolo*, a widespread shrub in our backyard. This juicy, succulent leaf had strong haemostatic property. My sister squeezed the juicy leaves and allowed their clear juice to drop directly into my wound. Within minutes, the bleeding stopped. We then thought about the way we had seen adults treat punctured wounds. They would heat the tip of a kitchen knife in the fire. When it was red hot, they would take it out and immediately drop palm oil onto it. As the drops bubbled and steamed on the knife, they would drop them onto the wound. And, terrified, this was exactly what we did. As the boiled oil landed on my wound, I saw hell. Every part of me felt it.

I needed to get out of the house after that, not just because I didn't want mother to know about the incident, but to prove that I was strong. My sister was already stressed. I wanted her to know that I was okay and she shouldn't feel guilty that she hadn't looked after me properly. So I took an aspirin, and my sister cut a piece from the old cloth that we used for cleaning and wrapped up my hand. Then, despite the throbbing and swelling, I dashed out of the house and soon found myself teaming up for a football match. I knew that my friends would ask questions, and no team would want to pick a person with a sore hand, so I took off the dressing before joining the boys and tried to ignore the agony. But it didn't go away.

In the middle of the night, it was as though all the pain that I should have felt in the day had waited for darkness to hit. My hand had become three times bigger and felt as if it were being cooked. I turned and tossed on the mat, but couldn't find any comfort. I sat up, placed my swollen hand on my head and started to groan. I knew then that I couldn't keep it from mother anymore. But just before mother asked questions, my sister explained what happened. And thinking that we were brave to handle it on our own, I informed mother of all the details that my sister would have omitted.

"Oh my God!" she exclaimed. "You children will kill me."

We didn't know what to do. My sister's eyes widened and her heart raced as mother stepped closer. I stared at the hand that now looked like a loaf of bread that had been soaked in water all day, as if I hadn't seen it before. Mother ordered me to get ready straightaway to follow her to the native doctor.

Within minutes, we arrived at the Urhobo herbalist's house. The solitary hut built with clay and a thatched roof stood at the outskirts of the village. There was no particular road leading to it. People had to make their ways by partitioning the tall elephant grass that surrounded the hut. As my mother tore her way through the shrubs, all I could think of was a python or tiger coming to attack us. But mother entertained no such fear. I simply followed as I held my swollen hand in my other hand for comfort.

The herbalist beamed a welcoming smile as he let us into the room. Of course, he knew my mother, and he sensed that something must be serious to make us come in the middle of the night. After inspecting my hand, he informed Mama that the fish had left its spirit in my hand, and unless we got it out, it would slowly eat up my flesh. He spoke something in his language that I didn't understand. Mama seemed to understand, as she nodded after the man had said the words. He hobbled into his inner room and came back with a basket of assorted herbs. After picking the ones that he needed, he hobbled back into the room to return the basket. He lit another bush lamp and started to check corners and hidden areas of the room. I wondered what he was looking for. But as he pulled away an old calabash from under an old wooden table, it became apparent that he had been looking for a spider in its web. He captured the monstrous spider and added it to the medicinal herbs that he had laid on the floor. Then he scraped half a handful of soot from the cooking area and blended all the ingredients in a mortar. And after abluting my hand seven times with a whole bottle of palm oil, he made twenty-one scarifications all over my hand. He then rubbed the medicinal paste on my bleeding hand. My hand must have been immersed in a gallon of sulphuric acid. I screamed and nearly brought down the roof, as he rubbed another layer of paste on my hand.

"It will soon ease," he reassured me, as he hobbled into the inner room.

I gnashed my teeth as Mama put her reassuring arm over my shoulder. Minutes later, the herbalist returned with a glass of herbal medicine.

"Drink this," he instructed, as he handed me the thick concoction.

I felt as though I had a glass of sewage in front of me. I had to pretend that my nose and my taste buds had ceased to exist as I gulped down the entire contents of the glass.

"Take. Apply the rest in the morning," the man instructed Mama. "And keep it dry," he said to me.

My stomach and gullet were at war as we made our way back home. I couldn't wait to get back. In true obedience to my sense of smell and taste, all my salivary glands opened up. In the end, my stomach won the battle and emptied its contents. With one retch, I emptied my stomach on the roadside. I then started to see double. I felt as though I was walking on molasses. My head pounded. I thought it had a tonne of atomic bomb in it ready to explode. Mummy held my hand and steadied my gait as we trekked the narrow, winding path back home.

There must have been more than twenty-four hours that day. I sat on the mat with my hand placed on top of my head, praying for the morning to come as my hand swelled by the minute. I turned from side to side, trying to find a comfortable position. I wanted to cry, but all I could do was grunt.

As the first cock crowed, I heaved a heavy sigh. "It's morning at last," I whispered to myself, as I gently turned the lock and let myself out of the room. I didn't want to go back to the medicine man, so I had to pretend that all was well. My siblings would soon wake up, and I didn't want Mama to know that I had suffered all night, so I went outside, coiled up on the pavement and held my hand on my head. The harmattan breeze provided a little comfort. Pretending that I was fine, I got my bible in preparation for the family's early morning devotion.

"How's your hand this morning?" Mama asked.

I knew, of course, that my mother would ask this question, and I knew exactly what to say.

"Oh, it's getting better, Mum," I replied.

"No, it's not," my cousin insinuated. "He was up all night."

How could he say that? How did he know that? I thought to myself. They were all snoring away whilst my hand throbbed. But, of course, that made Mama say what I had dreaded.

"I better take you back to Baba Urhobo," she informed me, as she held my swollen hand. "I think there's still some poison in it that needs to come out."

There was a knock on the door. We ignored it. It was a rule that we all knew. No one answered the door during our morning devotion. But the knock persisted, so Mama stopped the bible reading to greet the visitor who had refused to give up. With the excitement that she showed when she opened the door, we knew that it must be Uncle Dele. The whole house brightened up whenever he visited. Mama let him in with a large bag of goodies from the city. We all swarmed at him, pulling his ears, rubbing his elbows. Oh, we loved seeing Uncle.

"What's happened to your hand?" he asked me.

Before I could explain, Mama told him that a poisonous fish had stung me. Baba Urhobo had drained out the poison, but it seemed there was still some left in my hand. So she would be taking me back to him that morning.

My uncle took a good look at my hand. He turned it over and gently pressed it with the tip of his index finger. Then he felt it with the back of his hand.

"It has turned into an abscess," he announced. "He needs to go to the hospital."

"Hospital!" I exclaimed. "Oh no, Uncle. No"

I didn't want to go to the hospital. I didn't know what to expect there. I had never been to a hospital before. I saw hospital as the place where they took dead people. It was a common belief in my place that anyone whose illness was so bad that they had to take him to the hospital would die. So to be told that I would need to go to the hospital quickened my heart. But, of course, I knew that there was no way I would disobey my uncle. So, I prepared my mind to undertake the two-hour ride on Uncle's bicycle.

On arrival, we took our place in the queue to register for a card. There were patients with bandages on their limbs, heads and other parts of their bodies. I saw people crying in pain. Others were on trolleys waiting to see the doctor. There were mothers carrying their babies with running noses on their backs. People with smelly leg ulcers and malnourished children all queued for their turns. I remained on the spot, looking around, and I momentarily forgot my own problem when the boy standing behind us threw up and soiled himself. I covered my nose with my good hand, as his mother slapped him on the buttocks and dragged him away to the toilet.

After standing for an hour, I was glad when a man in uniform called my name. At first, I didn't hear him because of all the noise. The man was about to put my card back when my uncle raised his hand and rushed to him. I had thought that only nurses wore uniforms and doctors were all males. So, with the authority that this man seemingly had, I thought that he was a doctor.

"Are you deaf?" the man said to my uncle. "I have called your name several times."

My uncle explained to him that we couldn't hear because of the level of the noise there. He held my swollen, smelly hand and showed it to the man, pleaded that I was really sick, and told him that I had to wake up early in the morning to get there in time.

"When we tell them not to misbehave, they won't listen," the man groaned. "You will learn today in a hard way when the doctor cuts your hand."

My heart sank. I wanted to run back home. How could I live without my hand? And my right hand, the dominant one, for that matter. My hand throbbed more than ever now, but I tried to be brave. One thing I knew was that no one would cut off my hand. They would have to first cut off my head.

The man pulled my card out and handed it to my uncle. I couldn't believe how unkind he was. I looked at my uncle. He collected the card and looked back at me with an encouraging smile. I thought I was going straight to see the doctor, but again we took our seats on the long pew and waited for the messenger to call me in.

As we waited, I started to feel sick. My head pounded. I felt dizzy. Then I started to shiver. My uncle felt my forehead with the back of his hand. He called the attention of the messenger and expressed his concern. The man told my uncle that I was shivering because of fear for what they were going to do to my hand. He reassured him that it was the joke he made earlier that they would cut my hand that made me shiver. He said that I was having a panic attack.

Meanwhile, the doctor had finished with his patient, so there was no one in the room. My uncle seized the opportunity and went in to express his concerns that I was seriously ill. Judging my uncle's good grammar and the confidence with which he entered, Dr George must have thought that he was a big man in the community. The Egyptian doctor told him to bring me in immediately. By that time, I had double vision, was sweating profusely and unsteady on my feet.

My uncle carried me into the consulting room. As he gently laid me on the examination couch, my heart beat fast, everything started to spin. I was clammy. Dr George attended to me straightaway. After checking me all over, he explained to my uncle that the infection had spread from my hand and was now poisoning my whole body through my blood system. He told my uncle that my hand infection had turned into something called septicaemia, a life-threatening condition. The doctor ordered a pain-killing injection for the nurse to inject into my buttock. He set up an intravenous line and infused fluid as well as antibiotics into my veins. Later that afternoon, when I felt stronger, they took me to theatre.

I had been told before that doctors would put a patient to sleep before performing an operation, so I was surprised when the doctor sat me down in the small theatre, ready to operate on my hand.

"It won't hurt you," he reassured me and told me to turn my face away and tell him the names of all the fish I knew. He said that he would guess the one that stung me. As I kept reciting the names, the doctor incised my abscess in one thrust of the knife. Gallons of pus gushed from my hand. He then pushed a metal instrument into my hand and let out more pus. The pain hit me in the deepest part of my brain. But soon afterwards, my hand felt lighter and stopped throbbing. The doctor recommended daily injections of antibiotics and wound dressing. It was over.

I really admired what the doctor did that day. I felt more than ever that I would like to become a doctor when I grew up. I wanted to perform operations on people to make them better.

Chapter Two
SCHOOL

When the student is ready, the master appears.
Buddhist Proverb

My hand didn't quite reach my ear, so I wasn't ready to begin my education. That was the rule. A child would only be registered in the primary school when his hand touched his ear, with his arm over his head. Age was not the determining factor. Few parents knew their children's right dates of birth anyway.

I sat on the top corridor of our house, with my wrapper tied around my neck and a chewing stick between my lips, watching pupils trekking to school. The second bell started to ring. The antique bell in the old Methodist church was second only to the King's town crier, sounding all over the village. I noticed that all the pupils had their aluminium bowls as they raced to the only primary school in Shabomi. The six-class primary school was situated on the outskirts of the village. Why is everyone holding their bowls? I wondered.

With my sisters and cousins gone, l felt lonely, but I was never short of something to do. I got my catapult ready to hunt birds and lizards around the house.

I heard them singing in the school. I knew the Empire Day song. My sisters had practised the song all through the weekend, so much so that I knew every word of it. I hadn't realised that it was the Empire Day celebration. I knew food would be plentiful, but I hadn't yet started school. I wanted to join in the fun, though, so I searched the house to see if I could find a school uniform. I couldn't wear my sister's uniforms, and those of my male cousins wouldn't fit me. So I quickly washed my face, put on a vest that my uncle had passed down to me, and my old khaki shorts, and raced to the primary school. All the pupils had queued up when I arrived. I took my position behind them.

"You there, come over here," Mr Ladejo demanded. The

headmaster's command made me jump.

I marched to the headmaster and stood in front of him with my hands locked behind my back.

"What is your name?" he asked.

"Joseph," I replied.

"And your father's name?" he asked, narrowing his eyes.

"Baba Joe," I replied.

"So, you are Joseph Baba Joe!" He burst into laughter.

Although I did, as a matter of fact, know my father's name, I couldn't say it. I felt like it was an insult to call him by his name. In my place, children wouldn't call their parents by their names. So I had to tell the headmaster that my surname was Baba Joe, meaning Joe's father, as I heard people call my father. My primary reason for coming to school that day was basically to join in the celebration, although I had wanted to start school earlier.

Standing in front of Mr Ladejo was like being arrested by the police. I had expected him to take me into his office and give me a good flogging for trekking the half a mile on my own just for food. Instead, he held me by my hand and asked the pupils whoever was my sister or brother. Aunty Ileola, my eldest sister, raised her hand in embarrassment as other pupils laughed.

"Follow me," the headmaster ordered and led me into his office. "Your name is Joseph Williams, okay?" he said.

I nodded.

He wrote my name on a piece of paper and took me to the primary one teacher. The teacher found a place for me in the queue with the primary-one pupils.

After eating, all the pupils dispersed into their classes. I didn't belong to any class, but I knew some boys of my age group, so I stood behind and peeped through the class-one window. With only a few weeks to the end of the third term, the class teacher had to ensure that the pupils were up to scratch with their times tables. She stood in front of the class and called the pupils, one by one, to recite four times four.

"Jonathan," she called. "What is four times four?"

I knew Jonathan Najite very well. His father was a palm oil maker, and his mother had a stall in the market where she sold palm oil, pepper and other grocery. The only son among six daughters, his parents always treated him like a prince. You could call him a spoilt child. Whenever a teacher flogged him, his mother would come to make trouble in the school the following day. So whilst Miss Opelenge wiggled the cane in the air, she resisted the temptation of flogging Jonathan lest Mrs Najite came after her the following day.

After asking several times, Jonathan finally replied, "Four times four is eight."

Some pupils put up their hands to give the right answer. Miss Opelenge marched to Jonathan, who was now trembling.

"I did not ask you four plus four. I asked you four times four." Staring at Jonathan, she asked again, "Now tell me, what is four times four?"

Jonathan burst into tears and started calling, "Mummy," like a toddler, with his nose running.

"Four times four is sixteen," I shouted from outside.

Miss Opelenge turned to my direction, as if she had just realised my presence. "Come over, Joe," she commanded.

I didn't even know that she still remembered my name. I had expected her to give me a good knock on my head for answering the question that she didn't ask me. And, of course, I dreaded the possibility of her taking me to the headmaster for disrupting her class. I had heard my sisters and cousins talk about the headmaster. They used to say that he would make you hold onto his desk whilst he landed strokes of cane on your buttocks. Even parents would take their wayward children to Mr Ladejo to help them discipline them.

A thought came into my mind: to pretend to be coming into the class and run back home. But if I did that, I would be in a bigger trouble. No doubt, they would report me to my mother. My mother would kill me for causing trouble. A woman of high standard, she brought all her children up to be well behaved and to respect authorities. And she did everything she could to ensure that we didn't get into trouble. As I battled with these thoughts, I dragged myself in front of Miss Opelenge whilst all the pupils looked on in anticipation of what she would do to me.

"So, what did you say?" she asked and receded to her desk.

"Four times four, sixteen," I shouted.

"Okay," she said. "And what is four times five?"

"Four times five is twenty," I replied. And without waiting for her to ask me, I continued: Four times six, twenty-four; four times seven, twenty-eight, and so on, until I had recited the whole of the four times table.

Without saying a word, Miss Opelenge held me by my right hand and took me to the headmaster. I couldn't describe how I felt standing in front of the formidable headmaster after I had sneaked into the school when I was underage. I should have returned home and not loitered around the class. But somehow, although I dreaded the repercussions, I didn't regret what I had done. I was passionate about education. I always sat down with my sisters as my mother taught them arithmetic, reading, writing and spelling. Aunty Ileola, my eldest sister, was in primary six, and she was the head girl. So I learnt my times tables and spellings listening to my sisters and cousins.

Mr Ladejo stared at me for a very long time. Then after clearing his throat, he asked me to recite the times tables starting from one times one. I scratched my head, wondering why he would ask me to recite the one times table when I already knew the four times table. Nevertheless, I went through the whole times tables within minutes without faltering. He brought *Alawiye Book One* out of his drawer and asked me to read to him. This was the standard Yoruba book in the Western Region of Nigeria. I had read my sister's copy of the book so many times that I knew the content by heart.

The headmaster cleared his throat again. After testing me on spellings, he declared to Miss Opelenge, "He is fantastic. He is even better than some primary-three pupils." That was it. The headmaster had decreed it, and no one would change it. Not even my parents. Joseph Baba Joe was formally registered as Joseph Williams, to begin primary school education in the third term at the age of just under four years.

With the headmaster's approval, Miss Opelenge took me back to her class. It wasn't difficult to find me my chair and desk, as the class wasn't full. And so, I was formally registered to begin my education in Methodist Primary School Shabomi, only a few weeks before the end of the third term. Within minutes, word had gone around the school about the four-year-old boy who knew all the times tables.

I spent the rest of the day in Miss Opelenge's class. I felt like I had been in her class all the year. We learnt more arithmetic and spellings. I had no slate to write on, but our teacher made sure that I was included in all her teachings.

At the end of the day, we all assembled on the lawn in front of the headmaster's office. Although we were supposed to line up according to our heights, I chose to stay in the back. I had no uniform on and I started to feel shy in my old oversize uncle-passed-down-to-me vest. I guessed my senior sister, who was the head girl, was embarrassed too. She stared at me, at the back of primary-one line, with my bowl in my hand and my shaven head glistering in the blazing sun. But if she was embarrassed, she must have changed her mind when the headmaster informed the school of how well I had done and that he was proud of me and my parents.

I didn't have to explain to my mother. Of course, ours was a small village. All the families knew one another. But the headmaster came to our house just before our supper. Having praised my mother for giving me a good foundation, he urged her to get my school uniform ready. It was a Friday and so, there was enough time to make me look like a proper pupil on Monday.

That evening, after supper, my mother took me to Akure quarters to get the materials for my school uniform. She bought my slate and a pack of white and colour chalks. There was no need for shoes. None of the pupils had shoes. Only the three children of teachers had the privilege of wearing shoes. The rest of the pupils had to go to school barefooted.

The excitement of starting school soon disappeared, as I now had to deal with the disciplines that came with it. Although I still enjoyed the privileges of the first son in certain situations, by and large, my mother treated me no different to my siblings. I now had to do my homework like my sisters, ensure that my uniform was clean and ironed, my fingernails were cut short, my hair was short and I cleaned my teeth every morning. In our house, everyone had duties assigned to him or her. At the age of four, I had two morning duties assigned to me. Firstly, I had to wash the plates. And secondly, I had to sweep the sitting room. Although we were all individually accountable for doing our assigned duties, ultimately it was our senior sister who would bear the punishment if we failed to do our duties. Mother used to tell her: "If you supervised them properly, they would not fail to do their job." I guess Mummy was planting leadership skill into us even though we, especially my senior sister, thought she was too hard on us.

Each new day, I looked forward to going to school with excitement. I ran in my uniform, carrying my slate and a small bag containing my chalks, behind my sisters, in response to the school bell. My excitement wasn't simply because I was a primary school pupil. Of course, I was proud to go to school, but I enjoyed the lessons and liked my class teacher. Though strict, she also made me believe in myself and to always do my best. But that also challenged me, as I determined to work hard and not disappoint her. Sometimes, she would bring coconut pieces sprinkled with sugar for the 'good pupils'. I was sure to have my own coconut every day. But in fairness, all the pupils would have their share in the end. No one was left out, but I was always among the ones to receive theirs first.

It was soon time for the third-term examinations. I wasn't sure if they would promote me to primary two, as I only joined them in the third term. Thankfully, it wasn't as hard as I had anticipated, and I believed I would be promoted. I looked forward to using pencil to write. Of course, I had already started to write with pencil at home using my sisters' old lined papers.

The school year normally ended with an entertainment night in the Methodist church. The pupils would entertain parents and their guests with songs and drama. Our class drama was *The Good Samaritan*. This biblical story was one of the stories that mother had taught us. It was one of my favourite stories. My mother told us to always be kind to people whether we knew them or not, and to help like the Good Samaritan. The story was about a Jewish man who had been attacked by robbers. A Samaritan man found him on the road and cared for him. My part in the play was that of the Good Samaritan who lent a helping hand to the wounded Jewish merchant. I was excited to act this part. I promised myself that I would always be nice to people. I would always help people in need even if I didn't know them.

The end of year entertainment was also the time when they announced the results of the third-term exams. Pupils and their parents looked forward to this night. Prizes were given to pupils in the first to third positions. There were also prizes for pupils who came first in individual subjects and the overall performance for all the three terms of the year. The primary six pupils would sing their valedictory song, after which the headmaster would announce the names of the new prefects. He would also inform the gathering of pupils who had gained admission into the secondary as well as modern schools. In my primary-one exam, I came second in the class. I also got the following prizes: first in arithmetic, first in English language, first in religious knowledge, second in Yoruba and second in writing. I left the entertainment with a bag of prizes, pride of my parents, and great admiration from other parents and guests.

Going to school didn't change my lifestyle to any great extent. I still enjoyed playing with my friends. We still hunted rabbits and birds. We still fished, wrestled and played football. We were never tired of playing. There was always something to do. One thing I particularly enjoyed, living in our village, was the safety that we had. You could go out day and night without fear or danger. Most nights, we left our doors unlocked. Animals roamed about the streets. Your hen could lay eggs in someone else's backyard and it would be safe.

Fruits were also plentiful. They were fresh and sweet. It was fun sitting high on the top of orange trees with a penknife and peeling ripe oranges. We threw sticks up to pluck mangoes. Sometimes, we pulled guava tree branches for large ripe ones. Other times, we climbed the trees.

One Saturday afternoon, I went with my friends in search of guava. A particular guava caught my attention, and I decided to climb the tree. I was nearly at the top, and as I stretched to reach for the guava, my friend shouted, "Snake!"

I didn't ask "Where?" or "What?" I threw myself off the tree. Looking up, it became clear why my friend had alerted me. A boa constrictor had coiled itself around a branch behind the guava that I was about to pluck. I shook all over as I imagined what could have happened to me had my friend not seen the snake. I didn't have the courage to look for more guavas. As we made our way out of the bush, I felt as though the snake was following us. And every guava tree, every branch and even a piece of wood by the roadside, looked like a boa constrictor had hidden itself behind them.

I continued playing football, which was a good thing. Most of my friends were in the school, so we continued our competitive matches whenever we had the opportunity. We played at break times even if only for a short time, and we often stayed behind after school to have a good match. I later joined the school team, where I played in midfield.

Between my successes at school and the freedom to enjoy a childhood spent in the great outdoors, I had very little to complain about, but an unfortunate accident changed all that. It was time for the athletics. My favourite athletic sport was high jump. I always tried to maintain the championship by practising regularly and stretching myself to the limit. One day, I called some of the boys in my house to come with me to practise. It was during break. I jumped higher than I had ever jumped, which was great. In my excitement, I decided to jump over from the sandy pit backwards, but my feet caught the pole and I fell. The pole slammed down onto my head, leaving me with flashes of light and dizziness. But I wasn't knocked out. In fact, when the bell rang for the end of the break, I got up thinking that nothing had happened. But I felt something crawling down the side of my head, and when I touched it, my palm was red. The blood was flowing and my heart sank. I thought I was going to die. All the school gathered around me. My head pounded. I started to cry, thinking my head had split into two.

The health and hygiene teacher took out rolls of bandages from the first-aid box. He wrapped up my head in several layers, and within minutes, the bandages were soaked in blood. There was panic all over the school and the teachers tried to stop the news from getting out and causing mayhem in the village. There was no doubt that I needed medical help. Fearing that I was still bleeding, the headmaster decided that the safest thing to do was to take me to the dispensary. The nearest dispensary was at Igbotu, a journey of thirty minutes by canoe. He took me on his motorcycle to the beach on my journey to Igbotu. I sat in the boat, looking like I had a red turban on my head. My sister's reassuring arm remained on my shoulders, as the canoe driver paddled with all his strength. He tried to calm me down by telling stories and cracking jokes, but none of these would take my mind off what would happen to me at the dispensary. The pain was excruciating, but that wasn't the only reason I was so petrified. I had heard harrowing stories about the dispensary officer, and I still had horrific memories of my ordeal at the hospital with my poisoned hand. Friends had told me that if you went to the dispensary officer for a wound dressing, he would shut your mouth with soiled dressing if you cried. Someone had also told me that his needle was longer than a ruler. He would push the whole length of the needle into your body. These thoughts imprisoned me in a state of fear. I looked into the water by the side of the canoe, and the image that stared back at me took my heart out of me. I nearly jumped out of the boat. I looked like a red-headed masquerade with four eyes, a massive mouth and a nose that looked like that of a hippopotamus. I trembled all over. My sister gently turned my face away from the side of the canoe. "You will be alright," she reassured me.

The dispensary was on the outskirts of the village. We took our place in the long queue. With my bloody bandage, I was obvious to the health assistant. She came to us straightaway and took me to the dressing room. Soon, the dreaded dispensary officer entered in his white coat. The people called him 'Doctor', but he wasn't a medically qualified doctor. The middle-aged ex-serviceman used his military experience to help at the dispensary.

He carefully removed my bandages as the assistant prepared the dressing trolley. The bleeding seemed to have stopped, but when he pulled the last of the cotton wool, blood spurted over his white coat. The assistant fetched him a large piece of gauze, which he heaped on my wound and almost crushed my head, as he pressed hard on my bleeding wound.

"It will need stitching," he informed the assistant.

The assistant brought out an aluminium bowl from the large sterilising unit. As she took off the lid, a penicillin-smelling steam of needles and syringes filled the room. She picked a syringe and needle. Whilst the dispensary officer shaved my head, the assistant gave an injection of penicillin into my buttock. She drew up pain-relieving medication with the same needle and injected it into my other buttock. The officer threaded a long needle with a piece of black silk. As he pushed the needle through my scalp, I blinked several times. I must have visited hell, as he pushed five silk stitches into my wound.

The stories that I had heard about this man kept me going, and I tried not to cry so that he wouldn't shut my mouth with used dressings. I clenched my teeth as I agonised. The headache was killing, but I was glad that my wound had been stitched and the bleeding had stopped. I subsequently visited the dispensary every morning for penicillin injections.

That evening, the dispensary officer visited us to check how I was. He advised my mother to ensure that I kept my head dry. He had given the same advice to my sister before we left the dispensary that afternoon. He further advised that I should take the whole week off school. That wasn't a bad thing, as I hadn't fancied going out with head shaven and a large plaster to cover my wound. Nevertheless, the thought of not going to school also concerned me. It was close to our inter-house sports, which was the very reason I practised my favourite event that led to my head injury. No doubt, my house members would be disappointed if I was unable to participate. Everyone knew that I was favourite to win the gold for high jump.

After spending three days at home, I couldn't take it anymore. I covered my head with one of my father's old hats and waited until my mother had left for the market. The noise of people cheering and shouting was irresistible. Within minutes, I was back at school, cheering with the other pupils. Though I wanted to practise, the games master stopped me. Still, I was glad to be back with my friends again, cheering and laughing.

My sister was preparing for her primary school leaving certificate examination, so she couldn't accompany me to the dispensary for my daily antibiotic injections. As a matter of fact, I didn't need her to go with me. Almost all the people in Shabomi and Igbotu knew one another. The sister villages, belonging to the same clan, had so many things in common and were under the same monarch. So, all the canoe drivers knew my parents, and it was safe for me to go on my own.

Although I was used to the daily injections, I wasn't looking forward to having my stitches removed. So when the dispensary assistant said, "Come tomorrow to have your stitches out," my heart beat fast. I was glad, of course, to have them out, but what frightened me were the harrowing stories that my friends had told me. One of my friends had told me that the stitches must not snap. "If the stitch breaks, the bit that remains will sink into your head and cause fits." Another friend warned that if the stitches were not removed, they would turn into worms and itch me in the anus. Of course, I didn't want any of these to happen to me. So, I had to be brave. But as I sat down in the dressing room, I couldn't get those thoughts out of my head. They sounded fictitious. Still, I didn't want anything bad to happen to me.

The dispensary assistant washed my head with antiseptic solution. She then cut one end of the silk stitch. As she pulled it, my skin came with it. The stitches had stayed too long and my skin had started to grow into them. I started to reason that my friend was probably right that the stitches could sink into my head or even travel to my anus. As the assistant yanked out the first stitch, I felt as though my scalp was being ripped apart. She placed the stitch on a piece of white paper. I inspected the blood-stained black thread with a rim of skin on it out of the corner of my eye, wondering if there was any piece left behind that could get stuck into my brain.

"Steady your head or I'll pull out your brain," the dispensary assistant instructed. She then gave me a wooden stick to bite on. With my teeth clenched on the wood and eyes shut, she took out the rest of the stitches one by one. I thought that was all, but after removing all the stitches, she redressed the wound, this time with a small plaster. I didn't want a plaster on my head, as my hair had started to grow back. So, as soon as I got back home, I took it off.

As time went on, l continued to experience the good and bad of life. Like other people, I realised that it wasn't all about having fun or playing football with my mates. It wasn't even about academic excellence. Tragedies would come in different forms, as I found out one day after our morning devotion, when we were getting ready for our class teacher to take our roll call. I peeped out of the classroom and saw boys and girls running into the bush. When l looked back, I found that pupils started to jump out through the windows. At first, I didn't know what had happened. But, as three uniformed women entered the classroom carrying their brown bags, it dawned on the rest of us that it was vaccination day. The teachers always tried not to announce the day of vaccination in order that pupils turned up. But, despite their efforts, many pupils didn't come to school, and many tried to escape the needles.

That wasn't the first time that I had been vaccinated. Although I didn't like the needles, I knew, of course, that I mustn't run away. None of my siblings would want to face the consequences of running out of class in fear of the vaccination. Besides the strokes of the cane from the headmaster, we would have to explain to Mummy why we had done such a stupid thing. So, with my teeth clenched and my eyes tightly shut, I surrendered to the nurse as she drove the measles vaccine into my left arm.

That night, my aunt arrived with her twin babies, both of whom had contracted measles. They had weeping rashes all over their body and cracks in the skin that peeled like the scales of a fish. Their eyes were swollen with purulent discharge in between the interlocked eyelashes. The lips were cracked with cold sores in the angles of their mouths. Their breathing was shallow, and their chests were rattling. Each time they coughed, they cried and threw up. Then they struggled afterwards to settle down. They couldn't keep anything down. They had constant diarrhoea and sore bottoms.

They took the babies to Baba Urhobo. He gave them different kinds of native herbs. But in the early hours of the following day, one of the children died. The other one died later that afternoon. I felt like I could have done something to save them. We had learnt at school that immunisation could prevent diseases. I also learnt that there were many things that doctors could do that the herbalists couldn't do. I could still remember the problem with the fish sting. The herbalist tried all he could, but only the doctor could do the operation to remove all the pus. My cousins couldn't be cured of their measles. That day, as I joined my family to mourn the loss of my twin cousins, I promised myself that I was going to be a doctor so I could help to cure people's illnesses. Although I had no idea what it would take to become a doctor, this desire was strong in my heart.

A few days after my aunt lost her twins, we received the sad news that my sister's first son and her second daughter had lost their lives to measles. Although I had been vaccinated, I was still anxious about the possibility of contracting the highly infectious disease. Like our family, many other families in and around our village lost many children to measles.

I always looked forward to the end of year holiday. It wasn't so much the fact that the holiday spread over Christmas and the New Year, but it gave me the opportunity to spend part of it with Daddy in his station. It was also the time that Daddy took his logs to Lagos for sale. In my penultimate year in the primary school, I spent part of the holiday at my father's camp. This particular trip changed my outlook on life. I always enjoyed life in the camp. There was plenty to eat: different kinds of fruits and fish, all there for our free consumption. The game were easy to hunt. Our traps always caught a grasscutter or porcupine. With your catapult, you would certainly bring home one or two pheasants. The forest also teamed with snails. They were so easy to find. Just tease apart the dry vegetation and you find tens of large wild snails. One day, I went into the forest with one of my friends. Kamoru was about a year younger than me, but he was brave and knowledgeable. Despite living in a remote camp, he was current with the news and what was going on in the country. He knew everywhere in the forest. He even showed me fruits that I had never seen before. As we were tilling the leaves for snails, I heard a rattling sound coming from a heap of dry leaves. When I walked closer, I saw something vibrating in the middle of the leaves. It vibrated in sequence with the rattles. Meanwhile, Kamoru was busy picking snails as I stood admiring what I thought was a rattling worm. I had never seen a worm rattling, I thought. As I reached for it, Kamoru shouted, "Don't! Rattlesnake!"

I froze. I had never seen a snake incubating its eggs before.

I didn't have the courage to look for more snails after that. Every heap of leaves looked like there could be a snake hidden within it. Instead, we picked a few mangoes and went back home.

One thing I particularly learnt from my friendship with Kamoru was life skills management. The rattlesnake incident had given me nightmares; every long object in the house looked like a snake, but, of course, I knew there was no way I could avoid the bushes. That was life in the camp; we had to go to the farm; we needed to gather firewood, check our traps daily and fetch water from the brook. So, when Kamoru came to me the following morning, holding his catapult, I knew exactly what to expect. But I couldn't face up to the possibility of encountering another poisonous snake.

Kamoru smiled. "Snake is everywhere here," he said. "When you cannot change your circumstances, you have to try and make the best of it." He plucked a leaf from the shrub in front of the house. "We live in the bush with all sorts of poisonous snakes and insects. They mind their business and we mind ours." After throwing the leaf into the bush, he advised, "Friend, when life is tough, you've got to be tough."

This statement from Kamoru became my empowerment. It changed my perspective on life and from that point on I started to live fearlessly. I became stronger and ready to face any challenges that life might throw at me. I climbed even the tallest mango trees to get the biggest ripe mangoes. I had no inhibition to till the leaves to find the most matured snails. I was prepared to confront even the wildest animal.

It was three weeks to Christmas. Daddy had prepared his logs for the three-day transportation to Lagos, but they had to wait for the right weather. The Atlantic Ocean had to be calm, and there was no metro professional to predict the weather, only experience and instinct. It was a narrow window of safety that all timber magnates knew.

Although it wasn't the first time that I had been to Lagos, it was the first time that I had accompanied the logs, and I had heard terrible stories about journeys to Lagos by sea. I couldn't relax, always thinking of a big storm that would dismantle the rafts or a shark looking to prey on us, as I slept in a tent built on the logs with Daddy. All these thoughts and other stories kept me awake. Daddy must have known what was going on in my mind. He started to tell me stories. Some of these were his usual ones to make me laugh. But the one that really inspired me was the biblical story that I already knew. The story of David and Goliath was not new to me. What I really took away from Daddy's own version was his conclusion.

"Son, you will come across many Goliaths in this world," he advised. "But if you make yourself David, you will defeat them." He advised me to be tough and face my Goliath without a blink. After his stories, I saw life in a different way. I didn't worry anymore about a big storm dismantling the logs or a preying shark. I believed that whatever happened, I would be victorious like David.

We arrived in Lagos at dawn. After securing the logs at the jetty,

Daddy took me to Uncle John. Uncle John's house was a convenient walking distance from the jetty. After a quick bath, I was ready to explore Lagos. My cousins were pleased to see me and eager to hear about life in the village. The girls liked to spend time watching the television. The fifteen-inch, black-and-white television must have seen better days. It either blacked out or the screen became fuzzy. Whenever this happened, the girls would bang the box. That often cleared the fuzziness. Sometimes they had to switch it off and back on to restart it.

I wasn't allowed to sit in the sitting room. Of course, I could watch the television, but I had to do so from outside. Whenever popular programmes were showing, I would find a place among the neighbours' children to watch from the window. My uncle made the rule during one of my previous visits. On that day, the girls and I were watching the TV. I was sitting on the floor.

"You will dirty my carpet with your feet, village boy," he remarked. I thought he was joking until he showed me where I belonged: the window. Of course, I walked barefooted, but I washed my feet before entering the house. We all had played outside, although my cousins wore their slippers. Despite their slippers, their feet were just as dusty as mine. I washed my feet and also cleaned them on the doormat before entering the sitting room. Still, uncle chased me out of the room and allowed his children, who hadn't washed their feet, to sit comfortably in the easy chairs and watch the TV.

With the large number of the neighbours' children crowding the lone window, their pungent breath almost suffocated me. I didn't get to see much of the famous *Baba Sala*. Although this was my favourite programme, I didn't enjoy it with all the noise and body odours around me. In the end, I decided to go and help Daddy at the jetty with the sale of his logs.

Daddy had found buyers for most of his logs when I arrived and was having a discussion with one of his customers. Mr Bankole was calculating the number of planks that could be sliced out of a log using a reckoner. This figure table matched the size of a log to the number of planks. He was thinking aloud as he tried to do the calculations. Within seconds, I had made a mental calculation of the number of planks from the log. I knew how many planks you could get out of a twenty-inch log.

So, by simple multiplication, I worked out how many planks you would get out of an eighty-inch log.

"What?" Mr Bankole shouted.

I thought I was wrong even though I knew for certain I was right. Mr Bankole checked the reckoner again. "What class are you?" he asked.

"I am in primary five, sir," I replied.

"That means you will be writing your entrance examination to grammar school next year," he said.

"Yes, sir," I replied.

Then he turned to my father. "Your son is such a brilliant boy. He must go to a good grammar school. He is the kind of brain that goes to schools like King's College, Igbobi College, Baptist Academy and many other good schools."

"Thank you," my father said with pride.

After completing the sales with Mr Bankole, my father and I walked home.

"Son," he said, "I am really proud of you. You will go to big schools and even go abroad to study with white people. Just keep reading your books."

I promised my father that I would continue to do my best.

When we got home, my father was so excited. He informed Uncle how good I was and how I could calculate the number of planks without using the reckoner.

"Oh, that's good," my uncle said casually.

"Uncle, I would like to write the entrance exam to King's College, Igbobi College and Baptist Academy." I was impatient.

He almost jumped out of his seat. I thought I had said an abominable thing. "You must be joking!" he exclaimed. "Don't even try. The exams are of very high standards. I would not expect a boy from a village school to pass."

I scratched my head and looked at my father to rescue me. Although Dad certainly trusted my ability to pass any exam, including American or European exams, he couldn't argue with Uncle. He boasted to be highly educated even though he only had the old Standard Six certificate.

"I am sure I can pass the exams," I maintained.

Uncle stared at me with a look that said, 'How dare you argue with me?' I scratched my head again and kept quiet. "Okay. I will get the forms for you when the time comes," he finally admitted. I was excited and promised myself to really work hard so I could pass the entrance examinations.

Time seemed to go too fast. Although there were many interesting things to see in Lagos, I still preferred life in the village. I didn't enjoy the busy lifestyle in Lagos. Everyone seemed to be running after something or someone. The streets were never quiet, even at night. Eventually, I was pleased to return to the village with a new pair of shoes, a new *Platignum* pen, a bottle of *Quink* Parker ink and Christmas flashlights. Daddy also bought new releases by Ebenezer Obey, Sunny Ade and IK Dairo. And he bought all the children our Christmas clothes.

We always had a big celebration at Christmas and New Year, with plenty to eat and plenty of fun. Nothing would prevent my parents from celebrating with our large extended family, returning from all over the country.

My year in primary six went very fast. Although I was looking forward to finishing my primary education, I had a feeling that I might not have a post-primary education. At best, I had hoped to attend the modern school, on which successful completion would enable me to go to a teacher training college. My mother wanted me to go to the secondary school, but she had to have authorisation from my father, as she wasn't sure that he could afford it. Primary education was free in the Western Region, but secondary was not.

Pupils had started applying to sit the entrance examinations to secondary schools, and applications were closing fast. At this time, the Civil War had broken out. The panic and confusion that the war brought added to the uncertainties of my future. I wrote to my uncle in Lagos and asked him to collect the entrance examination forms of the schools that I had previously told him. I never got his response. Instead, he told me that he would advise my dad to try and get a place for me in the local modern school. I didn't bother trying admission into schools in other places. I liked such schools as King's College Lagos, Christ School Ado-Ekiti, Government College Ibadan, Government College Ugheli, Mayflower College Ikene, to mention but a few. But it was easy for my parents to talk me out of these schools. They were easy excuses: the war was ongoing and it would be too dangerous for me to go on my own.

I had resigned to the fact that I wouldn't be going to secondary school immediately after my primary school. Neither of my elder sisters continued beyond the primary school level despite the fact that they were brilliant and had excellent results in their primary school leaving examinations. Their inability to progress their education beyond primary school was a combination of poverty and the general belief in those days that girls didn't need more than basic primary education.

I was determined to further my education, but I was unsure that my parents would be able to afford my higher education. I thought of what I could do if in the end my parents decided that there was no money to send me to the secondary school. My first option was to go into commercial fishing. I knew I was good at fishing, so I planned to weave hundreds of raffia fish traps and purchase hooks and nets. It wouldn't be a problem for me to find a canoe. I had no doubt that my grandmother would lend me her own. The other option I considered was to purchase fish from the Ilajes and Ijaws fishermen and sell them to the mainland dwellers. I reckoned that I should be able to raise enough money doing this for one year. Finally, if these options proved nonviable, I would go and learn about mechanics. There weren't many good mechanics in the village, so that could be a breakthrough. Whilst all these thoughts were going through my head, I still hoped that something would make my parents make the decision to send me to the secondary school. I prayed every night for God to provide money for my parents in order for them to be able to sponsor my higher education. But I soon learnt from friends that all the entrance examination applications had closed, and I concluded that there was no hope of continuing my education, at least not immediately after my primary school education.

Then, one evening after school, I was playing draughts with my friends. The headmaster stopped over. Mr Joseph Obideyi was highly regarded by all the parents. A native of Ode Irele, a neighbouring town, he knew almost all the families in Shabomi. But that wasn't the only reason he was held in high esteem. He was a disciplinarian and had the best interests of the pupils always in his heart, always trying to make us work to our best ability. I was fortunate to have Mr Obideyi as my headmaster as well my class teacher in primary six. Although many of my friends got into trouble with him, I only did that once. That was when one of my friends absented himself from school without permission. Mr Obideyi asked him to come to the front of the class and write on the blackboard that he was sorry. Akin wrote*: I yam surry no come school yesterday. Becuss I get malarea.* I tried to contain my laughter. But, in the end, I burst into laughter. The headmaster called me to come and identify the mistakes in the sentences and to rewrite it in the correct form. I came out and confidently wrote: *I am sorry that I did not come to school yesterday. It was because I had malaria.* Despite the fact that I wrote it in the correct way, the teacher punished me, just to teach me about a certain aspect of multidisciplinary life. Don't make other people feel bad just because they are not as good or clever as you. Instead, you should support them as best as you can. My punishment was to write 'I am sorry' one hundred times on plain, non-lined paper, and the words must be on straight lines.

Normally, we would all fly away upon hearing the all-too-familiar sound of Mr Obideyi's Vespa, but we had written our primary school leaving certificate examination. There was no more homework. Technically, we had finished and were only waiting for the school to formally close for the year.

"Good evening, sir," we all greeted.

"Good evening, boys," he replied and switched off his motorbike.

"Looks like you are having a good time," he smiled.

"Yes, sir," we replied and smiled back.

The headmaster seemed to take an interest in our game, but I felt uneasy that the great disciplinarian was there encouraging us in a situation for which he would normally condemn us. Of course, he encouraged us to take an active part in extracurricular activities. Nevertheless, to be so friendly at around six o'clock in the evening, when we should be helping out in the kitchen, was unusual. I reasoned that perhaps it was because it was Friday, time for him to go to his family for the weekend break. After watching our game for about ten minutes, he switched on his motorcycle. He was about to drive off. Then he switched it off again.

"Oh, lest I forget, Joseph, which secondary school are you going to next year?" he asked, now with his normal headmaster's facial expression.

"I don't know, sir," I replied.

"You don't what?" he asked. He rolled his bike backwards closer to us. "All the entrance examinations have almost closed. And you are telling me you don't know?"

I scratched my head. "My mother has sent messages to my father, but we have not got his reply, sir," I replied.

"Is your father going to help you to do the test?" he asked.

"No, sir," I replied, "but he has no money."

"Did he say he would not allow you to go secondary school?" he asked.

"No, sir," I replied, "but—"

"But what?" he interrupted. "Get on my bike now," he ordered. "I need to have a serious discussion with your mother."

My heart pounded as I held onto Mr Obideyi on the back of his Vespa, even though it was an opportunity for me to be on a Vespa, something that I had dreamt of doing. I didn't know if I would get into trouble for telling the headmaster what I had said. I wished I had run away like we normally did whenever the headmaster passed by. Surely, I would receive my punishment after the headmaster had left, I thought. My mother had taught us to always watch what we discussed with outsiders, and I wondered if I had gone too far. Whatever my thoughts, there was nothing I could do. So I resigned to whatever happened.

My mother was preparing our supper when I arrived with the headmaster. As a primary-six-age boy, I no longer stayed in the kitchen when my mother was cooking. My sisters and female cousins were there to help. So what would have got me into trouble – that is, playing outside at that time – was no longer an issue. Still, my heart raced as I disembarked from the headmaster's motorcycle.

The headmaster marched confidently into the backyard, as I followed behind him. My mother rushed out of the kitchen, with water dripping from her hands, as she heard the headmaster's voice. I had known my mother long enough to interpret her facial language. I could sense the two questions on her mind: What had brought the headmaster to our house at that time of the day? Has Joseph got into trouble? Fortunately, Mr Obideyi didn't waste any time in telling my mother his mission.

"Joseph has not got admission into the secondary school," he said emphatically, rather than ask, "Why has Joseph not taken any entrance exam?"

I tried not to make any eye contact with my mother as she struggled to find the right way to reply. After wiping her hands with the hem of her wrapper, she cleared her throat. "I have sent several messages to his father, but I have not got a reply."

"So, if he doesn't reply till next year, then this boy will just stay at home. Is that it?" he asked.

"But …" Mother was hesitant. Then she looked away. And after clearing her throat, she said, "I'm not sure if we have money for secondary school. Maybe it's better for him to go to the modern school first."

"Modern school is not for pupils like Joseph," the headmaster said. "I think United Grammar School is still accepting applications for the entrance examination. I will head straight for the school and see if I can get him a form."

My mother had no idea how much the application would cost, but she must have thought that it would cost a lot. She scratched her head. "I will get the money ready for you on Monday," she said, but wondered where she would find it.

"You like United, don't you?" the headmaster asked me, as he was about to start his motorcycle.

"Yes, sir," I replied with excitement.

I felt like I was a new person. I wasn't sure if the entrance examination applications to UGS were still open, but that didn't stop me from daydreaming about life in the secondary school. I couldn't contain the feeling. I wanted to fly out and tell all my friends the exciting news. Mother must have realised that. She warned me not to go out that evening. She also advised me to always keep my information to myself until I was sure. "You don't count your chickens until your eggs have hatched," she advised.

Later, when we had just had our supper, I was with my siblings and cousins, tidying up at the back of the house. I had washed up the utensils, and I still needed to go and check my fishnets before the end of the day.

My mother had kept to herself in her room since the headmaster's visit. I needed to inform her that I was going to check my fishnets. I had no doubt that she would think that I hadn't heeded her advice if she called me and I wasn't around. But I also knew that she would tell me that it was too late to go and check my fishnets. Of course, I didn't want to do anything that would upset her, so I decided to tell her anyway, and if she objected to my going to the river that night, I wouldn't go.

Mother was on her knees in her room, praying. I didn't hear most of her prayer, but I heard when she said: "Please God, let that principal be considerate. I don't have any money right now, but I know you will provide it." I knew then that my mother had been praying for me. I decided not to disturb her. I would postpone checking my nets till the following morning.

I gently tiptoed back into the kitchen area, and then I heard the sound of a motorbike. I hadn't the slightest doubt that it must have been the headmaster's, since, of course, no one else had a scooter. But it was already late. I wondered why he had come back so soon. I zoomed to the front of the house. I guessed right. Mr Obideyi was parking his scooter.

"Good evening, sir," I greeted.

"Evening," he replied. "Call your mother," he said.

The headmaster informed us that the applications to UGS had closed, but he was able to persuade the principal to allow me to apply.

"Thank God for answering my prayer," my mother said. And turning to the headmaster, she said, "Thank you so much." And she really meant it.

The one-page form took less than five minutes to complete with guidance from the headmaster. I felt a new life come over me. Of course, I knew I still had to write the entrance examination. And if successful, I would still have to attend the interview, which was the final lap. Even if I was through with my admission, I was unsure if my parents would be able to sponsor my secondary education. Nevertheless, all these caveats did not stop my excitement.

Apart from passing by the gate of a secondary school, I had never been in one before, but I couldn't think of anything else. In a few weeks' time, I would be a secondary school student.

The headmaster advised that it would be better for him to take the completed form by hand to the school. Before he left, he informed me that the provisional date for the entrance examination was the following Saturday. "This is your only chance if you want to go to secondary school in January," he advised. "And you must not disappoint me," he added.

"Thank you, sir, I will not disappoint you," I promised.

My mother thanked the headmaster from the bottom of her heart. She also promised him that she would send a message to my father straightaway. But the headmaster advised her to wait until I had a confirmed place before informing Daddy. I guess he didn't want anything to stress me during my preparation for the entrance examination. He reassured my mother that not all the students in the secondary school were from rich families. He further encouraged her that if I did very well, I might even win a scholarship to fully or partially cover the cost of my secondary education.

Two weeks later, the headmaster brought the good news in a brown envelope. The most important information was contained in the first line of the one-page letter: ... *successful at the recently concluded entrance examination to United Grammar School, Ode Irele*... That was all that mattered to me. And for that moment, I believed nothing would stop me from going to the secondary school. But when I turned to my mother, her look brought the realisation to my perception that it wasn't enough to pass the entrance examination. That was perhaps the easiest of the tasks. I had had no doubt in my ability to do well in the entrance examination. Indeed, I dared to say that I could pass any entrance examination if I had the opportunity. The real issue was the school fee. That was the disappointment that my mother had expressed. To secure my place, I must complete the acceptance form and return it with a deposit of ten pounds by the deadline, which was two weeks from the date on the letter.

"Thank you, Headmaster," my mother said. "But please beg the principal to give me till the end of the month. I will be able to borrow the money from friends and pay back."

I knew then why my mother had looked sad after the initial excitement. It would be impossible to find ten pounds without borrowing.

"That's alright," the headmaster reassured my mother. "I will take care of that."

"Thank you very much," my mother said. "May God bless you. Please tell the principal that I will not disappoint him."

My mother had thought that what the headmaster meant by "take care of that" was to waive the deadline. What she didn't know was that he had offered to pay my deposit.

"I'll drop the form with the deposit on my way home. You don't need to borrow any money," the headmaster said. "I will come back to talk to Papa when he comes," he concluded, as he mounted his scooter.

I couldn't believe what had just happened. That the formidable headmaster had so much interest in my welfare would be a good plot in a fiction book. But it was real. It was no fiction and not a dream. I was still in my thinking mood when my mother called me.

"Keep the envelope in that cupboard until your father comes," she directed. "And don't discuss it with anyone."

"Why shouldn't I discuss it, Mum?" I asked.

"Well, I just feel that it's better for your father to hear about it from us rather than from outsiders. You see, not everyone likes your progress. These people could influence your father in a negative way. But if the headmaster could talk to him before the news goes around, then no one would be able to discourage him."

I understood my mother clearly. If these influential people had had my interests in their hearts, they would have helped with obtaining the entrance examination forms to popular schools. Among them was the uncle, who had told me that the famous schools I liked were not for 'boys from a village school'. If such people heard about my admission into a grammar school, they could persuade my father not to let me go, that I should go to the modern school instead. They could even tell him that only rich people could send their children to the secondary school. My mother knew all this, and of course, I could always trust her judgement. So I nodded and thanked her.

My mother received a message from my father, urging me to come to him in his station. That was lovely news. It couldn't have come at a better time. I knew that my father must have heard the good news of my success in the secondary school entrance examination. And I reckoned that he would have heard that Mr Obideyi had paid my deposit and confirmed my place in United Grammar School. If the headmaster had decreed it, that was it. So I had no doubt in my mind that my father had approved. But that wasn't the only reason for my excitement. At that time of the year, my father's logs would have been joined together in rafts ready for trawling to Lagos. As the workers wouldn't be engaged in felling trees, they would spend most of their time picking snails, fishing and hunting games. So I couldn't wait to join them in the camp.

I left home early in the morning. My journey started with a four-mile trek on the dusty road to Ode Irele. There, I caught the transport to Ore. I joined the other travellers waiting by the roadside to get lifts to Lagos. This was a common practice. As all the traffic going to the West from the Eastern part of the country passed through Ore, it was a strategic place to catch transport. We would wait by the roadside and stop an oncoming vehicle. We would then negotiate a price, usually much less than the normal fare. Occasionally, you could even be lucky to get a free ride.

Soon after waiting, a car sped past me, ignoring my wave to give me a lift. Then it stopped and started to reverse slowly, as one of the passengers beckoned me to run and join them. Music boomed out of the car. I was about to run to them when a bearded old man in a shabby looking *Danshiki* appeared from nowhere. He held my hand. "Don't," he said. "Those boys are probably drunk," he warned.

I couldn't explain how the old man had suddenly appeared. There were only three of us waiting, and we were all young people. I had been taught to respect the words of the old, for they were full of wisdom, so I obeyed the old man and refused to join the lads.

"Where are you going, Papa?" I asked. "Oh, just the next village," he replied. "My transport will soon come," he said.

Just then a Peugeot 404 arrived.

"That's a good one," the old man said and urged me to join them. He smiled and waved, "Safe journey," as the driver gathered momentum and sped away on Lagos-Benin Road.

The Harmattan period was not a good time to travel. It was chilly, and the blanket of dust-laden fog reduced the visibility greatly. Many of my co-passengers remarked about how slow our driver was.

"At this speed, we will never get to Lagos," one of them said.

"Can you not see the writing on my vehicle?" the driver asked. "Slow but Safe," he answered his own question.

"Even a bicycle can go faster," another passenger remarked. And we all laughed.

Looking ahead, vehicles started to slow down. People had put palm leaves on the roadside, something that they did whenever there was an accident. My eyes widened when we got to the scene of the accident. A Peugeot 404 was beyond recognition, as it lay crushed on its back, with no survivors. It was the car that the old man at Ore had stopped me from getting into. I couldn't thank God enough for sending the old man to me.

I arrived at Epe shortly after midday. The medium-size coastal town on the northern side of the Lekki Lagoon was a checkpoint for the timbers destined for Lagos. My father's timbers had docked, awaiting certification and stamping by the forestry guards. He was over the moon when I arrived.

"This is my son," he introduced me to the head of the Guards, beaming with smiles. "He is going to the grammar school in January," he said with pride.

I had no doubt then that my going to the secondary school had received my father's blessing. Nothing would make me not go, I believed, since my father had endorsed it. But it was still about six weeks to the start of the new school year, and it felt like it was six months. I wished the time could fly or the hours could shorten.

We spent about a week in Epe. After the registration of the timbers, my father's workers followed the trawling logs to Lagos whilst he and I went by road in a minibus. Before we left Epe, my father's friend, the chief forestry guard, called me into his living room.

"Your father told me the good news of your success in the entrance examination," he said. "Timber work is hard. You must not waste your father's money. Put your best efforts into your education so you can have a good career when you finish," he advised. Then he gave me two pounds and offered me best wishes for the future.

Lagos was always fun in the Christmas season. We stayed at Ebute Metta, close to the beach. Most timber magnates stayed there when they brought their timbers to Lagos. It was good to see my cousins and to enjoy city life. Within hours of my arrival, everyone had heard the news of my going to the secondary school at the beginning of the year. I had just turned ten then. I deliberately started to communicate with my cousins in proper English now rather than Pidgin or Yoruba. I wanted to behave like a college student, although I didn't know how a college student should behave.

One of my cousins, who was already in the secondary school, visited. She told me so many things about the boarding house, although she herself was a day student, and I didn't know if I should believe everything that she told me. Part of the story was that we would be made to live like prisoners. We wouldn't be allowed to go out until the holidays. Even our parents wouldn't be allowed to see us.

"Well, if they didn't allow me to go and see my mum, I would sneak out," I said to her.

She warned me that that would land me in trouble. They might even expel me. I then started to have second thoughts about boarding school. The excitement of the previous few weeks now dampened, I tried not to talk about secondary school anymore. Nevertheless, my ambition to be a surgeon eased the fear of boarding. Maybe it was different in the village schools, I reasoned.

One day, we were watching a film on my uncle's black and white television. In the film, a young boy's parents took him to see a surgeon. The boy with a swollen abdomen looked so thin and pale. The doctor told his parents that there was something growing inside him. Whatever he ate would go to feed the terrible growth. The doctor told the boy's parents that unless he performed an operation to remove that thing, the boy would die. Although my cousins turned away when the surgeon was doing the operation, I watched all of it. It fascinated me to see the object, the size of a watermelon, removed. The film went further to show the boy looking well weeks after the operation. I wanted to grow up to be like the surgeon in the film. I wanted to perform operations on people to make them better. My cousins laughed when I told them what I thought. But that thought never left my mind.

As the start of term approached, I discovered that my father had made his best sales that season. The price of timber had gone up phenomenally, and all my father's customers were already waiting for the logs to arrive in Lagos. In less than one week, he had sold all his logs. As he thanked God, he informed me that he had worked harder and taken more on than he had ever done. He said that he was committed to giving me the best that he could. He reassured me that I was destined to have further education. Not only did he make enough money for my school fees, he also planned to renovate the family house back home and buy land to put up a building in Lagos. "Your success in your entrance examination is a blessing in disguise," he said. "I thank God for His faithfulness," he added and made sure that I lacked nothing. I needed to get a bucket, a cutlass, a hoe, canvas shoes, sandals and a mosquito net. We bought a pair of everything that I needed. He also bought a large suitcase, a large tube of *Pepsodent* toothpaste, a jar of pomade and a *Vono* mattress. I bought a *Parker* fountain pen and one bottle each of black and blue ink. After shopping for my school needs, my father did the Christmas shopping. He bought a record changer to replace the old gramophone. And he bought a number of records to go with it. One of the records was 'Edumare soro mi dayo' (God has turned my misery to joy) by Chief Commander Ebenezer Obey. This record couldn't have come at a better time. God had truly turned things around for my father and the whole family. Then he bought the Christmas clothes and all the Christmas gifts. We spent a couple more days in Lagos before we left for the village.

We arrived home two weeks before Christmas. The excitement was unprecedented. With a brand-new record changer and tens of newly released Juju music albums, it all made for a perfect Christmas. My father slaughtered the fattest goat I had ever seen. He was proud to share our joy with the whole family.

Soon after we arrived, Mr Obideyi visited us. Even though my father had the sum of seventy-six pounds, ten shillings, the annual fee for the boarding school, the headmaster reassured him that he didn't have to pay it all at once. The school accepted payment in instalments. Even the term fee could similarly be paid in instalments. This was a great relief for my parents, as it was the main issue that had bothered them. There was now nothing to stop my secondary school education. My parents were grateful to Mr Obideyi, and truly so.

Chapter Three
SECONDARY SCHOOL LIFE

Learning is not attained by chance,
it must be sought for with ardour and attended to with diligence.
Abigail Adams

United Grammar School (UGS) Ode-Irele was far larger and grander than it had looked when I came to write the entrance examination and attend the interview. The co-educational institution extended beyond the two lawns, separated by a long path and blocks of classrooms. The girls' dormitory was situated behind the main school block with only the kitchen separating them. The principal's house was strategically situated, almost facing the main gate, whilst the teachers' residences were on both sides of the principal's house. The boys' dormitory, consisting of five blocks, was almost a mile from the main school block. The senior tutor, who was also the house master, resided in the first of the blocks.

I arrived in the boarding house on a Saturday. Only a handful of students arrived on that day. The rest of the boys arrived in the dormitory on Sunday. They were mostly the Ilajes, Apois and Ijaw Arogbos from the riverine area. We were all freshers, apart from the senior boy, Senior Gbade. They were all from the same place, and I felt alienated, so I chose to sleep on my own in one of the rooms.

"Don't you sleep in the same room with people?" Senior Gbade asked. He was the time prefect. He was tall, athletic and talked fast with a little stutter.

"I do, sir," I replied.

"Come on then, join us," he urged.

I learnt quickly that the junior students were not allowed to call the seniors by their names. You had to prefix their name with 'Senior'. The second-year students were now glad to have their own juniors, and I was realising that there were certain rules, written and unwritten, that I had to learn.

All the students from forms one to four lined up according to our classes. The form five students didn't line up. They stood at various positions as the head boy addressed us. The first thing that I observed was the wide disparity in the ages and sizes of the boys. I was one of the smallest boys in my class, so I stood in the front row. When I looked back, it surprised me that some of the boys, whom I had assumed were in senior classes, were in the same class as me. They looked so big and mature. If I hadn't seen them before, I could have mistaken them for teachers or final year students. Many of these men had taught for many years after modern school. Some had worked in factories or farms for many years to raise funds for their secondary education. Some others were already parents. I couldn't call them 'Senior', since they were my classmates, so I had to call them 'Brother', and truly so, since they were old enough to be my uncle.

At first, I didn't know the name of the head boy, and I dared not ask. All the students called him Galloper. That was his nickname. Even his classmates called him so. A six-footer with military physique, he was well-made for the post. It was after they divided us into our various houses that I knew the head boy's real name. Patrick Akinduro was to be head of Olofun House, where I was assigned.

At home, I never had to make my bed since I slept on a mat. All I had to do was simply fold the mat and tuck it away behind the door. Even that wasn't something that I did every day. My sisters used to do that most days. In the boarding house, every student had to make his bed.

It didn't take long to learn the daily routine. The bell rang at five in the morning, and all the boarders lined up according to their classes for the morning devotion. Every junior student had duties assigned to him, and he must complete his morning task before leaving the dormitory. My morning duty was to tidy the front of the housemaster's house. I had to sweep the fifty-metre lawn daily, as well as clear the weed. I would then make my bed before walking the one mile to the brook to fetch water. Like all the junior students, I had to make double trips as we had to fetch water for the seniors as well. I soon learnt from my colleagues the trick to avoiding making double trips. We would take our towels and soap with us and have our bath in the bush. We would then fetch a bucket of water for our seniors. The problem with this strategy was that if you didn't fetch your water before all the boys entered the brook, the water would become dirty. You would then have to wait for the water to settle again, which could result in causing your senior to be late. Should that happen, you would receive severe punishment.

I noted that one of my friends had two buckets. An older classmate, Michael Obamonire, was more mature than me. As a farmer's son from a polygamous home, Michael and I had a similar background. He was the first person that I made my friend. Inspired by Michael, on our first outing day, I bought a second aluminium bucket. I wrote my name boldly on the outside of my new bucket, like the first. Michael and I would then go to the brook with two buckets. We carried one on our head and the other with one hand. We had no pipe-borne water, so we depended on the brook for our daily water use, but sometimes, the water was so full of particles, we had to put alum blocks into the bucket to make the particles settle at the bottom and make the water drinkable.

It was much easier to get water in the raining season. You could fill your bucket with rain water. The problem was that boys, who were too lazy to come out into the rain, would steal your water whilst you were unaware. One morning, I didn't go to the brook with the other students since I had filled my buckets the previous evening. I had hoped to go to school early. But when I checked under my bed, where I had kept my water, one of the buckets was completely empty. Someone had emptied it. I had to give the other bucket of water to my senior, so Michael and I shared his bucket of water for our bath.

We had a tank in which water collected in the raining season. One day, I was desperate for water, but as I lifted the lid of the tank, several dead toads rose to the surface. That put me off drawing water from the tank. It was better to trek to the brook than drink water littered with decomposed toad carcasses.

We were thirty-five students in form 1A. I had thought that I was the youngest and smallest student in my class, considering that those that I had seen in the boarding house were much older, much bigger and more mature than I was. As the day boys and girls joined in, I realised that I was among the smallest, but not the smallest student.

Our first subject was English literature. Our literature teacher, a beautiful lady in her early twenties with NCE teachers' qualification, was inspiring. We were meant to read a book entitled *Kidnapped*. The book was familiar to the older students, as it was their standard book in the modern school. They could narrate the whole story. Some of them had almost the same understanding, if not better than the teacher. I had always thought that I was a bright student, but meeting these students, who seemed to know more than the teacher, knocked off my confidence. Subsequently, I started to lose interest in English literature. Our teacher must have sensed this, as I wasn't as enthusiastic as I had been when I started.

One day, I helped her to carry notebooks to the staffroom, and she remarked that my scores were below her expectations.

"Don't let those modern school leavers beat you," she advised.

"But they seem to know everything," I replied.

"Not for long," she said. "Just try your best."

I didn't understand what she meant by 'Not for long' until later when we started a new book, *Lorna Doone*. They hadn't read the book in the modern school, so it was new to all of us. They became less enthusiastic, as they struggled like the rest of us. I was even more confident as some of them came to me to help explain some parts of the book that they couldn't understand. We were meant to read and summarise the chapters as we read them.

My experience with English literature was the same in other subjects, but I didn't allow them to intimidate me. Whenever they showed off in the class, I recalled our English literature teacher's advice: "Not for long." And true to her words, things started to level out, where their modern-school education no longer created an unfair advantage. By the second term, we were all on level ground, and we knew who the brightest students were.

It wasn't hard for me to make friends, as I had an interest in so many social activities. I joined the Boys Brigade and participated in all its activities. I was a member of the Lilliputians, the School football team of young boys who were not big enough to play for the main school team. I joined the literary and debating society, and I was a member of the dramatic society. I did high jump for Olofun House and won trophies. And I was in the school choir and the Christian union. So I made friends, not only among my classmates but also with my seniors.

Having friends in the senior classes was particularly useful. Our boarding house was like a military school. A military school was probably better, as there was supposed to be discipline. That wasn't the case in my boarding house. The seniors turned themselves into tin gods, doing whatever they liked with no one to control them since we were isolated from the main school grounds.

One incident of such unruly behaviour occurred when one of the seniors punished me for serving him a part of the fish he didn't like. Senior Galadima was the senior boy at our table. It was the duty of the form-one students to serve, and we took it in turns to do so. After preparing the food, the cooks would place the pots of food on each table for the juniors to share out. On this day, it was my turn to share out the meal of white rice and fish stew. It was an unwritten rule that every junior server knew: the seniors must have the largest share and best part of the food. I dished out each person's portion. The dry mud fish had a head more than twice the size of its body. Thinking that the senior should have the largest portion, I dished out the head part of the fish to our table head, covered the bowl and placed it at his side of the table. After the head boy had said the grace, we all sat to have our meals.

We were in the middle of our supper when Senior Galadima arrived. He panted heavily and looked like a tiger that had been on the chase all day, sweat streaming down his forehead.

"Who is the idiot who has done this?" he asked, after taking off the lid of his bowl.

I didn't know what he had seen that upset him. No one seemed to understand what he meant, so we all ignored him.

"I mean, who is the server?" he roared.

"I am," I replied.

"So, you are the one who has served me operculum!" he barked, and threw the lid like a flying saucer at me.

I had anticipated that he would throw it at me. When Senior Galadima was angry, he could do anything. He reached boiling point in a twinkle of the eye. Whatever he held when he boiled became his weapon. His anger knew no bounds. So I ducked and let the saucer fly over my head. It crashed onto another table, but didn't hit anyone. He asked me to stand on the table with my bowl of food on my head and eat from it, ignoring my pleas that I had served him what I thought was the best part of the fish. I apologised for my wrong judgement.

I had thought that that was all my punishment for serving Senior Galadima a fish head. The time was eleven in the night. The time prefect had rung the lights-out bell at ten o'clock, after which all lights must be switched off and everyone must be in bed. Then the bell rang.

"Forms one to four, come out and fall on your lines," the time prefect announced.

I ran out, still a bit drowsy, to join the other boys. All the prefects and seniors stood in front of the students, looking like they were ready for a battle. We didn't know the reason for this emergency call-out. But, judged by the looks on their faces, we reckoned something serious must have happened. We stood on our lines according to our forms, yawning and slumbering, as we waited for them to tell us what the matter was. Senior Paddy, the head boy, arrived after about thirty minutes, wearing his sports uniform. All his mates moved back and left him to take charge of the gathering.

"Tonight, a boy was fortified with courage to contravene the law of hospitality and generosity," Senior Paddy addressed. "The disciplinary committee of the form five students has met, and his punishment will be irrevocable," he resolved.

My sleep disappeared as the most powerful student stood to attention like an army general. Like the rest of the boys, I stared at Senior Paddy, wondering why he had summoned us at this time of the night.

"You, Dingory, fall out here," he gestured at me.

"What have I done?" I asked.

"You have the audacity to ask the head boy a stupid question!" Senior Galadima landed his long, heavy hand with a knock on my head and brought a hundred sparks into my eyes. My legs turned into jelly. It was as though an asteroid had landed on my head.

"Kneel down there," he commanded.

"I will not," I said, "as I have not committed any offence."

"Oh, I see! So you thought you would go scot-free after serving me operculum, idiot," he roared.

That was when I realised that it was because of me that they had summoned all the students. But I couldn't understand why they had to punish all the juniors for the offence that I had allegedly committed. Just as I thought this, the form-four students started to leave the assembly. Forms four and five students always quarrelled over the smallest issues. Despite the head boy's repeated threats, they continued to leave. Soon, all the form five students came out to reinforce their position. By the same token, the form three students joined in. Within minutes, a brawl had ensued as the seniors tried to establish their authority. Although the principal lived about a mile from the boys' hostel, he often came to the hostel unannounced. The night guard, a middle-aged Ijesha man, whom we called Baba Olode, paraded the school grounds as well as the staff quarters and the boys' and girls' dormitories. Although we often found him snoring away in his small hideout, he always boasted of his supernatural power.

"That I shut my eyes does not mean that I sleep, you know," he often said. "Kerosene does not ever sleep." And when you found him snoring, he would say, "Oh, I was having a meeting with the spirit."

One other reason we all revered him was that whatever went on in the boys' dormitory would become known to the principal. Even things that seemed to be secret would reach the principal. All the students, and even some teachers, believed that the Ijesha man had a supernatural power.

The head boy did everything he could to pacify his classmates and the class-four students. As he had anticipated, Baba Olode arrived with his dog and shotgun. But by the time he arrived, all the boys had dispersed into their hostels. The head boy reassured him that there was no problem. He told him that it was a routine Friday-night gathering.

I heaved a sigh of relief, as I thought that the night guard had saved the day and tucked myself under my blanket. But as I was about to dose off, I heard Senior Galadima roar, "Where is the Dingory?"

My heart stopped. What now? I wondered. With an angry stretch of his hand, he pulled me out of my blanket, and dragged me out of the bunkbed. "Follow me to my hostel," he commanded.

Senior Galadima directed me to kneel on top of pebbles that he had piled up in one corner of the room. I pleaded to him, with tears running down my cheeks, but he turned deaf ears to me. I even promised him that I would bring him bigger and better fish after the holidays. Of course, fish was no problem to me. And he knew that. As riverine dwellers, our main source of protein was fish. So it was something that I found hard to understand, that someone would treat me with so much cruelty for something that was so easy to catch in my village.

Meanwhile, Senior Paddy went from dormitory to dormitory to ensure that all the boys were in bed after the hullabaloo. He was furious I wasn't in my bed. A few strides of his long legs, and he was face-to-face with Senior Galadima.

"Let him go back to his bed now," he roared.

"I will release him when I'm satisfied," Senior Galadima roared back.

"That's when he's dropped dead. Right?" The head boy raised two angry folds on his forehead.

He took two long steps. Now within an arm's length of Senior Galadima, who had stood to face him like a boxer in the ring, he advised, "I have protected you tonight."

"Don't be ridiculous," Senior Galadima narrowed his eye.

"By not telling the principal the reason for all the trouble tonight," the head boy said. "And if you don't release this boy immediately, you will have some explanations to make to the principal as well as his parents," he commanded.

"Is that a threat?" Senior Galadima barked.

"No, it is not a threat. It is an order," the head boy roared. And turning to me, he ordered, "Now, get up and fly to your room."

My knees felt as if all the pebbles had sunk into them.

"Yes, sir," I said. And with hot, swollen knees, I leaped out of Senior Galadima's dormitory.

My roommates were already snoring when I arrived back. I hadn't tucked in my mosquito net when Senior Galadima had pulled me out earlier on, so when I returned, my net had become a haven for the mosquitoes. I tried unsuccessfully to get rid of them, and in the end, I dragged my tired body up into my double bunkbed for the sleep that it desperately yearned for.

Two mountain gorillas were in a tournament in front of the boys' hostel. There were no spectators. I was the umpire.

"Where are the boys?" I asked myself.

One of the gorillas looked twice as the other. His look was deadly. How could I officiate when two monsters were fighting? What if they both decided to turn on me and make a meal of me? I must find a way of escape. As these thoughts were going through my mind, the smaller gorilla freed himself from the larger one and charged towards me. His bloodshot eyes made my heart stop. I trembled all over. He stretched his massive hand and grabbed my neck.

"Come down, Dingory," Senior Galadima commanded as he grabbed my ankle.

I blinked several times, my heart still racing, and banged my head on the side support of the bed. My sleep quickly disappeared. It was no more a nightmare. It was now the real human gorilla, Senior Galadima, ready to devour me.

I thought I had overslept and failed to hear the morning bell, but when I turned to look at my bedside clock, it had just gone past two-thirty.

"Take this," he said, as he handed me a tablespoon.

I stared at him, wondering what I had done to deserve the gift of an aluminium spoon. I knew I hadn't left a spoon in his room. And if he wanted me to keep his spoon, that shouldn't make him wake me up and drag me out of bed.

"And this," he added, pointing to an empty bucket on the floor.

I pulled a questioning eye, still trying to piece together what he meant. What should I do with a spoon and an empty bucket? I wondered.

"Right, I will leave this bucket under my bed," he said. And then with his large hand around my neck, he instructed, "Now, go to the brook and fetch water with the spoon into the bucket. You will do that until the bucket is full."

I wanted to cry, but there was no use. This man was the gorilla in my dream. My nightmare.

"Okay," I said, but I knew I would certainly disobey him. Nothing would make me walk the one mile to the brook on my own. I would rather die in this man's room than get swallowed by a python or eaten by a wild beast. But I left his room with the spoon in my hand and made him think that I was going to go to the brook. At first, I thought of going to report to the head boy, but I wasn't sure if he would support me. Senior

Galadima could even make up a story just so that his colleague could believe him. In the end, I turned in a different direction – towards the principal's house.

I had been gone for three minutes when I saw two torchlights shining in the opposite direction. My heart sank. I wondered who the people were. I knew that many of the seniors used to stay behind in the classroom after prep to do their reading. But my main worry was whether these were bandits looking for someone to kidnap for ritual sacrifice. So I withdrew and stood in front of House One, the first of the dormitories. As the people walked closer, it became apparent that they were two seniors: Senior Loyola, the games prefect, and Senior Ojo, my college father. Whilst Senior Galadima had spent the whole night punishing a form-one student for serving him a fish head, his colleagues were busy preparing for their West African School Certificate Examination (WASCE).

"What?" Senior Ojo screamed.

I couldn't say anything. I simply stared at the tablespoon in my hand.

Senior Loyola was a brilliant, easy-going prefect. Unlike most of his colleagues, he rarely punished the juniors. He was a brilliant student and a fantastic footballer, and all the students loved him. I had no doubt in my mind that, if he was in the hostel when the seniors called me out, he would stop their reckless behaviour.

"You mean, Galadima asked you to go to the brook at three in the morning to fill a bucket with spoonfuls of water?" he asked, after I had narrated everything that had happened to them.

I nodded.

"Right," he said and tore his way to the head boy, who was fast asleep, unaware of what Senior Galadima had put me through.

Senior Ojo raced to Senior Galadima's dormitory. He almost tore his mosquito net as he dragged him out of his bed. Still drowsy, Senior Galadima staggered to his feet.

"How dare you disturb my sleep?" Senior Galadima shouted.

Senior Ojo stood in front of him. His muscles twitched as he tried to suppress the urge to strike him. After staring at each other for nearly five minutes, he reached for Elijah, my classmate. Elijah was the junior student assigned to Senior Galadima. He slept in the bunkbed on top of

Senior Galadima's. Senior Ojo dragged him out like he had done Senior Galadima. He got the spoon that Senior Galadima had given me.

"Now, take this spoon," he commanded. "Go now and fill a bucket with water from the brook."

"What have I done?" Elijah protested.

"Well, ask your Senior," Senior Ojo said.

Just then, the head boy and Senior Loyola marched into the room.

"Galadima, this thing must be brought to an end now," the head boy said with authority.

"Are you telling me I don't have the right to punish a good-for-nothing junior who has been disrespectful to me?" he roared.

"You," the head boy said to me, ignoring Senior Galadima's outburst, "go to your room and see if you can get some sleep." And turning to Senior Galadima, he said, "You can have my fish portion tomorrow if you like. Right?"

I raced out of the room and prayed that there would be no more events. It had gone just past three-thirty, and I would have to wake up at five like the other students.

The head boy decreed to move me from Senior Galadima's table to Senior Ojo's table.

Better, But Not Good Enough

The fear and threat to my confidence by the modern-school leavers became easier, and I scored top marks in most subjects in the first year. In fact, I faced no real challenges in the first year, and my promotion to form two was not a question, but I aimed to be in the A class. In UGS, students were assigned to their classes according to their exams results.

Victor Onoviran joined us in form two. A modern-school leaver, he was among the oldest students in our form, but he looked like one of the youngest. Soon after joining our class, Victor showed his brilliance. I was no longer a local champion, as I now had to compete with Victor for the first position at each examination. This was, in a way, good for me, as it made me work harder.

Despite our academic rivalry, Victor and I were good friends. We had so many things in common and shared friendships. Victor joined the Boy Scout and rose to the rank of a Scout Master. I went as far as the rank of a lieutenant in the Boys Brigade. We were both active in the literary and debating society, in which we were always on opposing teams. He was an all-rounder student excelling in all subjects, and he had an incredible memory. I learnt from him how to commit things into memory. This was the case when we challenged each other into memorising the whole of Shakespeare's *Julius Caesar*. We later acted the play, in which Victor and I took prominent roles. He was the overall best student in my year.

I had close friends in senior classes too, many of whom were role models who significantly impacted my performance. However, the attitude of one particular senior to mathematics had a less than positive impact on me. He gave me the impression that mathematics was a useless subject, and there was no need for it, as it would lead me to nowhere. What was once my best subject became something that I struggled with.

That year, my form-two year, Victor beat me to the second position in the promotion examination from form two to three. I wasn't pleased with my performance, as I had hoped to come first. As we broke up for the third term, I went home determined to beat my only rival the following term.

Although I wasn't pleased with my results, my parents were. All that mattered to them was that I was in the first three.

"We are happy with first, second or third," they reassured me. "Just make sure you don't fall behind," they said.

As I folded my report sheet and was about to tuck it away in the long brown envelope, my uncle breezed into the room. Papa Zacchaeus was my father's immediate younger brother. A tall and handsome man, he was highly regarded by all of us. My father always trusted his younger brother, particularly in matters relating to educational discipline.

"Our son has done very well again," he reported and focused on the A4 paper like you do when you are reading an interesting story in the newspaper. I smiled as I watched him nodding and smiling. But my heart dropped as I watched his smiles disappear into a frown. I didn't have to be told that he had spotted my Mathematics 18%.

"Come here," he ordered. "Eighteen percent in Mathematics?"

I scratched my head. I knew the reason, but I simply stared at him, praying that he didn't land his large hand on my head. My parents didn't understand why Uncle would react that way. After all, I had done well coming second in the third-term examination with my promotion guaranteed. That was the only thing that mattered, as far as they were concerned.

"Look at this!" he exclaimed. "You have top marks in French, history, general science, health science and literature. And your marks in the other subjects are impressive too. Surely, you must have neglected your mathematics. I am sure if you had scored a high mark in mathematics, you would have come first."

My uncle had hit the nail on its head. Of course, I knew that, and I feared the repercussions from this no-nonsense uncle. I had already determined to get back into gear with regard to mathematics. I had promised myself that I would never ignore any subject. And I would never again let anyone have a negative influence on me.

"Well, no Lagos for you this holiday," he said, as he handed my report sheet back to me.

Although I loved to spend my holidays in Lagos, I really wasn't bothered this time. We were not short of things to do that time of the year. The village boomed with people coming from the city for Christmas. It was also the time when farmers harvested yams, so I didn't plead to go to Lagos. In any case, I knew, of course, that even if I wanted to go to Lagos, once Uncle had declared it, even my father wouldn't overturn it. So I was resigned to spending the whole third term holiday in the village.

Later that evening, Uncle called me to the lounge. The table had been set for him and Daddy. I thought it was unusual for me to dine with them.

"Have," my uncle said, as he handed a Clark's Combined Mathematics book to me.

I stared blankly, wondering why my uncle should reward me with a new book despite my woeful performance in mathematics.

"Thanks, sir," I said.

"You like it?" he asked.

"Yes, sir," I replied. "That's what they use in Stella Maris College."

"Right," he said. "That's your project this holiday. You will remain in the village. I will be back before the end of your holiday." Then he handed me an A4 exercise book. "And when I return, I want to see that you have read all the chapters and written your answers to all the questions in this book," he decreed.

Solve all the questions? How could I? We hadn't even done some of those topics in the class. I was only a form-two student. How on earth could I start doing form-five students sums? These were among the countless number of questions that caused my tongue to stick to the roof of my mouth, as I stared at the hardback, white and green book of mathematics.

Daddy simply nodded, as his brother pronounced my judgment. I knew, of course, that they must have discussed it. Uncle must have explained to my parents that mathematics was an important subject. He must have told them that scoring high marks in the rest of the subjects was not enough. Scoring high marks in all the subjects, including mathematics, was what would guarantee a good grade in my WASCE.

I went straight to my room. I sat on the bed with my back leaning against the wall. At first, I hated my uncle's decision. It was the long holiday, the Christmas holiday, time for fun. How could I finish a whole book of O-level mathematics in less than three months? As my anger melted away and my senses returned, I considered the fact that this man had cycled ten miles to buy the book from the only local bookshop in Okitipupa. He must have bought it with his own meagre funds. But I already had mathematics books. The ones the school had supplied us were in three separate volumes: algebra, arithmetic and geometry. That was what our school had recommended to us, and that was what all the UGS students used. The one that my uncle had just bought wasn't even up to the size of the algebra volume of CV Durrell's mathematics book. Why would my uncle spend his own income on a book that probably didn't cover the whole syllabus? Nevertheless, I opened the book. And as I looked through it, page by page, I said to myself, "My uncle has bought me not just a book but a teacher of mathematics." He must have been genuinely concerned. Surely, he wanted me to do very well. He knew that I had potential. And, of course, I myself knew the cause of my poor score in mathematics. I liked everything about the book. I wanted to prove to my uncle that he was right that I could do better. But, more importantly, I wanted to endorse the philosophy that my parents had planted into me, that nothing is impossible. I should never say, "I can't." They had taught me to take away doubts and get on with it. So, I resolved to touch every page of the book and, at least, attempt every question. I unwrapped the notebook that Uncle had bought with the mathematics book, wrote *WASCE Mathematics* on the back and began my assignment.

I needed to have a distraction-free place to study. By this time, we had moved out of the main family house close to the beach, into my father's newly built, large-storey building. I had a single room to myself. But that time of the year, our house was never short of visitors, and Father would call me to greet every visitor.

The primary school was only a five-minute walk from our new house. The primary-six room was at one end of the row of bungalows. All the windows were intact, the roof wasn't leaking, and the door could be securely shut to provide all the privacy that I needed. So I chose to do my studies in the primary school.

Since I started secondary school, my mother had relieved me of most of the housework that I used to do. I didn't have to help with cooking or washing the plates. My siblings and cousins now had to do all those things. So after having my bath and breakfast, there was nothing else to hold me back. I went straight to the primary school and locked myself in the primary-six classroom for self-teaching in mathematics.

I had an easy ride in the first few weeks, since the topics were those that we had covered in forms one and two. I didn't struggle with any question. What that showed me was that I wasn't actually weak at mathematics. And like my uncle had said, if I could score high marks in the other subjects, I could do so in mathematics. My confidence returned, and I looked forward each day to doing more sums. In addition to spending time in the primary school, I also woke up around four o'clock every morning to do more sums. Sometimes, I would stay up into the night, finding solutions to particularly difficult questions. I had no one to help me with the questions, and in some cases, it could take me several days to find the answers. I had a great sense of satisfaction when I eventually solved the questions. I couldn't believe how my interest in mathematics had grown in just a few weeks. And that was a great impetus that motivated and provided me with daily encouragement.

As I watched the notebook filling up, I had no doubt in my mind that I would complete the assignment, and I was grateful to my uncle for spotting my weakness and for the academic discipline that he had imparted in my life.

I completed the whole book four days before Christmas. Uncle returned from Lagos on Christmas Eve. He hadn't expected me to have completed the book. I guess he only really wanted me to brush up my mathematics, perhaps a way of testing my responsibility and problem-solving ability. I decided not to tell him straightaway. I wanted him to call me and ask me in the presence of my parents and uncles and aunts. That was the best time for me to show off, I thought.

I didn't know why Uncle didn't ask me. I wondered if it was because he didn't want to spoil my Christmas, thinking that I might not have finished. It was also plausible that he didn't see the need to ask so soon. After all, we still had a few weeks to the end of the holiday. One thing that was certain was that he hadn't forgotten. My uncle never took anything that pertained to education lightly. And he would always carry whatever plan he had made to the end. For my own sake, I wanted to submit my assignment because if I didn't, I would be expected to lock myself away from the Christmas and New Year festivities in my room to swot.

"I have finished, sir," I said, as I handed the exercise book to my uncle.

If Uncle was surprised, it didn't show on his face.

"Sure?" he asked.

"Yes, sir," I replied.

I stood before him, my hands tucked behind my back. After clearing his throat, he wiped his glasses and opened the notebook containing my answers to the questions in Clarke's Combined Mathematics.

"I will call you when I finish," he said, after scanning through a few pages, and dismissed me.

I waited all through the day for Uncle to call me, but nothing happened. We celebrated Christmas as usual. Still, nothing happened. So I took my mind off it, thinking Uncle had made me spend my holiday studying when I should be playing. One observation I made was that he said yes to whatever requests I made. Even when I sought his permission to go to the local music bands' show in Ode Irele, he didn't object. Western Dandies and Rosy Star were famous among the youth in those days. Everyone looked forward to their Christmas parties. I also observed that he often told my cousins and siblings to emulate me whenever he reprimanded them. So I concluded that whether Uncle had looked at my answers or not didn't matter. The fact was that he set a target for me to finish the assignment by the end of the holiday, but I set my own target to finish before Christmas. And I did. That was what mattered to me. And that gave me a great sense of satisfaction and fulfilment.

Saturday after the New Year celebration, around about five o'clock in the morning, I had a knock on my door. I was already up, reading a novel in bed. My heart sank as my uncle breezed into my room, holding a notebook in his hand, wondering if he had come to give me another assignment. I blinked several times as my eyes settled on the notebook in his hand, the notebook containing my mathematics assignment.

"Good morning, sir," I greeted and pushed myself out of my bed.

"Morning, son," he said. "God bless you." He pulled out a chair and sat by the table. "I am impressed," he observed. And after clearing his throat, he asked, "Now tell me, have you reflected on this issue? I mean have you looked back to know why you didn't do well in mathematics?"

"Yes, sir," I replied.

I explained to my uncle that some of my seniors made me neglect mathematics. I told him that they had wrongly advised me to spend more time on other subjects, as mathematics wasn't that important. I expressed my sincere regrets. My uncle advised me to always be myself. I must endeavour to do the right thing and to be truthful, no matter the intimidation or temptation. Moreover, he advised me to believe in myself and to continue to aspire to greater heights. Then he handed me five pounds.

"You've got to learn from successful failures," he advised. "Failure is in successful men's portfolio. True failure is when you fail to learn from your failure. Son, you have learnt and so, you have not failed," he said as he gently tapped my shoulder.

"Thank you, sir," I said and really meant it.

I had personal satisfaction for setting a target for myself and meeting that target. That gave me personal gratification. I learnt valuable life skills from this experience. I would never allow bad influences to change my circumstances. And I promised I would continue to do my best in everything, no matter how hard it was.

The Game Changer

I started form three with high hopes and confidence. I now had two sets of students referring to me as 'Senior'. Although I still had forms four and five to contend with, I found that not to be a big issue.

Those weren't the only changes that occurred in the new term. We were informed before we broke up that the principal would be leaving. A new principal had been appointed during the holiday. We also had a new mathematics teacher, who was also to take up chemistry. The French teacher had left, and there was no replacement. Likewise, there was no teacher for Latin. And, of course, we had a new set of prefects.

The new principal arrived in the school assembly in his academic gown with *MA Durham* obvious to everyone from the distance. A middle-aged man, with bushy moustache and a pair of wide-framed glasses on his narrow face, Mr Joseph Olagokun stood in front of the assembly. He looked tough. He was determined to transform United Grammar School.

We stood still according to our forms, listening to the principal, like the Israelites listened to Moses reading out the Ten Commandments, as he promulgated the decrees aimed to bring radical changes to the school. He had spent his time studying students performances whilst the schools were on holidays, not only in the WASCE but also in the term examinations. A thorough man with a great attention to detail, he knew exactly why the students did badly in the WASCE despite good term performances. It was obvious to him that most of them failed in mathematics and very few got credits in English. But the grading rules in WASCE were clear: to have a grade one, a student must have at least a credit in English and mathematics. Whatever your scores in the other subjects, failure in both subjects would automatically push you into grade three if you were lucky. As a matter of fact, there were no grade ones in the set that had just finished their WASCE. So, Mr Olagokun's first change was to introduce the grading system into the term examinations, exactly as in the WASCE, and do away with the traditional first, second, third, etc, performance model. As he stated this, it hit me like a bullet. If our promotion exam had been our WASCE, then I would have had no chance of a good grade, despite coming second. And I thanked my uncle for his visionary thoughtfulness.

"English is very important," he said. "It is fundamental to all the other subjects, even mathematics." He paused and adjusted his glasses. "You can't learn a language without speaking that language," he continued, after clearing his throat. Then he announced that he would take on the teaching of English for classes three to five. He also decreed that we must speak in English at all times. Anyone caught speaking in vernacular would be punished. And he encouraged us to read novels. This was at variance with hitherto practice. Some of our teachers and seniors had made us believe that reading a book other than the recommended literature text was a waste of time. The seniors went about seizing any novel found with students. But, with this declaration by the new principal, we had the liberty to read novels, as long as it had no offensive content.

After emphasising the importance of these two compulsory WASCE subjects, he was quick to add that all the subjects were important too. "Every subject offered in this school is important," he said, "and none of them must be neglected."

Finally, he reminded the school of the need for discipline. He advised that we all maintained good conduct and promised severe punishment for any student who failed to uphold our values. "The seniors should be mentors to the juniors, not terrors," he concluded.

With my new-found confidence in mathematics, I began my class three with eagerness. The new mathematics teacher was a 'son of the soil'. An NCE graduate, Mr Adetuwo was highly regarded in the community. He was also the games master and the Boys Brigade leader. Having a teacher with so much respect and credibility, and who had the best interests of the students at his heart, further increased my interest in mathematics. I had already covered the whole syllabus on my own during the long holiday, so mathematics lessons were like revision to me. When the teacher asked us to solve a sum, I was almost always the first person to answer. I sat in the front row, and it was easy for me to jump to solve problems that our teacher had written on the board. Later, our teacher decided not to ask me questions, and often ignored my raised hand, to give other students the opportunity to answer questions and learn.

My newly acquired high standard in mathematics brought its own problems too. Whilst some of my friends and classmates were happy that

I was readily available to help with their homework, others became jealous. The mathematics teacher often ridiculed some of the senior students whenever they struggled with their mathematics, saying, "I will call a form-three student to come and solve it." And one day, he did just that. He was teaching a group of seniors during break. I marched into the class with all eyes on me. "I'm sure you know the answer," the teacher urged me. It was a question in trigonometry. I had done it before. It took me less than three minutes to prove that one angle was equal to the other and to calculate their values. After writing *QED* at the end of my answer, "Easy," I said and took my leave.

The teacher often told the students that if I took the WAEC mathematics, he would expect me to get an A. This got into my head. But I didn't realise how my success was aggravating some of the senior students until one day, when a senior wanted to punish me for not switching off my light when the lights-out bell rang.

"No wonder you couldn't solve simple sums," I said to him. This spelt my doom. My punishment was to sleep under his bed. The mosquitoes had an easy prey to feed on, with hundreds of them hanging on the walls the following morning, with their bellies looking like prunes. That taught me a great lesson: Humility.

One of the projects that the school embarked on was the expansion of the class arms and the building of a new kitchen and assembly hall. The need for these facilities had been earmarked by the governor body, but there was no funding. So everything was put on the hold until funding became available. But Mr Olagokun believed that we could do it even with the limited funds and ordered that the students made the blocks. We had just finished our second-term examination. My allocation, like boys of my age, was to mould twenty bricks. My friends and I decided to help one another, and we completed our numbers within three days. We had nothing more to do than to mess about, making fun of those students who hadn't completed their numbers or whose bricks were crooked. But, as the saying goes, the devil finds work for idle hands. One day, after we had completed moulding our bricks, I went with my friends to pluck mangoes and avocados. That time of the year, the mango and avocado trees were heavy-laden with matured fruits. But the trees were tall, so we had to throw sticks at the fruits to make them drop. We managed to pluck a few, and the five of us sat on the windows of one of the uncompleted school buildings to eat our fruits. Just then, three police officers passed by. They were on their way from Ode Irele to Ebute Irele. For no apparent reasons, Simon started calling them names. We all joined in. After abusing them, we threw sticks at them and jumped into the bush. We did this several times before the officers were out of our sight. After about ten minutes, the officers returned and followed the same route that they had previously taken. And we did exactly what we had done before, shouting at them, calling them names and hurling sticks at them.

The following day, the principal called the five of us into his office. He narrated the whole event that had occurred the previous day, exactly as it was. How could he have known? I wondered. But everything he said was true. He kept no details away. He asked each of us what we knew about the 'ugly scene', as he put it. My friends denied their involvement, claiming that the person who reported us to the principal must have made up the story to discredit us because we had finished moulding our bricks before them. I was the last person that the principal asked. At first, I wanted to deny it, just as my friends had done. But I thought there was no point denying it. I was brought up to always tell the truth, no matter what. Besides, for the principal to give such a graphic and detailed description of the scene, he must have either seen us himself or whoever had informed him must have had a clear view of the event.

"I was there, sir," I confessed. "I am sorry, sir."

I felt like the ground could just open and swallow me. There was no need for a grave. But my mind was at ease after confessing. And if the ground could swallow me, I would go with the truth said. After my confession, the principal asked my friends again, and they all confessed.

"I know how hard your parents have worked to find the money to send you to school," the principal said. "So I will not expel you. But I will teach you a lesson you will never forget."

The principal called in Mr Akinduro, the agriculture master. We took off our clothes, leaving only our pants on. The principal gave each of us ten lashes of the canes on our buttocks whilst Mr Akinduro held our hands to prevent us from protecting ourselves. As each person received a lash, the principal would ask, "What is the school motto?" And the person would reply, "Integrity, culture and industry." After we had all received our lashes, the principal ordered us to follow Mr Akinduro. He took us to a large, flamboyant tree and ordered us to uproot it.

It took us over one week of hard work to uproot the tree, and only three days now remained until the second-term holiday. The principal called me into his office. I thought he was going to give me a letter of expulsion or a letter to my parents, informing them about my bad behaviour.

"Look outside," he directed. "What can you see?" he asked.

"It's raining," I replied.

"Yes, it is raining," he said. "Sit down." He directed me to one of the chairs in front of me. "Your father is probably in the jungle in the torrents of rain, working in the most treacherous conditions so that you may have a better life." He removed his glasses, and after wiping his face, he put them back on. "You are a brilliant student. I have seen your term results, and I am pleased. You must not join a bad company. And you must learn to say no when friends want you to join them to do bad things."

I had tried not to cry, but I couldn't hold it in as I listened to this fatherly figure that most people had seen as a tyrant. I had no doubt in my mind that he was a good man, and whatever he did was for good. He told me that he knew that I was not the ringleader. And he was right. On my own, I could never have conceived the idea of abusing anyone, let alone police officers. Simon started it. We thought it was fun. Then the rest of us joined in. But, in retrospect, I could have stopped Simon or left if he didn't stop. What Mr Olagokun told me changed my behaviour. He made me promise him that I would never join bad groups, I would be well behaved, respect authorities and work hard to reach my potential. And I did.

The reformation that Mr Olagokun brought to UGS touched every aspect of our school life. He was an iron man, a no-nonsense principal. But that was what a school at the brink of academic decadence and moral delinquency desperately needed. He repeatedly reminded us of the school's motto: Integrity, Culture and Industry – to be honest, respect our moral values and do everything to the best of our ability. With his team of committed teachers, UGS was holistically transformed. For the first time, there were many students with high grades in the School Certificate Examination and in the compulsory subjects, including mathematics and

English. We also excelled in intercollegiate activities, including athletics, football and literary competitions.

Medicine Without Physics?

Among the new teachers that started with the new principal was Mr Ayoade. Like many of our teachers, he had just done his A-Level examination. He took the temporary teaching job whilst awaiting his results and a place in the university. A teenager, he was younger than many of my classmates. Yet he was highly respected.

On his first day in the science class, he asked each person to introduce him or herself. So, one by one, the students stood up and announced their first names, surnames and what they hoped to do after their secondary school education. Some students wanted to be teachers, accountants, clerical officers, agricultural officers, and so on.

"And you?" Mr Ayoade pointed at me.

I stood up and told him my first name and surname, like the other students.

"I want to go to the university and study doctor's course," I said, after clearing my throat.

"You mean, you want to study medicine," Mr Ayoade corrected me.

"No, I don't want to be selling medicine," I argued.

I had mistaken medicine for pharmacy. I had thought that pharmacists studied medicine and doctors studied 'doctor'. As a matter of fact, I didn't know that one needed to go to university to study pharmacy. My understanding of a pharmacist was that of a patent medicine seller or a dispenser in hospital. I had thought that the doctor did everything, including diagnosis, treatment and preparing the medicine.

Mr Ayoade couldn't help laughing at my ignorance. My colleagues joined in, even though very few of them had had career guidance and very few, apart from those that had transferred from other schools, knew the courses available in the university.

Mr Ayoade shook his head in pity as the laughter died down.

"Medicine without physics? How can you study medicine without physics?" He shook his head again, and my classmates again almost blew up the roof of the classroom with their laughter. Mr Ayoade had to control them, lest the uproar reached the principal.

Throughout the science lesson, I couldn't help thinking over what the new teacher had said. "Medicine without physics?" occupied every inch of my brain, so much so that there was no room for anything else. I was crazy. I was frantic. I needed to do something. I had to talk to Mr Ayoade. I needed his advice and guidance. I knew I had to talk to him without my classmates. I couldn't wait for the bell to ring for lunch break. I knew that Mr Ayoade would be in the staffroom during lunch. But, at that time, most of the teachers would be there also. I refused to let their presence intimidate me.

Mr Ayoade's seat was at the far end of the room, which meant that I would have to walk through the middle of the large common room. But to my advantage, it was directly opposite the main entrance. As I stepped into the room, Mr Ayoade beckoned me over. I wasn't sure if he was expecting me, but I really didn't care. I marched to his seat, ignoring the questioning demeanour of his colleagues.

Mr Ayoade pulled a seat close to his table and asked me to sit down. I told him that I was concerned by what he had said about how to become a doctor. I emphasised my passion for medicine and my dream to become a doctor. Mr Ayoade advised me that physics was an essential subject for medicine, and since we didn't offer that subject in my school, it was an impossible dream. But if I really wanted to study medicine at the university, the best thing to do was to change school.

Following the meeting with the science teacher, I wrote applications to many schools to transfer. Most of them did not reply. Some of those that replied wanted me to repeat form three. Others wanted me to sit examinations with form-two students, while one wanted me to start in form two. The term was almost getting to the end when I got the replies. I had another meeting with Mr Ayoade and updated him.

"I have been doing some thinking," he said. "You could do physics in the GCE."

He informed me that I would need to have six credits to be eligible to study medicine. And that included physics, chemistry, biology, mathematics and English. As I was not going to transfer to another school, the best option for me was to enter for six subjects, including physics and the other compulsory subjects in the GCE. He advised that I could do that either before my WASCE or after. But, as it was a tough examination, it would be best to do it before the WASCE. Doing it after the WASCE would be more difficult, as there would be too many distractions.

The following week, Mr Ayoade called me to the staff common room. He had the Cambridge University GCE O-Level form for me. He also gave me his old copy of Principles of Physics by Nelkon and Parker.

"You can do it," he encouraged me.

The plan was for me to sit the examination the following year, the end of my form four. He offered to give me private lessons in physics. Although he was only going to be in our school for a short time, as he would be going to the university the following September, he reassured me that he would try his best to give me a good grounding in physics before leaving. He had obtained the games master's permission for me to spend part of the games period in the evening with him, so he could offer me private physics lessons.

The *New Kitchen* Scandal

I chose to do my private studies in the new kitchen that was under construction. This was a convenient place for me to study as it provided me with a distraction-free environment. Although it was a hideaway, I was visible to the games master and the prefects. Since Mr Ayoade had sought the games master's permission to excuse me from games to enable me prepare for my Cambridge GCE, I had no problems with the prefects. Nevertheless, I had to make myself obvious to assure them that I utilised the time for my private study and nothing else.

One afternoon, I was in the new kitchen as usual. A junior student brought a problem in mathematics. My newly achieved competence in mathematics brought with it fame that went beyond my class. I not only helped many of my classmates but also junior students with their homework. Earlier in the day, I had helped a number of her classmates, so it didn't take me long to solve the problem in trigonometry. As Vicky left the room, I heard someone coughed behind the window. I got up, and when I looked out two boys, Vicky's classmates, ran off. One of the boys was among the students I had previously helped. I didn't understand why they behaved that way. I reasoned that they must have thought that I would report them to the games master for roaming about when they should be doing their games.

The games period was over. The time prefect rang the bell, confirming it was time for supper. I hurried to my classroom to lock away my books before making my way to the canteen.

As I approached the canteen, I noticed boys and girls gathered in small groups. That wasn't unusual. It was the opportunity for friends to catch up with gossip and rumours. What was unusual was that they stopped chatting when I moved closer. And after I had passed by, they shouted, "New kitchen!" and giggled.

I didn't realise that all the gossip and taunts were about me until the head boy called me into his room. Apparently, the rumour had dominated the gossips across the genders that Vicky and I were involved in sexual activities that afternoon when I helped her with her mathematics. The principal had charged the head boy to question me whilst the head girl interviewed Vicky.

I told the head boy that nothing happened between us. I was still a virgin, and even if I was going to do any such thing, as had been alleged, that was neither the right time nor place for it. I enjoined him to trust that I had told him the truth and was prepared to swear on the bible. The head boy stared uncomfortably into my heart. Then after what seemed like eternity, he gently rested his hand on my shoulder.

"I believe you," he reassured me.

"What, sir?" I stared at him. I heard what he said, but my brain gave a different interpretation to the auditory impulse.

"You see, I am a grownup man. I have done that thing before. I mean, I have slept with a woman before." Then he smiled and added, "But from talking to you, I have no doubt that you've never slept with a woman, let alone with Vicky."

I didn't know what it was that I said, or what my body language told him to convince him of my innocence. Nevertheless, I was glad that he believed me. He reassured me that the head girl, after interviewing Vicky, had also concluded that she was innocent.

"How could people be so wicked?" I asked. "Why would they make up such an unkind story?" I scratched my head. I was close to tears.

My vindication by the head boy did nothing to stop the taunts. Boys still shouted "New kitchen!" whenever they passed by. They taunted in groups, as individuals and from their hideouts.

I lost confidence. It was beginning to affect my concentration and sleep pattern. I was up all night. I tried to be brave to confront my detractors and punish them for the untrue rumour, but that was bound to make it worse for me. If the principal caught me fighting, he could bring up the matter to the school assembly, irrespective of my innocence. He could expel me from boarding or even completely from the school. So, I tried to keep to myself and limited my interactions to a smaller circle of friends: the few that believed in me and were convinced of my innocence. These friends, most of whom were older and bigger than me, fought on my behalf to stop the rumour that had spread all over the school like a wildfire.

I had no doubt that the teachers would have heard about it. And if they had, so would the principal. Although I felt bad about the issue, I felt worse for Vicky, an innocent class-two girl who had sought the help of a form-four student and had become an object of ridicule.

My fear materialised the following week when our biology teacher called me for a meeting with her. Mrs Ogunbameru, a highly regarded and much-loved teacher, sent for me. The meeting took place in her residence at the staff quarters. She offered me fried plantains, after which she sat me down and interviewed me. Just as the head boy had done, she reassured me that she believed my story. Prior to chatting with me, she had already spoken to Vicky. She believed that we were both innocent. She further advised that she knew the ringleader and the boys who perpetrated the rumour. She had asked them. They admitted that they didn't see us doing anything together, but they saw her coming out of the new kitchen. So they thought she must have had sexual activity with me since I was on my own. I thanked her for trusting me and promised her that I would, at all times, endeavour not to do what would bring dishonour to myself, my family, the school and most importantly, God.

The following day, the principal called me to his office. Having had reassurances, firstly from the head boy and latterly by the respectable Mrs Ogunbameru, I hadn't expected things to get to the highest authority, but they did. Indeed, as the principal informed me, he heard about it the very day that the rumour started. This frightened me and endorsed the belief that all the students had – that the principal had the supernatural power to know everything that went on in the school.

"Sit down there." He directed me to one of the chairs, as he took his own seat behind the large desk. This was unusual. Normally, when you came into the principal's office or the staffroom, you had to stand with your hands locked behind your back. To give me a chair to sit, and be told to make myself comfortable after such a serious allegation of misconduct, was unprecedented. I had expected him to dismiss me summarily. Instead, he allowed me to tell him what had happened. I told him exactly as it was, exactly as l had narrated it to both the head boy and the senior teacher.

The principal stared into my soul, reading the part of me that no one could see – the part where all my secrets resided. My heart quickened, but my spirit was unshaken. I was innocent and would maintain that even if it meant being expelled. Then he smiled.

"I believe you," he concluded.

I didn't know how to react. I froze like a carcass buried in the Antarctic. My eyes welled up. I wanted to jump over his desk and give him a hug. The man whom everybody regarded as a difficult principal had just revealed his soft part: the kind heart of a caring father. He stood up and came over to my side. He placed his hand over my shoulder as tears ran down my cheeks.

"In life, people will say bad things about you. They will make up stories to discredit you. These unkind words are damaging," he said.

He turned and faced me. And resting both hands on my shoulders, he advised, "Go and face your studies. Nothing will come out of this. I will instruct the prefects to be on the lookout, and anyone caught calling you names will be severely dealt with."

I left the principal's office dazed. I felt the way astronauts must feel when they step on the moon. It was breaktime. My friends had waited for me, and as I entered the class, they rushed to me like chickens when thrown a cup of grain. They wanted to have the full gist, but I simply informed them, "All sorted."

My Final Year in Secondary School

I sat the Cambridge GCE examination, as planned, at the end of my form-four year. Mr Ayoade had since gained admission into the university to study engineering. The results came out just after we resumed the new academic year. I had credits in all the six subjects, including physics. With this result, I had fulfilled the requirements to sit the concessional entrance examination into the university to do a preliminary course in medicine. I felt on top of the world, but kept the secret away from everyone. Although theoretically, I could leave school and not bother to have the WASC, I decided to complete the five years. Also, I learnt from my teachers that the minimum age to go to the university was sixteen, and I wasn't old enough yet.

I became the social and chapel prefect. I couldn't understand why I should be two prefects in one. But, of course, I couldn't refuse to be a prefect. It was an honour, and I vowed to carry out the duties to the best of my ability.

Being a social prefect made me popular in and around the school. I had to organise social events, which were often challenging, as ours was a mixed school. In conjunction with the head boy and head girl and other prefects, I had to make sure that boys and girls conducted themselves within moral bounds and that there were no fights. I was also in charge of organising the literary and cultural activities. We had social events every Saturday evening. Apart from disco, the event that most students liked was the Balloon debate. This involved debate among students, representing various professions. The question was: Imagine you were to fly to an uncharted destination, who would you like to take onboard with you: doctor, engineer, teacher, lawyer, farmer or mathematician? Each candidate would try to convince the audience that he or she was the most important profession. At the end of the debate, every student would cast a vote, and I would announce the winner.

I also organised school excursions. Our most famous one was the visit to Aiyetoro Community. With a population of probably around a thousand, this communist island was situated on the coast of the Atlantic Ocean under the leadership of a king. They did everything in isolation from the mainstream Nigerians. They had everything that they needed and didn't depend on the government. They even had a landing place for the helicopter. Everything was free. They even ate their meals at the same time.

The two-week excursion was paradise on earth, and students looked forward to it. Students went in batches. It was not only fun, but it also showed us how they practised communism. We also learnt to respect authority and community values.

At this time, members of our literary society were invited to a play in Ibadan. We had previously staged *The Trial of Brother Jero* in our school. This time it was to be staged at Mapo Hall, Ibadan, with Ibadan Grammar School hosting us, which was a much bigger school. But I found the same student behaviour, with junior students at the mercy of their seniors. From the little that I could see, I found that the Higher School Certificate (HSC) students were able to curb the excesses of the form-five students, unlike in my school, where they were a superpower.

I sat with a form-five student, Ishola Balogun, who was a little smaller than me but a year older. Like me, he hoped to study medicine at university. He informed me that Ibadan Medical School, the premier Nigerian University, was one of the best in the world, with international recognition. He further informed me that his sister was a nurse at the University College Hospital.

Our trip to Ibadan Grammar School gave me a great deal of enlightenment. Ishola told me that the students had career advice. Through him, I learnt that medicine was a six-year course. The first year was preliminary. However, in his school, the students had the opportunity to do the HSC, where they did A Levels, which would provide them the opportunity for direct entry to the university. He even knew about other courses offered in the university and their requirements. Like me, he hoped to go to the University of Ibadan. I was glad that I made the trip. As I travelled with my fellow students back to our school, I was more determined than ever that I would study medicine, and by the grace of God, I would do that in the great University of Ibadan.

The Snake in my Box

As the WASC Examination approached, our teachers encouraged us to do our revision together. With my GCE results, I wasn't under any pressure, and I didn't think I needed to put much effort in. We were to share our knowledge and solve questions. Whoever had a difficult question in mathematics would write it on the blackboard. Anyone who knew the answer would write the solution on the board. One day, I arrived in the classroom, and someone had written a query on the board. I knew the answer straightaway. It was a question in geometry. I knew exactly where it was in my mathematics book. I knew I had solved it before, and in my usual scholastic enthusiasm, I took a white chalk, and within minutes, I was in front of the large blackboard, calculating the value of the empty angle, but one of my classmates disagreed with me, and we went into a protracted argument. I had no doubt that I was right. I told him that I knew exactly where that question was in my book, and I would go and get the book to convince him that I was right.

It was a hot afternoon. The teachers had stopped formal teachings and we had started our revision, so I could leave the classroom without having to obtain permission. I wanted to show and convince my colleagues that I was right. I raced to the dormitory in the blazing sun. I had locked my mathematics book and other books away in a large carton and placed my suitcase on it. All the prefects each had a separate room. That was where I slept and had all my belongings. I wanted to go back to the classroom before the school broke up for the day, so I yanked the door open and removed my suitcase and the other effects that I had placed on the carton. I swept up the books as I looked for the mathematics book. A striped object in the middle of the box caught my attention. My school tie. I had been looking for it and was sure that I had now found it. But as I reached for it, the bolted window unbolted itself, screeched to open, and as the rays of light settled onto the depth of the carton, I saw, to my horror, that what I thought was my tie was a viper.

I dropped all the books that I had held to my chest onto the deadly snake and flew out of the room. I didn't have the courage to go back to the classroom – I felt as though the snake was after me – so I stood outside the house one block in an open space, praying for the boys to arrive. Soon, they arrived one by one and in groups.

No one believed me when I told them there was a snake in my room. To find a snake in our school was not unusual. We encountered them

94

every day and they were everywhere. But, to find one in a room such as mine, with smooth, plastered walls and an elevated entrance, seemed unusual. And for the snake to climb a three-foot carton, and bury itself among the books, beat everyone's imagination.

Upon my insistence, the boys decided to look for the snake. One of the boys, a form four student, slid a magic ring onto his index finger and led the other boys into my room. He reassured all of us that if indeed there was a snake in my room, he had the power to charm and overpower it.

Within minutes, the boys lifted the box and brought it out of my room, as the rest of us watched with eagerness. They turned the carton upside down, and as they separated the books, the snake lay in their midst, with its head on page 322 of my mathematics book, the very page where I would find the answer to the question on our blackboard. The boy with the snake-charming power asked me if I wanted him to send the snake back to the person who had sent it to harm me. I declined. I didn't see the need for that. God had performed His miracle. Who unbolted the window? It had to be God. So, rather than use evil to fight evil, I thanked God for saving my life and prayed for His continued deliverance and protection. But I was shaking all over. I didn't have the courage to go back to my room. I couldn't do anything. Why would someone try to harm me with black magic?

The news got to the principal. As it was a Friday, he granted me permission to go home for the weekend, knowing how disturbed I was.

Mummy hadn't expected to see me come home when my School Certificate Examination was less than three weeks away. I didn't want to keep her in suspense, so I narrated everything to her.

"Thank you, my God," she said. "You are truly alive."

Mummy told me that she was on her way to the market that morning. It was around five-thirty. A white-robed priest stopped her and urged her to go back home and start fasting. He warned her that one of her children was in great danger. So Mummy called off the market and returned home to start her fasting and prayer.

"I still cannot understand how a window that I had bolted from inside would unbolt itself," I said.

"That's God's work," my mother said. "He sends his angels to rescue

95

His faithful ones and plants them on their paths."

At last, I completed my five years of secondary education. As friends hugged and bade farewell to one another, I hoped to meet my friends again, but the reality dampened my excitement, that the parting we were making could be forever. As said by William Shakespeare in Julius Caesar, "If we meet again, we shall smile! If not, well then this parting was well made."

I had had a fantastic time in UGS. Apart from the operculum issue I had not had any real problems with the seniors. I hoped that I would meet Senior Galadima someday, perhaps when we were both matured, and he would apologise for maltreating me. But even if we didn't meet again, I had forgiven him, and I thanked his colleagues who tried everything they could that night to save me from his recklessness. With regard to the *New Kitchen* scandal, I was still hurt, but I knew that I had to move on, and so, I forgave the boys even though they never apologised.

As a young school, UGS had limited resources, but we were fortunate to have a team of dedicated teachers who had made it a good place for learning. I had met talented and incredibly brilliant students not only in my year but in the years below and above. Had these students attended a school with more facilities, they would have undoubtedly come out with fantastic results in their WASCE. Nevertheless, I was thankful to God for bringing me to this school that I was proud of. I had learnt a great deal of life skills that I believed would prepare me for the next stage in my life journey.

Chapter Four
AFTER GRAMMAR SCHOOL

*Desire is the key to motivation, but it's determination and
commitment to an unrelenting pursuit of your goal – a
commitment to excellence – that will enable you to attain the
success you seek.*
Mario Andretti

Like most people after the School Certificate Examination, I moved to
Lagos to find work. The secondary school academic year was different
from that of the university and polytechnics; the school year ended in
October for the secondary schools, whilst for the higher institutions, it
ended in June. That meant that a secondary school leaver would wait for
nearly a year before entering the university. During that time, students
who didn't progress to the Higher School Certificate (HSC) or the
polytechnic for their A Levels would look for employment. The best
opportunities for such jobs were found in the cities, particularly Lagos.

I took up a job at Chellarhams Supermarket in Marina, Lagos. The
job was not tedious. It involved stocktaking and bookkeeping. With a
salary of twenty pounds ten shillings, I felt on top of the world. I could
buy shirts, shoes, trousers, soap and toothpaste without asking my
parents. A sense of independence and maturity came upon me. I planned
to save most of my earnings, as I looked forward to going to the
university in a year's time. I decided not to take more than one pound to
work. One day, I put my only one pound in my breast pocket. As usual,
in the mornings in Lagos, the traffic was hectic. The rain was heavy. So
when the bus arrived, it was total chaos, with everyone trying to squeeze
into the overfilled bus. Soon, the conductor went around to collect the
fares. I dipped my hand into my pocket, but I couldn't find my one pound.
Someone had stolen it during the struggle to get onboard.

"Get out, you thief!" the conductor shouted, despite my pleas that
someone had stolen my money. He waited until we reached a traffic hold-

up and pushed me off the bus. I felt disgraced and embarrassed. That was all the money I had. I didn't know whether to go to work or back home. Whichever decision I made, I would have to trek in the rain, since I had no money. I decided to trek to work rather than back home. Just as I turned to start trekking to Lagos Island, a motor cyclist stopped in front of me.

"Jump on," he urged. It was Uncle Kola, the one who found me the job at Chellarhams. That wasn't his normal route, but that morning, he had to drop his wife in the hospital, and it was easier for him to go that way. He then told me about the accident: just before the Carter Bridge, a bus had summersaulted, and many passengers had been injured or worse. This was my bus, and I would have stayed on it and risked death if I hadn't lost my money.

"When something bad happens to you, don't despair," he encouraged me. "It may be to prevent something worse happening to you."

I couldn't agree with him more. My father had always said it to me. Bad things happen to both good and bad people. The rain spares no one, and it respects not the magnificence of a palace.

"When hard times come, allow God to be in control," Daddy used to say. "He will reveal why He has allowed that to happen to you."

I was used to the routine of waking up early, setting off by six to beat the traffic. Although I still had the ambition to go to university, I began to feel that there was no urgency. I was getting absorbed into city life, and I enjoyed the fact that I had earning power. One day, I had just arrived home from work and was playing with my nephew in front of the house when one of my father's tenants called me. Mr Earnest Egbuna was a kind-hearted gentleman who had a great interest in seeing that young people did not waste their talents. On my first day in the city, he had interviewed me, and was pleased that I had passed the GCE and had the ambition to study medicine. And from that day, he started calling me The Doctor.

"So you've started working," he observed.

"Of course, yes," I said, thinking it was obvious.

"I think you should apply to do the HSC this year instead of working," he advised.

I felt disappointed that he would offer such advice. After all, I was good enough to pass the concessional entrance examination. He advised that whilst that was a good plan, there was no guarantee that I would pass. And whilst he appreciated how well I had done, he would advise that I didn't put all my eggs in one basket. I could do the concessional entrance examination in the lower six, and if I passed, I could choose not to progress to the upper six. But if I failed, then I could progress to the upper six and sit the A Levels, which would grant me direct entry into the university. He gave me the names of three schools that were still taking on students from other schools and arranged for their interviews.

I had a successful interview to do my HSC at Ansar-u-dean College, Isolo. The Muslim co-educational school made UGS look like a primary school. Each form had classes A to H. The HSC students had a separate block. The science laboratory was well-equipped. In UGS, we only had one microscope for the whole class. In Ansar-u-dean, each science student had a work station with individualised equipment, including a modern microscope. All the teachers were experienced graduate teachers.

The term had long begun when I joined Ansar-u-dean College, Isolo, but it took me no time to catch up with my classmates. Being from another school, everything was at first strange. The principal, an elderly and respectable Alhaji, ensured a high standard of discipline. I was used to a strict principal anyway, so that was not a problem to me.

I settled down very quickly and made friends. All the students called me Dr Joe. Even the principal addressed me by that name. I couldn't tell how it started, but I loved it and enjoyed my popularity.

As a Christian, it wasn't compulsory for me to go to the mosque. I had the freedom to go to church on Sundays. We even had a Christian Union in the school. That atmosphere of free worship and practice of one's religion made the school a great place to learn. But, despite the freedom, I chose to attend the mosque and worship with the Muslims. I wanted to know about their religion. I even fasted with them during the Eid festival. The non-discriminatory values at Ansar-u-dean College made it a fantastic institution for both Christians and Muslims.

My lower-six year went quickly. It provided me the opportunity to have a better understanding of physics, chemistry and biology. I had AAB in the end of year examination. And that was what the teachers had predicted for my A Levels, although I was capable of making all A's.

I was undecided whether to sit the concessional entrance examination until the last moment. With my first-year results and the predicted grades, I thought it better to progress to the upper six and sit the A Levels.

"And what happens if you don't make the required A-Level grades?" Mr Egbuna narrowed his eye when I informed him of my plan.

It was as if I had lost my focus and someone had shone a torchlight on my dark path.

"Go for it, my friend. You can pass it," he encouraged.

"Yes, I will," I resolved.

A Near Miss

I took up a vacation job with the Nigerian Breweries, Lagos. During this period, I stayed with my eldest sister with her family. Working with a team of enthusiastic and funny colleagues in the laboratory was just what I needed to make the time go fast. I was in the quality assurance area. My job involved taking samples from the beer before it was bottled and checking the alcohol content to ensure that the samples were within acceptable alcohol strength. We also checked the bacteriology at different stages of production to ensure that the beers were fit for consumption. Situated on the first floor, far from the mainstream factory, we were isolated from the rest of the workers, which made those of us working in the laboratory close. It took no time for me to make close friends.

One of the friends that I made was Kayode Akinlawon. Like the other workers, he was a West African School Certificate holder. Although slightly older than me, we jelled and I respected him a lot, as he showed much maturity. I found him to be someone that I could confide in, and I entrusted him with my secret: my work colleagues believed that my appointment was permanent; it was only Kayode that knew that I didn't intend to stay long, and he never disclosed this to anyone.

Having Kayode as my friend was great. As a more experienced laboratory staff member, he was readily available to assist me, especially during my induction. It was also easy to swap our shifts, and our friendship soon extended beyond work. He lived ten minutes' walk from my house, and we visited each other daily, often spending long times with other family members.

Nigerian Breweries was a convenient place for me to do my vacation job, as I didn't have to get the bus. Although at first, I didn't like the idea of walking along the railway line, I soon got used to it, seeing that it was the normal route that people took to cut short their journey and avoid the hectic Lagos traffic. And, of course, whenever Kayode and I finished our shifts at the same time, it was great to walk home together. One such day was after a Saturday afternoon shift. Like all the laboratory staff, I had plenty of beer to drink, but I wasn't used to drinking, and I lost all sense of decency. I knew that I shouldn't walk on the rails, but that was just what I did. Then I sat down there completely out of my senses, despite Kayode's advice to get off the railway tracks. I hadn't heard the sound of the approaching train. And when it horned, I was stiff, too frightened to move. With one determined pull, Kayode dragged me from the tracks, as the old locomotive zoomed noisily past. I blinked several times. My brain-computer rebooted itself, as the effects of alcohol left me. Kayode then stayed with me, ensuring that I reached home safely, before going to his own home.

I went straight to bed to sleep off the alcohol. I tried not to remember the incident, but as the alcohol gradually cleared out of my system, I realised how foolish I had been and how close to death I was. When I woke up, I joked about it with my friends but kept it from my senior sister so as not to upset her.

That same day, at about seven o'clock in the evening, while my sister was preparing supper, I played table tennis outside. Saturday evening was always busy in front of our house. Young boys waited to take turns, shouting to encourage the winners and booing the losers. The table tennis belonged to us, so I didn't have to pay the 'five pence a go' to play. Besides, I was better than most of the boys, so I always played whilst the other boys took it in turn to compete with me.

"Joseph, can you come in," my brother-in-law called me, holding a newspaper. "I want to have a word with you." His neck veins stood up, and his face bore no smiles. My heart sank, wondering if he had heard about my drunkenness and risking my life that morning. But how could he? I wondered. As I dragged myself behind him into the house, I was determined to be honest. I would confess to my stupidity, and I had already vowed never to drink excessively again.

"Why did you not tell anyone about this?" he queried, as he slapped a page from the *Sunday Times* on the central table. I scanned through the two-page black and white sheet, whilst my sister and her husband stared at me in expectation of an explanation. I blinked several times as I allowed my eyes to settle on a name on the second page. *The following candidates were successful at the concessional entrance examination...* That was my name, one of the fifty-one names under *Medicine, University of Ibadan.* I felt like Archimedes must have felt when he exclaimed, "Eureka!"

I explained to them that I had no idea that the results were out. Of course, it was a thing of joy and excitement – a wonderful achievement by the grace of God. There was no reason to keep it to myself. My brother-in-law explained that it was by sheer luck that he came by the paper. He wasn't supposed to do the shift that he had just finished. The person who was down to do that day had been taken ill. My brother-in-law, therefore, had to cover for him. "It wasn't too busy," he informed us, "so I decided to go to the toilet." He picked up the paper and after shaking his head, continued, "I just wanted something to read in the toilet. And I just pulled an old copy of *The Sunday Times* from the pile in the reception, gathered for disposal. I don't know what made me pick this one. But I guess that's the work of God."

I was on top of the world. We all were.

The following day, we set off for the village early in the morning to take the good news to my parents. We left home at five in the morning to avoid the heavy traffic in Lagos. We checked into a Peugeot 404 Pickup at Ojota. They only needed two more passengers to be full. So we were there at the right time. I had no idea of the cost of university education. I imagined it would be too costly to study medicine. I wondered if my parents, who had struggled to send me to the secondary school, would be able to afford a six-year medical course. What if Daddy objected to my going to the university? What if he advised me to finish my HSC first? What if he wanted me to work first, like many people did before proceeding to the university? A hundred 'what ifs' filled my mind. And suddenly, my excitement disappeared, as a feeling of disappointment descended surreptitiously into my mind.

The journey to Shabomi took less than the usual three hours. My parents had just come back from church when we arrived. Uncle didn't want to keep them in suspense, so he told them the exact reason we had come: the good news that their beloved son had passed the highly competitive concessional entrance examination to study medicine in the prestigious University of Ibadan.

"Excuse me," Daddy said, as he hobbled into his room.

Within minutes, he returned, holding a large brown envelope with both hands.

"The postman brought this a few weeks ago," he said, as he handed the envelope to me.

That was my letter of admission to the University of Ibadan. My father thought that it was an important letter. And so he had locked it away in the cupboard, to keep it safe until he could find a trustworthy person going to Lagos, or when he next went to Lagos. And that could be several weeks, if not months.

I tore open the envelope with shaking hands as others watched. My head felt doubled, as I read the first line of the letter of admission. But as I read further, my smiles wore off. The deadline for acceptance of the offer, and payment of the deposit, was twelve noon on Monday – the following day.

My dad felt bad that he hadn't sent the letter to me straightaway. He wished he had opened it. But he had chosen not to, since he couldn't read and would have to depend on someone else to read it to him. Doing that could mean that other people would know information that I would prefer to keep secret.

"Thank God tomorrow is the deadline. And thank God I have enough money in the house for the deposit," my father reassured me.

"If we set off very early in the morning, we will get to Ibadan before the deadline tomorrow," Uncle added.

I nodded, though one part of me doubted if it wasn't too late.

"And if we are a little late, we can plead for them to show some understanding," my father encouraged.

My father directed us to pray. He thanked God for my success in the examination. He prayed that God kept our journey safe, and for the staff in the admissions office to show kindness.

There was no direct transport to Ibadan, so we took the earliest taxi to Ore around four o'clock in the morning. Within minutes of arrival, we found transport to Ijebu-Ode, from where we joined another transport to Ibadan.

We arrived at the university around nine o'clock. I heaved a heavy sigh of relief as the taxi dropped us at the terminus. But as we walked towards the admissions office, my heart started to race. I sweated all over. I started to pant, my fingers were tingling, and my vision became blurry.

"Everything will be fine," Uncle reassured me. "God has made this day possible for you and will not let anyone take your place," he prayed.

My strength returned, and my hope rekindled. As we drew close to the office, I kept repeating the prayer that Uncle had just prayed in my heart: "God will not let anyone take your place."

"Why are you just coming?" the young receptionist asked.

"As you can see, we have come from a long distance," Uncle explained.

"That's not an excuse," the girl said, and didn't bother to take my acceptance form from me. Within minutes, people had queued behind us. We refused to leave the queue, insisting that we were still within time. Then a middle-aged gentleman walked into the reception.

"What's holding up the people?" he asked.

"I have come to submit my letter of acceptance, sir," I replied, before the receptionist could answer. "But she said that we were late."

"What faculty?"

"Medicine, sir," I replied.

"Okay, come over." He directed us to his desk.

After matching the name on my letter with the one on the admissions sheet, he stamped my acceptance letter.

"Congratulations," he said. "Follow me."

He took us to the cashier office to pay the deposit. That confirmed my admission. I was the happiest and luckiest person on earth.

Chapter Five
PREPARATION FOR UNIVERSITY

God will not allow any person to keep you from destiny. They may be bigger, or more powerful, but God knows how to shift things around and get you to where you're supposed to be.
Joel Osleen

The long holiday seemed unending, and all I wanted was to start my medical course. I couldn't wait to start making diagnoses, treating people and performing operations. I wanted to start my reading, but I didn't know what to read. I went from bookshop to bookshop and scanned through any medical book that I came across, including general health and nursing books. My life was no longer the same. All I could think of was life as a medical student and a career as a doctor.

Although I still worked at the brewery's laboratory, I knew that was the last time I would work there. My time there was temporary, even though I was on the permanent staff list. I decided to break my exciting news to Kayode and no one else.

Daddy came to Lagos about three weeks before the end of the holiday. He was full of excitement as he tried to absorb the wonderful news, that one day he would be the father of a medical doctor. In my community, you don't keep good news away from people. Certainly, you mustn't let your relatives hear the news as second-hand information. It's got to come directly from you. So Daddy took me to see Uncle John. That was the same uncle who had advised me a few years previously that a village boy like me wasn't good enough for a secondary school in the city. He had just had his Sunday lunch when we arrived. Fortunately, he was sat outside on the balcony, which was a good thing, as I didn't fancy taking off my shoes to enter his sitting room. After prostrating to him, I stood away and allowed Daddy to break the news.

"My son is going to be a doctor," my father informed Uncle John, with excitement.

"Going to be what?" Uncle exclaimed, as though Daddy had spoken a forbidden word. "I don't think so," he said, and leaned back.

"Yes, he's passed the examination to study medicine in University of Ibadan," my father confirmed.

"That's prelim, isn't it?" He turned to me.

"Yes, sir," I replied.

"That can't be right," he said. "A boy from that mushroom secondary school cannot pass that tough examination," he said, as my father and I looked on. Then, turning to my father, he warned, "They will weed him."

"What do you mean by that?" my father asked him.

"Prelim is tough. Most students fail and are not allowed to progress from the first year. That's what I meant by 'weeding'," he explained.

"Oh!" My dad's voice showed obvious disappointment.

I took two steps forward and picked up my letter from the pavement, where he had placed it. And as I put it back in the envelope, I said to him, "Thank you, sir, but they will never weed me." And looking straight into his eyes, something that, hitherto, I dared not do, I said, "Only fifty-one candidates out of several thousand passed the examination. Even if I was the fifty-first of them, I think the village boy has done well. I don't need any other proof that I have got what it takes to study medicine, *sir*." And without waiting for him to ask how I dared talk to him like that, I took my leave. When I turned back, I saw my father walking to catch up with me.

"Well done, son," he said. "No one could stand up to John the way you have done. Oh, it's so good to be educated. It empowers you." Then with his hands on my shoulders, he prayed, "God in heaven will not let them weed you."

"Amen," I said.

My father's prayer touched the deepest part of my heart. I felt a chill throughout my body. It was a prayer that came from his heart. A sincere prayer that I had no doubt touched God's heart too. I was determined, more than ever, to work hard and make him proud. Even if what my uncle had said was factual, I wouldn't let that discourage me. I had already stepped on destiny road, and no one could block the way that God had opened.

My father left for the village the following day. I had one more shift left at Nigerian Breweries. I had anticipated that it wouldn't be possible to resign, but I was honest with my boss. He was over the moon when I broke the news to him.

"This kind of job is not for someone like you," he said. "You have done your job here with a great deal of enthusiasm and diligence. I have no shadow of doubt that you will be successful in the university." He advised me not to bother about the one-month notice that I was expected to give. "I will sort that out with the personnel department," he reassured me.

I went back to the village one week after my father returned. I had bought most things that I needed, so I decided to spend one week with my family in the village. When I arrived, my father had gathered the whole family in his lounge. They had slaughtered a goat and prepared pounded yam to give me a send-off party. My father announced that I was the pride of the family. After praying for me, he made a pledge, that if God would keep me safe and allow me to successfully complete my intended course, he would gather the people together again to thank Him.

The night before my departure, my mother came to my room. "Thank you, Mummy," I said to her, and really meant it. "You made this possible."

"Oh, no, I didn't make it possible," she said, with tears of joy streaming down her cheeks. "God did."

After wiping her tears with the hem of her wrapper, she prayed for me, as I knelt down before her. "The God that we worship is the true God. Fear not, my son. He will protect you like He has always done. He will put His angels along your path to pass your baton of success from one angel to another. You will not be short of helpers."

"Amen," I said.

She unwrapped something that she had tucked under her armpit.

"Take and always cover yourself with this wrapper," she said, as she handed it to me.

I had never seen this *Adire* wrapper on her. I was unsure if she had worn it before. But it looked beautiful. And it was even more beautiful that it was a special gift from my mother's heart. My mother left my room after drying her tears. I knew she was excited by my success. But I had no doubt that she felt like she was losing me. For the moment, my excitement at going to the university dampened as I watched her close the door behind her. I tried not to cry, but as I turned over the patterned wrapper, tears streamed down my cheeks. "Thank you, my mummy," I said, as I tucked it away safely at the bottom of my suitcase.

I spent the last few days in Lagos. I didn't know what to expect at the university, but I made sure that I had a new toothbrush, a tube of toothpaste, two bath soaps, body cream, hair cream, a brand-new pair of shoes and a brand-new pen. I was all set to go.

On my last day in Lagos, I woke up in the middle of the night with severe pain in my abdomen. I felt as though my bowels were in knots. At first, I thought it was due to the excitement of going to Ibadan in the morning. So I ignored it. The pain came in waves, and was getting worse by the minute. Then I started to throw up. I felt dizzy. My brother-in-law and my sister became concerned, so he called for a taxi to take me to General Hospital, Lagos.

The doctor, who saw me in the medical emergency department, thought that I had an acute abdomen, so he admitted me into the ward after giving me a pain-relieving injection. Despite my severe pain, all I could think about was my university course. If I had an operation, I wouldn't be able to go to Ibadan the following day as I had planned. I probably wouldn't be fit to start my course for at least a few weeks. I wondered what implications that would have on the course. What if they told me that I was too late and deemed unable to start? I prayed to God not to make me undergo an operation. "God, if it was you that made it possible for me to gain admission into the university, please don't let me have an operation," I prayed.

Within minutes of praying, my pain eased and I fell asleep. An hour later, the cold hand of the surgeon on my forehead woke me up. After taking a detailed history from me, he pressed all over my abdomen. He pressed as hard as he could, but I felt no pain.

"Please, sir, I don't want to have an operation," I pleaded, with tears running down my cheeks.

"Are you frightened of operations?" he asked, smiling.

"No," I replied. "But I don't want anything that would stop my university course."

"Oh, you are an undergraduate." He narrowed his eyes.

"Not yet," I replied. "I am due to start medicine tomorrow," I said.

"Wow!" the doctor exclaimed. "What university?"

"Ibadan," I replied.

The doctor informed me that he, too, studied medicine in Ibadan. He advised me that Prelim in Ibadan was tough, and I should put all my efforts into my course. He also advised that I handed in my assignments on time and didn't let my work pile up. I felt as though I had known Dr Bambo for years and thanked him for his valued advice. He told me to wait for an hour or so, to allow the effects of the morphine that I had been given to wear off, and he would return to re-examine my abdomen. He promised to discharge me if everything was alright. As I watched him leave in his white coat and a stethoscope dangling on his neck, I was more determined than ever to be a medical doctor. I wanted to be a listening and caring doctor like Dr Bambo.

Chapter Six
LIFE AS AN UNDERGRADUATE

Challenges are what make life interesting and overcoming them is what makes life meaningful.
Joshua J. Marine

After the excruciating wait was over, the day finally arrived. Like hundreds of other taxis, our taxi driver drove us to Nnamdi Azikiwe Hall, and I saw for the first time just how big the University of Ibadan was – so much bigger than I had envisaged. Although people had told me that it was a big campus, I never expected it to be the size of a large village. It was indeed a village on its own. Thankfully, the driver seemed to know the geography of the campus at his fingertips. He knew exactly the shortcut from the main gate to the halls of residence, avoiding the traffic hold-ups and multitudes of students and families. When we parted ways, I took my place in the long queue at the porters' lodge to collect the keys to my room. The returning students knew exactly what to do. They had chosen their rooms at the end of the previous year. They simply picked their keys and went straight to their rooms.

"Welcome to Nnamdi Azikiwe Hall," the chief porter said, as he handed me the key to room B32 on the second floor. "Zikites don't take nonsense," the man said.

"Yes, when Zikites cough, all other halls catch cold," a returning student wearing a black hat said.

"In fact, the whole university has fever," another student added.

It didn't take long for me to start hailing fellow hall mates, "Great Zikites!"

My roommates had arrived before me. I was pleased they were both medical students. They had successfully completed their prelim year, and they were due to start their first-year preclinical medicine. They both had a large number of used books, including notebooks and textbooks, handouts and tutorial notes. They welcomed me like we had known one another before.

I was curious to know why the students in Zik Hall greeted each other with 'Great Zikites'. My roommates informed me that there were many activists in Zik Hall. Most of the student demonstrations tended to start in Zik Hall. They warned me that there would be a lot of distractions, but I mustn't let them tamper with my academic year. "Prelim is hard," they warned. "You can't progress to the preclinicals if you fail your prelim year." Of course, I already knew that. I guess that was what my uncle referred to as 'weeding'. And I already knew that I would work harder than ever to disappoint my uncle, by not allowing myself to be weeded.

The lecture theatres and laboratories were far from our hall of residence. On Monday, after breakfast, everyone disappeared into their various faculties and departments for registration. I headed for the main taxi pick-up place, holding a large envelope containing the originals of my GCE certificate and the WASC, and the letter of admission. I stood in front of the Trenchard Hall, waiting for the bus to the University College Hospital. Whilst waiting, I heard two students talking as they passed by me. One of them looked so young that I didn't think he was one of us, until I heard from the older student, saying, "You medical students have got so many departments to register at." I realised then that the seemingly young-looking boy was a prelim medical student like me. But why didn't he join me to catch the bus? I wondered.

"Are you not coming to register?" the boy asked me.

I didn't know him. I wondered how he had known that I was a medical student.

"Register where?"

"Medicine," he replied.

I screwed my eyes, wondering how he knew that I was a medical student. But if he was also a medical student, why wasn't he going to the UCH?

"My name is Yinka Omigbodun," he said. "I stood behind you in the queue yesterday and overheard you when you mentioned to the chief porter that you were a medical student."

"Wow!" I was ecstatic. "So, you too are a medical student."

Yinka told me the registration took place on the main campus. The prelim students had all their teaching there. All the preclinical courses took place on the main campus. It was only in the clinical years that students moved to the teaching hospital. I had wondered how Yinka knew so much about medical education in Ibadan, and I knew so little. But I later got to know that he had attended the famous Loyola College, a high-standard grammar school in Ibadan.

I relied on Yinka to lead me to the preclinical department for registration. As we trekked the distance, we bumped onto other freshers trying to find their ways to their departments, everyone holding the envelopes containing their certificates. Some freshers had quickly made friends. Others from the same schools had no problems, as they continued as friends. I wasn't just the only student from my school, but also the only person from my area. So having Yinka as my friend was great.

"Many people regard this department as a dumping ground," the head of department said. "But without the teachers, even the most eminent professors would not get to where they are."

I turned to Yinka and raised my eyebrows. "We are in the wrong department," he whispered to me.

We hadn't realised that we were in the department of education. Luckily, we had sat on the back row, so we quietly sneaked out through the back door.

The queue had built up when we arrived to register for the preliminary subjects: chemistry, physics and biology. We positioned ourselves in the queue, as the students went into the room, one by one, to register. Each registered student emerged carrying a folder with all the information, including the rules of the department, the lectures and tutorial times.

Yinka went in before me. Like the student before him, he came out smiling, as he held his own folder.

"Next," the usher said to me.

I entered the large office. There were four stations: each for the faculty and the departments of chemistry, biology and physics respectively, and the fourth one for the faculty of medicine. All the prelim medical students had to register at each of the stations.

"United Grammar School!" the official, a bearded, obese man, exclaimed as he inspected my credentials. "Where is that in Ibadan?"

"It must be one of those mushroom schools," his colleague, a young woman with a thick layer of eye shadow and plaited hair, said.

I waited as they passed my certificate from hand to hand, as if it were not authentic.

"How did he manage to get in?" another official asked with a broad Yoruba accent. Whilst the gossips went on, I decided not to say anything. They had thought that I didn't understand them since I had an unusual dialectical Yoruba surname. Perhaps if they had checked my middle name, they would not have said all they had said.

"You have wondered where United Grammar School was," I said, loud enough for everyone in the room to hear. "I am sure you can see *Ode Irele* on the certificate."

"Oh, it's not for a bad reason," the bearded man said. "I was just curious, as I saw that your results were better than so many of the students."

"Will you please tell the lady there that I may not have been lucky enough to attend a posh school, but I am here by the grace of God," I said to the bearded man.

"Of course, and we are happy for you," the bearded man said.

The rest of the registration progressed without any event, ending with "Congratulations!" as they handed me my own information pack.

Prelim Year

When lectures began in earnest, there was no time to play around, and although I was used to studying on my own, I soon realised that I needed to work with my peers. The volume of work was getting bigger by the day. I needed to meet deadlines, attend tutorials and contribute to group discussions. Being in the same class with the fifty-one of the most brilliant boys and girls in the country was a great privilege, but that threw a big challenge. Whilst it wasn't a race to be the best student, I knew that I couldn't afford to make a mess of my prelim year. I constantly reminded myself of my uncle's statement that they would weed me. Whenever this came into my thoughts, I could see my uncle's wry smile, and I turned my anger into an impetus that took away hunger, tiredness and sleep. I also remembered Dr Bambo. I had promised myself that I would work hard and one day, become a doctor like him. I also knew, of course, that everyone in my village was aware that I was studying medicine. My failure would devastate not only my family, but the entire community. So I determined to work hard and beat the odds like I had done before.

When we had completed the first modular examination, the results were pinned to the departmental noticeboard. I hadn't expected to find my name on the first sheet of the A4 paper, which contained the names of the students with top marks, so I was checking the results from the last sheet. My heart stopped when my eyes caught my name on the first sheet bearing the names of the students with top marks. This was a turning point in my university education. In fact, it was a game-changer in my entire academic life. I started to believe in myself. Whilst I respected my peers' WASCE results, I told myself that if I had been privileged to attend the same schools that they had attended, with all the facilities, I would have done much better than I had done. But we were now under the same roof with the same facilities, so I had more confidence in myself, and I was determined to remain in the top-marks group.

The matriculation ceremony was something that every new undergraduate looked forward to. I had collected my academic gown, but I needed the other things to go with it. I needed a nice long-sleeve shirt, a complete suit, with matching tie and a pair of shoes. With my limited funds, my only realistic option was to buy them from second-hand shops.

The university taxi bay was busy the day I planned to go to buy the clothes for the matriculation. The taxi drivers were cashing in on the fact that so many people wanted to go out. Instead of offering a direct service to Dugbe market, they were offering short services, which cost more, as passengers would have to pay for the number of stops before getting to their final destination. As I waited, Emma Elueze joined me. He was one of my classmates, a prelim medical student. He too was going to Dugbe Market, but not to buy second-hand clothes like myself.

As we waited, I heard a Danfo bus conductor shouting, "Oremeji, Oremeji!" I noticed that people were trooping into the bus. Oremeji in Yoruba language means 'Two friends'. Emma, a non-Yoruba-speaking person, didn't understand. So I told him the meaning, and we both reasoned that the taxis probably preferred to take two friends or two persons going to the same destination. So we jumped into the Danfo, relieved that we had eventually found a taxi, after waiting for nearly an hour. After about twenty minutes, the taxi stopped, and all the passengers got down, as the conductor began shouting, "UI," to take passengers back to the campus. It was then that it dawned on us that there was a place called Oremeji in Ibadan. The previous calls by the conductor were for people going to Oremeji. It wasn't for two friends travelling together. Luckily, soon after disembarking at Oremeji, a Danfo arrived and we were able to take the remaining two seats. We arrived at Dugbe market within twenty minutes.

I had very little money. Although my parents were able to pay my university feels I had only twenty naira left for my upkeep. So I decided to purchase a second-hand suit and a new pair of shoes. The second-hand clothes trader directed us to the Lebanese traders on the southern part of the market, where I found an affordable shirt and tie. The return journey to the campus was straightforward. Having realised the taxi drivers' gimmicks, we decided to look for direct transport to the campus. It didn't take long before we found an overloaded Danfo. We got back with just enough time to grab our lunch and rushed in the blazing sun to the lecture theatre for the afternoon lectures. I couldn't stop thinking about the matriculation ceremony taking place the following day, but I was no longer worried about what to wear. The excitement showed up on the faces of every fresher, and it was the subject of everyone's discussion.

The brown Lennard's shoes that I bought were exactly my size. The grey suit was slightly oversized. The yellow shirt was a size smaller, so I couldn't button the top of it, and I couldn't tie a tie anyway. I didn't want to make my roommates aware of this, so I waited until they had both left the room and knotted it as best as I could, but when I checked in the mirror, it looked like I had tied a rope round my neck like a tethered cow. I had just undone the tie for the tenth time when I heard a knock on my door. Emma was already dressed, looking handsome in his suit. He laughed at my tie, which now looked like a used paper crumbled to be thrown in the bin.

"I'll help you with that," he offered. After ironing out the creases, he knotted the tie for me and taught me the technique of knotting a tie properly. With Emma's approval of my well-knotted tie, we set off to join the other freshers in Trenchard Hall for the matriculation ceremony.

We rose in majestic tranquillity as the Vice Chancellor, Professor Oritshejolomi Thomas, led the procession of the university senate. I looked across the hall. There were boys in their suits and ties of various sizes, shapes and colours, girls in their gowns of various colours and styles, all wearing the prestigious university academic gowns. I had no doubt in my mind that we all felt privileged and honoured to be there.

"Over twenty thousand candidates applied to study in this citadel. You have worked hard to get here. You must count yourself lucky," the Vice Chancellor said.

As I listened to the professor's matriculation address, I couldn't stop thanking God. If it were possible, I would be on my knees, praying and thanking Him. I wanted to sing and dance for the Lord, that I could beat the odds by His wonderful grace. I knew that the journey had only just begun. I couldn't be sure that I heard the whole of the speech, as my mind had travelled far away, reflecting over my bumpy road and God's goodness. I prayed at heart for God to give me the opportunity to come back to Trenchard Hall to listen to the VC, delivering the convocation speech and handing me my MBBS certificate.

It didn't take me long to make friends. As the number of prelim students was small, it was easy to get to know everyone and to get on with one another. We needed to share knowledge and study techniques. Having trustworthy friends also helped me whenever I had financial difficulty. My parents did all they could to ensure that I had money to pay for the university fees and books. However, having to pay for unexpected expenses often made me to run out of cash. Despite the fact that food was heavily subsidised by the government, I often struggled with money and had to miss meals or depend on cracker biscuits. My close friends often offered to pay for my meals, but I felt uncomfortable with this, and I tried to avoid having to depend on them by giving excuses that I wasn't hungry or that I didn't like what was on the menu.

The prelim year was tough, but it was also full of fun. Our practical chemistry was particularly interesting. The lecturer realised that students shared work, especially results of chemistry experiments. Though a European, having lectured in Ibadan for so many years, he had learnt what students said to one another whenever they wanted to share their results. Friends would go from station to station asking, "Ki lo get?" meaning, "What did you get?" So during practical sessions, the lecturer would warn us, "I don't want 'Ki lo get' method." To ensure that we didn't steal each other's results, he gave each person chemicals of different strengths. Whilst I never covered up my work or prevented anyone from comparing my work, I never copied any other person's work. Those who did ended up having poor marks, before they believed that the lecturer meant it when he advised to not use 'Ki lo get' method.

My prelim year wasn't all work and no play. Campus life was great. The new-found freedom was fantastic. We were treated as adults, with liberty to do just anything, even though I had only just turned seventeen. We were never tired of finding something to do. Being a Zikite, a name coined for a resident in Nnamdi Azikiwe Hall, I couldn't escape the hot and more often chaotic life in Zik Hall. Most of the students' crises began in Zik Hall. We shared the same canteen with the neighbouring Independence Hall. Invariably, whenever trouble arose in Zik Hall, Independence Hall students would be quick to join in.

The twenty first of February was a special day in the life of the University of Ibadan. It was the anniversary of Kunle Adepeju, a student of the Department of Agricultural Economics, who got killed by a stray bullet during a previous student demonstration right in the front of Queen Elizabeth II Hall, University of Ibadan, on the 1st of February, 1971. This day was honoured by the National Union of Nigerian Students (NUNS). It was not just to honour the life of Adepeju, but it was also an opportunity to lay our grievances before the military government. One of my friends, Soji Ogunjobi was a student of Political Science. He was an activist like many of the political science students.

On the eve of the February 21st demonstration, I went with Soji to join other students at the University of Ibadan Students' Union Building, popularly known as the Kunle Adepeju Building. The structure was one of the most beautiful buildings in the university. Its location seemed to be deliberate, to remind every student there was a vibrant and progressive student body that would always defend their rights and put a check on the government. But this building also meant different things to many people. Some students saw it as a place that had produced politically smart and calculative heroes. Some others saw it as the bedrock of student militancy and radicalism. But whatever people's opinions were, it was a place free for everyone to share viewpoints and to make friends.

On this day, the students gathered together in the Kunle Adepeju Building. There were so many issues that the students cared much about: apartheid in South Africa, the struggles in Rhodesia and other places where black people were maltreated. But students were most concerned about the military dictatorship in Nigeria, clamouring passionately for an end to dictatorship, and return to democracy. The meeting went on till late and continued in Zik Hall. It was agreed by the student body to carry out a demonstration on the anniversary.

I went to bed late after the meeting. I had never been involved in a large-scale student demonstration before. The only one I had ever been involved in was when we protested in the secondary school against the changes that they introduced to our menu. The school had added oats to our breakfast. The students preferred pap. Many of us had never had oats before. We marched to the principal's house with pots of oats and mashed beans and emptied them in front of his house. Several students were expelled from the boarding house. The ring leaders were expelled from the school. The prefects were relieved of their posts. The remaining students were made to sign an undertaking that we would never be involved in any such violence.

I had heard stories about Kunle Adepeju Day, so I was looking forward to an exciting day. That night, I only had a few hours of sleep, but it felt like I had slept all day. It was a deep, resounding sleep in which I dreamt so many dreams. I couldn't remember most of the dreams, but the last one that woke me up gave me a great deal of concern. I dreamt that the university was shut down and students had to leave the campus. I packed out of the campus, like the other students, for the indefinite closure of the university. The first bus that appealed to me was a white Peugeot pick-up. I sat on the only remaining space, by the driver between two beautiful girls. No sooner had we set off than we had an accident. The van summersaulted. Everything blacked out after the incident.

I woke up, my heart racing. I lay in my bed, too afraid to get up. At first, I brushed it aside as one of those countless dreams that give our minds a scare but will never come true. I tried to reassure myself, but the image of the Peugeot pick-up van kept creeping into my vision. My roommates had already woken up. Our room was on the second floor of the B Block, and so provided a strategic position to see not only the beautiful front lawn of the hall but far beyond. I came out to the front corridor. Students were trooping to the canteen for a quick breakfast before the demonstration. Members of the Black Nationalist Movement, in their black berets, were busy mobilising people and encouraging everyone to join in. In some instances, people who expressed reservations about the demonstration were threatened with reprisals. I dashed to the bathroom, had a quick shower and got into my jeans and a black vest. Within half an hour, I was all prepared and joined the mainstream students, discussing the pros and cons of the demonstration.

The Students Union president assured us that it was going to be a peaceful demonstration. I joined in for this main reason: peaceful. But I was also curious to see what was going to happen. I also felt proud to be seen as an undergraduate student of the University of Ibadan. The procession started from Nnamdi Azikiwe Hall. As we left the Zik Hall, other students joined in, chanting all sorts of songs with themes on freedom from military dictatorship, corruption in the country and other issues. The procession then left the main campus and progressed to the city. Some bystanders clapped in support of our cause. Others joined in. I observed that some demonstrators started to bang on people's cars. They were looting from stalls and beating people. I wasn't happy about this. I sensed trouble brewing and receded to the rear of the procession, thinking of a way of escape. Soji seemed to feel the same way. Just as this thought came into my mind, military vans arrived in their tens with soldiers armed with live ammunition.

"Go back!" the soldiers ordered.

"No!" the students shouted, and taunted them.

A fracas ensued. The students were determined to continue with the demonstration, but the soldiers had filed up on our way. They threatened to kill us if we made any move. This only made matters worse, as the students now went berserk, tearing down shops and setting up fires. Ibadan city centre was turned into utter chaos, as the students dispersed into various places, running for their lives.

I didn't know much of Ibadan. The soldiers were searching for students. They were ready to kill whoever challenged them. Although we could find a taxi back to the campus, Soji advised that it was not a good idea, since the soldiers were stopping and searching taxis and buses. No matter how you disguised yourself, they would recognise you as an undergraduate, and you could not deny that you were part of the demonstration. With Soji showing the way, we got back to the campus through the Polytechnic.

Soji disappeared into the group of the Black Nationalist Movement members that found their way back to the Zik Hall to plan another strategy. As for me, I had had enough. I wouldn't have taken part in the demonstration if I had known that it would be violent. I lay in bed reflecting over the event, wondering how something that started as a peaceful demonstration for a good cause suddenly degenerated into utter chaos and violence. I was just about to dose off when Soji ran into the room.

"They have closed down the University of Ibadan," he informed me. "We must quickly pack our stuff and leave."

"But why should they?" I asked.

"Don't ask," he advised. "The soldiers are going from room to room, battering students and throwing them out. Just get a few things, and we can escape through the polytechnic."

I knew that the soldiers were ruthless. They could kill anyone, and no one would ask questions. After all, they killed Kunle Adepeju and got away with it. If they could detain prominent individuals, such Taiye Solanke, Gani Fawehinmi, Fela Anikulapo Kuti, Professor Wole Soyinka, Professor Awojobi and many others who had campaigned for a return to democracy, and against the level of corruption in the country, who was I, an unknown village boy, privileged to go to the university?

We had just jumped into the bush when the military vehicles arrived. And like Soji reported, they ransacked the hall, going from room to room, fishing out students indiscriminately and beating them up with a great deal of malicious heavy-handedness.

Molete Garage was busy with everyone trying to find transportation to various destinations. It didn't take long for Soji to find a lift to Abeokuta. The term 'lift' referred to when you stood by the road and someone offered to take you part way or the whole of your journey, either free of charge or at a fare lower than was charged in the bus station. As for me, I had to go inside the station to find transport to Lagos.

As news of the closure of the university got to transporters, they all inflated their fares. At that time of the year, the fare to Lagos should normally be one naira. With the university closure, and the consequent large numbers of students wanting to go to Lagos, commuter drivers were charging at least four times the fare.

The time was around five in the evening. I didn't want to travel too late, so I boarded the van, a Volkswagen commuter that charged three Naira, among the lowest fares. I sat in the middle seat, hoping for more passengers to join so we could set off. After sitting for over an hour, only four passengers joined, despite the conductor almost ripping his vocal cords shouting for passengers. I was becoming impatient. As I contemplated going to find another, perhaps a smaller bus that would fill up quicker, a white Peugeot pick-up van pulled up a few yards from me, its conductor shouting, "Lagos, one Naira." Like the other passengers waiting in my van, I picked my luggage to board the newly arrived, smaller, faster and cheaper van. I was about to jump out when it hit me like watching a film that you have seen before: A white Peugeot pick-up with two girls in the front and an empty seat between them. Exactly what I saw in my dream, fresh in my image memory. Still, I brushed it aside, thinking it was a coincidence.

"Don't join them, son," an old man said.

The man of advanced age was the first person to sit in my vehicle. I met him in his seat. Apart from a nod of acknowledgement to my greetings when I joined him, he had uttered no word. Even with all the noise in and around the van, he was deeply asleep. He opened his eyes briefly and smiled feebly when the other passengers were disembarking.

"I can't wait any longer here," I said to him. "At this rate, we are not going to get to Lagos until late into the night."

"Oh, this one too will soon fill up," he said, with sleepy eyes, like someone struggling to keep awake from the effects of alcohol.

"That one is cheaper," I protested. "See, everyone has left us."

"I know," the man said. "But don't worry, I will ask the driver not to charge you since you've remained with him."

How could a fellow passenger ask the driver not to charge me? I wondered. Maybe he is the owner of the vehicle, I reasoned. Or maybe he will pay my fare. But why will he do that?

Whilst I was struggling with those thoughts, the man picked up his luggage, which consisted of a small sack. "I'm going to get some food. Will be back before the driver returns," he said.

"Do you want me to tell the driver to reserve your seat?" I asked.

"Don't worry, he won't go without me," he said. "But make sure you don't leave this bus."

I concluded that he must be an important person, even though he didn't look it.

As I battled with these thoughts and the urge to go and take up the remaining seat in the Peugeot van, the driver of our van arrived, only to find that everyone else apart from me had left. He urged me to remain with him and not join them in the Peugeot van. And because of my loyalty, he said he wouldn't charge me any fare. And so, I remained in the van and watched the Peugeot van fill up quickly and disappear into the Lagos-Ibadan road.

Just then, a group of students arrived and occupied all the seats. I reminded the driver of the old man who had occupied one of the seats.

"Which old man?" the van driver asked.

"The man who was sitting over there." I pointed to where the man was sitting.

"I don't know of any old man who sat there," the driver said.

I scratched my head. I knew I had a dream when I slept. But I hadn't slept that afternoon. He was a real man. His voice was real. Everything was real. I felt like asking the driver if the old man had told him to waive my fare, or if he had indeed paid for me. In the end, I decided not to ask him. I recalled that the old man took his luggage with him. He said he was going to have some food. Where? What food? Why now? Perhaps he had intended not to come back. Maybe he had found a lift to Lagos. I met him in the van. The driver was in the van when I joined. How come he didn't see him? Strange.

We were about thirty kilometres into the journey when we saw palm leaves placed on the road, signalling that an accident had occurred ahead of us, and all the vehicles had slowed down, leading to a traffic build-up. We crawled behind. Everyone was curious to know what had happened. At last, we reached the scene of the accident. The Peugeot pick-up van that the mysterious old man had prevented me from entering had summersaulted by the roadside. Rescuers were trying desperately to free wounded passengers from the wreckage. The front of the van was unrecognisable. I learnt from our driver that the van nose tipped before landing on its roof. The driver and all the front seat passengers had died, and most of the rest of the passengers had suffered serious injuries. The realisation that I could have been one of the victims brought my heart to my mouth. I looked up and thanked God for His miracles. This was not the first time that I had been saved from having an accident, and it made me realise that God really loved me and He had a good plan for my life.

After eight weeks, the government reopened the University of Ibadan, as well as the other universities and polytechnics that had been closed down because of the university students strike action. We were made to sign an undertaking that we would not go on strike again. Lectures resumed. We had to undertake extra lectures, tutorials and practicals to cover the syllabus before our end of session examination. At this stage, my confidence had developed. I no longer felt threatened by the students from posh schools. We were all going to write our examination on level terms. I found all my classmates to be outstanding. I had no doubt that UI had chosen the best of the best. I had no doubt that we would all fulfil the academic requirements to progress to the next stage of our medical education, and I was right. All but one prelim student made the grades to progress to the preclinical phase of our medical education.

The Preclinical Years

That year, the Gowon Government announced that they wanted to produce one thousand doctors every year. It was a good plan to increase the output from the medical schools. But typical of most Nigerian governments, it had to happen 'with immediate effect'. So the university was forced to increase their intake immediately. The university authority protested but to no avail. There was no room for discussion, but the facilities were not there to support the large intake. Once the military government decreed it, no one could change it, and there were no plans to increase the facilities. The government was only interested in the number, so the university increased the intake as commanded. Over two hundred students began preclinical medicine, more than double the maximum capacity. Our class was dubbed Dugbe Class – a large class like Dugbe Market.

Over two hundred students had to take lectures in lecture rooms with maximum capacity for a hundred students. We had to squash ourselves into the lecture theatres, with hardly any room to swing your hand. To find a seat, you had to come very early or sit on the window, and the lectures were often noisy. We no longer enjoyed the organised lectures presented in a comfortable environment that we had in the prelim year.

Despite the difficult conditions, I was enjoying the challenges of preclinical study. Anatomy fascinated me, and I was curious to learn about the structure of the human body, and doing so brought me to my first contact with a cadaver.

We were split into groups consisting of eight students per cadaver. Students from the senior classes offered useful assistance in these practicals, and when I had previously mentioned to one of the senior students that I wanted to be a surgeon in the future, he had said to me, "Oh that means your anatomy must be sound." So I couldn't wait to start.

I had seen bodies before. Dead bodies. Bodies from drowning, road traffic accidents, thunder-struck victims and war victims. I had seen bodies of new-born babies and stillbirths. But I had seen them only from the distance. Never touched or felt a dead person. Neither had I seen so many bodies, even during the war.

I had grown up with the belief that there were ghosts – the spirit of the dead person going about in the world. It sees and knows everything we do.

Like the rest of my colleagues, I stood by the body assigned to us, a young woman, probably in her forties. I wondered if my colleagues knew what I was thinking. Questions. These were people like me. They had arrived in this world at different times. Beautiful clothes, makeup and nice shoes. Leaders and servants, valiants and cowards, winners and losers. Now they were laid on the table as cadavers, for the would-be doctors to dissect. All the dignity now gone, only bodies now and not people.

I couldn't keep my eyes off the beautiful body in front of me. Her eyes were wide open, pleading to be left alone. I wondered if her ghost was hovering over her body, waiting for the first person to make the cut. What was she when she was alive? How did she come to this fate?

"You are starting with the anatomy of the lower limbs. So the task today is to dissect the long saphenous vein in its entirety from the venous plexus on the dorsum of the foot to the sapheno-femoral junction in the groin," Professor A.B.O Desalu, the head of the anatomy department, instructed. I took in only part of the instructions, as I was transfixed in all sorts of imaginings as to what she could have been when she was alive. She looked so beautiful and innocent. And I wondered whether her spirit had gone to heaven or hell.

"Get started. Everyone feels the way you feel, but you will get used to it," Sam Ajulo, the senior student assigned to our table, said to me as he tapped my shoulder.

That awakened my senses and brought me back to why I was there: to learn about the human body. I had expressed my emotions for the bodies. I would never know who they were, where they came from and what caused their death. And so, with one brave strike of the scalpel, I incised the skin below the inguinal ligament, to expose the sapheno-femoral junction, where the long saphenous vein joined the femoral vein. My colleagues joined, each doing a bit of the dissection, exposing the tributaries of the saphenous vein along its course. We also identified its valves that ensure that blood flows only in one direction, that is, towards the heart, and also its perforators, connecting the deep veins to the superficial veins.

I left the cadaver room with mixed emotions. I couldn't clear my mind of the picture of the fifty bodies or so, lying on the tables for the medical students to tear apart without mercy, to study every bone, muscle, nerve, artery and veins. Their chests would be split for us to study all the organs encased by the rib cage. Their abdomens would be split from the chest to the pelvis, and the brain would be liberated from the encasing skull. Every organ, the whole body, was there in the anatomy laboratory for us to study. No part would be exempted. That was the exciting bit – foundational and educational. But it put me off eating meat for several months. The smell of chloroform followed me about. It was as though my nose too was embalmed. But I soon got used to it. I soon got used to seeing and touching human bodies, preparing me for a lifelong career of cutting and stitching: surgery.

The preclinical years were tough, really tough. I continued with the friendships that I had formed in the prelim year, but I also made new friends, all supporting one another to climb over the huddle of the preclinical studies. And despite my ability to study alone, I realised the importance of my colleagues' support. We formed study groups and visited the anatomy laboratory in the middle of the night to study the bodies. I no longer feared being alone with bodies, whether day or night.

As my friendship circle widened, so did my social life. We established Club d'Operandi, a social club, dubbed Club D. I had wanted to join the Zigma Club or one of the other prestigious clubs, but I found the financial commitment to be too burdensome. So when my friends discussed establishing Club D, I embraced it. The rest of the members of Club D were not medical students. Although we made UI the base of Club D, it was not an UI club.

One of the first few friendships I made in my prelim year was with Wole Kukoyi. He looked deceitfully fragile with a thin physique. But he was strong and funny. Wole could give his heart to anyone. I wondered how his tiny body frame could harbour such a big heart. He was kind and generous. He always left his cabinet open for everyone to help themselves. A student with incredible memory, he was also hardworking. He wouldn't succumb to sleep if he had set himself a target. An ex-student of Molusi College, he introduced me to many other Molusians both in the UI and other institutions. Other members of the club were Segun Adeleye, Femi Adewale and Bayo Adetiloye. A handsome man, looking intelligent behind his glasses, Segun was brilliant and calculated. Femi and Bayo joined us in the first preclinical year. Bayo transferred from the Jos campus after successfully completing his prelim. Femi had a direct entry after passing his A Levels with flying colours. The last person in our group of friends was Wunmi Omoniyi. Wunmi was in my prelim year. Although Wunmi was not an official member of Club D, he took part in many of the activities of the club. He was diligent and intelligent. He spoke very little and showed more maturity than the rest of us. Bayo was from another hall, but he often came to join the rest of us in Zik Hall. Femi was easy-going and full of fun. His aunt lived in

Ibadan, and we were often able to borrow her car on weekends. As the only licensed driver, I often drove Femi's aunt's car on those crazy weekends.

Despite the difficult preclinical years, I had a fantastic time with my friends. The club brought a high degree of social dynamism into my life and extended my friendship far beyond medical students. As the public relations officer, I had to engage with every event that the club was involved in. God really blessed me with these wonderful friends and those that were not within the first concentric friendship circle. All of them contributed one way or another to make my undergraduate life socially and academically fulfilling. Our presence in any birthday party or other events brought transformation. We would never allow any disco to be boring. We were not silly or disorderly in any way, but we made our presence known in a positive way, bringing fun and showing people how to make the moves.

Despite my active social life, I ensured that my academics did not suffer. I always ensured that I finished any assignments given to me on Friday, knowing that I would be spending time with my friends on weekends. This sometimes meant that I had to swot all night. Another strategy that I had was to spend the day with friends and go to bed early. Then when everyone was snoring away in the middle of the night, I would go to the reading room to put hours into my reading. By so doing, I was able to have maximum university fun but also put the best to my academic work – winning in both worlds.

One Saturday, I planned to go with a group of friends to Ilorin for a birthday party. I was in the middle of preparation for the second MB, the examination that every aspiring doctor must pass before beginning their clinical work. After passing this examination in Ibadan, students would transfer from the main campus to the prestigious University College Hospital (UCH) for their three-year clinicals, which completed their medical curriculum. I had planned with friends to leave the campus around six in the evening after supper. I had a lot to cover that weekend, but I didn't want to let down my friend, whose girlfriend's party we had planned to attend. Although he wasn't a medical student, he knew that the preclinical subjects were tough, since one of his former roommates, now crossed to the UCH, was a medical student. I rushed my meal so I could join the boys in the taxi, waiting in front of Trenchard Hall.

The canteen was full to the brim. I sat in my favourite place, directly facing the service area, so I could see the sizes and combinations that people had ordered. Unknown to me, a student that I had never seen was standing behind me with his food tray, waiting for a seat. As I got up to go to get more tea, I knocked his food off, and I was covered from top to bottom with his okra soup. I had already dressed up for the party, and that was my only party outfit – my one and only – the best. I pleaded for the boys to wait for me so I could wash the stains from my shirt and dry it with the iron, but they didn't. I felt let down. They left me behind. I was upset and decided not to follow them in another taxi. If they were true friends, they would have waited the twenty minutes or so to get changed.

I was on my way to the front of the campus to find transportation to Ilorin when I met my friend, Gbenga Ojo, coming back from the city. He informed me that our friends had had an accident, with many of them suffering serious injuries, and one had died. So I turned back, thanking God for bringing the boy whose food spilled on my shirt. Without the event in the canteen, I would have been in the taxi with the boys. I was angry with my friends for leaving without me, but the news of the accident and the loss of a friend took away my anger. I could not think straight, but one thing I knew was that God had intervened, like He had done so many times, to rescue me from danger in His own divine way. I learnt a good lesson from this event, which remains with me all through my life. No disappointment is a disappointment. Every disappointment has a reason. I view disappointments as God's appointments. God sometimes brings disappointment in order to teach us some life skills. Other times, it is God's way of telling us that He is working behind the scenes. Many things we call chances are simply divine interventions at unexpected times.

Chapter Seven
CALABAR HOLIDAY

My uncle invited me to spend my holiday with him in Calabar. I had planned to do so after my preclinical examination. But he insisted that I come before then. So I set off on a Monday morning to spend the last holiday before my Second MB, the exam that all medical students would have to pass before they transferred to the teaching hospital for clinical medicine.

I arrived at Iddo Station in Lagos at five o'clock in the morning to board *Iyang Ete* Bus to Calabar. It was a misty, cold Harmattan morning. I wore a blue shirt, grey jeans and a patterned jumper that my uncle bought me when I previously visited him. And with a baseball hat on, and my camera dangling on my neck, I looked forward to another fantastic holiday in Calabar. But as I lifted my luggage to the rack, a tout snatched my camera from my neck and ran away.

"Pursue am!" the other touts urged me in Pidgin English.

I was about to pursue him when a man standing by put his arm across me. "Don't!" he restrained me.

I didn't know what the man was doing there. I guessed he must have accompanied a passenger to the bus station. He could have been a worker at the station. Whatever his reason for being there, he was certainly there at the right time. As he explained, the boy was a member of a gang of touts. Their plan was for him to take my camera and lure me away from my luggage. His friends had urged me to pursue him, expecting that I would leave my luggage to run after him. Once I was out of the sight, they would gang up and not only take whatever they found on me, including all my money, but they would also beat me up. Meanwhile, other members of the gang would make away with my luggage. I was grateful to God for putting this man there at that time, and for his timely intervention.

I settled into my seat next to a middle-aged man. Although he was smartly dressed, he spoke very little, and that was only in Pidgin English. I tried once or twice to communicate with him in proper grammar, but he maintained the communication in Pidgin. He seemed to prefer being on his own, as he struggled to respond to issues that I brought up for discussion. Even when a motorcyclist nearly caused our bus to have an accident, and everyone in the bus discussed the nuisances that motorcyclists caused on the road, he simply nodded and resumed his sleep.

Police stopped our bus in Owerri. We had just left the Owerri depot of Inyang Ette Bus, where we refuelled and had a break. They told us they were carrying out a routine check and ordered all the passengers to disembark. No one knew for sure what the police were looking for. We stood by our luggage as the police conducted their inspection inside the bus. Then they came out and went from passenger to passenger.

"Open your box!" the officer ordered me.

"Yes, sir," I said and opened my suitcase.

"Ritualist!" the officer shouted, as he pulled out a skull, part of the human skeleton in my box.

"What?" I wondered.

Within seconds, his colleagues left the other passengers and came to join him. They turned my box upside down, revealing the rest of the bones to complete a human skeleton. At first, I thought they were joking. My smiles disappeared when other passengers and even passers-by surrounded me.

"Imagine a small boy like you dealing in selling body parts for rituals," one of the officers alleged.

"I am not a ritualist," I protested. "I am a medical student, a student doctor."

"Well, you will confess when you reach the station," the senior officer threatened.

I showed them my medical books and my student's identity card. Still the police insisted they would take me to the station, threatening to charge me with illegal possession of a human body.

Just then, the man who had sat with me on the bus squeezed through the crowd and came to me.

"The boy is not a ritualist," he said. "He has told you and confirmed

130

he is a medical student. What more information do you need?"

I couldn't believe that the man could speak so fluently. The few times that we had spoken with each other, we had spoken in Pidgin English.

"Who called you to defend this criminal?" the senior officer shouted in Pidgin English. "If you don't get out of here, I will charge you with obstructing a law enforcement agent whilst discharging his lawful duties."

"Oh, I see," the man said. He then pulled a card from his wallet and flashed it in front of the officer. "Are you still charging me?" he asked.

"No, sir," the officer said and gave him a salute.

The police then stopped their inspection, and we all returned to take our seats on the bus. I hadn't realised that the man who had sat with me for over eight hours was an inspector of police. I couldn't thank him enough. He informed me that his roommate in the university was a medical student and his nephew had just begun his medical training in University of Lagos. As we chatted throughout the rest of the journey, he told me that he would normally fly to Calabar, but he decided on that occasion to take the bus.

We arrived at Oron early in the morning and took the ferry to cross to Calabar. My uncle and his driver had waited at the marina for the ferry to dock. I was about to inform my uncle about the inspector, but that was unnecessary as they hugged.

"What a small world!" Inspector Patrick said when my uncle informed him that I was his nephew.

My uncle was grateful to his police friend, and I was grateful to God for putting Inspector Patrick at the right place at the right time.

My uncle had arranged a vacation job for me at St Michael's hospital. This was a full-time job, but I changed it to part-time as I needed to study for my upcoming second MB. I worked with Dr Armstrong, an Ibadan product. As a preclinical student, I was only shadowing the doctor, but it was exciting to be called 'Doctor'. The patients thought that I was a doctor, and often remarked that I must be really brilliant to have become a doctor at my young age. Even some hospital staff thought that way, and Dr Armstrong didn't correct them. He simply encouraged them to regard me as such, and I enjoyed it. The six-week job geared me up to work harder to pass my second MB. I worked two days a week, so I had sufficient time for my studies. I really liked the clinical environment and couldn't wait to cross to the UCH. At the end of my time at St Michael's hospital, they gave me a white coat and a gold-plated pen.

The second MB took place two months after my return from the holiday. The holiday had helped to take away much of my exam stress. I was confident that I would be successful.

Chapter Eight
CLINICAL YEARS: THE STUDENT DOCTOR

I had made it, so I thought, but not quite so. I had only turned a corner on the road to my medical career. I passed all the subjects in the preclinical school with flying colours, among the top marks. I was also glad that all my friends made it. I was proud to be called a Brownite, referring to students resident in the only medical students' residence in UCH, the prestigious Alexander Brown Hall. It was a different kind of campus life, a more mature and respectable lifestyle. Although we still discussed topical issues and politics, students were more focused on their studies and patient care. As prospective doctors, we were meant to dress and behave like respectable gentlemen and ladies, who would command patients' and people's respect. Also, we didn't have to automatically join in whenever there was a student crisis on the main campus. One of those crises was the 'Ali must go' crisis in 1978, when students demonstrated against the increase in accommodation and feeding fees. It was a fifty kobo increment.

The crisis spread throughout the institutions of higher learning in Nigeria. Students were highly disappointed and lost confidence in the then Federal Minister of Education, Col Ahmadu Ali, himself an alumnus of Ibadan Medical School. In April 1978, as soon as the negotiations on the increase in accommodation and feeding fees broke down, the National Union of Nigerian Students (NUNS) decided to have a showdown with the federal government. They decided on a boycott of lectures from Monday April 17 1978. When this proved ineffective, some of those at the University of Lagos decided to sneak out in the early morning of Tuesday 18 April 1978 against the directive of the university authorities and the law enforcement agents, that under no circumstance would students be allowed to demonstrate outside the campus. The senseless killing of five students by the armed police led to much hues and cries.

The murder of the students caused more problems for the government, as the students refused to be cowed by the gun-wielding murderers sent to control the situation. The protest slogan, ALI MUST GO! became spread across the country, as the Minister of Education was believed to be the cause of the crisis that led to the students' deaths. Taxi drivers, market women and other people joined in to shout ALI MUST GO! The students fought running battles with the mobile police stationed outside the gates of the university. For over a week, they boycotted classes, throwing stones and taunting the 'godo-godos', as they called the ferocious, mobile, anti-riot policemen.

After about a week of this standoff, the government closed the universities and students were advised to leave the campuses. It was painful and inconvenient for students who came from afar to study at the various universities and polytechnics across Nigeria. At first, I thought the medical students would be exempted, so I didn't leave immediately. But it was nationwide. We all had to evacuate the campus, and I headed for Molete garage to find transport to Lagos. Luckily, I found transport as soon as I got to Molete, despite the number of students wanting to escape from Ibadan. I hadn't realised that Lagos was also in chaos, but as we approached Ikorodu Road, the whole place was in disarray. The driver wanted to drop all of us out of panic, but I pleaded for him to try and at least get to Yaba. I could find my way home from Yaba by trekking along the railway line. My heart sank as the traffic moved further. There was mayhem on Ikorodu road. Heavily armed mobile police engaged in running battles with the ordinary citizens who had come out to sympathise with the students, especially when they heard on the news that several students had been killed by the mobile policemen, who had fired live bullets at the students demonstrating at Ife and Lagos Universities.

The people of Lagos were charged. On Ikorodu Road, thousands of people boldly confronted the Nigeria Police Force and engaged them in battle. Ironically, some policemen changed camp and joined the people to shout, "Ali must go!"

The Danfo driver drove bravely through the angry crowd, pretending to be part of the demonstrators. The mobile policemen were armed to their teeth. I had to find a way of disguising my undergraduate identity.

They were beating and arresting students indiscriminately. If they found out that I was an undergraduate, particularly from the University of Ibadan, they would, no doubt, arrest me to join the hundreds of students in detention. Fortunately, the traffic got easier after we passed Palmgrove, and the driver dropped me at Yaba. I had to walk the almost three miles along the railroad from Yaba to Ebute Metta.

As there was a great deal of public support, the Obasanjo Government was shaken. It was the first time a military government in Nigeria had ever been so vehemently challenged by the people, and now under immense pressure, they responded to the people's demands by removing Col. Ali as Minister for Education. In addition to that, they announced a number of reforms.

The institutions of higher learning were reopened after about a month. I returned to the university and our course resumed immediately. Several student leaders were arrested and detained. They were charged with all kinds of offences. Many in the Students Union Executive Committee were expelled from the university.

It is arguable whether it was worth all the violence in response to a small increase in the menu fees. Even with the increase, it still seemed cheap. I guess the students were simply expressing their disappointment in the government. It was even concerning that despite the increase, the standard of the meals plummeted. For many months, all we had on our rice was boiled fish, no stew because there was no oil to make it. To some of us, fifty kobo was a lot of money. I, for instance, only had a maximum of twenty naira for the term. Moreover, whilst I didn't support violence, I believed that the students were fighting for a just cause. They were simply expressing their disgust with the dictatorial government that was so impotent to fight the ills in the country, including indiscipline, corruption and abuse of human rights. Finally, I didn't think the government could justify, under any circumstance, ordering soldiers to fire live ammunition at the protesters. It was unfair to deny the students' leaders the right to complete their studies.

As I am writing, I cannot but shake my head pitiably at the deplorable situation in my beloved country. University education was fun and it brings a smile to my face as I reminisce, but it saddens me that despite "Ali must go," and other crises, student life continues to decline.

Nevertheless, during my time, life was still, in the main, enjoyable and adventurous. I met fantastic people, many of whom have become my life-long friends. I also enjoyed a qualitative education delivered by excellent teachers.

I don't like politics. Even when I was on the main campus, I wasn't interested in student politics. However, I spent hours with friends debating topical and political issues. I was a member of the student union, but I wasn't a member of the executive. I was driven to be active by my non-medical friends, many of whom were studying political science and were current and always critical of the military government. I didn't have the courage to vie for a post in the student union executive. Despite the fact that I believed that I could make an impact, I knew that my studies would suffer, and should I run into trouble, I had no influential persons to rescue me. I also wondered how my parents would react to my going around universities all over the country for meetings. My father had never been interested in politics, and the political crisis in the sixties, in which houses were burnt and people were killed, was still fresh in everyone's memory in my town. So my father vowed he would never get into politics.

We resumed our studies, but had to face the challenges of catching up with the lost weeks of lectures and clinical postings. The library was always packed with students, and we were everywhere in the theatres, on the wards and clinics. Life returned to the university, but it was never the same. Some of my friends on the main campus graduated that year. Unfortunately, some of the front liners in student politics were not allowed to return to complete their education. I lost contact with them for ever.

As the political frenzy calmed, my training continued, and I was finding clinical medicine incredibly interesting. As the premier Nigerian university, and the premier medical school, we had a team of well-led lecturers and clinicians with international recognition, whose standards of teaching were comparable to British and American standards, and we had visiting professors from the UK, Europe, America, Canada and reputable African Universities. I learnt early that your skills as a doctor couldn't be found in your textbooks. As one of my teachers, a distinguished professor of surgery, put it, "Your patients are your textbooks. They are all you need." Much of medical training is passive learning. You learn the art through watching someone doing it. I spent a lot of time on the wards, learning from senior students, resident doctors, consultants and nurses. I knew, of course, that being compassionate is part of being a good doctor, and the nurses were particularly helpful, showing me the practical basics of health care that you don't find in books and your senior colleagues don't teach you. Hands-on experience in wound management, giving injections, blood-pressure measurement and other basic care activities were taught daily by nurses.

During one of my visits to the ward, I was asked to examine a patient who was on the professor's operating list. The twenty-one-year-old man had been on the medical ward for several weeks, where he had received treatment for his duodenal ulcer. He was transferred to the surgical ward to undergo an operation for gastric outlet obstruction. As I was taking his history, I felt a hand on my shoulder.

"So what has this patient got?" Professor Ajao, the senior consultant, asked me.

"Gastric outlet obstruction, sir," I replied.

"Very good," the professor said. "Will you show me how you knew that?"

"I read it in his case notes, sir," I said.

Of course, the eminent surgeon knew all about his patients. He wasn't asking me to read to him. All he requested of me was to diagnose gastric outlet obstruction at the bedside. Two colleagues of mine, who were examining a patient nearby, had been listening to my conversation with the professor. They had anticipated that he would call them and ask the same question. So they pretended that they didn't see him and decided to leave the ward without looking in our direction. But they couldn't escape the keen eyes of the brilliant surgeon.

"Come over here," he ordered them.

Professor Ajao gathered us together. Other students on the ward joined us. In a moment, ten students had gathered around him to learn how to examine the abdomen.

"Imagine the abdomen is divided into four quadrants," he taught. "Before palpation, you must look. You will then palpate the abdomen, quadrant by quadrant, in sequence, ensuring that you palpate any painful area last."

Then he showed us how to diagnose gastric outlet obstruction at bedside. With the patient on his back, he asked us to look carefully. And when we did, we, indeed, found a swelling on the top part of the abdomen. Then he felt the abdomen, and we all felt it one after the other the way he had taught us. After we had all had our turns of palpation, he showed us how to demonstrate a 'sucussion splash'. Again, we took it in turns. Each person would gently rock the patient's abdomen from side to side with our ear placed close to his abdomen and listen for a splash. This was definitely present.

"Now you know how to diagnose gastric outlet obstruction at bedside. Good day," Professor Ajao said. And after checking my notes, he left us to spend more time on the patient. The news went around among my colleagues who were doing their surgical posting, and I spent much of the day showing them how to conduct an examination to elicit a splash.

With a large number of students, we had to hustle to get our learning. In theatre, we had to struggle for a good place to watch a procedure, but there were also opportunities to assist in operations, which was a privilege. Most students, however, tried not to assist, as this would expose them to being asked a barrage of questions. Of course, some consultant and senior doctors created a not-so-friendly learning environment, as they insulted you when you gave a wrong answer. They made you look stupid in the presence of your mates, even though your colleagues also wouldn't know the right answer if they were asked the same question. So no one wanted to be in the forefront. Only the ones who dared would show up in the front. But, one day, I was determined to assist at a partial gastrectomy and gastroenterostomy, the operation that Professor Ajao had planned to perform on the patient with gastric outlet obstruction that he had taught us on the previous day. I had spent the night reading about peptic ulcers, its diagnosis and management, including the indications for surgery and the complications of gastric surgery. The professor arrived just after me.

"So, you now know how to examine the abdomen properly?" he asked.

"Yes, professor," I replied, with a shaky voice.

I couldn't believe that he still remembered my face. I wished I could fly out of the changing room before he had any chance of asking me questions. I had wanted to assist, to see and feel a live stomach, not a cadaveric one. But now, face-to-face with the eminent professor of surgery, I regretted my decision. I wanted to be like my colleagues, to disappear into the crowd, swallowed by the Dugbe Class, my face hidden behind a brave one.

"So you are assisting me this morning," he said.

I didn't know if this was a request, a question or an order. Of course, he knew that by coming so early, I must have been keen to assist.

I had never assisted at any operation. We were taught how to scrub up on our first day in theatre, but I hadn't done it since that day, and I wasn't sure if I could do that properly. Wearing the gloves was also a challenge. It had to be done aesthetically and thoroughly. I was relieved when the registrar and the SHO arrived. With them both being around, there would be no place for a medical student, I thought. But that was wishful thinking. Professor Ajao was impressed by my keenness and bravery. Just as I was about to take a leap and disappear among my colleagues, who were now almost standing on one another to find a strategic position, the professor called one of the theatre nurses to supervise my scrubbing and gown me up.

As the third assistant, I watched every step of the operation. All the while, I kept my hands on the edge of the operating table. Resting my hands on the table made me feel included and prevented me from touching unsterile surfaces, particularly when gesticulating.

The theatre was hotter than an oven. It was as if someone had poured hot water on me. And the patient's stomach looked like an overfilled leather bag as it glistened under the beaming theatre light.

"Have a feel," the professor directed me.

That was the moment I had been waiting for: to feel the real stomach, a live stomach – not the dead, chloroformed cadaveric stomach. It was warm with every sign of life in it. I couldn't imagine how distensible the stomach was, more than five times the ones I had seen in the anatomy laboratory. I had expected the professor to ask me questions, but he never did. Instead, he taught surgical anatomy, bringing those things I had learnt on the cadaver into their practical application.

The operation took about two hours, and I was glad that I was given the opportunity to assist. It helped to build my confidence, and I no longer hesitated in assisting other surgeons.

Chapter Nine
Ibarapa Project

Medical training in Ibadan involved rotating through various specialties within the UCH. It also involved a block of rural posting in Igbo-Ora. This training – the *Ibarapa Project* – was unique to medical training in Ibadan. It was one of the special aspects of Ibadan that made it stand higher than other medical schools, both nationally and on the international stage. During this six-week posting undertaken in the penultimate year, students undertook the duties of a doctor under the supervision of a senior doctor. Dr Pearson, a generalist, was a delight to work with. British trained, he had worked in rural Igbo Ora for decades. He taught us how to practise medicine even with the barest facilities through reasonable improvisation. I learnt so much under him. The experience that I acquired in Igbo Ora has been a great asset in my medical career. The natives regarded us as doctors, and they had so much confidence in us. Being addressed as 'Doctor' by patients really inspired me. I couldn't wait to complete my course.

One particular case that remained in my memory was that of a young man who had contracted rabies. I was on call that night. Dr Pearson confirmed the diagnosis and advised that there was no cure for rabies. I watched the patient barking and struggling with his breath, wishing I could do something. But sadly, there was nothing I could do. At about four o'clock in the morning, the barking and grunting had stopped. His pupils had dilated and didn't respond when I shone light on them. He had stopped breathing. I couldn't feel any of his pulses, and his heart had stopped beating. I confirmed his death at exactly 4:15 a.m. I left the patient in the room with a heavy heart. Dr Pearson patted me on the shoulder.

"That is it. You can't cure rabies once the patient is symptomatic," he said. "You cannot save every life. So put that behind you, son, and try your best to save those that can be saved."

I grew up in the medical profession with this philosophy. No matter how much you try, you can't save all the patients. But whilst you sympathise, you must summon courage, and put yourself in the right frame of mind, so it doesn't compromise the care you offer to subsequent patients.

Although we were busy in Igbo-Ora with clinical work, we also had fun. While at Lanlate, the satellite village, only a few miles from Igbo-Ora, during the World Cup football matches, we all gathered in the common room, shouting with excitement as we watched the matches live. But work always took the priority. I was on call when my favourite team, Brazil, played in the finals and couldn't watch the match. A fifteen-year-old boy presented with severe pain in his abdomen due to a burst appendix. I assisted the surgeon as he carried out an appendicectomy on the boy. Unlike in the UCH, I had the opportunity to handle surgical instruments, feel the tissues, cut the stitches and stitch the wounds. I came out of the theatre feeling accomplished. I had saved a life. I said to myself, "Surgery is about saving life," and I made up my mind there and then that was what I would be – a surgeon in the 'saving life' business.

The Final Lap: The MBBS (Ibadan)

My final year in medical school went so fast. The house officers were men and women that were students only a few months previously. They were now real doctors, not the honorary 'Doctor' that they were called when in Igbo-Ora. As I watched them marching up and down the wards, looking after their patients, I pictured myself too, in a white coat and a stethoscope over my neck, as I pushed the trolleys up and down the wards, taking history from patients, conducting physical examination and taking bloods. But my confidence took a big knock when I became aware that some of the students in the final year failed their final MBBS examination. Many others had references in major subjects and would have to retake the papers. These were the students that I rated very highly. Some of them had even taught me both in the preclinical and clinical years. Although I had remained among the top students in my year, I realised that I couldn't take anything for granted, and I prayed daily and committed everything to God. I put everything I could into my preparation for the final exam, especially since ours was the largest class in our generation, and the university could afford to fail up to half of us and would still have a large enough number of doctors graduating.

Everything went well, I thought, until my paediatrics clinicals. I had anticipated that it was going to be tough after realising that I had been allocated the dreaded professor of paediatrics. Rumour had it that most of my friends in the year before, who failed paediatrics, had their clinicals and vivas with him.

My first case was a child with a heart condition. After taking a detailed history from the parents, I examined her and reported to the examiner that she had a systolic murmur.

"Listen again!" the professor shouted.

"I heard a murmur, a systolic murmur, sir," I said, after placing the diaphragm of my stethoscope on the apex of the heart.

The professor brought out a piece of paper. He was about to scribble something, I believed *Fail*, when Dr Nottidge, the second examiner, placed the bell of his stethoscope on the child's chest just to the right of the midline at the fourth intercostal space.

"What can you hear?" he asked calmly.

"A mid-diastolic murmur," I replied.

"Yes, diastolic," the professor said, like someone who had just received anticipated news. "A diastolic murmur, not systolic."

I nodded.

"So what has she got?" he asked.

"Mitral stenosis," I replied.

The professor burst into laughter.

"Say that again," he said.

"Mitral stenosis," I repeated.

And the professor laughed again. He seemed to be enjoying himself whilst I sweated under my armpits. I couldn't figure out what made him laugh. It was only when Dr Nottidge corrected my pronunciation of 'mitral' that I realised that he had been laughing at my Yoruba accent.

"So now, what has this child got?" the professor asked, now softened.

"Mitral stenosis," I said, this time with the right pronunciation.

"Yes, mitral stenosis!" he said, with excitement. "What is the other

142

name for the mitral valve?" he asked, after adjusting his bow tie.

"Bicuspid valve," I replied. And without allowing him to ask me why it is called bicuspid, I explained, "The valve has two flaps. And that is why it is called bicuspid valve."

"Very good," he said. "Why is it called mitral, then?" he asked, and laughed after teasing me by pronouncing the word with the Yoruba accent, the way I had previously done.

I scratched my head. I stared at him. I knew I had read something about it. But at that moment, my mental faculty had switched off in resignation.

I looked at Dr Nottidge with the corner of my eye. He smiled and gave an encouraging nod.

After clearing his voice and adjusting his tie again, he wiped his forehead with a white handkerchief. "The mitral valve is named after the mitre of a bishop, which resembles its flaps," he informed me.

The professor asked me several questions, including: what could have caused the stenosis? We discussed rheumatic fever, its symptoms, how to recognise a patient with the disease and its treatment. We also discussed the short-term, as well as the long-term, sequelae of the disease and how to prevent them.

We were supposed to have a minimum number of cases. Consequently, a student needed at least a pass in this minimum number to pass in that subject. I was only able to see two more cases: a child with kwashiorkor and the other with Down's syndrome. Dr Nottidge placed a reassuring hand on my shoulder, but I couldn't be reassured, as I realised that many of my colleagues had seen five or six patients, and I couldn't complete the last one before my time was up.

I had been confident that I would have no problem graduating with my colleagues, but after the paediatrics clinicals, everything changed. The excitement of finishing my medical education became drowned by the real possibility that I could, indeed, fail the final examination. One mind was telling me that I had done enough to pass – after all, I was one of the best students. But a more powerful thought was telling me that anything was possible. After all, even brighter students had experienced negative surprises.

Alone in my room, I prayed to God. It was not a long prayer, but one from the bottom of my heart, a sincere one. I could still remember the exact words. I was straight with God. There was no need and no time to beat about the bush. It was a prayer in desperation. I asked Him for what I wanted, the way I would ask my earthly father. "Papa God, please give me the MBBS Ibadan." That was all I said. I knew I had no power over the fearful professor, but I believed God would answer my prayer. He would use someone as an angel for my cause.

The results were released on a Friday afternoon. The list of successful students was placed on the medical school noticeboard. I had just had my lunch, and I couldn't go to check. In fact, I pretended that I didn't even know the results were out and decided to go to town with no specific thing to do. I just wanted to get out of the campus, hoping that by the time I returned, all my colleagues would have seen their results, and no one would see me when I went to check what I had expected to be a failure. As I was about to leave the entrance of ABH, three of my close friends shouted at me, "Joe, we've made it!" I didn't know whether they alone had passed or the 'we' included me. They knew I hadn't seen my results.

Two of the three students were very close friends, and they wouldn't be celebrating if I had failed. Also, they knew about my concerns regarding my paediatrics examination.

"We've made it," they repeated. "All of us."

I felt like a million-tonne weight had been lifted off my chest and needed to confirm what my friends had told me. Not that I disbelieved them. I knew they would never make up such important and sensitive information. But I wanted to see it for myself. I wanted to see my name written and posted on the famous noticeboard, among the successful students, one among the newly qualified doctors.

That afternoon, all the newly qualified doctors and dentists gathered in the medical school main auditorium for a swearing-in ceremony. The University of Ibadan maintained the traditional swearing of the newly qualified doctors to the Hippocratic Oath. The ceremony usually took place soon after the final examination results were released. The mood in the fully packed hall was electric. It felt like it was only yesterday that I had started my medical education, yet I had just completed a six-year course.

I had seen the Hippocratic Oath before, but it didn't mean much to me. Reading the oath loudly with my colleagues, however, in the presence of the medical school authorities, was something I would never forget. The serenity and the respect accorded the oath made me feel special. Together with all the newly qualified doctors, I read:

I swear to fulfil, to the best of my ability and judgment, this covenant:

I will respect the hard-won scientific gains of those physicians in whose steps I walk, and gladly share such knowledge as is mine with those who are to follow.

I will apply, for the benefit of the sick, all measures which are required, avoiding those twin traps of over-treatment and therapeutic nihilism.

I will remember that there is art to medicine as well as science, and that warmth, sympathy, and understanding may outweigh the surgeon's knife or the chemist's drug.

I will not be ashamed to say 'I know not', nor will I fail to call in my colleagues when the skills of another are needed for a patient's recovery.

I will respect the privacy of my patients, for their problems are not disclosed to me that the world may know. Most especially must I tread with care in matters of life and death. If it is given me to save a life, all thanks. But it may also be within my power to take a life; this awesome responsibility must be faced with great humbleness and awareness of my own frailty. Above all, I must not play at God.

I will remember that I do not treat a fever chart, a cancerous growth, but a sick human being, whose illness may affect the person's family and economic stability. My responsibility includes these related problems, if I am to care adequately for the sick.

I will prevent disease whenever I can, for prevention is preferable to cure.

I will remember that I remain a member of society, with special obligations to all my fellow human beings, those sound of mind and body as well as the infirm.

If I do not violate this oath, may I enjoy life and art, respected while I live and remembered with affection thereafter. May I always act so as to preserve the finest traditions of my calling and may I long experience the joy of healing those who seek my help.

I completed my medical education with permanent smiles on my face, and I knew that my friends would drag me out of my room for the desperately needed drink. But before party time started, I sneaked into the toilet and locked myself away from all the hullabaloo. I knelt down, and with tears of joy and gratitude falling down my cheeks, I gave God the glory, thanking Him from the bottom of my heart.

Chapter Eight
HOUSEMANSHIP

Do all the good you can,
By all the means you can,
In all the ways you can,
In all the places you can,
At all the times you can,
To all the people you can,
As long as ever you can.
John Wesley

I was given a place to do my housemanship at the UCH. This was exciting and humbling, but it put a split between my heart and my brain. I had to decide whether to do my house job in the teaching hospital or a general hospital. Doing my housemanship in the UCH had the obvious advantage of working in a familiar environment. I knew all the departments and many of the nurses. I also had a fair idea of the characters of most of the senior doctors. However, I thought that there would be less respect from the nurses, who had known me as a student. Some of them had been present at teachings and ward rounds, when I had given incorrect answers to consultants' questions. So I thought I might lack confidence, at least, at the beginning.

As I couldn't make up my mind, I sought advice from one of my friends, two sets before us, who was a medical officer in a general hospital. He advised that working in the general hospital would offer me the opportunity for more hands-on practical experience than a teaching hospital. He further advised that by the time I had completed my housemanship in a general hospital, I should have become competent at common surgical procedures such as appendicectomy, bowel resection and anastomosis, hernia repair, hydrocoelectomy, testicular fixation for torsion, haemorrhoidectomy, suturing techniques and trauma and fracture management. I should also be able to manage complicated labours with Caesarian sections, forceps delivery and episiotomy. I should have done salpingectomy for ectopic pregnancy, manual evacuation of the uterus and dilatation and curettage. He informed me, as a matter of fact, that having this experience empowered him, as the only doctor in the village hospital where he served during his NYSC. Since I didn't know where they would post me for my NYSC, I thought Dr Babatunde Ade's reasons for doing his housemanship in the general hospital sounded appealing to me. I wanted to gain those experiences so I could offer a wide range of skills during my NYSC, even if I wasn't the only doctor in the hospital that they would post me to for my NYSC. My heart was for the UCH, but in the end, I followed the dictate of my brain. I turned down the job offer at the UCH and accepted the one at the State Hospital Akure in Ondo State.

I left the students' hall of residence to spend time with my family before starting my job in Akure. My parents knew, of course, that I would be finishing that year, but they didn't know that I had, indeed, finished and passed my final examination.

I got home on Sunday in the afternoon. My parents had just come back from the church. Daddy was having a drink with his brothers and family friends, and Mummy was in the kitchen preparing the Sunday lunch.

"I am now a doctor," I informed my father. I couldn't let his questioning look persist. He had wondered why I had come home with all my stuff. The last time I did that was when the university was shut down during the 'Ali must go' crisis. Even then, I didn't come to the village. I went to Lagos. So when I arrived this time, he must have wondered if there was another crisis.

"Glory be to God," he acknowledged, as his grimace turned into open, fatherly arms, into which I jumped, feeling his breath of love. We both realised our pledges to each other. Promises that we made six years previously on my valediction – he, to provide all my care and financial needs, and I, to work hard to pass all my exams.

We were still locked in our embracement when my mother walked onto the balcony with the tray of food for Daddy and my uncles. I withdrew from Daddy's embrace and nearly knocked the tray out of my mother's grip. I didn't have to tell her. She knew that history had been

148

made. She had produced the first doctor in the family, the first doctor from Shabomi and its environs, and the first doctor from United Grammar School. She was happy and proud, and she had every reason to feel that way.

"Thank you, my God," she said, with tears of joy streaming down her cheeks. "I know I serve a living God who does not sleep." Then, looking straight into my eyes, she said, "Thank you, son, for making us proud."

I couldn't find a word to thank my mum enough. What could I say for all her bravery in the community, where women had no say in any decision? How could I thank her for convincing Daddy that to continue my education was a must, and giving Daddy all the support needed to ensure there was financial provision for my education?

"Thank you, Mummy." That was all I could say. But that came from the deepest part of my heart and touched the deepest part of hers.

Within minutes, the news had gone around the whole village. Every household had heard that Shabomi had produced a medical doctor.

That afternoon after the Sunday dinner, I took a stroll to the primary school. That was the school that had given me the very foundation of my education. I sat alone on the lawn at the back, and as I gently rubbed my hand on the petals of the hibiscus flower, I allowed my memory to take me back to my first day in school, as an unregistered four-year-old boy, wearing oversized, second-hand clothing.

"Thank you to Miss Opelenge and Mr Ladejo for believing in me and giving me the chance to be enrolled on that day."

Everything changed the moment my people heard about what God had done. Some of our family members visited to congratulate my parents and me. People began to show me a great deal of respect. But I didn't allow that to get into my head. In my place, we valued respect. I was brought up to show respect to my elders. I couldn't compromise that no matter how big I had turned. But whenever I tried to prostrate to greet an elder, he would restrain me, saying, "Doctor, don't prostrate." I found this to be humbling, and I thanked God for giving me a new life and a new status.

The following Sunday, the day before leaving home for Akure, my father called family and friends for a thanksgiving gathering. The time had come for him to fulfil the pledge he made six years previously: to gather family and friends together to celebrate and thank God for the successful completion of my medical education.

Father slaughtered a big goat for a large celebration. Earlier in the day, we had a thanksgiving service in our local church. I knew my parents were proud of me, and they had done all they could to show it. But I was prouder of them for being fantastic parents and the envy of other parents.

Life in Akure as a Young Doctor

I had been to Akure once before. That was when I went to take my driving test two years previously. I wouldn't say that I really knew the city. There had been a great transformation since it became the capital city of my state, Ondo State. An average size city with a central location in the state, it had a good road network connecting all the areas of the state.

On my day of arrival, the taxi dropped me at the hospital after signing all the paperwork at the Health Management Board. The hospital was similar to the one in Okitipupa but bigger, with separate departments for medicine, surgery, paediatrics and obstetrics and gynaecology. The Principal Medical officer (PMO) was Chief Dr Anikulowo Kosanu, a British-trained gynaecologist and a native of Akure.

As I didn't have a car, I would have preferred one of the houses on the hospital grounds, but the houses had been taken by the doctors from the University of Lagos. Their curriculum was about three months shorter than those of other universities, thus they began their housemanships earlier. I was given a two-bedroom flat shared with my friend, Dr Nimbe Akinro in Oluwatuyi quarters, a set of two-storey buildings in a quiet place, within walking distance from the hospital. It felt like being in Alexander Brown Hall in UCH, as most of the doctors were graduates of Ibadan Medical School. Apart from a doctor from Ahmadu Bello University, one from University of Nigeria and four pharmacists from University of Ife, the rest of us were from Ibadan.

As I began my medical career, I remembered the speech given by Professor Akande, the provost of the medical school, at our swearing-in ceremony.

"The University has prepared you with foundational knowledge. The real learning begins now, and it will continue throughout your career," he had said. I also recalled the Hippocratic Oath, to not do anything to harm my patients; in other words, to keep safe all the time. I made a candid determination to make these my guiding principles throughout my career.

I learnt very early in my career that surgery is an art. Like art, you see beautiful ones and ugly ones. There are ugly artworks, but there are also magnificent ones. I also recalled the man who called himself a doctor in my village. 'Dr Willy' lacked the concept of oral and parenteral administration of medications. For example, if you had a sore on your foot, he would give a penicillin injection into your foot close to the sore. Likewise, if you had a sore on your thumb, he would administer antibiotic injection into its proximity. As I practised medicine, I began to have flashbacks of how I had seen medicine practised in uttermost unacceptable ways that were not in line with the Hippocratic Oath: Firstly, do no harm.

One day, I was the resident doctor-on-call. An elderly man was brought in with a bodged inguinal hernia repair. He had had the operation privately in Idanre. I had already done enough hernia repairs under supervision, and was competent to do simple, uncomplicated ones on my own. As I took off the heavy heaps of dressings from the man's groin wounds, I clenched my teeth to stop myself from saying what I wanted to say. Looking at the inverted Y-incisions, I had no doubt that the surgeon had no understanding of the anatomy of a hernia, and I doubted if he had ever been taught how to do one. That night, I took the man to theatre, assisted by my consultant surgeon. I did most of the operation. As I was stitching the skin, the consultant asked me, "So what's your plan after your housemanship?"

"I will go for my National Service," I replied.

"I know that," he said. "I mean, what will you be doing afterwards?"

"I would like to train to become a surgeon," I replied.

"I think you will be a great surgeon," he said, as he gently tapped my shoulder with his blood-stained, gloved hand. "Go and get your training in the UK," he advised.

From that moment, I planted that ambition somewhere in my brain and let it grow, as I continued to build my experience. I pictured myself being in the UK, working with eminent surgeons, doing big operations and doing them the right way. I knew, of course, that it wasn't going to be easy. I would need money to go abroad. My parents would never be able to sponsor my postgraduate surgical training in the UK. I didn't even have a clue how to go about going abroad. My parents had done enough to get me so far. It would be absolutely unfair to ask them to put all their money on me when, of course, I knew that I still had so many siblings coming behind me. And they all deserved to be educated. So whilst going abroad for surgical training was my desire, I had to focus on the immediate and take things one step at a time. I had to have full registration, and that could only happen after the successful completion of my one-year internship. So whilst being a surgeon was my ultimate goal, it was important that I gained experience in other aspects of medical practice. Even at this early stage of my career, I believed that I needed broad-based, general experience to be a good surgeon.

A surgeon needed to master the art, and the art is not simply to cut and stitch. To be a good surgeon means to master the principles of surgery: that is, knowing that all systems and organs in the body are interrelated. When a patient presents with a hernia, a good surgeon sees not just the hernia, but the person as a whole. As a good surgeon, you must know who to operate on, what operation to perform, when to operate and when not to operate. You must prioritise your list according to threat to life or function. You must provide a good pre-operative work-up, ensuring patient's fitness for a particular procedure. And you must provide good post-operative care to ensure a pain-free recovery and return of function.

The government had just cancelled the car loan scheme when I finished at the university. This was a blow to new graduates. When I was still a medical student, it was one of those things we admired – to see the newly qualified doctor cruising in his brand-new car after work or when on call. That was one regrettable incentive that had been taken away for ever.

I never thought of the need for a car until I met Mr Obe, the proprietor of a new nursery in Akure. He set up the nursery following his retirement after decades as a teacher in Lagos and appointed me as physician there. I conducted visits to the nursery twice a week. During each visit, I would check each child, looking for signs of malnutrition, check the child's temperature, look for signs of anaemia, as well as treat any child who might have an acute illness. I was paid two hundred naira a month for this retainership, with additional payment for treatment. Most times I trekked. Other times, I took a taxi to the nursery. One day, Mr Obe called me to his office after one of the visits.

"Doctor, I think you need to have a car," he advised.

"Why?" I asked. "A car is not my priority right now," I said. "Besides, I've only just graduated. I will need to save money to buy a car."

"Well, you need a car because I have introduced you to many individuals and companies in Akure, and they would like to appoint you as their personal doctor," he said. "It would be easier for you if you had a car."

"But the government has cancelled the car loan facility. So I'm unable to afford a car until I've made enough money," I said.

Mr Obe advised me that I needed to be mobile to have the financial rewards for my popularity. He further advised that I didn't have to buy a new car. He would take me to Lagos, where I would find an affordable second-hand car. He showed me a Toyota Crown that he had bought from the same dealer.

Mr Obe took me to Lagos as promised. I bought a ten-year-old Datsun 120Y, ex-taxi for eight hundred naira. The car had a good body, but the engine was pretty old. So I bought a new engine to replace the old one. The car had an inscription on its back: PAPPY JOE. I decided to keep this inscription. It was as though the car was made for me, with my first name being Joe.

The vibrant yellow colour, and its coincidental inscription, gave the car its uniqueness and made me even more popular on the social circle.

I soon made friends and had a busy social life. Having a good network of friends provided me with a great deal of opportunity to make money. Even as a doctor with only a few months of clinical experience, I was a much sought-after doctor in Akure, but I didn't allow the financial incentive to take away my primary responsibility as a doctor. Nothing could take away my feeling for my fellow human beings. I owe it to God to use the talent he has endowed me and the miraculous way he has made it possible for me to become a doctor. All I can do in appreciation of God's goodness is to do all I can to save life and to alleviate human suffering.

One Saturday evening, I was getting ready to attend my cousin's girlfriend's birthday party. We had packed the music set in my car. As I was locking the door, a Peugeot pick-up van pulled up on the drive. An elderly woman came out of the van. She looked up and raised her hands.

"Thank God," she said. "Thank God, I met him at home. They have said that if I could meet him at home, he would help me."

I didn't understand what this woman meant. I wasn't on call, and I had a party to attend. The woman opened the back of the van as she cried for help. She didn't have to say anything. I totally forgot about the party that I was going to attend. A young woman was crying in labour, with the foetal hand showing and blood pouring out from her introitus.

"I am not on call," I said.

"He would not come unless we paid him three hundred naira," the woman cried, "but we don't have it. Please help us," she pleaded.

I couldn't believe how a doctor could be that callous. How on earth could a doctor refuse to save a life when he could, just because the patient couldn't afford it? And that the doctor was the most senior doctor and principal medical officer (PMO) of the hospital, beat my imagination. Health care was supposed to be free and so the doctor should not have demanded any payment, particularly, as the woman had a potentially life-threatening obstetric complication. The doctor's callousness made my muscles twitch several times, but I had to remain calm to help this woman who would certainly lose the baby and probably her own life if there was any further delay.

"Follow me," I said to her as I drove to lead the van to the hospital. I knew I would get into trouble with the PMO, who had refused to manage a patient with a hand prolapse in spite of being the doctor on call. Normally, he would need to be informed about any obstetric or gynaecological patient that needed to go to theatre. Only after he had given the authorisation, which was after the patient had paid him, could the junior doctor take the patient to theatre. The theatre nurses, the ODA and anaesthetist knew that. However, I was fortunate that I was friendly with the theatre team on duty. They, like me, disagreed with the way the chief gynaecologist was conducting his practice – putting money before life.

I informed them of the woman's plight, but I wasn't sure if I could still save the life of the baby, which would be a miracle, having had a hand prolapse with antepartum haemorrhage for several hours. I sent the driver to call the senior medical officer on call for his assistance in the no-simple Caesarean section that I was about to carry out. Although I had performed fifteen sections on my own previously, I had never dealt with such a complex case as the one I was about to undertake. I was in confrontation with the very person whose signature I needed at the end of my housemanship, to advise the NMC that I was registrable.

After waiting for a further twenty minutes, and the SMO hadn't turned up, we all agreed for me to carry on with the section. Whilst the woman was being anaesthetised, I hid myself in the toilet for a minute prayer. I acknowledged to the Lord that I was undertaking a procedure that should be undertaken by a senior doctor. I told God that I was not doing it for money, but out of compassion and necessity, despite risking my own registration and the chance of carrying on as a doctor. I asked God to be my assistant, and it would be to His glory if I could save the lives of the woman and her baby.

Just before I began, I listened to the woman's abdomen, and I could hear the foetal heartbeat. The midwife listened and confirmed it. I proceeded with the Caesarean section. Despite its indication, it was the quickest section that I had performed. I delivered a two-pound baby who cried straightway. I was stitching up the uterus when the SMO arrived. I wondered why he scrubbed and gowned, when all that was left was to stitch up. But he did that in order for the PMO not to take drastic action against me for undermining his authority. The SMO was satisfied and pleased that I was able to save both mother and child. With nothing left for him to do, he left me to finish up.

"Well done," he said. "Make sure you write in the case note that you had informed me about the patient before taking her to theatre."

"Yes, sir," I said.

"And remember to put my name down in the operation note as your assistant."

"Yes, sir," I said again. "Thank you, sir."

"You have gifted hands," the theatre sister remarked.

"Oh, to God be the glory," I said. "Thanks."

Pleased that everything had gone well, I returned to my flat. I had a quick shower, after which I went to join my friends at the party. My presence at parties always made a difference. I was often the DJ. But even when I wasn't, my choice of popular music would transform the party. As soon as I entered, everyone shouted, "Pappy Joe!" I took over the DJ role, and as I slot in my first cassette, the dancefloor was full. I was crazy and made everyone go crazy, as I was overwhelmed by what had just happened. It was a crazy night and a fantastic weekend.

I was just about to set up a drip on a child with gastroenteritis on Monday morning.

"Doctor, the PMO wants you in his office," the secretary said.

The PMO's secretary was powerful. He behaved like a deputy to the PMO. Sometimes people had to bribe him to make an appointment to see the boss.

"I am in the middle of setting up a drip on this dehydrated child. Please tell the boss that I will be there as soon as I set up the drip," I said.

"Is this child more important than the chief?" he asked.

"No, the child is not more important than the chief," I replied. "But saving his life is more important than having a meeting with the chief."

"Oh, I see," he said, and marched away.

I struggled to find a suitable vein to insert a cannula in this severely dehydrated child, who had had diarrhoea and vomiting for nearly a week. His mother sat by the bed, watching her almost lifeless, ten-month-old boy as I tried every vein in his body to insert a cannula. In the end, I found one vein on the back of his hand. As I was about to connect the rubber tubing to the cannula, I heard from the door, "Doctor, the PMO is waiting for you in his office." That was the secretary with the same order as before. As I turned to answer, I dislodged the cannula that had been so challenging to insert.

"Tell your boss I am busy with the most important duty of a doctor – saving life," I spat.

"Oh, I see," he said, and marched back to his office.

I knew I had got myself in trouble with Dr Kosanu, but I would rather I was at loggerheads with him than leave this baby to die. My muscles twitched, my bowels were in knots, but I had to maintain my composure. I couldn't allow the situation to cause me to make mistakes. I shaved the baby's head, so I could try to cannulate a scalp vein.

"Doctor, you have the audacity to undermine my authority," Dr Kosanu thundered.

All the staff stood up as he stepped into the ward. The baby's mother, who had sat by the baby's bed both times that the secretary had called me to see the boss, knelt on both knees to greet him.

"Good morning, Chief," I said to him, without taking my eyes off the baby, whose head I was shaving. "Sorry I couldn't come straightway, sir. This baby is pretty ill."

He stepped closer. He pulled on the baby's skin, rubbed his hand over his head, feeling for the sunken anterior fontanelle. He pressed on his forehead and let go to check the capillary return time. All eyes were on him, hoping that he would help to find a vein in this baby whose veins seemed to have disappeared. He turned his hands forward and backward. And he checked his feet. Finally, he slapped his head several times. Still, he couldn't find a vein. So he left me with the baby. He turned to the baby's mother, who was visibly sobbing at her baby, whose life depended very much on quantitative and qualitative rehydration and electrolyte replacement.

"You Akure women, you have no problems finding a man to impregnate you," he said to her. "But when the baby comes, you cannot look after him. You have been advised to boil your water and wash your bottles properly. You can see the result now, can't you?"

The woman looked up briefly. She wanted to say something, but she couldn't. Instead, she bowed her head and sobbed in desperation.

"Right, come to my office when you finish," he ordered.

"Yes, sir," I said, "I will come straight after setting up the drip."

"I think you need to do a cut down," he advised, as he breezed out of the ward.

"Thanks, sir," I said, and refocused my attention on the sick baby.

I tried the same vein on the back of the baby's hand that I had previously successfully cannulated. Although I managed to get back into it, fluid leaked around it, and within minutes, his hand started to swell up. I turned to the sobbing mother and reassured her that I wouldn't give up on her baby. I turned back to the baby. A blue line stood up close to a pulsating artery on his right temple. Though I couldn't feel it, I thought it couldn't be anything other than a collapsed vein. I raised the foot of the bed. With the baby's head now lower than the rest of the body, the blue line stood out more. I ran my index finger over it to confirm that it was a vein. And with a determined strike and a steady hand, I went straight for it. The cannula went in smoothly, and blood flew back into the rubber tubing. I held my sigh, not wanting to raise the baby's mother's hope, as I had done before. I secured it with criss-cross plasters and applied a bandage to prevent any cannula dislodgement. Having calculated the baby's fluid requirement as per his body weight, I made a final check on the cannula. Satisfied that everything was alright, I made my way to the PMO's office.

As I came out of the ward, I saw Dr Abitoye. He was walking in my direction towards the children's ward.

"Have you seen the chief?" he asked.

"No," I replied. "I am on my way to his office."

"Jolly good. I'm glad that you've not been. That's why I was coming to find you. I have just left his office. He accused you and me of conniving. He said we received payment from the woman that had an emergency C/S and shared it between ourselves."

I opened my mouth; my jaws were almost in two pieces.

"Well, there's nothing he can do to you," he reassured me. "Just go and see him. I have warned him that if he did any bad thing to you, I would not only report him to the NMC, but would make sure that all the market women fill up the whole hospital. He knows, of course, that when I mean to do something, I carry it out with enormity. So go and see him. But be calm. Okay?"

I nodded and thanked the SMO for his help and for being understanding. I couldn't believe that a doctor could be so callous. How could he let a patient die for the sake of money? And how could he raise his head so high when the most junior member of the team had done what the consultant couldn't do? These and other ethical questions challenged my thoughts. I promised myself that I would keep my calm, but if he showed any nastiness, I would return it in equal measure.

His secretary sat at the usual place when I arrived. His office was in the forefront of the administrative block.

"I have come to see the PMO," I reported.

"Sit down there," he beckoned, with a wry smile, to an empty seat next to the main entrance, after checking the time on his wristwatch.

I narrowed my eye at the secretary's lack of respect, but took my seat as directed, next to a patient, in my white coat and a stethoscope dangling from my neck. The patient looked at me strangely. She must have wondered why a doctor should sit with the patients. She probably also wondered why a man should be waiting to see a gynaecologist.

The secretary seemed to ignore the fact that I was busy on the ward. He was in and out of the PMO's office, ushering appointees in and out. He would have quiet moments with some people outside his office and would openly receive brown envelopes containing money. People were not seen according to their times of arrival, but at the dictate of the secretary.

I waited for nearly an hour, but the secretary didn't send me in. I doubted if the PMO was even aware of my presence. By then I had asked the secretary thrice when he would let me in, or if he would ask him if I should come back at a later time. He kept giving me the same reply: "The boss will see you when he's ready."

I decided to go in without the secretary's approval. A woman had just come out, and while she was filling a form for the secretary, I decided to take the liberty of going into the room. He hadn't expected me to come in, as he was counting his money. He yanked the large naira-filled envelope, hauled it into the drawer and slammed it.

"Where is the money you collected from that woman?" He stretched out his opened hand.

"I don't understand what you mean, sir," I said calmly.

"You took a woman with obstetric complication to theatre on your own. She needed nothing less than a consultant level of input. You have undertaken a procedure beyond the level of your competence. Now, my boy, you've got two options. You either give me the money or else I deduct it from your salary," he threatened.

"I repeat, I did not receive any money from the patient," I maintained.

"Alright then, I will report you to the NMC. I know everyone there.

I will simply inform them that you are not a safe doctor and basically terminate your career," he threatened.

"What about the consultant who is paid by the state but refused to discharge the duty for which he is paid, by refusing to assist a critical patient, just because she couldn't pay an illegal fee?" I was defiant and ready to give it whatever it took.

"Okay, let's come to an agreement. You give me the money and we pretend nothing has happened. Or I deduct it from your salary," he resolved.

"If I had taken money from the patient, I would have condescended. But since I have taken nothing from the patient, I have nothing to give you, sir," I said.

"Shut up your smelly mouth," he roared. "My informant told me that you took advantage of the vulnerable woman and demanded three hundred naira from her. That was the reason you operated on her despite being not on call."

"I did not take any money from the woman," I maintained. "You did not need any informant to inform you that I did what I did out of necessity. Who is guilty: the consultant who refused to save the life of a mother and her baby or the junior who went out of his way to save their lives?"

"Where is the money?" he demanded, and gave three angry strikes to his desk.

"I did not receive any money," I maintained.

"Alright, I know what to do," he said and lifted his handset. "When the police arrive, you will bring the money," he threatened.

"If you call the police, then the whole world will know about this case," I said. "I am sure this will be a good story for my brother to write in the *Daily Times*."

I had no journalist brother, but that sank heavily into him. It was as if I had poured a gallon of oil on his wings, his feathers so stuck, he couldn't fly. There was an eerie silence. We were both staring at each other. I couldn't tell how long this went on for. It must have been at least three minutes.

"You know I am a chief, remember," he broke the silence.

"And I am a royal, a prince," I said.

He blinked several times, pulled out the drawer that he had pushed in before, and then pushed it back again. Then he pushed the telephone away and struck his desk several times with a pen.

"I am sure you have got things to do on the ward," he resigned.

"Of course, sir," I said and left his office.

For several weeks, Dr Kosanu wouldn't answer when I greeted him. I knew he would be looking for an opportunity to punish me, but I never let that come to pass. The woman that I sectioned had no complications, and her baby was well. They were both discharged a few days after.

One Sunday afternoon, I had just woken up after being on call on Saturday. A white Peugeot 505 pulled up on the drive. A man wearing a flamboyant white *Agbada* lace was getting some stuff from the boot of the car, whilst an old woman, accompanied by a young woman carrying a baby, stood by. It was the woman that I had sectioned six weeks previously, the young woman with a hand prolapse. I watched as they emptied the large boot of the car of large tubers of yams, plantains, bananas, pineapples, fish, oil, gari and rice. These were the gifts, just for me.

I ushered them into my flat on the first floor. They told me that they brought my 'son' to see me, and to thank me for all my kindness. "You will always find favour with God. Whenever you need help, you will find it," they prayed.

The father of the child introduced himself as Mr Tola Babalola, a bank manager. Of course, he could afford what Dr Kosanu had demanded. Unfortunately, he and his family lived in Ibadan. He had had to travel to Porthacourt on a business trip. He had sent his wife to Akure to spend that weekend with his mother. They didn't have enough cash, and they couldn't get through to him in Porthacourt when she was in labour.

"I want to thank you from the bottom of my heart," he said. "I know there is nothing I can give that can adequately reward you and show my appreciation, but have this token gift," he said as he handed a brown envelope to me. I counted six hundred naira. I put the money back in the envelope and handed it back to him.

"That is very thoughtful of you, sir," I said. "But I can't take this money. You have done enough. Even bringing my 'son' to see me is enough for me. And look at all the gifts you have kindly brought."

Mr Babalola insisted that I took the money, but I refused to take it on ethical grounds. Firstly, I did what I did voluntarily out of necessity, and on the grounds of compassion. I had not done it for my financial gain. Secondly, if I were to do it for money, I would not have charged six hundred naira. Finally, God had used me in the process of answering their prayers. So they should show their gratitude to God and not to me.

"Okay then," he said. "I will not force you against your moral principles. But if there's anything I can do for you, please do not hesitate to contact me if you need any help," he added, as he handed me his business card.

I decided to share the gifts with the PMO. So on Monday morning, I packed them in my car. There were a lot of them. He was already in his office when I arrived. So I wanted to catch him before he left for the ward round. His secretary wanted me to wait in his office as usual, but when I informed him that I had something for the boss, something he had demanded from me, he went into the boss's office to inform him. The boss must have thought that I had brought the money that he had demanded from me. Within seconds, the secretary emerged.

"You can go in now, Doctor," he ushered me in, smiling.

"Good morning, sir," I bowed.

"Morning," he said, with a shallow smile. It wasn't the smile of a friend, but that of a tiger watching a sheep pass by. "So?" He narrowed his eyes.

"I have come to give you what I received from the woman after I did her section," I spat.

"You are a good chap," he said and stretched out his hand with an open palm.

"Can I show your secretary, sir?" I asked.

"My secretary?" he braced up.

"Yes, sir," I replied. "They are all in the boot of my car. Too many to carry on my own, sir."

"Gabriel!" he called his secretary. "Follow him."

I opened my boot and showed Gabriel its contents: five tubers of yams, two bunches of plantains, two bunches of bananas, five coiled smoked fish, a gallon of palm oil and a bag of rice. His jaw dropped when

I told him, "Please, tell the boss these are what I got from the woman and I will give all of them to him. Ask him where he wants me to put them," I said. "I will wait here for you."

The secretary went back into the office whilst I stood by the opened boot. He returned soon afterward.

"Doctor, he wants you to come back to him," the secretary reported.

Dr Kosanu made a further demand for money. He believed that they must have also given me money. "If they were rich enough to give you that much, they must have given you money as well," he reasoned. "Where is the money?" he roared.

I pulled out my wallet and brought out the card that Mr Babalola had given me. "Here is it," I said, smiling wryly.

He looked up and stared at me. "What's this?" he wondered.

"That's his card with his phone number on it. You can phone him to ask him how much he has given me," I said calmly.

He picked up the card. And after inspecting it front and back, he handed it back to me. "You can share your gifts with your friends," he said.

"I intend to do just that, sir," I said.

Apart from the incident with this woman, I wasn't in any further confrontations with Dr Kosanu. My goal was to acquire skills in the common surgical and obstetric and gynaecological procedures. And I was pleased, by the end of my housemanship, that I had acquired those skills. The other consultants in surgery, medicine and paediatrics had endorsed my competencies and approved my recommendation for full registration with the NMC.

Dr Kosanu refused to sign his own part of the form. At first, I thought it was because of the incident with the woman that I took to the theatre. I visited his secretary daily to check if he had signed my registration form, but each time I asked him, he gave the same reply: that the PMO was busy. We had only two weeks left for the NYSC, and I had to be fully registered before undertaking the service.

"Will you please tell me why the PMO has not signed my form?" I asked. "It's been two weeks since I submitted it. This is going to delay my youth service," I pleaded.

The secretary went into the PMO's office. He came back with my unsigned form. "You should have asked your colleagues to show you what to put on the form," he said.

I believed I had completed the form the way I should. After all, other consultants had signed.

"I can't see what's left to be completed," I said.

"Anyway, I will just help you because people have said nice things about you," he said. Then he showed me one of my colleague's forms that had been signed. "If you write all he has written on his form, *Oga* will sign it."

And so in the places for the consultant obstetrician and gynaecologist and the PMO, I inserted *Chief (Dr)* and added to his two lines of accolades: *FFPH and Certificate of Family Planning.* Satisfied that I had put everything on the form, the secretary took the form back to him and returned in a few minutes with my signed form.

Chapter Nine
THE NATIONAL SERVICE

It is the Lord who goes before you.
He will be with you;
he will not leave you or forsake you.
Do not fear or be dismayed.
Deuteronomy 31:8

I had hoped that I would be posted to one of the northern states for my National Youth Service. I would love to have served in Bornu, Gongola or Sokoto. I couldn't tell why I preferred those states. I suspect it was curiosity. I believed in the principles of the NYSC, one of which was to see how people in other parts of the country lived: to know and understand them. I can speak or at least understand most of the major southern languages. Serving in the north, I had hoped, would afford the opportunity to learn Hausa, a language that is spoken in most parts of the north. When I received my letter of posting, however, I was to serve in Bendel State. Of course, there was nothing wrong with that. I loved Bendel, a state unique for its ethnic diversity and hardworking civilised people, and I had no doubt in my mind that I would enjoy my time there.

Four of my colleagues were also posted to Bendel. We were expected to report at the NYSC office in Benin at eight o'clock on Friday morning, to receive our postings. I could have driven early in the morning, but two of my colleagues had friends who were finishing their service in Benin City, and they suggested that I joined them on Thursday, so we could travel together in my car. I didn't know anyone in Benin, and their friend would host us for the night. We could then all go to the NYSC office together. That sounded good to me. So I agreed for all of us to travel together.

My colleague's friend was not only hospitable, she was also a great cook. She prepared a delicious dish of jolloff rice with goat stew and fried plantains. We had a late night, snacking and drinking. She told us so much about Bendel State and advised us to try and get to the Youth Corps Office early, since they tended to allocate corpers to nice places before the other less popular places. She gave us the names of two officials at the office, telling us that they were nice and would post us to Benin or any other nice places of our choice. So we went to bed and planned to get to the office before anyone else.

As planned, we got to the office just after seven o'clock in the morning. The office opened at seven thirty. We agreed for me to stay in the car to prevent someone breaking into it and stealing our things, and they promised to speak for all of us, so that we could all be located in Benin. We were all looking for fun, and it would be great if all of us were posted to Benin City.

I waited in the blooming sun, sweating profusely, hoping all would be as we had planned. Just around lunchtime, they emerged one by one from the Youth Corps Office, each smiling as they announced their posting. As each of them informed me, he would grab his luggage and wave goodbye to me.

"What about mine?" I asked.

"They haven't finished the allocation of places," they said.

I waited until the last friend came out. It was the same reply. So all of them removed their luggage from my car, happy with their postings, and I was left on my own with only my stuff and my car. Three of my friends were allocated to Benin City, and one was posted to Warri. Unfortunately, they had the sheet of paper that Dupe, their friend, had scribbled the names of the Youth Corps officials who could help. They had helped them to be posted to good places, leaving me to try on my own.

I left my car with its contents in it, risking burglary or even theft of the car. They stopped me at the reception downstairs and prevented me from going upstairs to talk to an official. The young lady at the reception asked me to confirm my name. She went upstairs and was back in less than five minutes. She handed me my letter, stating that I was posted to Kwale.

"Kwale!" I screamed. "Where is that?"

"It's about two hours' drive from Benin," she informed me. "Have you got a car?" she asked, with a wry smile.

I nodded feebly.

"It's a pity you will not be able to take it with you," she said. "Also, be careful there, because the people eat human beings," she warned. "But I think you will be alright. They have never eaten a youth corper."

"Why is it that out of the five of us I am the only one posted to such a remote place?" I asked. "Surely there are many corpers who have no car. They would have been better suited for Kwale," I said.

"Well, I can't help you. The allocations have been finalised and I can't change yours," she said.

"Okay, can I see the boss, so I can explain to her?" I requested. "Maybe she would be able to change it."

"That is not possible, sorry," she said with an emotionless face.

I knew there was nothing I could do to persuade this young woman. I had to be on my way in order to get to the hospital before closing time. It would be too dangerous to travel at night, since she had warned me that the people were cannibals. So I would be able to drive back if Kwale was what she had described.

I sat in my car, completely dazed. I had prayed and asked God to make it possible for me to be located to Benin, Warri, Sapele, or Asaba. If I were given the opportunity to choose, those would be my choices. It seemed to me that God had not answered my prayers, and I was greatly disappointed. Why would God abandon me? Why would He allow me to be thrown into the lion's den? I wept bitterly. In the end, however, I accepted my fate and let God do as He pleased. I rested my head on the steering wheel and prayed this prayer:

"Oh God, you have not granted my request.

My friends have betrayed me.

I am abandoned and left to fight on my own.

I do not hate them even though they hurt my heart.

But I know that I cannot question you.

I have no right to accuse you, my God.

You are the one who has brought me this far.

Your ways are not human ways.

That is why you are God.

Only you understand what you do.

Only you can make things happen.

And only you can change things.
Humans see the immediate.
But you see far beyond.
I am going to Kwale.
I will not change it.
I will go in faith, because I trust you.
I trust you will not abandon me.
Dear Lord, please send your angels,
So they can run your errands,
And let me see your hands in action.
Amen."

If I had known then of the opposition and dangers I would face in Kwale, I might have run for the hills and begged for a different position, but after praying this prayer, I dried my tears, and my energy returned, driven by my renewed faith in the Almighty God. I pulled out of the NYSC office's drive and hit the Benin-Abraka road to face my destiny, trusting God had made things go that way, and it was for a purpose, which I might not know at that time. I trusted God to reveal that purpose later.

The traffic was busy. I liked it that way, as I didn't want to be lonely on the road. I passed through a number of villages. The people seemed to be friendly.

I got to Kwale at about two in the afternoon. The road was motorable throughout. I didn't come across any rivers and didn't have to park my car anywhere. The journey itself took less than an hour, and the people seemed to be nice. So none of the things that the girl at the Youth Corps Office told me was true. I wondered why she had lied to me. She should have encouraged and not frightened me with rumours that were fabricated on the premises of ignorance. I was determined there was no need to worry over my posting. To humans, it seemed wrong, but to God, it was for a purpose. God's way is always right, no matter how unreasonable it may look from human perspectives.

General Hospital Kwale was at the outskirts of the town and well signposted, so it wasn't hard to find. It had a similar look to the other post-independence hospitals. It was much bigger than the one in Okitipupa. The staff quarters were large, where most of the non-medical staff resided. Some local council staff with their families shared the estate with the hospital staff. Clinical sessions had finished when I arrived, and the PMO had gone home. One of the gatekeepers described to me how to locate the PMO's house.

The PMO's house was exactly as the gatekeeper had described it: about a mile from the hospital, a large bungalow opposite a patent medicine store on Abraka Road. As the PMO emerged, my fear disappeared into a big smile on his face that infected my face, causing a bigger smile. Dr Vincent Odeda was my senior registrar in UCH. To meet someone that had taught me before, now my boss in the place where I thought I knew nobody, gave me a great deal of excitement. He was busy with his private work, so I didn't want to take too much of his time. Besides, I wanted to unload my car and get to know the people. As I drove to the NYSC doctor's residence, I felt something that I couldn't explain. I felt uncomfortable and despite my initial excitement, something didn't seem right. I had a mental picture of his smile and there was something about it that made me think that it wasn't genuine. Moreover, no matter how busy, I had expected him to offer me at least a bottle of Coke or a cup of water knowing how thirsty I must be. I sensed that he was going to be a money-crazy doctor and a thorn in my flesh like Dr Kosanu. Nevertheless, I brushed the feeling aside and decided to give him the benefit of the doubt.

The NYSC doctor's residence was a three-bedroom bungalow opposite Eke Primary School on Ashaka Road, a stone's throw from the main market, Eke Market. Capital of Ndokwa Local Government, Kwale was a small town surrounded by the Ukuwani people in towns and villages. After unpacking, I connected my music set to the electricity plug in the sitting room, but nothing happened when I switched it on. The Kwale people had not had electricity since their plant, which they had during the time of Governor Ogbemudia, had broken down.

As the day drifted to an end and darkness began to set in, I had to find somewhere to eat. I was hungry and exhausted; I could swallow a cow. The Mainland Hotel was a walking distance from my residence. Although I had dismissed other fears that the girl at the Youth Corps Office had created, I couldn't get the fear of cannibalism out of my mind, so I thought it better to have fish or chicken at the hotel. Unfortunately, they only had beef. As the only option, I ordered for eba (gari paste) and vegetable soup, praying they didn't swap human flesh for beef.

The staff were friendly. They recognised me as the new doctor. I wondered how they knew that, but that gave me some relief, as I believed that they would respect and protect me. It would have been better if I could have swallowed my meat like I had done my eba. I nearly cracked my molars when I took a voracious bite on my piece of meat. I couldn't carry on with the meal. It was as if they had sprinkled the meat with sand and pebbles instead of table salt.

The following day, on Saturday, I went to Eke Market to buy things to prepare my meal. Like most markets in Southern Nigeria, most of the traders were women. Interpersonal communication was mostly in the Ukuwani language. But, like in many parts of Bendel, most people could speak Pidgin English. Thus, doing the shopping on my own wasn't a problem. I bought pork, rice, gari, yam, ripe plantains, salt and oil. As there was no electricity, I had to buy ground dry pepper. I prepared a stew that afternoon with the dry pepper. The stew was so peppery that I had to take out the meat and wash off the stew to be able to eat it.

The day went with no one to talk to, and as darkness fell on the town, I felt so lonely. I hardly slept for one hour. Whenever I managed to grab a few minutes of sleep, I would be woken up by a nightmare that made me regret even trying to sleep. Better to be awake. Then I could flee or fight should I have an attack in the night.

I knelt down and prayed to God. I told Him I had had enough. I had obeyed Him, but nothing had happened. If it was the will of God for me to be posted to Kwale, then God should show me the signs and send His angels.

I woke up on Sunday morning with heavy eyes. My head pounded and my body ached. I felt like I had had enough. There was nothing in this place to interest me. I asked God: Oh God, have you abandoned me? What about my prayers? My friends who don't believe in you had good placements. What have I done to be so punished? I resolved to go to the national headquarters of the NYSC in Lagos. Maybe I had to play the game that they all played.

I loaded my car. The sky was bright. It was sunny and dry, a good day to travel. As I was about to lock the door, a man, probably my age, arrived on his motorbike. His bushy moustache exaggerated his smile, but his smile was genuine. I raised my eyebrows, wondering what he wanted from me.

"Doctor?" he smiled, as he parked his motorbike close to my unlocked car.

"Yes?" I raised two huge, questioning ridges on my forehead.

"I saw you when you arrived at the hospital on Friday, and I liked you," he said. "My name is Ikechukwu, but you can call me I.K. That's what people call me."

"I am Dr Joe," I said, with a warm handshake.

"You've packed your stuff," I.K observed. "Don't you like it here?"

"Definitely not," I said, without any diplomacy or political correctness.

I.K. informed me that he was the landlord of the Youth Corps doctor's residence. He saw me when I arrived at the hospital, and there was something good about me, something unique that he couldn't explain. He also told me that many people who saw me when I arrived made good comments about me. He reassured me that his people were good. Kwale people looked after their strangers well. He promised me that I would not regret coming to Kwale. His wife had prepared food, and he had come to invite me to eat with the family. I didn't want to be rude to him, so I agreed to honour his invitation. He told me that he didn't live far away from my house. I agreed for him to park his bike safely in the lounge, and for us to go in my car.

We had just passed Eke Market when he stopped me. "I am going to introduce you to your 'town people'," he said.

"Town people?" I wondered.

"Yes, Yoruba people," he said.

I never thought I would meet my people in a place so far from Yorubaland. Yet these generations of Ijeshas had lived in Kwale for decades. Some of them had married Kwale women, and they spoke Ukuwani fluently.

I.K. stopped over at a restaurant. We were only three minutes' drive from his house.

"These are your people," he said.

"Welcome, Doctor," they greeted.

I wondered how they knew I was a doctor. I guessed I.K. must have told them that he was going to bring me. I had a full bowl of goat pepper soup and palm wine. They were very friendly, something that I needed at that time. They assured me that their doors were open for me to visit whenever I liked.

I.K. lived in a large, well-maintained bungalow with his wife and fifteen-month-old baby. The well-appointed mansion occupied a strategic site on the popular Umusamu Road. His beautiful wife had prepared the meal when we arrived. Darlington, I.K.'s fifteen-month-old baby, jumped out of the couch where he had been asleep as soon as he heard his father's voice. He toddled graciously towards us and stretched out his hands to me rather than his father. I wondered why he wanted me rather than his father. I wondered if he was confused between his father and me. We had similar sizes and shapes of moustache, bushy and long sideburns. I carried him. He refused to go to his father when he stretched his hands.

I.K.'s wife was a great cook. She knew exactly what I liked and what I needed at that time: my favourite pounded yam and egusi soup. Prepared with large chunks of mud fish, she ticked all the boxes. It would have been an insult not to finish my portion, considering the great efforts she had put into preparing such a delicious meal, so I gulped large well-moulded balls of pounded yam and washed them down with fresh palm wine. I hadn't had a meal like that for a long time. I couldn't have imagined I.K.'s family's hospitality and generosity and how gracious his wife was.

After the heavy meal, all I wanted was to have a nap. I had brushed aside the plan to leave Kwale for the time being. I.K. had promised to make me enjoy Kwale, and I had had the first taste of it. After the meal, he left me in the sitting room to play with Darlington while his wife cleared the plates. Shortly afterwards, he returned in a clean pair of jeans and a clean, white shirt.

"I want to take you around," he said, with a smile of reassurance. "You need to meet the important people."

"Okay," I said, without any hesitation.

We set off on our familiarisation tour in earnest. Although I didn't know where exactly I.K. was taking me, I had decided to trust him. After all, his family had received me with warm hearts, and I had dined with them, and he looked to me to be an honest person who was genuinely caring. So I drove as he directed. Every so often, he would direct me to stop. He would introduce me to a man, a woman, boy or girl as their new doctor. He would tell them in their language that I was a good doctor, tell them where I lived and urge them to patronise me. When they replied in their language, he would interpret what they said: "He's young and handsome." Some would say, "I like his smiles." Others would say, "He's a Yoruba man. Oh, I like Yorubas." It was all good remarks, even though I hadn't diagnosed malaria in any of them, taken an appendix or repaired a hernia. Still, these people had started building confidence in me and had high expectations. At first, I didn't feel comfortable to have myself advertised. I thought it was unethical to do so as a registered doctor. But I wasn't the one doing it. I didn't initiate it. The ultimate motive was to make people know about me in order for me to enjoy my National Service, so I didn't stop I.K. doing what he was doing.

The first person we visited was the Onotuku, the traditional head of Kwale. I learnt quickly from I.K. how to greet elders or respectable persons in Ukuwani.

"Ajeh!" I greeted and bowed, as I.K. did, as we entered the palace of the Onotuku. In Yorubaland, you wouldn't greet a king by standing up. You would fall and lie flat on your abdomen. In the Ukuwani custom, you wouldn't do such things. You would simply bow and say, "Ajeh."

Onotuku was pleased to see I.K. I was impressed by the warmness with which he received us. I.K. introduced me to him and his family as their new doctor. He told the High Chief that I loved the people of Kwale. That was why I had accepted to come to serve them. Onotuku broke kola nuts and prayed that nothing bad would happen to me. He reassured me that I would be protected in Kwale and advised me to let him know should anyone maltreat me. He also gave me the same advice that I.K. had given me earlier: that his people were nice to non-natives, but I must do everything I did with honesty.

We visited many more chiefs, councillors, patent medicine dealers, the principal of the local grammar school, the magistrate, the head of prisons, the DPO and the head of the market women. We also visited some youths and the principal of the technical college. The time had gone past six in the evening when we returned. I dreaded living on my own again without electricity, although I had decided I was going to stay. When we arrived, however, there was light in the house, and we wondered who had entered the house in my absence. As I tried to park my car, the front door opened.

"Hello, my name is Yakubu Mohammed," a handsome man with afro and goatee said with a gracious smile. "I am the pharmacist corper. I arrived this afternoon."

I shook hands with him and introduced myself as the Youth Corps doctor. I had thought that I would be the only occupant of the three-bedroom bungalow, which would provide an extra room to be used as a consulting room. Nevertheless, I was pleased to have someone from the north to share the house. I also felt that having a pharmacist sharing with me would give me professional benefit in my private practice.

Yakubu had the same but a newer model of my car. He had already prepared Irish potatoes and fried eggs, but he waited for me to return so we could eat together. This was very thoughtful of him, and I had no doubt in my mind that we would get on very well.

I.K. was about to take his leave when a man arrived on his bike with another man on the back. The teenager was bleeding from a laceration on his forehead. I had nothing in the house to manage the wound, which needed to be stitched. But when I told him this and signposted him to the hospital, the boy refused to go, thinking that I didn't want to treat him, perhaps because I thought he couldn't afford it.

"Doctor, someone has directed me here. They told me that you were a very good doctor. I can pay any amount you charge me," he pleaded.

"Of course, I can stitch your wound, but—"

"You can get all you need from Harrison, the patent medicine dealer," I.K. interjected. "His shop is in the building behind this house."

He told the boys to wait whilst I went to get everything I needed. The boys, of course, knew I.K. and they agreed with his suggestion. I.K. took me through a narrow footpath, and we were at Harrison's in three minutes. The middle-aged man with permanent smiling creases on his cheeks emerged from behind the counter of his shop. The shop was his sitting room that he had adapted into a shop. I.K. introduced me to him. He said that he had heard about me, and as a matter of fact, had tried to visit three times when I was out with I.K.

Harrison had everything that I needed to manage the wound. He also supplied me with medication for common illnesses: chloroquine injections, tablets and syrups, novalgin injection, paracetamol tablets and syrups, phenergan injection, tablet and syrup, piriton, ear- and eyedrops and various antibiotics. Harrison knew all that I would need. As I looked at the pile of medication on the counter, my heart beat fast. I was delighted that Harrison had all these things, but I wasn't sure if I would have enough money to pay for them.

Harrison must have noticed my anxiety. "I know you need time to settle down," he said. "You don't have to pay now. You can pay later."

I thought the boys must have left, but they waited. The injured boy had put pressure on the wound with his fingers as I had instructed before we went to Harrison, and the bleeding had stopped.

With Yakubu joining, there was only one spare room left. He agreed for me to use the spare room as my clinic. We moved the kitchen table to the room and displayed the drugs and my diagnostic set, making it look like a consulting room. I shaved around the boy's wound, and after checking that there was no foreign body in it, I stitched it up with silk. I would have preferred to stitch it with nylon, but that was all I could get from Harrison. I charged the boy a hundred naira, and he paid straightway. As he left, I took another look at the hundred naira on the table and couldn't believe that I had made the equivalent of my salary in one case.

"You are not going anywhere, Joe," I said to myself. "Thank you, God. I know you have brought me here for a good cause." And so my private practice ensued.

That night, I had three more patients. Two patients came to see me before I went to bed. The first patient, a thirty-year-old woman, had malaria. I offered her injections of chloroquine, novalgin and phenergan. She paid me fifty naira. The second patient, a forty-two-year-old woman, came to see me just as I was getting ready for bed. She had a boil in her ear. She was in a lot of pain. I received a payment of forty naira. The third patient, a teenager, was the daughter of a chief. Her parents woke me up around four o'clock. She had dysmenorrhoea. Her parents were concerned that she could have had an abortion. After examining her, and with a negative pregnancy test, I reassured them that she truly had dysmenorrhoea. I received a payment of a hundred naira for this. So on my first day, I made a total of nearly three hundred naira. It couldn't be any better. I couldn't go back to bed. I thanked God for bringing me to Kwale and for bringing I.K. to stop me making the decision to quit. I looked forward to starting my first day in Kwale General Hospital.

I arrived at the hospital before any other doctor, and the staff and patients wondered why I started work so early. They were used to doctors arriving late and leaving early. Making patients wait for a long time before the doctor arrived accorded the doctor a sense of being special. This conflicted with my own philosophy. It also challenged my belief that everyone deserved to be treated with dignity.

I learnt from the matron that the doctors were semi-independent. "How much you do depends on your experience," she informed me. "The head of the hospital is a specialist gynaecologist. He shows less interest in anything else apart from gynaecological procedures. You need not inform him about a surgical case. You can independently take patients to theatre, or if it was something beyond your competency, you could refer it to the specialist hospital."

I had two healthcare assistants assigned to me. They helped to call the patients in, as well as acting as interpreters. The male assistant, Mr Aguye, a middle-aged man, was with me most of the time. He seemed to know almost everyone in Kwale, and they regarded him highly.

I have always held the notion that the best way to communicate is to speak in the language that you both understand to avoid confusion. I often shake my head when I listen to an interpreter translating information into a language that I understand. They often twist the words and sometimes fail to convey the meaning as the speaker has said it. So one of the things I set out to do from the start was to learn the Ukuwani language. I wanted to be able to talk to the ordinary people in their own language. Patients also liked to be able to share secrets with only the doctor, preferring not to speak in the presence of a third person.

After seeing the first few patients, I learnt how to say a few words and sentences in the native language. I knew how to say 'Hello,' 'What is wrong with you?' 'How many days?' I knew how to say 'Yes' and 'No.' I could say 'One tablet one a day, twice a day or three times a day.' I knew the words for headache, back pain, abdominal pain, diarrhoea, blood and worms. My interest in the Kwale language enthused Aguye. He made me start each consultation on my own and joined in to bail me out when I was stuck. The patients were also impressed. By the time my colleagues arrived, I had seen all my patients and most of theirs, who had moved to my side.

I thought it was a good start until Aguye came into my room, looking like someone who had not slept for one week. I couldn't understand how he would change in less than fifteen minutes. I waited for him to talk. He simply packed the case notes of all the patients that I had seen and left the room. I didn't stop him. I had no reason to. I didn't know how the system worked. Maybe that was how it was done. But why would he change his demeanour? What had happened to him? I decided not to think too much about it. He would explain to me when he was ready. I decided to go to the pharmacy to chat with Yakubu and to get to know the senior pharmacist and all the staff. But before doing so, I thought it best to see the PMO and inform him that I had started, and also so he might brief me as to how he wanted me to work.

I was just about to step out when Aguye arrived, panting and sweating.

"Doctor, the PMO wants you in his office," he reported between his pants.

"Oh, I was actually on my way to see him," I smiled past Aguye.

Dr Odeda's office was exactly like Dr Kosanu's. You would have to pass through the main office where his secretary sat close to the door to the inner room. The matron had been waiting in the main waiting room to see him. A middle-aged woman in Florence Nightingale style nursing uniform, with a motherly look, Mrs Iyasele stood up as I entered the main office. Her sweet and warm smiles blessed my day. She gave me a warm welcome and congratulated me that the patients were already singing my praises all over the place.

"Keep it up," she said. "Can I see you before you go home today? Otherwise, I can see you tomorrow."

"Okay, Ma," I replied.

Dr Odeda sat behind a mountain of case notes and files. He looked up briefly as I entered then resettled his look on a file he had opened in front of him.

"Good morning, sir," I greeted, smiling.

"Morning," he said, without looking up.

I cleared my throat, wondering why he had given me such a cold reception. He kept on flicking the file from page to page, like someone looking for his car in the park of a large supermarket, completely ignoring my presence.

"You started so early this morning." He broke the eerie silence, with his eyes still focused on the file in front of him. "I know when you start a new job you want to impress the patients, so that they can all come to you, but I think you are overenthusiastic."

"I don't understand that, sir," I said and raised my eyebrows.

"You came early this morning and stole all the patients," he said. "All the other doctors have complained that you have stolen all their patients."

I stared at him, trying to find the right thing to say. In situations like this, I always tried not to say the first thing that my brain sent to my tongue. I would wait and let my central processing unit process and reprocess before I opened my mouth. I scratched my head, pretended no one was in the room and let the good part of my brain bring out the right words, and also to ensure no sparkling to cause an outburst.

"Oh, I am sorry if I have broken the local rules," I said calmly. "Sir, I will be grateful if you will give me an information pack on what my duties are. I promise you, I will carry out my duties according to the rules."

"Your duties are the duties of a doctor." He raised his voice.

"In that case, with due respect, sir, I have performed my duties," I said. I tried to control myself. It was my first day. That wasn't what I expected from an Ibadan product. I couldn't understand why my starting work early should upset anyone. All the patients were happy. That was the most important thing.

"Well, see only the patients assigned to you and don't poach other doctors' patients. Just a piece of advice, because I want you to enjoy your service," he said, smiling wryly.

"Thanks," I said. "But how do I know those patients that I must not see?" I scratched my head.

"The staff will let you know," he replied, rolling a pen between his fingers.

"And if they choose to see me?" I narrowed my eyes.

"You are asking too many questions," he replied and drew the discussion to an end.

The main office had filled up when I came out of the PMO's office. They were people waiting to see him for various reasons: nurses from the ward, officials from the health office, prison officers, police and patients all waiting in the queue to see him. Mrs Iyasele was still in the room. She too was waiting. I gave her a final wave with a smile as I took my leave.

I put on a brave face as I returned to the outpatient department and pretended that the conversation with Dr Odeda hadn't taken place. Mr Aguye and his colleagues watched me with an expectant look, but I decided I wasn't going to tell them what I had discussed with the boss. Two more patients had registered to see me whilst I was with the PMO. One had ringworm. The other had an eye infection. After finishing my consultation, I thought of going to see Yakubu. Just then, there was a tap on my door.

"Hello! My name is Dr Odebatu." He stretched out his hand for me to shake. "Ibadan?" He narrowed his eye, like you do when you want to recollect a face.

He didn't need any more introductions, and I recognised him very well, although he had put on some weight since I last saw him three years previously. He finished from Ibadan two years before me.

"Yes," I replied. "Hello." I gave him a warm handshake.

"I am going for lunch," he said. "You want to come?"

At first, I was reluctant to go with him. If he had reported me to the PMO for seeing the patients that I had seen, he wasn't the kind of person that I would like to have as a friend. I also felt that he might be finding a way of making me say things that he could then pass on to him. But he looked like a decent gentleman. Unlike Dr Odeda, he had given me a warm welcome and even offered to take me for lunch. I thought his motives were genuine.

"That's great," I condescended.

Dr Odebatu lived in a slightly larger than Odeda's, colonial DO's style mansion, just off the Asaba-Warri motorway, with his wife and their eighteen-month-old baby. Mrs Odebatu had prepared a large pot of jolloff rice with huge chunks of tropical fish. I couldn't be sure if she had expected that her husband would bring me to have lunch with them. She ticked all the boxes with her jolloff rice, and with the amount of warmth that the Odebatus gave me, I couldn't imagine that he would have said those things that Dr Odeda had alleged. A decent gentleman like Dr Odebatu wouldn't have reported to Dr Odeda that I poached his patients. I wanted to ask him, but didn't know how.

"So how has your day been?" Dr Odebatu asked me, as we drove back to the hospital.

"I thought I started well until Dr Odeda told me that I didn't," I spat.

That was the opportunity I had been waiting for. I had to tell him exactly what Dr Odeda had told me, but when I told him the full story, he laughed so hard that he almost lost control of the steering wheel.

"Crazy!" he said, in between his laughter. "He has made that up. Neither Dr Isiozor nor Dr Enebeli would say such a thing. I will introduce you to them, and you will see how nice and supportive they are."

"So, does that mean he has made up the story?" I queried.

"Of course," Dr Odebatu reassured me, "it's all made up, just to discredit you for his own gain."

"I don't understand that," I said.

We were now only a few minutes' drive to the hospital. He pulled up by the roadside.

"Listen to what I am going to tell you. This man is dangerous. He will do anything for the sake of financial gain. I had a similar experience when I started here. Then there was a consultant surgeon here as well. He was a decent gentleman. He has been transferred to head the hospital in Asaba. A no-nonsense man, he was able to put Odeda in his place, and the rest of us were able to find breathing space. Now he cannot treat me like that anymore, and he tries not to cross my way, although that doesn't matter to me anymore."

"It doesn't matter anymore?" I wondered.

"Oh, yes," he informed me, "because I am leaving next month. I have been appointed the medical officer at Abraka College of Education."

I felt like I had known Dr Odebatu for a long time. It was sad that he was leaving. He advised me to ignore Dr Odeda and continue to practise good medicine. He would give up after trying and eventually leave me alone.

"But don't undertake any procedure that is beyond your competence, because he will be on the lookout for your mistakes," he advised. He further reassured me that I could come to see him at Abraka anytime.

Dr Odeda had finished and gone when we came back from our lunch. I didn't have many patients booked to see me. That was a good thing, because I.K. had planned to introduce me to more people.

Yakubu was home before me. He was having *Dodo* and fried eggs. Although I told him in the hospital not to prepare anything for me, he still made two portions with mine left on the cooker. I thought it would be a disservice not to eat the meal that Yakubu had prepared. He had put great effort into its preparation, and it was thoughtful of him. So when I.K. arrived shortly afterwards, we devoured everything within minutes.

That afternoon, we went to the local government office. It was close to closing time, so the workers had started to wind up. Still, we managed to see most of them. Many of them openly promised me that they would change their doctors and come to register with me. Words had gone around Kwale about the 'friendly and smiling' doctor. Whenever I.K. introduced me, they would say that they had heard about me. That was a good thing. But it also gave me a fright. If good word could spread round the community in less than a week, by the same token, bad words could also go around. So I promised myself, I would never do anything to drag down my reputation.

I realised from the first day that I needed to buy a generator, but I hadn't the slightest idea how much they cost, which one to buy or where to buy one. I.K. and I planned to go to Onitsha once I made enough money to buy one. Judging by how much I made daily from private practice, I reckoned that I should be able to purchase one the following week. Meanwhile, I.K. took me to a local mechanic, where I bought a second-hand car battery. I connected this to an electric lamp, which provided me with a few hours of electricity to run my clinic in the evening.

Every evening after work, I.K. would take me to see new places. Within two weeks, I had visited most influential chiefs and business people, not just in Kwale, but in the Ndokwa Local Government area at large. He had also introduced me to the youths.

In my third week, I.K., Yakubu and I had planned to go to Warri. Through I.K.'s connection, we got to know of a large dealer in Warri, where I would find a good, affordable generator. But that evening, Dr Odebatu visited. He told me that he would be leaving Kwale for Abraka that weekend. His accommodation in Abraka was ready, and his employer had agreed for him to move in even when he hadn't officially started. He could commute to Kwale daily till the expiry of his resignation notice. He wanted to dispose of some of his medical equipment, and I could come and see if I was interested. I told him that I wouldn't be able to come on Saturday, as I had planned to go to Warri to buy a generator.

"Good timing," Dr Odebatu said. "I won't need my generator in my new house. I can sell it to you. It's only about six months old."

"Wow! That's terrific." I couldn't contain my excitement. I didn't ask how much he wanted for it, but I believed I should have enough money to buy it. And if I fell short of the asking price, I didn't think he would mind me paying in two or three instalments.

Dr Odebatu couldn't spend more time with us, as he had to go and pick up his wife from the hairdresser. IK arrived soon after he left, and I broke the good news to him. We cancelled the trip to Warri. Instead, Yakubu and I made a fresh plan to go to Asaba, where one of Yakubu's former classmates was serving. He promised to take me to Onitsha Market to shop for my drugs, equipment and other needs for my clinic.

The week seemed to be too long. Saturday seemed to never want to come. I had bought electric bulbs and fitted them in their sockets. I bought jerrycans of diesel in preparation for the arrival of the electricity generator. At last, the hours drifted to Saturday, and everything became a reality. Dr Odebatu had disconnected the 25Kw Yamaha generator and packaged it at the entrance of his garage, together with a jerrycan of leftover diesel. He had also packed clinic equipment in one room: examination couch, operating table, sutures and needles, syringes and needles and some other stuff. When I asked him for the price of the generator, he said to me, "I have made back the money that I spent on it. Just give whatever you can pay." This was a give-away. I paid a meagre one hundred and fifty naira. He informed me that he had passed his private practice to me and directed all his patients to come to my clinic after he had left.

That Saturday, we gathered a few friends after my evening clinic and threw a disco party. The presence of a powerful generator transformed our residence, and we felt as though we were in the city. It transformed my clinic too. I could see patients far into the night. It was as if the patients knew about it, as there was a great influx of them.

At the end of the first month, I had to go to the NYSC camp to undergo the mandatory orientation programme. This was a compulsory part of the Service. As doctors and pharmacists had started our services before the other graduates, we had to suspend our clinical work and join the rest of the corpers for the events of induction.

The Abraka campus was converted into a quasi-military camp, where we received basic military training, as well as information about the ethnic diversity in Bendel State. It created a suitable environment for the corpers to meet new people and build relationships.

We stood at attention, listening to Captain Abdullah as he gave us instructions about our orientation programme. The stern-looking, no-nonsense military officer, dressed in combat uniform, gave me the scare of my life. He read out the rules as we all stood at attention in our brown khaki uniforms:

"I know that you are book people with big degrees, but you are here to take orders from me and my officers. You are here, and you will spend the whole month here. You are expected to remain in the camp throughout the month. You must not leave the camp without my permission. As you know, this is a compulsory part of the National Youth Service. It is tough training. I advise you to co-operate with us if you want to enjoy your time here."

I had informed my patients in Kwale that I would be coming to run my evening clinic. So hearing from the camp commandant that we were not free to leave the camp posed a great challenge to me. I had to figure out a way of sneaking out. But this officer meant his words, and I didn't fancy being the first corper to get into trouble with him. I didn't know what the repercussions would be for anyone who broke the rules. So I elected to see how things went. There had to be a way out, I resolved.

We didn't do much on the first day other than the drill from Abraka to Obiaroko, a distance of about a mile. We were divided into our troops. We spent the rest of the afternoon getting to know one another and having a good orientation to the NYSC. We had guest speakers, invited to brief us about the various ethnic culture in Bendel. After our supper, there were no official activities, leaving us to spend our evening as we liked.

I bumped into Yakubu as I came out of the canteen.

"Old boy, shall we go for a drink in the village?" he asked.

"Oh no," I replied. "The officers will not open the gate, you know."

"That's not going to be a problem," he reassured me.

Yakubu told me that from the marks on the commandant's face, he knew where he was from, and he could speak his language.

"Follow me," he directed.

I followed him to the officers' quarters, without asking any questions.

"Sannu," Yakubu exchanged greetings with the gatekeeper. They exchanged greetings in Hausa, and said other things that I didn't understand. Then the gatekeeper let us in. Captain Abdullah was having a drink with three officers when we arrived. Yakubu exchanged greetings with him in Hausa, as if they were old friends. Captain Abdullah was no longer the tough-looking officer who had addressed us earlier in the day. He was now a fun-loving young man, relaxing with his friends. Yakubu introduced me to him as a doctor and a close friend of his.

"You are welcome to have a drink here after each day's activities. And if you want to go out, just let me know," he said to us.

At first, I thought he was probably under the influence of alcohol. Maybe he was out of his senses. But he was the boss, the commandant. He had the final say on anything, the only one that could make the rules.

"Sir, can I have your permission to go to Kwale every evening and weekend to run my clinic?" I asked Captain Abdullah, with all the courage in the world. This was the opportunity I had looked for, and I had to seize it.

The officer pulled out a bunch of exeat cards from a drawer and gave one to Yakubu and one to me after signing them.

"Show this to them at the gate whenever you want to go out and come in. But make sure you don't sleep outside, and don't stay too far into the night," he said.

I felt like a million-tonne weight had been lifted off my chest. As we trekked back from the officers' quarters, I had another look at the green-white card with the officer's signature on it and felt incredibly privileged.

"Thank you," I said to Yakubu, and really meant it.

Yakubu offered to accompany me to Kwale. Patients were already waiting when we arrived. It would have been a big disappointment if I had failed to come. I saw more than twenty patients, and we arrived back at the camp just before midnight. The gatekeeper officer saluted as he let us in after inspecting our exeat card. Most people were already in bed when we arrived, but that didn't bother me. I had a quick shower, and in a twinkle of the eye, I was in dreamland.

I made daily trips to Kwale. By special permission, I was allowed to spend whole days on Saturdays and Sundays. The gatekeepers had recognised me as a friend of Captain Abdullah's, and they ceased to ask for my exeat card. They recognised my car, and as soon as I showed up, they saluted and lifted the bar.

By the end of the orientation month, my private practice had become well-grounded, and I couldn't cope with the volume of work. I employed two school-certificate holders, a boy and a girl, to help with administrative work, and a registered nurse to help with clinical work.

Also at this time, my car had started to show signs of ageing, thus becoming unreliable for a long-distance drive. Although I had made enough money to buy a new car, I worked for two more weeks. I followed my father's philosophy. As he often advised, "When you want to buy a car, always ensure that you have enough money to buy a second one." Father believed that it was better not to have a car than to have one and be unable to buy a replacement should anything happen to it. That was exactly what I did. After buying my Nissan Estate, I still had more than enough money in the bank.

When we returned from the orientation camp, another pharmacist had been allocated to join myself and Yakubu. Sam Mba was a pharmacist doing his internship. At first, I didn't like the idea that we were now three people in a house that was meant for just me. But having found Yakubu to be a nice person, despite my initial reservations, I felt that I should give Mba a chance. Certainly, my first impression was that he seemed to be a nice person. And he truly was. In no time, the three of us became inseparable, doing our shopping together, cooking together and eating from the same pot at the same time.

The presence of two pharmacists was a good boost to my private practice. Unfortunately, having all the rooms occupied left me no room for my practice. So, with the agreement of Yakubu and Mba, I converted our sitting room to my consulting room. This caused some limitations in my practice. I therefore approached I.K., seeking to rent a separate apartment.

"That's not a problem," I.K. reassured me.

There was a five-room block beside the main house. One of the rooms was vacant. Fortunately, the tenancy agreement of the other rooms was ending the following month. They were happy to move out. As an incentive, I.K. excused them of one month's rent. Having a whole building dedicated to my clinic transformed my practice.

My friends, with whom I first went to the NYSC office, heard about my buoyant private practice, and they came for a weekend visit. At first, I was angry with them for the way they treated me on the day of our allocation. I wanted to punish them for the betrayal of my trust. But then I reasoned that I shouldn't blame them. That must have been God's plan for me. Even if that wasn't His plan, He certainly turned things around. God had turned my cries of disappointment into tears of joy.

I recalled Joseph's story in the Bible, when his brothers sold him into slavery. But God prospered Joseph. His brothers meant him harm, but God turned it around. God can turn a bad situation into good. And he has a plan for everyone's life. Joseph understood this, and he forgave his brothers. Like Joseph's brothers, my friends meant me harm, but God had other ideas. I had no option but to forgive them, though, and we resumed our friendship and did what youth corpers did: partying and having fun.

My friends informed me of their regrets about where they were posted. Unlike my experience in Kwale, they were not loved, and they made little or no money above their two-hundred naira salary. As for me, the NYSC salary was nothing compared to the income from my private practice. Many of them regularly came to borrow money from me. I never asked for repayment, and they never paid back. It was my pleasure to help them, and I thanked God that I was able to use my position to help. More importantly, I was able to send money to my parents and support my siblings' education. And as I reflected over my humble beginnings, I felt privileged to have such financial independence within a short space of time.

We had discos in our house every Saturday, and all the other non-medics in the neighbourhood soon heard about me and became my friends. I provided the music and sponsored the parties without any stress. I couldn't thank God enough.

The Fitting Child

Despite my busy practice, I made time to relax and enjoy life with friends. One Saturday night, after our usual disco, I had just gone to bed when several knocks on the door woke me up. I thought I was in the middle of a dream. At first, I ignored the person. The time was around three in the morning. As the knocking persisted, I opened the door, and a woman fell on her knees with her fitting daughter.

The four-year-old girl had been having recurrent fits from birth. She had taken her to see several doctors near and far, but nobody could help. She had spent all her money and even sold her market store and all that she owned to raise money for her daughter's medical care.

On her knees, she pleaded for me to show kindness to her. She had been to two doctors that night, who had turned her down as she had no money to pay for her daughter's medical care. So she had come to me as the last resort. Just as she pleaded, the child had another fit. I rushed her straight into the treatment room. She settled after administering intramuscular paraldehyde. I discharged her and advised her mother to bring her back in the morning. As I was expecting her to bring back the child in the morning, I hadn't billed her, hoping to give a final bill when she came back.

I couldn't get back to sleep, all the time thinking about the causes of status epilepticus in a child. I knew they were not febrile convulsions. I thought of all sorts of causes and reasoned that whatever had caused the convulsions must be congenital. I reflected over everything that she had told me. She had been impoverished by her daughter's illness. I could just imagine her having sleepless nights and missing her meals. Her husband didn't accompany her. This could mean that he was fed up and had abandoned mother and child or had to stay at home to look after the other children.

I was in the middle of my breakfast when one of my workers knocked at the door. "The woman who came to see you last night has returned," she reported.

"Is that why you have come whilst I am having my breakfast?" I asked.

"Sorry, sir," she said.

"Tell her to wait. I will see her after breakfast," I said.

"But her daughter is seriously sick," she said. "She is having fits again."

I stopped my breakfast and raced to my clinic. The child was twitching again like she had done in the night. Like before, I administered a dose of paraldehyde. The twitch stopped, but I wasn't happy that I hadn't found the cause of this child's fits. As I parted her eyelids to check for pallor that might suggest anaemia, I noticed dark rings that appeared to encircle the iris of the eyes. Could these be Kayser-Fleischer rings? And with a yellow tinge (jaundice) on the white part of the eyes (sclera), I wondered if this child had Wilson's disease, a rare inherited disorder that causes copper to accumulate in the liver, brain and other vital organs.

Wilson's disease is inherited as an autosomal recessive trait, which means that to develop the disease you must inherit one copy of the defective gene from each parent. If you receive only one abnormal gene, you won't become ill yourself, but you're a carrier and can pass the gene to your children.

I told the girl's mother that I just might have found the cause of her daughter's fits and advised that I needed to refer her to the teaching hospital for confirmation of the diagnosis and treatment. The woman accepted my diagnosis but declined referral to the specialist centre. She believed that if I couldn't treat her child, no one could. I explained to her that I had neither the facilities to confirm the diagnosis nor to treat her. She knew, of course, that I had not issued her any bill for the care that I had given her daughter, so she thought that I wasn't interested in treating her because she hadn't paid me. I made her aware that I would never refuse treatment because of inability to pay and urged her to trust me to do whatever I did. Whatever advice I gave was in her best interest. After much persuasion, she agreed to be referred. I did a referral letter, with a suspicious diagnosis of Wilson's disease, to the paediatrics department at the University Teaching Hospital.

Six weeks later, I had just finished my breakfast when a taxi pulled up in front of our house. I came out to advise the passenger that I would be unable to see them that morning, as I had to go to the hospital for my normal government practice. If they needed to see a doctor urgently, they would be better off going to the hospital, but if it was for something that could wait, they could come back to see me after work.

A mother emanated from the back of the taxi, holding the hand of her child. I thought I had seen her before. As I pondered, the driver started to off-load the stuff in his taxi.

"Doctor, I know you are busy. I came early, as I wanted to catch you before you left for work," she said.

I raised a questioning eyebrow.

"I have come to thank you for all you have done," she said. "The doctor in the big hospital also said that I should give this to you," she informed me, as she handed a brown sealed envelope to me.

I hardly recognised the mother of the young girl whom I had referred to the specialist hospital. Her daughter had been discharged after six weeks in the specialist hospital and had been fit-free for three weeks. The woman, who had shown up with only a wrapper on and unkempt hair, now looked so different, much younger, with well-plaited hair and make-up. Her daughter smiled shyly as her mother told her, "Say thank you to the doctor."

I watched the driver arrange all the gifts she had brought at one corner in the kitchen: two large bunches of matured plantains, one large bunch of ripe bananas, ten large tubers of yams, one whole roasted porcupine, four large frozen Murtala Muhammed turkey limbs and two racks of matured smoked mackerels. My eyes welled up as I read the letter that the consultant paediatrician had written to me:

Thank you for sending this 'once in a doctor's lifetime' case. Your diagnosis was spot on. It has also provided learning opportunity for all of us. The patient's mother said so many nice things about you. I am sure she will sing your praises all over the place. If after your NYSC you need a training post in paediatrics, I will be able to secure a place for you in my department. If there is any other way I can be of assistance to you, do not hesitate to contact me ...

The woman thanked me and promised to come again. I gave the young girl a final hug and advised her mother to keep her follow-up appointment with the specialist. I also advised her to ensure that her daughter took the medication that the specialist had prescribed.

My involvement with the care of Abigail was a turning point for me. It brought a transformation to my practice. Like the professor stated in his letter, Abigail's mother had become my self-appointed public relation officer. She had recommended me to all the market women, and through them, my name had spread around Ndokwa and beyond. All the taxi drivers knew about me. My attendance was explosive. Patients came in tens from as far as Rivers State. My reception room became too small. People queued up to the roadside, with my evening clinics sometimes going on till twelve in the night.

I became the family doctor for most of the chiefs and politicians. The only bank in Kwale, The National bank, dropped their previous doctor and gave the retainership to me. I also had the retainership for Agip Oil Company. So many businesses registered with me. Even people working in Lagos and other cities registered their families living in Kwale with me. But my new-found fame brought me in direct confrontation with Dr Odeda. He had called me to his office a number of times and raised his concerns that I was beginning to be too popular in the town.

"Wherever I go, people talk about the 'nice new doctor'," he reported.

"That cannot be a bad thing, sir," I said. "You must be proud of me."

"What did you say?" He stood up and gripped the edge of his desk, after blinking like the devil.

"I said, you should be proud of me," I replied sternly.

"How can I be proud of you when you have bribed all the riff-raffs in the town to advertise you to poach all my patients?" he roared like a wounded lion.

"I see," I said calmly. "So, the issue here is to do with money." I shook my head in disgust.

"Anyway, listen and listen well. If you continue like that, I will make you see hell," he threatened.

"What does that mean?" I asked.

"You wait and see," he replied.

"Okay," I said. "Can I take my leave now?" I asked.

He replied with an angry shove of the pile of files on the desk in front of him.

That evening, I ran my clinic as usual. Yakubu came to see me in the consulting room.

"You won't believe what is happening," he hinted.

"What?" I asked.

"Just come for a minute before the next patient, because you need to see things for yourself," he insisted.

I thought I was dreaming, but, of course, it wasn't a dream. It was six o'clock in the evening, and Dr Odeda leaned on his white Peugeot 504 parked in front of Eke Primary School, directly opposite my clinic, counting the number of patients who had come to see me. Yakubu reckoned that he must have been standing there for at least an hour. My first thought was to go and challenge him. But on second thought, I decided to ignore him, leaving my success to be his headache. Yakubu agreed that was a wise decision, and I returned into my consulting room. Yakubu later informed me that he left shortly after I returned into the consulting room. We speculated that either he had realised that we had seen him or he could no longer bear to see the number of patients waiting to see me and those that I had seen.

The following morning, I arrived in the hospital at eight o'clock, as usual. Dr Odeda's car was already parked in the PMO's parking area, which was unusual, as he normally started work no earlier than eleven o'clock. Judging by what I saw the previous night, I could sense trouble coming, and I had to brace myself. I was about to call for my first patient, when the door was pushed open. I thought they had used a bulldozer. Dr Odeda stood at the door with a sardonic stare. Aguye and the other outpatient staff stood behind him. Aguye placed his hands on his head. Some of the staff scratched their heads. Others simply stared into my room. I had no idea what they knew or what they anticipated.

"I have been talking to you as a small man," he barked. "See me at the Health Management Office at noon. I will talk to you then as a big man."

Then he slammed the door and marched away. I thought he was going to start his clinic. Instead, he drove back home to run his private clinic.

Aguye and the other staff came into my room. They told me that they overheard everything he said. They reassured me that the Kwale people loved and trusted me, and there was nothing he could do about it. Aguye revealed to me that he had threatened to recommend my transferral to the NYSC Office, but all the staff promised me that if he attempted that, they would call for his transfer. I felt valued. This was a humbling experience, and I appreciated their support.

Yakubu had arrived, and he came straight to my room after hearing about the event that morning. Although I appreciated the support that the staff had given me, somehow I found it hard to trust them. They had known Dr Odeda long before me, and I was only three months into my twelve-months service. He was their boss with power to sack them. For those reasons, they could betray me to protect their jobs. So I decided not to talk to Yakubu in their presence. Instead, we went to the pharmacy staffroom for a chat.

Mba and the chief pharmacist were in the staffroom. The chief pharmacist, an American-trained pharmacist, was a disciplined person who was highly regarded by the hospital staff. Through Yakubu and Mba, I had formed a friendship with him. Although in his thirties and a married man, he and his wife had visited us and attended our parties a number of times. I trusted his advice and integrity, so I was happy to bring up the issue in his presence. Like Aguye said, he reassured me he would be digging his grave if he made even the slightest move to request my transfer.

"He should have known by now that Kwale people are nice, but they can also be nasty if you provoke them," he said.

Yakubu offered to accompany me to see Dr Odeda at lunch time. At first, I declined his offer, since I believed I could handle him on my own. But Mr Igbeke, the principal pharmacist, advised that having a third person there would act as a restraint. Also, that person would be my witness should he make up a story to discredit me.

"What if he makes up stories, for example, that you threatened his life or that you called him names? It will be his word against yours," he advised.

This made sense, and I agreed for Yakubu to accompany me.

Dr Odeda was already in his office when I arrived. Before I could inform him that my colleague, Yakubu, had come to support me, he said, "I am seeing just you." I found that to be strange. Surely, if there was something so serious or a major decision to be made, he should at least have his secretary to minute our meeting.

"I have seen that you are not busy in the hospital. That is why you can spend all your time running an illegal clinic," he said and paused to measure my response.

I wanted to respond, but when I looked at Yakubu through the window, he signalled to me to keep calm and let him say everything he needed to say before responding.

"I have made the decision to change your job plan," he continued. "Starting from tomorrow, you will be running the mobile clinic," he said.

"Can I start next week?" I asked.

"No," he bleated.

"Okay, I will start tomorrow," I said.

Again, I looked at Yakubu, who nodded in agreement.

"By the way, why next week? Is it so you may tell your patients not to come to the General Hospital?" he asked, as if he had had a brain wave.

"So the real reason for pushing me into the mobile service is so patients may not come to see me. Isn't it?" I asked.

"You may say so," he replied. "You have taken all my patients. Can you imagine a patient telling the outpatient staff that she preferred to see the youth corper!" He slammed the table.

"You are the consultant," I replied. "I am only an ordinary youth corper. It is a pity that you have seen me as a threat to your private practice."

"Shut up, and don't argue with me," he roared.

"I am not arguing with you," I said. "I requested to start next week so I can plan my itinerary."

"You don't need any itinerary," he thundered. "The driver knows everywhere. Where do you know anyway? After all, you are only a foreigner."

"Why would you refer to me as a foreigner? I am no less a Nigerian than you," I said, trying very hard to control my breathing, which had become fast.

"You are not a Bendelite," he roared.

"My mother is an Urhobo like you. So she is a Bendelite, which makes me a Bendelite too," I said. "After all, you are not an Ndokwa person. So we are both aliens on Ndokwa soil."

Yakubu was no longer just sitting on the bench. He stood up and looked directly into the room. I smiled when my eyes caught his nods of encouragement. Dr Odeda looked at the direction of my gaze. His eyes caught Yakubu's, who gave him a wry smile. He sat down and tightened his fist. Just then, the secretary knocked at the door.

"Hello, our lovely doctor," he greeted.

"Hello, sir," I greeted him.

From his body language, I sensed that he must have heard some, if not all, of our conversation.

"We are hearing good news about you," he remarked.

"I don't think that the PMO shares that with the people," I said. "Thank you, anyway."

"I am sure—" the secretary said.

"I was about to call you to update the file," Dr Odeda interrupted. "He has been moved to the mobile clinic. He will set off tomorrow."

"That's not going to work," the secretary cautioned. "This needs to be properly planned."

"What do you mean?" he snapped. "The driver is from Kwale. He knows everywhere in Ndokwa. So all the doctor has to do is to see patients."

"With due respect, sir, it is not just that," the secretary advised. "The commissioner requires us to make monthly itineraries. There's a separate budget for the mobile service. The drugs and diagnostics come directly from Benin. All these have to be in place before the team sets off. Also, each visit is supposed to be pre-planned, and the people need to be informed of the visit so they can get ready."

That was exactly what I said to the PMO. I was glad that the secretary showed a good understanding.

"Okay, how long will all these preparations take?" Dr Odeda asked, looking like a defeated boxer.

"At least one week, maybe two," the secretary advised.

"He can start on Wednesday or Thursday, then," Dr Odeda said.

I watched as both men discussed the issue. Dr Odeda had no idea how to run a mobile service. If he did, he must have allowed his selfish interest or his jealousy for my thriving private practice to cloud his judgement.

"No, that won't work," the secretary maintained. Then after scratching his head, he said, "May I suggest you give the doctor enough time to plan with his team, collect all the things that they need from Benin and draw up an itinerary to cover the whole of the local government area?"

"Who is the boss here?" Dr Odeda asked, looking like he did when he came to my room that morning.

"You, of course," the secretary replied.

"And who makes the rules here?" he roared.

"You, of course," the secretary replied. "Sir, I am not telling you what to do. I am only pointing your attention to the directives from Benin. As you know, the mobile clinic service is an important agenda of the UPN, and we are expected to provide a feedback at the end of the year."

"In that case, he can start tomorrow from Kwale or Ashaka with some drugs from the hospital stock," Dr Odeda said.

The secretary maintained his stance. He advised that if Dr Odeda insisted on changing a state-wide government policy, he should obtain an approval from the headquarters. This was a hit below the belt.

"Alright then, get everything in place so that he can start on Monday," he resigned.

I asked if I could take my leave. He agreed, but that I should see him in the hospital. He needed to talk to me. After agreeing a meeting with the secretary the following day, for briefing regarding the government's aspirations about the mobile service, I took my leave. Yakubu had waited for me, and he was pleased with the way that I had handled the issue.

Chapter Ten
THE MOBILE SERVICE

I decided to see Chief Otobo, Secretary of the Health Board. He had said some nice things about me, to the disappointment of Dr Odeda, during our meeting. I also noted that Dr Odeda did not invite any of the secretariat staff to the meeting he had with me. That suggested to me that whatever he had planned to do was unlikely to be favoured by them.

I needed Chief Otobo's advice. I didn't know why I thought I could trust him, but that was what my mind told me, and I was reassured when he beamed a warm smile as he welcomed me to his office. He advised me not to be intimidated by Dr Odeda. "The people like and respect you," he said, "and he cannot change the people's perspectives, no matter how hard he tries." He reassured me that he would do everything possible within his power to ensure that I enjoyed my new role as the medical officer in charge of the mobile clinic.

With a large map of Ndokwa Local Government on his office wall, he showed me the entire area. The community is divided broadly into two: the mainland and riverine people. He advised that how I ran the service was entirely my prerogative, and I was at liberty to draw up my itinerary as long as the local government areas were all covered.

Apart from the driver of the van that carried the drugs and equipment, I had the liberty to choose the driver of the car that would carry me. I was also allowed to choose my nurse and health assistant.

Ben, the driver of the van, was an Itshan man in his thirties. I didn't know much about him, but he had a likeable personality. I had no problem choosing my health assistant. I trusted Aguye. He was an experienced health assistant and highly respectable. I also admired his chats. He knew so much about Ndokwa people. The driver was Frank, a twenty-eight-year-old Kwale man, I.K.'s cousin. My nurse was Pat, a thirty-year-old, highly experienced and intelligent staff nurse, also from Ndokwa. She was the only nurse in the outpatient department who had stood up to Dr Odeda. When I first met her, I didn't like her. I thought she was too full of herself. But as I got to know her, I found out she was a delightful and caring person.

Upon my suggestion, Chief Otobo had approved funding from the Mobile Service allocation for provision of our meals. This pocket of money came directly from Benin City. So Dr Odeda had no power to stop us spending it that way. I gave Pat the responsibility for providing our daily meals. She also made daily checks of the drugs and equipment, making good documentation of their usage and restocking after each visit. The drivers and Aguye made out weekly itineraries and passed them to me for approval.

Running the mobile clinics made me even more popular. People who had never seen me, but had heard about me, had the opportunity to meet me. Wherever we went, I made sure that I met the head of the village and explained the purpose of our visit. I would then give him some vitamin tablets after Pat had checked his blood pressure and dipped his urine to screen for diabetes. Every place we visited, the people received us with a great deal of enthusiasm. We worked from morning till late afternoon, always making sure we saw everyone who needed to be seen. We never turned anyone away.

Dr Odeda's decision to move me to the mobile clinic was a blessing in disguise. His motives were bad, but God turned them to good for me. I didn't have to do any advertising; the mobile service was *de facto* a seller. It provided a useful opportunity for people to consult me. Also, people who would normally see me in the general hospital, and those who would not see the other doctors, came for private consultations outside of mobile clinic sessions. People trooped into my clinic from all over Ndokwa. I was busy day and night. And with a booming private practice, I decided that I would stay behind in Kwale after my NYSC.

On one of the visits, I saw something that challenged my thoughts regarding my future career. A forty-year-old woman was brought to see me. Although I had observed her when we arrived, I never knew how bad things were with this woman. The story was that the woman had been attacked by a tiger because she was a witch. She went to the bush to fetch firewood, when the tiger attacked her and beat off her breast. The husband had thrown her out and taken in a new wife. It was abominable to touch her. She had confessed under duress that she was a witch, and had caused her husband not to prosper. So, apart from her two daughters, whom the husband had driven out with her, she had no one else. As the two young daughters helped their mother into the van, I fought hard to hold my tears.

"You have a bad cancer of the breast," I informed her. "The story of tiger attack could not be tangible. A tiger that could beat off your breast, no doubt, would take the whole you."

The woman confessed that it was not caused by a tiger. In fact, she had never seen a tiger, let alone been bitten by one. She had seen all the doctors, and visited all the herbalists and spiritualists. She was a condemned person waiting to die, and her remains would be fit only for the scavengers in the jungle. Her eyes sparkled with hope when I told her, "There's something eating up your breast. It is called cancer."

"Doctor, please give me a strong injection to make it go," she pleaded.

I advised her that she needed to go to the specialist hospital, and she agreed.

I never returned to that village, so I didn't know what happened to her. One thing I did know was that she trusted me, and I had no doubt that she would have gone to the teaching hospital with my referral letter. Although at that stage the cancer was incurable, I was glad that I made the diagnosis and signposted her to the right place.

One Monday morning, Frank came to pick me up for the day's trip. He looked worried as he handed a brown envelope to me.

"Good morning, Frank," I said. "You look like someone who has just got the sack. Is everything okay?"

"Good morning, Doctor," he said. "The PMO asked me to give you this letter. He said that you must read it before we set off today."

In the three-line letter, Dr Odeda stopped my admitting rights to the Kwale General Hospital. He ordered that any patient needing admission must first be referred to him. What that essentially meant was that if I saw a dehydrated child in my mobile clinic, or any other patient who needed admission, they must see him first. This invariably meant that if he wasn't in hospital, they would have to see him at home. Of course, they would then have to pay before they could be admitted. I folded the letter into the envelope and tucked it into my pocket.

"Is everything alright?" Frank asked.

"Of course," I replied. "Please take me to the hospital."

On the way to the hospital, Frank informed me that he had heard Dr Odeda telling his secretary that I had been having too many patients for operations since I started the mobile clinics. He had to stop me using the theatres and hospital beds. He said he would wait and see where I would operate on my patients, and where I would admit them. It was after that he signed the letter his secretary had typed and passed on to me.

Dr Odeda was about to get into his car when I arrived at the hospital. He must have come unusually early, so he could catch the driver to ensure that I received the letter that morning.

"Good morning, Dr Odeda," I greeted. "I have come to see you."

"If you want to see me, book an appointment with my secretary," he said.

As he was about to start his car, I pulled his car door open. "I saw your letter. I just want you to know that I totally disagree with you," I said.

"I don't need you to agree with me. It is an order, which must be obeyed," he snarled.

"And if I don't?" I narrowed my eyes.

"Then you must face the consequences of insubordination," he warned and drove away.

We were nearly late for the day's trip. Patients would already be waiting. Unless we started on time, we would finish late. We always ensured that we saw everyone who came to see us. We never turned anyone away. So I decided to put the issue away somewhere in my mind, just as I had tucked the letter in my pocket.

The clinic went well, as planned, and I tried not to allow the issue to affect my interaction with the patients. They trusted and respected me. And they deserved to have my full attention. Fortunately, I had no cause to admit anyone to the hospital. Had that situation arisen, however, I would have ignored Dr Odeda's order in the best interests of the patients.

I.K. was playing draughts with Yakubu and Mba when I arrived back from the mobile clinic. The news had reached them. That was the real reason I.K. had come. He had waited for me to confirm the rumour that was going around. The rumour that circulated was that Dr Odeda had planned to send me away from Kwale. I explained to I.K. that was not the case. As he already knew, I had been charged with the responsibility of running the mobile clinics which, of course, I enjoyed. I then gave the letter that I had received that morning to I.K. He almost hit the roof after reading it. He passed it to Yakubu, who in turn gave it to Mba to read.

"This man is crazy," Yakubu and Mba commented simultaneously.

"He will be the person to leave, not you," I.K. resolved.

"So, what will happen if you need to admit patients?" Mba asked.

"I don't see that as a problem. I will admit the patient. I don't think he will come and drive the patient out of the bed," I replied. "My only problem is if he has instructed the nurses on the ward not to admit my patients."

I.K. promised to hold a meeting with the chiefs so they could petition Dr Odeda to the State Health Management Board in Benin. I didn't want to make any trouble. As Dr Odeda had said a number of times, I wasn't a Bendelite, and soon my service year would come to an end. Then, like other corpers, I would be released into the world to build a life and career for myself.

Many of my patients mentioned the rumour that was going on, that I would soon be leaving. I wasn't the first doctor to serve in Kwale, and I had expected them to know that the NYSC was for one year only. At the end of the year, my time would be up, and it would be someone else's turn to serve. Nevertheless, my patients believed that it was Dr Odeda who had planned to send me away from Kwale.

The following week, I received a letter to attend an urgent meeting with the Chairman of the Health Board, together with Dr Odeda in Benin. My heart sank when I read the letter signed by the Chairman himself. I wasn't bothered about whether I remained in Kwale or not. I was more bothered about my reputation and my future career. Dr Odeda was a son of the soil, a Bendelite with everything in his favour. He had all the power and influence, and he had professional seniority. I was no match in the political boxing ring, so I needed moral support in case they terminated my service. At first, I thought of inviting I.K., but that could be blown out of proportion if the market women were mobilised. So I decided not to inform him. I knew Yakubu and Mba had been supportive, and they were in the healthcare profession. They had heard and seen how Dr Odeda had behaved, and they would play a key role as my witnesses. Although both of them were prepared to accompany me to Benin, only one could realistically go, otherwise there would be no pharmacist to work that day.

The meeting was scheduled for ten o'clock in the morning, and we went in Yakubu's car. That was a good thing, since Yakubu was a better driver on rough or busy roads than me. Such was the case whenever we went to Onitsha Market or Warri. We arrived at nine, and I almost had a heart attack as the office assistant led us into the waiting room and was greeted by I.K., who smiled as he rose to give me the warmest hug. Seated, waiting for the Board Chairman, were Chief Ben Obi, Chief Otoboh, Chief Chiyennemba and Chief Oligbo. They had all been mobilised by I.K. to come and testify to their petition against Dr Odeda.

Dr Odeda arrived just before eleven, almost an hour late. He entered like a cockerel that had been in the rain all day. I couldn't tell what he was thinking, seeing the presence of the Kwale chiefs. He took the only standalone seat and gently rested his briefcase by his side.

"You must have received a copy of the petition that the people of Kwale have submitted," the chairman said, without giving Dr Odeda any chance to explain why he was almost an hour late for an important meeting. "So what have you got to say about it?" he asked.

"I feel that a case like this should have been discussed between you and me, not in the presence of everyone," he protested.

"Is that all you want to tell all these respectable chiefs who have taken time to come and find a solution to the dispute between you and your colleague?" The chairman raised his voice. "You arrived one hour late, yet this is all you can say."

"Sorry, but I just feel that I should be left to discipline the doctor for his disobedience." Dr Odeda was defiant.

"I am sure you recognise all these people," the chairman reminded him. "These are the people who will chase you out of Kwale if you want things to go that way."

"If I had known that the boy was going to bring his friends, I too would have brought mine."

The chairman reminded him that he was the chairman of the board, and he had the power to strip him of his post as the principal medical officer. He couldn't understand why he had been so hostile and unsupportive towards a fellow doctor like himself. He was supposed to look after me as a youth corper. After all, he himself had served in another state before. "I had never met this doctor until today, but I have heard about all the good work he has been doing. Even the governor himself has heard about him," he said.

Dr Odeda turned to look at me. He gave a threatening stare and turned back to face the chairman. He knew, of course, that the chairman meant what he had said.

"So, what are you going to do now?" the chairman asked.

"Well, I just want him not to be disobedient," he said.

At that juncture, I asked the chairman if I could respond. He accepted.

I told the chairman and everyone present that I had nothing against Dr Odeda. In fact, I was excited when I arrived in Kwale and found out that he was the PMO. I knew him in Ibadan. We both qualified from the same university. I had expected that he would be my mentor. Anyone who knew me well would confirm that I would never be disobedient. But, as a doctor, my primary duty was to my patients. Kwale people had been so good to me. All I had done, and was doing, was for the good people of Kwale.

"I am humbled by the tremendous support of these chiefs, and I am grateful to them," I said.

"I have done that for longer than you have done. I don't think Kwale people would say, with their hands on their chests, that I had not helped the Kwale people," Dr Odeda interjected.

"We have been quiet since," Chief Obi said. "Kwale people love our doctor. Let me pass the mandate of the people. If you hurt the people's doctor, you hurt the people," Chief Obi warned.

"I have treated your wife before," Dr Odeda said to Chief Obi. "But since this boy came, all of you have left me."

"So that is the issue, isn't it?" Chief Obi asked. "You know that he is a good doctor. But you want to discredit him for your own gain."

The chairman had sensed where the meeting was heading, with the other chiefs wanting to join in. That wasn't the purpose of the meeting.

He certainly didn't want to worsen the already bad situation, so he had to do something.

"Doctor, the people of Kwale love the young doctor," the chairman said to Dr Odeda, "and I can't see what you can do about that. I advise you to stop the harassment and work together for the sake of peace and for the patients that you have sworn to care for."

"Yes, I know he is a good doctor," Dr Odeda confessed, "but it gets to his head sometimes."

Yakubu pinched me to confirm that he heard what the boss had said. I believed he had made an honest admission to my professional skills. But I didn't understand the latter part of his sentence, whatever he meant by 'gets into his head'. Nevertheless, I didn't let that bother me.

"I implore you to let peace dwell," the chairman said to me.

"Yes, Chief," I said.

The chairman thanked everyone. Dr Odeda was the first to leave. When I came out, he had driven out of the compound. I thanked all the people who had come to support me. We took our leave. I promised to catch up with I.K.

The following day, Frank told me that Dr Odeda wanted to see me before setting off on the mobile trip.

"What is it this time?" I couldn't help asking.

Frank shrugged his shoulders. "I think he is a crazy fellow," he said.

"You are probably right," I said, and took my usual position in the back seat.

Dr Odeda was busy giving instructions to the outpatient staff when we arrived.

"Oh, talk of the devil," he said, as I came out of the Volkswagen Beetle.

"Good morning, Dr Odeda," I greeted.

"Follow me to my office," he ordered, without returning my greeting.

"You are now so powerful," he remarked. "Even more powerful than me. You spoke where I could not speak," he sighed, and smiled wryly.

I didn't want to have an argument with him that morning. I simply nodded and let him say whatever he wanted to say. He told me that the doctors couldn't cope with the work in the outpatient, so I should change how I worked. I should spend two days in the hospital and three in the mobile clinic. I advised him that I had already drawn up my itineraries for the rest of my service year. But despite my pleas, he insisted on reducing the number of days that I went on mobile clinic. He promised to reinstate my admission rights, but I wasn't sure if this was a bribe to make me accept the changes or a bow to pressure. Whatever his motive, I agreed to do two days in the hospital and the rest of the week on the mobile clinic.

Meeting with the Man of the Underworld

After the morning clinic, I went with Yakubu and Mba and our friends who had come to visit us, to Bamboo Inn to have pepper soup. We had a good time, and after our friends had left, Yakubu, Mba and I returned to our house. I had wanted to have a nap before my evening clinic. It was a hot afternoon, and I needed to switch on the electricity generator, so I could use the air-conditioner. As I opened the door to the engine room, however, I couldn't believe what I saw. Someone had stolen my generator. I raised the alarm. All of us checked the bushes. We looked for it everywhere but couldn't find it.

I drove to I.K. and reported the burglary. I.K. reassured me that if the burglars were local, we would recover the generator. He took me to see a man with the nickname of Pilot. The middle-aged man lived alone in an isolated, storey building in Ashaka, which was about one and a half miles from Kwale.

As the man emerged from his room upstairs and looked down over us from his balcony, I thought I had seen the Devil himself. If he wasn't the Devil, then he must have a full DNA copy of the true Devil. There were many stories told about this man who had tight control over all the criminals in the land. One story was that his burnt face was the result of a plane crash in which only he, the pilot, survived. Another story held that he got burnt during a piracy event. Yet another story was that he had acid thrown at him during a burglary. None of these stories held water. Whatever the cause of his scarred face, all I could say was that you wouldn't want to see that face in your dreams. He stared at us as he drew in a large breath of cannabis. After what seemed like an eternity, he beckoned us to come upstairs.

As we climbed the narrow stairs, I didn't know what else to do other than pray silently as my feet wobbled and my heart raced. "God, my life is in your hands," I sighed.

All the while, I.K. didn't say anything, though he suspected that I was frightened. He simply smiled and winked. Within seconds, I was facing the head of the gangsters in Ndokwa. He and I.K. shook hands and then hit each other's chest. Then he focused his gaze on me, like the Devil would when he had found a prey. I put up a shallow smile. That was simply to keep my heart, which was rearing to jump out of my chest, in its place.

"My friend, Dr Joe," I.K. introduced me.

"I have heard about him," he said. "He is a good doctor."

I didn't know whether to nod, smile or thank him. But when he stretched out his hand for a handshake, I knew he meant good.

"It's nice to meet you, sir," I said to him.

"It's nice to meet you, too, my friend," he said, and shook my hand again as he led us to his balcony.

Pilot had chosen the right place to build his house. Standing on the balcony, you could see the whole of Ashaka and far beyond. You could also see any visitor coming to the house from more than two hundred metres away. A brick wall surrounded the entire building, making the ground floor look like a prison. He lived alone in the big house, and I guessed the unoccupied ground floor must be where he kept the spoils from the burglaries that his agents brought to him. All the ground-floor windows and doors were securely locked with massive padlocks.

"Your boys have taken the doctor's generator," I.K. reported, without any equivocation.

He smiled wryly. "My boys can't take what belongs to Dr Joe," he said, after drawing long on his marijuana. "They mustn't do that to him, because he is a nice man, and I like him."

"Yes, that's why I have brought him to see you," I.K. said.

Pilot told me not to worry and disappeared into one of his rooms. When he came back, he told us that when I returned home, I should check the bush behind my clinic and I would find it there. I.K. brought out forty naira from his pocket and gave it to him, that it was from me for a drink.

He and I.K. shook each other's hand and beat each other's chest once again. And after a final shake of hands with me, we took our leave.

At first, I didn't believe Pilot. The whole thing must be a joke, I reckoned. And then I worried that I.K. was a member of his gang or maybe he used to be in his gang. They were, at least, friends. I wanted to ask him, but didn't know the best way. I didn't want to upset him. But, going out with a notorious gang would affect my credibility. It would also give Dr Odeda grounds to report me to the NYSC secretariat or even to the NMC for an act of dishonour to the medical profession.

"You looked like a lamb in the front of a tiger in Pilot's house." I.K. broke the silence that we had kept since we left the man's house.

"What did you expect?" I asked. "The guy looked like the Devil. He smiled the smile of a tiger sizing up its prey, and he lives in hell," I said.

"Life is survival of the fittest," he replied. "But sometimes to survive you have to make friends with both the good and bad people. You see, the community is made up of good and bad people. Sometimes you need the good people. Other times you need the bad people to appeal to the bad people."

"But I don't want to be friends with bad people. I don't want to join the gang," I said.

"I am not in their gang either. As long as you recognise and respect them, they will take care of you. Don't cross their way, and they won't cross yours," he said. "The chief of the underworld has recognised you, and he liked you. All you need to do is buy him drinks from time to time. Put something in the envelope for him. Whenever you see his boys, be good to them."

"How will I know his boys?" I asked.

"You will know them when you see them," he reassured me.

Yakubu and Mba were in the front of the house when we arrived. Patients had started to arrive. I.K. and I headed straight for the bushy grass behind the house. It was like magic. My Yamaha generator was there waiting for me. I couldn't contain my joy. But it also frightened me. The thieves stole the machine in broad daylight and returned it in the broad daylight, without getting caught. Pilot promised to bring it back, and he did without a step out of his hell palace. I resolved to do as I.K. had advised: to treat them with respect and keep them happy, but at a distance.

Chapter Ten
AFTER THE NATIONAL SERVICE

The steadfast love of the Lord never ceases;
his mercies never come to an end;
they are new every morning;
great is your faithfulness.
Lamentations 3:22-23

I was in two minds as to what to do after my National Service. At that stage of my career, I had performed at a standard far and above that of most of my local counterparts. I had won and maintained my patients' trust, and they were all faithful to me. I had a thriving private practice, and I had formed good and trustworthy friendships. I was happy. But my second mind warned me that I was too young in the profession to go it alone. I had always had the ambition to undergo training to become a specialist surgeon. Going into full general practice wouldn't make this ambition happen. These thoughts kept creeping into my head in the weeks leading to the end of my service.

One Monday morning when I wasn't on a mobile clinic trip, I had just settled into my consulting room, and someone pushed my door without knocking. Dr Odeda stood at the door.

"You are already here," he said, smiling wryly.

"Of course," I replied. "I am always here at this time."

I couldn't understand why he had said it. He knew, of course, that I was always the first doctor to arrive in the morning. As a matter of fact, this was the first thing he moaned about. So making a remark about my early arrival seemed out of context, especially at this late stage of my placement.

"You must be looking forward to going back to the west," he said. "I felt like that when I was serving in the west. I had to return to Bendel State because my people needed me. So I think your people need you like mine did."

I didn't know what to make of what he had said. One thing I knew was that it wasn't for good. He couldn't have meant good for me, given his attitude to me since I came to Kwale. But whether my people needed me or not wasn't his problem. That was my problem, and my people's. Why would he make it his problem?

"Thank you for your advice," I simply said.

"I will give you a good reference to help you get a good job in your state," he said.

"I don't think that will be necessary," I said, "but thank you."

"Does that mean you will be going back to your state?" he asked.

"Yes," I replied.

"Very good," he said, and smiled wryly, before closing the door behind him.

Minutes later, I saw him driving out of the hospital, suggesting that he had come that early solely to talk to me. I sat on my own, trying to piece everything together. I had no doubt that Dr Odeda wanted to get rid of me. If he was sincere with his acknowledgement of me as a good doctor, he would be doing everything he could to keep me in Kwale. But encouraging me to leave gave me a good insight into his true character. He had seen me as a threat to his malpractices, but more seriously, to his bank account.

Although I did, as a matter of fact, plan to go abroad for specialist surgical training, I felt like I wasn't ready yet, and conflicting with my ambition to become a specialist surgeon was my genuine feeling for the Kwale people. For many years, they had been deceived and had their trust betrayed by a doctor who lacked conscience and had no respect for the traditional doctors' ethics. My presence in their midst had opened their eyes. They had seen the other way, the better way of practising medicine. Being a doctor should be seen as a privilege and opportunity to serve. You are part of the people, and not above them. Much as I tried to take these thoughts out of my mind, they kept creeping into it and refused to leave my consciousnesses.

"Are you alright, Doctor?" Aguye asked. "You haven't spoken since Dr Odeda left. I have been waiting for your instruction before sending the first patient in."

"Oh, I am fine," I replied. "Just trying to sort out something in my brain."

"I heard everything," Aguye said.

"Everything?" I wondered.

"Yes, everything Dr Odeda said to you," Aguye confirmed.

If Aguye had heard everything, he must have been eavesdropping, and the whole thing would soon spread like wildfire all over the place. But I didn't think Dr Odeda minded. Perhaps that was his plan. He had deliberately confronted me in my consulting room with the door open. If he could make me say bad things, then he would have witnesses. When I told him that I would be going back to my state, he had hoped that the news would spread and patients would start returning to him out of panic. As they would become desperate, he could take a punitive advantage and charge them more.

"Don't worry, my friend. Everything is fine," I said. "Please call in the first patient."

"Doctor, is it true you are leaving us?" the patient asked, before I could ask her what she came for.

"Who told you that I am leaving?" I asked.

"That is what everyone is saying out there," she replied.

"Don't you want me to go back to my people?" I asked.

"But we are your people," the patient said.

Almost all the patients that I saw that morning asked the same question: "Is it true you are leaving?" And almost all of them wanted me to remain in Kwale.

I battled with what decision to make over the following few days. I couldn't sleep. I knew I had to make a decision, but I found it hard.

That weekend, I decided to see my mother. I knew I could trust her to help me look at the pros and cons of my options. As she used to tell me whenever I couldn't make a decision, "Put them on a balancing scale and present them to God through prayer, and it will swing to where God directs it."

Mother hadn't expected to see me that weekend, as I had visited the previous weekend, though she was happy to have me. As always, she had so many people around her. I had planned to go back the following day, but I changed my plans, knowing that I might not get the chance to have private time with her that Friday night.

My mother made it easy for me.

"Pray and sleep over it. Whatever your heart tells you when you wake up, that's God's will," she advised.

"What if after praying and sleeping over it, you still cannot make up your mind?" I wondered.

"That means you're not ready to make the decision," my mother replied. "In that case, wait upon the Lord, and He will make the right decision come into your heart."

That night, I prayed before going to bed and asked God to give me the right decision in the morning. When I woke up, nothing had changed. My heart remained the same, divided, and my brain couldn't think clearly. I had to wait on the Lord, like my mother had advised. He would provide the perfect decision at His own precise time. So I tried not to think about it.

"Have you made a decision?" my mother asked, after dishing out my breakfast.

"No, Mummy," I replied.

"The Lord will reveal it in His time," she said.

I had thought of going to catch up with my friends most of the day, but I changed my mind. I would be passing through Ibadan and Akure to see my friends. I would also spend time with the chaps in Benin City. So I decided to spend the day resting – a lazy day. I had a heavy lunch, thanks to my mother. A large portion of pounded yam with okra soup and stock fish was just right for the afternoon. I couldn't finish my bottle of Schweppes bitter lemon before I dosed off, and then I had a dream. An oba (king) paid me a visit. I sat on my own on the front pavement of my house in Kwale. The king wore a glorious crown of lustrous diamonds and gold. He wore a large, immaculate, white Agbada. The tail of the Agbada trailed many metres behind him. His shoes were shining. The king was on his own. He had no bodyguards and no entourage. Yakubu and Mba were not in the house. As the king walked towards me with his majestic regalia, I wondered why a king would visit an ordinary person on his own. I lay flat on my stomach and greeted, "Kabiyesi!"

"It's not yet time to leave this place," the king said. "Kwale people need you."

"But my people need me, too," I said.

"Of course, they do," the king said. "But their time will come."

"I don't think Dr Odeda will let me stay," I protested. "He will do everything possible to make sure I leave Kwale."

"Leave that in my hands," the king said.

"I plan to undertake postgraduate surgical training. So I am sorry, I can't stay," I said.

"I know that, and you will do it. But not just yet. You will make a fortune in Kwale, but invest only a small amount of your fortune in Kwale. When the right time comes, you will go abroad for your studies," he said.

"How will I know when the time comes?" I asked.

"You will know when the time comes. It will be a quick decision. No one will be able to talk you out of it," he concluded.

"Can I get you a drink?" I asked.

"Oh, yes, I would love a glass of cold water," he replied.

As I turned around to get cold water from the fridge, I woke up. It felt like I had slept a whole day, yet I had only had a nap after a heavy Sunday lunch. At first, I brushed it aside, thinking it was either a manifestation of my heart turmoil or the consequence of overeating. But then I lay on my back, trying to remember the details of my dream. It looked and felt so real, and I didn't know what to make of it, so I told my mother about it. She advised me that it was a divine revelation. It was a clear instruction from God. She informed me that when I had sought her advice, she had wanted to urge me to stay behind in Kwale, but she decided to allow me to be convinced that I was making the right decision.

I left Lagos in the early hours of Monday morning. I planned to stop over at the Bendel State Health Management Board. I wanted to hand in my application to work as a medical officer in Kwale. There was no need for me to arrive early in Kwale that morning since we had no trip planned for the day. It was the day that the driver had planned to service the mobile vehicles. The nurse also needed the day off for stocktaking. I was to use the day to catch up on administrative matters, so I wasn't in a rush to leave the health board.

I sat down at the reception, waiting to hand in my letter of application. I introduced myself to the receptionist as a doctor and told her that I needed to go back to work that morning. The receptionist ignored me, saying, "I am busy right now."

Then a thought crept into my head. "Can I see the chairman please?" I requested from the other receptionist who looked more approachable.

"Have you got an appointment?" he asked.

"Yes," I replied, without a blink.

"Your name, please?" he asked.

I told him my name.

"I cannot find your name on the appointment list," he observed, after scanning through a bookmarked page of his diary.

"That's strange," I said. "I am sure the chairman said it was alright for me to come today. Will you please tell him that the youth corps doctor from Kwale has come back to see him?"

Just then the chairman came out of his office. He stopped briefly at the reception on his way out.

"Good morning, Chief." I stood up and walked towards him.

"Oh, our lovely doctor. Nice to see you," he said.

The chief took me back into his office. I knew he was in a hurry to go out, so I was straight and direct.

"No need for an application," he said.

I scratched my head in disappointment.

"Oh, I see," I said, thinking that perhaps Dr Odeda had blocked it.

"The Chairman of the Ndokwa Local Government, who is my good friend, has recommended you to be offered an appointment as a medical officer stationed in Kwale. I think you are a blessing to the Kwale people," he said.

After shaking my hand, he took me back to the reception and asked them to give me all the necessary forms to complete. That was it. My post-NYSC job was secured.

"God, you truly love me," I said, as I sat behind the wheel of my Nissan to drive back to Kwale.

On Friday of that week, I decided to stop over in the hospital to check the patients on the ward before going home. Yakubu was still at work. Mba had left. He had planned to spend the weekend at Warri. As Yakubu hadn't finished, I let the driver go and park the car. I would go home in Yakubu's car. I only had four patients on the ward. They were all ready for discharge.

As I came out of the ward, Dr Odeda beckoned me from outpatients. He seemed to be in a rush. He stood there, checking his watch every second.

"I hear you have gone through the back door to get the job here," he said.

"I don't understand you, sir," I said.

"What do you mean by you don't understand?" he asked. "Everyone is calling your name at the health office," he reported.

"Oh!" I narrowed my eyes.

"Well, we'll see," he said. "Good day."

He turned around, shaking his head as he walked towards his car. It was obvious that my appointment was a threat to his income from private practice. It was also a threat to his medical standard of care and an embarrassment to his authority. But that didn't surprise me. He had made no secret of his dislike for my presence in Kwale, but I didn't let that bother me. I had survived him for nearly a year. I could only get stronger, and I wouldn't take any further intimidation from him.

St Joseph's Clinic

At last, the NYSC came to an end. I had a handshake with Professor Ambrose Alli, the Bendel State Governor, and an award for the meritorious service to the people of Ndokwa Local Government. At this time, Yakubu and Mba returned to their states. As I saw them off, a huge cloud of nostalgia surrounded me. I felt lonely and wondered if I had made the right decision, but I trusted my mother's judgement. If she told me I had made the right decision, that meant I had. And the king in my dream was not a fiction; it was a revelation. And for the Kwale people to clamour for my stay was humbling. So I put away my NYSC hat and began my role as a medical officer in General Hospital Kwale.

My work schedule in the hospital remained the same, but I was no longer running the mobile service. Unlike my service times, I had scheduled ward rounds, outpatient and theatre sessions. Also, I became more accountable for my actions.

My NYSC year had prepared me well for life as a medical officer. I had attained competency in common surgical procedures, including appendicectomy, hernia repairs, laparotomy and a lot more. This was one of the reasons Dr Odeda didn't want me around. But that was the reason for my confidence. It was also why patients clamoured to see me.

One Friday afternoon, I was just about to leave the hospital when news of an accident hit. As was typical of many road traffic accidents, the patient, a sixteen-year-old girl, was brought to the hospital in a taxi. A car had knocked her down when she tried to cross the road, and she had suffered multiple rib fractures. She also broke her pelvis. She was said to be knocked out after the accident, but when she arrived, she could answer to her name. The accident had occurred over an hour before they could find a taxi to bring her to the hospital, and the girl was critically ill, but we had neither the facilities nor the surgical expertise to manage this complex trauma. We therefore advised them to take her to Eku Baptist Hospital.

Tragically, I received news the following day that the girl had died en route to Eku. This incident reignited my ambition to undergo further training, which would have put me in a position to save her. I also felt that I wasn't getting professional satisfaction, even though I was making money.

Five months into my appointment as medical officer, Dr Odeda sent for me.

"I am considering sending you to Ashaka. I am unsure if Dr Enebeli will agree to come to Kwale," he said. "I think you will be more useful there."

"Do you think the Kwale people will agree to that?" I asked.

"I don't need their permission to transfer you to Ashaka," he replied.

"But why do you want to transfer me?" I asked.

"Who is the boss here?" he asked.

"You, of course," I replied. "But it just sounds strange that you want to transfer me for no reason."

"Alright then, if you want to know," he said. "Working in Ashaka will reduce your private practice."

"So, it's all about private practice," I said.

"You could say that," he confessed.

For several weeks, Dr Odeda kept reminding me at every opportunity that he would transfer me, although I had decided to take the medical officer job because the Kwale people wanted me. They fought to make me stay in Kwale, and I therefore resolved that if Dr Odeda continued with his agenda of harassment, I would resign and go fully private. I didn't tell him that. But that was my plan.

That weekend, I.K. visited me. He informed me that Dr Odeda had planned to move me out of my residence. His plan was to move me into the nurses' quarters in the hospital. I.K. advised me that he would terminate the tenancy agreement with the health authority if I was willing to rent the house. He also told me that if I wanted, he would terminate the tenancy in the other adjacent bungalow. So I would have both buildings for my exclusive use. I agreed with I.K. He promised to terminate the health authority's tenancy with immediate effect.

That night, I reflected over all that had happened. I had no doubt that Dr Odeda didn't want me around. He had been open about it. He didn't like me. He wanted to frustrate me. He was a local champion. My presence in Kwale was a threat to his dominance. He would not relocate. To do that would be to hand victory to me without a fight. And he had the power and influence to win the battle. I was up all night. Then at three in the morning, I decided to get out of his way. I would resign from the government service and go into full-time private practice. I.K.'s buildings were large enough for the premises that I needed. I had already built a large patient population. I had won the patients' trust, respect and loyalty. And so, I wrote my letter of resignation.

I didn't have to think twice about the name for my hospital. I believed St Joseph's Clinic was the right name. It was as though a heavy weight had lifted off my chest. As I lay on my back, I had no doubt that I had experienced divine intervention in my affairs. I was certain that I had made the right decision.

Dr Odeda was hit below the belt. He had planned to move me into the two-bedroom nurses' quarters the following week. Dr Enebeli had refused to leave Ashaka. Even though Dr Odeda was senior to him, he knew, of course, that he dared not confront him. He was a Ndokwa indigene and people liked him. So the only option Dr Odeda had to frustrate me was to humiliate me by moving me into the hospital quarters.

"That won't be necessary," I said to him. "I have tendered my resignation."

His eyes sparkled. I saw a smile on his face for the first time in the eighteen months or so that I had been in Kwale.

"Congratulations!" he sighed. "I knew you would."

"So you really hate me this much?" I shook my head.

"I don't hate you. I don't hate people. I just don't like what you do," he said.

"It's about money, isn't it?" I shook my head.

"You could say that," he said.

I decided not to inform him that I was setting up my private practice. I left him to find out himself. He had assumed that my resignation meant that I would leave Kwale. That was what he had wanted. I wondered how he would respond to my decision to set up St Joseph's Clinic.

The news of my resignation spread through the hospital like wildfire. Staff streamed in and out of my consulting room. They promised to petition Dr Odeda like they had done before. They would mount pressure for him to be transferred from Kwale. But I didn't want to involve anyone. It was my decision to work in Kwale, and it was my decision to resign. What I did was my decision, and I couldn't hide things anymore, so I informed them that I was setting up my private hospital, the first one in Ndokwa Local Government area. Immediately, many of the staff offered to come and work in my hospital, but I advised them not to resign as I didn't know how things would go. I would be willing to offer them locum positions if I needed their help.

Later that day, I was walking to the car park when one of the messengers ran to catch up with me.

"Doctor!" he called between his panting, "Dr Odeda wants to see you in his office."

"What, again?" I asked.

The man scratched his nose. "I don't know," he replied.

"Your friends have informed me you are planning to set up a private clinic in Kwale," Dr Odeda snapped.

"Is that a question or a statement, sir?" I asked.

"Well, whether you consider it to be a question or a statement, I have got to warn you about the plan," he said.

"Have you got a problem with it?" I asked.

"Yes, a big problem," he replied. "You cannot set up a private clinic since you are less than five years qualified. You must be qualified for at least five years before you can set up one."

"Why are you making that your problem?" I asked.

"Because I am the senior doctor here. And if I see someone breaking the law, I must report him," he said.

"Sorry, Senior Doctor, sir, I don't need your permission to set up my practice," I said.

"Well, if you set it up, I guarantee you it will be closed down. And you could be imprisoned for setting up an illegal clinic," he threatened.

"Have you finished?" I asked, as I prepared to leave.

"So?" he raised a questioning ridge on his forehead.

"So," I said.

We both stared at each other like sworn enemies. I had to get out of his room. He had annoyed me so much. I couldn't stand his naked hatred. If I stayed any longer, I could say or do things I would regret. So without seeking his approval, I pulled the door and closed it behind me.

I knew he meant what he said. He could cause the authorities to prevent me from registering St Joseph's Clinic. True, I hadn't been qualified for five years, and I needed someone to advise me, someone that I could trust. There had to be a way around it. I needed to see Dr Odebatu. He had been helpful on several occasions, and I trusted that he would give me the right advice. So instead of going home, I headed for Abraka to see him. At that time of the day, I expected he had left the hospital, so I decided to go and see him at home.

"Rubbish!" he said. "That is not a big issue. Even nurses open private clinics, so you can, a qualified, fully registered doctor."

Dr Odebatu advised that I could get a doctor who was in full private practice to register my clinic, either as his own or as an annexe of his existing clinic. Once I was five years post-qualification, the doctor would then reregister it in my name. That sounded good. I was grateful to him.

The first person that came to my mind was Dr Abitoye, my mentor when I was in Akure. He had rescued me from the wrath of Dr Kosanu. I had maintained my communication with him after I left Akure, so I had no problem visiting him any time. As expected, Dr Abitoye eagerly agreed to cover me. He even offered to follow me to Kwale to see Dr Odeda, whom he knew very well. Dr Odeda was his junior in the medical school. I discouraged him from doing that. His agreement to help me register my clinic was all that I had needed. I could handle Dr Odeda and all the other issues myself.

Within two weeks, all my papers were filed with the Ministry of Health, and I was given a provisional registration certificate, pending the inspection of the clinic. After six weeks, I received a letter from Benin that following recommendations from Dr Abitoye and references from the Chairman of Ndokwa Local Government, there was no need for the proposed inspection. And within two weeks, I received the certificate of registration of my eight-bed hospital and maternity unit. As it happened, Dr Odeda was driving to Ashaka the day they put up the signboard of my clinic that read: *St Joseph's Clinic, Ashaka Road, Kwale.*

I was happy that I had made the decision to leave government service, and we were busy day and night. Patients attended from far and wide. Pat, my nurse at the mobile clinic, offered to work for me part time, and she was an asset as a dual-qualified nurse in midwifery and general nursing. Another retired nurse, Carole, joined me. Pat and Carole helped me to train two school-cert teenagers to work as auxiliary nurses.

Dr Odeda no longer had the chance to confront me after I left the hospital, but he didn't stop his habit of driving into Eke Primary School. He would park his car in front of the central block, lean back and watch, sometimes for hours, as patients came in and out of my clinic. But I never allowed that to bother me.

Warri Road Incident

After a busy week, I decided to take a break. I drove to Lagos to spend the weekend with my parents and travelled back to Kwale on Sunday night. I got to Benin at about two in the morning and decided to take Warri Road, as it was a better road to drive on at night than Abraka Road and less busy than usual. I was about twenty minutes into the road, driving at top speed, wanting to get home in time. As I beamed into the distance, I saw plantain stems sprawled across the road. At first, I thought there must have been an accident, and that was a warning for drivers to slow down. But it was an unusual sign for an accident. Normally, whenever an accident occurred, people would put palm leaves on the road. I also wondered if the police had mounted a checkpoint.

As I approached, I reduced my speed but wasn't going to stop unless it was a police checkpoint. About fifty metres to the roadblock, I looked into my driving mirror and saw four men coming out of the bush, swinging machetes in the air. I realised that the plantain stems were placed with the leaf part to one side. The men were running towards my car, as a white Peugeot 504 reversed into the road. I put my car into gear and started to race away. The men climbed into the Peugeot to pursue me, and it was a do-or-die race. I accelerated to the end of my speedometer as the bandits tried to outmanoeuvre me.

We were the only two vehicles on the road, driving as though we were Formula One racers, and as I tried frantically to get away, I kept praying to God to rescue me. If they caught up with me, they would harm me and take away my car. At the speed that I was driving, if I had a crash, it would be a miracle to survive. But I was determined not to stop, trusting that God would either make them give up the chase or He would send an angelic help to my rescue.

When we were about seven kilometres from Warri, the driver of the Peugeot, in desperation, nosed the rear of my car. Then one of them fired a gun into the air to scare me. But I maintained my composure and held the steering wheel with steady hands. I pressed the horn continuously to alert other road users nearby, but no one showed up. Their car was so close that a direct shot at me would, no doubt, hit me. But I kept on praying. I checked my driving mirror again. This time, the car was no longer in my view, and a van surfaced at the terrain. The flashing lights and sirens brought my heart back to my chest.

The van with armed mobile police stopped me.

"Doctor!" the senior officer exclaimed. "What are you doing on the road this time of the night?" Inspector Alao was the head of the mobile unit. He was an unmistakable Ijesha man with his tribal Ijesha marks conspicuous on his cheeks even in the night. As a Yoruba man, the inspector was frequently at the Ijesha man's restaurant, like most of the Yorubas in Kwale. And we addressed each other as 'my brother' or 'my sister'. The bandits must have noticed them before me, hence they turned and raced in the opposite direction. Inspector Alao informed me that there had been two incidents on that road that night. In both cases, the victims suffered fatal machete injuries. So armed policemen were parading the road to catch the culprits. He gave me an armed officer to escort me to Kwale.

The Decision to Leave Kwale

For many months, although Dr Odeda still came most Sunday evenings to spy on me, he hadn't confronted me. As a matter of fact, he tried to avoid me. One such situation was when we met at the Travellers Cafe. The hotel, situated along Aboh Road, was a popular social place for the elites in Kwale. I was there with friends from Lagos. The staff at the hotel knew me, and most of the customers recognised me.

Dr Odeda arrived with his friend and two women. Neither of the women was his wife. I was with the boys. We were drinking and laughing. I was at the bar, waiting to buy drinks for my friends. Dr Odeda stood behind me.

"You've had enough time in Kwale. Time to go back to your state," he whispered.

"My decision. Mine and mine only, not yours," I whispered back.

"We'll see," he smiled wryly and marched away with his glasses of beer.

I told my friends what this doctor had just said. I had told them about him before, but they hadn't seen him until that night. They couldn't understand why he hated me so much. And they couldn't believe that he could be so mean and tribalistic. They wanted to confront him. I pleaded with them to ignore him. Silence, it is said, is the best answer for a fool.

That night, I had a dream. I was working as a surgeon in a big hospital. The hospital was in a white man's country. Patients queued to see me, just as they did in St Joseph's Clinic. It was a beautiful city. Electricity was on all the time. The air was clean. After the operation, the people didn't want me to go back home. I was happy to live with them.

The following day, Saturday, about midday, a sixty-year-old woman came to see me with her family. She had a huge goitre with extension into her chest. They had come so I could do an operation to remove the goitre. This operation was far beyond my level of competency, and I wasn't going to dabble into such a major operation. The woman and her

220

family were highly disappointed. They had undertaken the two-hour trip from the far Delta on recommendation. When I advised that I was prepared to refer her to the teaching hospital, they declined. Her son opened a briefcase with a stack of naira notes and laid it in front of me.

"Take as much as you want," he urged me. "If that's not enough, we will fetch you more."

I refused to accept the money, and advised them that although I sympathised with the woman, the operation and care that she needed were beyond my level of expertise and hospital facilities. The patient had been told that if I couldn't do it, then no doctor could. They had a large sum of money, so they just couldn't understand why I should turn her down.

After a long talk, they finally accepted the referral. But from the look on their faces, I knew that they were still unconvinced that I couldn't do the operation. I never heard about her again, but I suspected that they never took her to the teaching hospital.

This case was a turning point for me. Of course, I was making so much money and my patients loved me, but I felt that I should be able to offer a higher standard of care. I didn't go into the profession simply to make money. Of course, I thanked God for providing me the opportunity to make a good living, but my primary aim was do my best to offer the best possible care.

I had seen the medical art practised in the most deplorable way. I myself had suffered the consequences of poor standards and inadequate knowledge, such as the case of the doctor who incised and drained my palmar space abscess without anaesthetic. I also still clearly remembered the bodged hernia operation in Akure and the young girl with chest trauma who could have been saved. So I realised early in my career that I should strive to acquire a more specialised skill. I wanted to make a difference.

I was still young and offering basic care for patients. That was the level that most doctors in the private sector offered. But someday, a young trained surgeon could come back from overseas, and I wouldn't be able to compete with such a doctor, who would be performing more complex procedures. And it wouldn't be long before patients noticed my limited surgical skills. I could be too old or perhaps married with children. At that time, I would find it difficult to go for specialist training.

I resolved to go abroad to undertake specialist training in surgery, but I had no clue how to go about it. I also faced the dilemma of closing down my lucrative clinic. I had only established my practice for two years, and I was doing well. What more did I need? That was the thought that came into my faculty all the time. Why leave certainty for uncertainty? What if my training didn't go well? Who would look after my clinic during the four or five years of postgraduate training? What if the people didn't like me anymore when I returned? What if someone had become more popular in my absence? These were the questions, and many more, that troubled my heart. In the end, I rationalised that I probably wasn't ready for the change. I believed that God would provide me with a clear decision at His appointed time. And like He had done so many times, He would provide an angel to lead me to the great heights in my vision. Until then, I decided to put the plans on hold and continue to do my best in St Joseph's Clinic.

Six weeks later, I visited my parents. I needed to clear my head. Going to see my parents always helped whenever I needed to chill out. Being in the midst of my friends helped to destress me, but spending time with my parents and my family always helped to declutter my head.

On my way to Lagos, I decided to pass through Akure to catch up with my friends. I bought a copy of *The Tribune* newspaper. I always enjoyed reading this newspaper. Whenever I came to the west, I always made sure that I grabbed a copy. I didn't find any particularly interesting article to read, so I threw it on the pile of rubbish on the back seat of my car.

When I got to Ore, I bought some roasted corn from the roadside sellers. I didn't trust them with clean wrapping papers, so I decided to tear off a page or two from my Tribune. On the back of one of the sheets there was a small advertisement:

Ondo State Government is offering sponsorships to doctors for specialist training overseas…

This couldn't have come at a better time. It was just what I needed. This was exciting news. But as I read further, I noted the conditions that the State Government had stipulated. The doctor must be an Ondo State indigene. He must be under the employment of the Ondo State

Government, and must have worked for at least three years in the state service. So for me to have a realistic chance of the award of state sponsorship, I had to be employed by the state. In essence, I would have to either close down my clinic or employ a doctor to run it for me.

I drove home with mixed feelings. My brain told me to seize the opportunity and re-join the Ondo State Health Service, but my heart reminded me of my commitment to the Kwale people. They would feel let down if I closed down my clinic and left them.

I could discuss most things with my parents. They would always give me valuable advice and guidance. But I chose not to discuss my plan to pack up my private practice with them. I feared that they would look at my immediate success rather than the bigger picture. As far as they were concerned, I was successful at my career, and they were proud of my achievement within the short time that I had been qualified. If I told them that I was planning to go abroad, they would be more than likely to discourage me. They would probably consider that I needed no more training.

I had a number of friends that I trusted. I could discuss most things with them. But on this occasion, I feared that they would be more interested in the social aspect of my life. By this I mean, they would be happy for me to come back to Ondo State, provided I took up an appointment in Akure. Then we could resume our partying and all that we did when we were newly qualified. In the end, like I always did whenever I needed to make a decision, I knelt down in the middle of the night and prayed to God to help me.

I left things on hold for the time being and carried on as normal. New patients continued to register with me. My practice got bigger. The people truly appreciated what I did for them. I tried on a number of occasions to hint to the patients indirectly that I would leave, and their responses weighed heavily on my heart, so I began to have second thoughts about my plan to go for further training.

I considered applying to the University of Benin Teaching Hospital for my residency. The professor of paediatrics, the consultant who had looked after the girl with Wilson's disease, had promised to help me get into the residency program in UBTH. Maybe this was the time to seek his help. If I could get a place on the program, I could hopefully still run my private clinic, albeit on a part-time basis. I could employ a doctor who would help to run the clinic either on a permanent basis or to hold it while I trained in Benin. So I planned to make time to go and see him by the end of the month.

One night, two weeks later, at two thirty in the morning, there was a knock on my door. At first, I ignored it. Normally any emergency that came in the night would first report to the night staff who would then contact me if it was something that needed my attention. So I ignored the first few knocks, but they continued. There were so many things about the knocks that gave me cause for concern. Firstly, it was the main door on which they knocked. Secondly, it was a bang rather than a knock. My staff normally knocked at my bedroom window. They were gentle knocks. They knew they didn't have to bang the door since I wasn't a deep sleeper.

I tiptoed to the sitting room and peeped through one of the windows. What I saw brought my heart to my mouth. I shivered like someone who had received an electric shock. There were three men. Two of them had guns in their hands. They wore masks. I watched them as they paced the corridor. The third man sat in the car behind the steering wheel with the engine running. One of the men urged them to leave as he didn't think that I was in the house. The third, that is the driver, came down to join them.

One of them suggested they broke into my door, but the oldest man cautioned him, reminding him that they hadn't come for burglary. They walked round my house, and after a few more knocks, they decided to call it a day with the plan to come back the following night.

I plastered myself to the wall as these assassins argued among themselves, praying that they didn't decide to go to the clinic to query the night staff, or for the staff not to come out at that time. They could pretend to have brought a patient and urged the staff to call me. Even if they didn't do that they could force him to reveal my whereabouts. In the end, they decided to leave. I didn't know who had sent them, but their mission was clear. It was to get rid of me. And they promised to come back the following night. As I watched them reversing their car, I heaved a sigh of relief and shook my head, wondering why human beings could be so heartless.

The attempted assassination was a turning point. It eased my decision. I had to leave Kwale. And I had to do so with immediate effect. I couldn't go back to sleep. The night was not yet over. Although they planned to return the following night, they could come back if the person who had hired them insisted. So I crept back into my bed and prayed that they stayed away. In the morning, I informed the staff on duty that I needed to travel to Lagos urgently. Fortunately, there was no one on admission. I instructed them to contact my friend and former classmate to look after things whilst I was away.

Chapter Eleven
BACK TO THE WEST

We can make our plans,
but the Lord determines our steps.
Proverbs 16:9 NLT

I never went back to Kwale. It wasn't the best way to leave a place that I loved, where the people adored me, but I had no choice. God had rescued me from a threat to my life. The criminals had received part payment and had resolved to carry out the errand in order to receive their full payment. I just couldn't stay.

I went straight to the Ondo State Health Management Board. The Chief Medical Officer embraced my intention to come back to the service, and I got my letter of appointment the same day. I had hoped that they would post me to Akure. Instead, they posted me to my local hospital, General Hospital, Okitipupa. It wasn't that I didn't like my people. Of course, I did. But like most young people in my place, I liked to work away from home. People had their own reasons for that. Some people thought that by working far from home the witches wouldn't find them. Others thought that they would have too many unwanted and unsolicited visits. As for me, it wasn't any of those reasons. I felt that I wouldn't have the respect that I had enjoyed. "A prophet is not respected in his place," I reasoned. I also felt that my people would give me too much trouble. They would bring all their troubles day and night. They would expect me to treat without charging, and I wouldn't have any rest. But I accepted my posting because my area was neglected. No one wanted to go and work there, and I felt that my people would be blessed by my presence. I needed to give back something for their investment in me. I owed it to them.

"I accept my appointment," I informed the CMO.

"To Okitipupa?" he narrowed his eyes.

"Yes, to Okitipupa," I confirmed.

The CMO was surprised at my level of enthusiasm to work at Okitipupa. He promised me that he would make sure they gave me good accommodation. He also advised me to let him know if I had any problem.

I thought it was best not to reveal my whereabouts to those in Kwale, fearing that they might look for me. I had no doubt in my mind that if my patients knew that I had relocated to Okitipupa, many of them wouldn't mind the distance. They would travel the one and a half to two hours journey, just so they could see me. But I kept away, even from my friends. With the help of Uncle Olola, I hired a van but didn't accompany him to pack my personal effects from Kwale. I warned him not to reveal my whereabouts to anyone. If anyone asked, he was to tell them that I had gone abroad.

Medical Officer, General Hospital Okitipupa

The last time I was at the General Hospital Okitipupa was when I had a hand infection from the fish fin injury nearly twenty years previously. The hospital hadn't changed much, reminding me of the pain that I had when the doctor incised and drained my abscess without anaesthetic. I had now learnt to do a better job than that doctor.

I joined a team of four other doctors, and it didn't take me long to settle down. I grew up and schooled locally, so I knew so many people. Those that I didn't know, or those that didn't know me, knew my family members. My uncle, Mr Olola, had become a local businessman after retirement as a police officer in Calabar. My former games prefect, Senior Ilesanmi (alias Loyola), was an engineer at the local palm oil mill. My friend Mike was a medical officer. My cousin, Shina, and my good friend, Prince Deji Adetu, were nurses. Deji worked as one of the theatre nurses. Shina worked at Ilutitun, a few miles from Okitipupa.

The Health Board provided me with a detached, six-bedroom bungalow. It had another self-contained apartment annex to its side, and my old friends and family helped my resettlement. Within weeks, I had built my private practice here, becoming even busier than I was in Kwale.

Contrary to my reservations, my people received me with a great degree of enthusiasm and showed me a great deal of respect and value.

Even when I offered to give free treatment, they would insist on paying something. I was encouraged when one of my cousins came for a hernia repair. I offered to do the operation free of charge, but my uncle insisted on paying.

"You must not be wretched when other doctors who are from other places are making money," he said.

Life couldn't be any better. I was happy to serve my people, and two of my siblings came to live with me. I was glad that I could sponsor their upkeep, including their education. I went to Shabomi at least three times a week. My parents often came to spend weekends with me. News about me spread like wildfire, with friends and family acting as unofficial PRs. I was inundated with patients coming from far and wide.

I then bought many acres of land, on which I planned to build a hospital. I also bought another piece of land and started putting up a two-storey building.

One Saturday morning, I had just had my lunch when a green Peugeot 505 pulled up in front of my house. As the passengers came down one by one, I knew that they had brought a patient to see me. I knew, of course, that there was no chance for my afternoon nap. Working in the hospital and running my own busy private practice meant that I hardly had any time for recreation. But I couldn't turn any patient away. If they needed my help, it was my commitment to serve them, irrespective of whether they could afford it or not. It didn't matter to me whether it was convenient or not. It was the sacrifice I had to make as a doctor, and the price for having a busy practice. So I received the visitors into my consulting room with a welcoming smile.

"Doctor, we need your help," they said.

"What can I help you with?" I asked.

"Our mother is seriously sick," they reported. "We wanted to check that you were at home and would be able to treat her before bringing her out."

I had expected that they must have wanted me to repair a hernia or remove a lump since none of them looked ill. But that wasn't the reason they had come to see me. They were three men and a woman. The oldest man introduced himself as a businessman man based in Sapele. The others were his two younger brothers and sister. They informed me that their mother was under the care of a herbalist, where she was being looked after as she had been struck by *Ayelela*, the goddess of truth. She had been under the spell of Ayelela after the allegation that she was a witch. Many people in my area worshipped Ayelela. They trusted the goddess to help them settle their grievances and avenge the evils done by people.

"So, Ayelela has struck your mother and she is at the shrine," I said. "How can I cure Ayelela?" I squeezed my eye.

"All the people believe that there is no disease that you cannot cure. They have advised us that you will be able to heal her," the eldest brother said.

"Doctor, money is not a problem," the sister said. "Please, help us."

"Yes, we will pay any amount," the eldest son said.

"Okay, go and bring your mother," I directed them.

I hadn't expected them to come back, but they did. Normally, when a condemned person had been under the care of Ayelela priest, the person would remain there until she died. And when she died, her family wouldn't be allowed to touch her body, which would be cast into the wilderness. So it surprised me that they could take the discharge of their mother from the shrine.

They arrived about two hours later with their mother. The sixty-year old, struggling with her breath, arrived supported by her children. She was full of fluids, looking thrice her size. The woman clearly had congestive cardiac failure, and I admitted her for in-patient care. Within a week, she was back to normal.

The news about the cure of this woman's cardiac failure flew the community. They had never seen a doctor who could cure Ayelela. Consequently, patients trooped to my clinic from the riverine area, from where the woman had come. These were patients who, hitherto, would have sought help from the herbalists and spiritualists rather than a medical doctor.

One such case was that of a teenager with testicular torsion. The sixteen-year-old boy was getting ready for his West African School Certificate Examination. A severe pain in one of his testicles woke him up. As he was the only son, and the younger wife's only child, the boy's father and family members alleged that the first wife, who was childless, had caused the boy's pain. The woman swore to Ayelela that she knew nothing about it. From the history, I suspected that the boy had a testicular torsion, and after examining him, I advised his parents that he needed an emergency operation. The boy's testicle was still viable and I fixed it. He made an uneventful recovery early enough to sit his examination.

On another occasion, a man brought his father to see me. He had a lump on his back that had been present for over ten years. They had seen a spiritualist, who had advised them that it had been put there by the man's estranged wife. They had offered goats, money and other things to the herbalist, but to no avail. So they decided to come to me. The man had a lipoma on his back. I removed the lipoma the following week.

I also treated a man in his fifties at one of my evening clinics. He was my last patient for the day. The reason for coming late at night was clear after examining him. He had a hydrocoele. Many people knew him as 'the man with swollen scrotum'. A few years previously, he allegedly committed adultery with another man's wife. The woman's husband sent a juju known as *Kukubaku* to him. Despite his confession and payment of fines, his scrotum remained swollen. I successfully operated on his hydrocoele and restored his happiness and confidence.

These are a few of the interesting cases that I had. But some cases were beyond my level of competence. Such was the case of a woman who believed that she had been pregnant for five years. The spiritualist had told her that her husband's second wife had tied up her womb, preventing her from delivering her twin pregnancy. When I examined her, I discovered that she had a fibroid uterus, the size of a twenty-week pregnant uterus. I referred her to the specialist hospital, where she underwent a hysterectomy.

A fisherman's son consulted me with a swollen hand. As I listened to his story, it brought back memories. Two decades previously, I, myself, sat in front of Dr George with a pulp space abscess of my hand. The stories were similar. A fish's fin penetrated his hand. The hand swelled up. They took him to the herbalist, and the hand became infected. But in his case, I incised and drained his abscess under general anaesthesia, and he didn't have to suffer like I did.

My parents were very proud to hear everyone talk about their son, and I felt incredibly privileged to help my people. I was grateful to God that He made that possible, and I resolved to involve myself in the community in other ways. I became the chairman of the board of governors of one of the secondary schools, and member of many others. I became an important member of the community, one that high chiefs and royals, teachers, bankers, police officers, lawyers and magistrates, businessmen and women, politicians and church leaders wanted to make their friend.

Working in Okitipupa also had its challenges. As in Kwale, my people delayed coming to see a doctor. They believed so much in superstition, spiritualism and witchcraft. So if the doctor offered to refer them to a bigger or specialist hospital, they would prefer to go to a herbalist or spiritualist with the belief that someone had hands in their problem. It was beyond what the hospital could deal with, so it needed spiritual intervention. Such was the case when one of the wives of our theatre nurse's father came with obstructed labour. We advised for her to have a caesarean section. But whilst we were preparing to do this, she discharged herself and went to a spiritualist who had advised her that her labour had been made difficult by her husband's other wife. According to the spiritualist, she would need to undergo spiritual cleansing to make her assailant release her grip on her womb. Here was a short woman with a small pelvis and a large baby. Nothing other than a timely caesarean section would save her and her baby's lives. But she ignored our professional advice, preferring to go to the spiritualist, where she died.

Unlike in Kwale, the doctors at Okitipupa were more co-operative. I teamed up with my friend, Mike, himself also an Ibadan graduate. He was a brave surgeon with a wide range of surgical experience. We supported and learnt from each other. Teaming up with Mike was something that I instigated, and there was a story behind it. There was a dangerous rumour circulating among the hospital staff and the wider community.

One day, one of my cousins attended the hospital. He was booked to see Dr Mike. He had been diagnosed with an inguinal hernia. He booked him to have the hernia repaired by himself. That evening, my cousin came to see me at home with my uncle.

"Whoever Dr Mike operated on would die," they informed me, with a great deal of concern. That was the rumour circulating, so my cousin had a good reason to have concerns.

I had seen Mike operate. I had no doubt that he was a fantastic surgeon. And since I joined the team, I wasn't aware of anyone he had operated on that had died. So I found the rumour, at best, to be baseless, and at worst, to be unkind. But I couldn't persuade my cousin to remain with Dr Mike. They wanted me to move him to my operation list. Despite my reassurance that he was a good surgeon, he couldn't be persuaded.

In the end, I suggested that I would assist Dr Mike in the operation to make sure that he did it properly. They accepted my suggestion. After that, I suggested to Mike that we worked together. The agreement was that we would assist each other at operations, and also look after each other's patients on the ward. I didn't tell him the reason for joining him. I didn't know how to divulge the information about the rumour that was all over the place without hurting his feelings. So I left things as they were, hoping that he would hear about the rumour himself. Subsequently, Mike and I did many operations together with successful outcomes.

As a result of the deprivation in Okitipupa and its environs, there were many underground quack medical practitioners. These included nurses, registered and unregistered, patent medicine dealers and herbalists. They were all involved in illicit abortions. Even boat drivers and taxi drivers took part in this supposedly lucrative but criminal practice. Consequently, we had many cases of incomplete abortions, septic abortions and even perforated uterus. The latter cases were so common that we dubbed them 'spoke injuries'.

Like many general hospitals, we had limited facilities. Though we had a large laboratory and a full-time laboratory technician, there were no reagents for something as basic as full blood count or urea and electrolytes. There was a blood bank, but no chemicals with which to group and cross match the blood. Anyone who needed blood would either go and buy it from the town or be referred to Ondo State Specialist Hospital in Akure. Such was the case of a chief's wife with ruptured ectopic pregnancy. The twenty-eight-year-old mother of two had collapsed in the market. Although her ectopic pregnancy had ruptured, she was still clinically stable, but not in the right state to undergo the one-and-a-half-hour drive in a taxi to Akure. There was no ambulance. Her best chance of survival was early intervention.

When Mike and I opened her up, we confirmed a ruptured ectopic pregnancy and carried out a salpingectomy. The whole procedure took us less than twenty minutes, but the woman needed an urgent blood transfusion, so her husband left us to start the operation while he went to buy blood. We stood by her, trying to support her as best as we could. Four hours later, the husband returned with four bags of blood. But his wife breathed her last as his car pulled into the park.

I was furious after this event. It was a preventable death. I wondered just how many people had suffered the same fate as this woman. The reagents that were needed to type and cross match blood were cheap. Even when I was running my hospital in Kwale, I had a large supply. I couldn't believe that these facilities couldn't be made available in the general hospital.

I called a meeting of the elders and chiefs to see how we could prevent things like that happening again. We all agreed, even if the government couldn't provide them, they were affordable, and we should be able to buy them ourselves. But the enthusiasm died even before I left. I heard a chief telling other chiefs that there was no point spending their money to put things in the government hospital. As he said, "We would only succeed in enriching the doctors by so doing." That was it. That was the end of the agreement. Nothing would change.

Chapter Twelve
PREPARATION TO GO ABROAD

Behold, I am the Lord, the God of all flesh;
is anything too difficult for me?
Jeremiah 32:27

Despite my lucrative practice and the good life that I was enjoying, I still felt unfulfilled, and so I rekindled my ambition to travel abroad. Contrary to what I had read in *The Tribune*, Ondo State was only sponsoring selected people. The criteria were not clear. It seemed like it was on a who-you-know basis. So I decided I would do it myself. Money was no longer an issue. I had enough money in my savings to sustain me abroad. My only problem was that I had no clue how to go about it.

I decided to write to the foreign embassies in Lagos, and I got positive responses from a few of them. My first choice was Canada. I also liked the UK and Ireland, but it was not clear how to go about my training. Although I had loved the idea of going to the US for my undergraduate education, it no longer appealed to me. Also, I wanted to go to Australia and New Zealand. But like the British, their programmes were unclear to me.

The Canadian system was much appealing: just one exam, the Visa Qualifying Exam (VQE.) Once you passed, you would be offered a visa and admitted into a postgraduate training programme.

I put all my efforts into preparation for the Canadian exam. I then sat the two-paper examination at the nearest centre to Lagos. That was Abidjan, the capital of Ivory Coast.

The results came a few weeks later, and I passed. I had hoped that I would automatically be put into a training programme, as I had been advised by the embassy. Instead, I had a letter advising me that the waiting list for surgical training was five years. That was unacceptable to me. I was given the option of going into a different specialty, but all I wanted was surgery, so I began to explore opportunities in other countries. I wrote to my uncle who was living in London to find information about surgical training in the UK. Uncle Festus was not a doctor, but being a friendly character, I hoped that he would be likely to have doctor friends.

I got a reply from my uncle within two weeks. As I read his letter, a smile of relief and hope crept into my face.

After passing the PLAB, you will be registered with the GMC, and can then work and earn whilst you are doing your training, he wrote.

This was the breakthrough I had been looking for. I had never heard about PLAB before. The Professional and Linguistic Assessments Board test, or the PLAB test, helps to ensure doctors who qualified abroad have the right knowledge and skills to practise medicine in the UK. He also obtained the forms and information about the surgical fellowship course organised by the Edinburgh Postgraduate Board for Medicine and the Royal College of Surgeons of Edinburgh. That was all the information I needed. I applied to Edinburgh and received their reply within a month, offering me a place on their course.

I knew that my friend, Mike, had also been trying to find a training opportunity abroad. He had told me in previous discussions that he was looking to going to Canada. His brother lived there, and he had visited him before. His plan was to stay with him until he found a place on the Canadian training programme. I couldn't keep the information I had just received from him. Mike embraced my breakthrough information and applied to Edinburgh. He too was given a place. With both of us now going to the same place, we began to make our preparations together.

I kept the information about going to the UK to myself. Of course, it was good news. But I didn't want to count my chickens before they were hatched. I wouldn't tell anyone until all my paperwork was through.

The letter of admission provided the information that I needed to obtain the visa. However, the Federal Government at that time had placed an embargo on going abroad for postgraduate medical training. Anyone planning to go abroad for specialist training had to obtain approval from the Federal Ministry of Education that the proposed course was not available locally in Nigeria. This was a big obstacle for me. Of course, I didn't need a visa to travel to the UK for a visit, but I needed to pay for my course. I also needed money for my sustenance. I needed to process my foreign exchange. Everything had to pass through the Central Bank of Nigeria, and the Central Bank would only approve foreign exchange for educational purposes if the applicant had a letter of approval from the Federal Ministry of Education. The latter would make its recommendation only if I could provide a letter from a Nigerian University that the proposed course was not available in the country.

This was a big blow to my plan. Of course, postgraduate surgical training was available in Nigeria under the Nigerian College of Surgeons and the West African College of Surgeons. The Edinburgh course would be starting soon. I had to confirm my acceptance of the offer. I also had to get the approval from the Federal Ministry of Education. I felt like I had reached the end of the road. I was on my knees most nights. I prayed like I had never done before. I prayed to God for a breakthrough. He had brought me this far. I trusted He wouldn't let me down.

Up until then, I hadn't paid my deposit, and the deadline was close. As I was having my shower the following morning, a thought came into my mind. There were expatriates working at Igbokoda fisheries and the glass factory. I believed they would have accounts in their countries. I wondered if one of the engineers would be able to send a cheque in pounds sterling if I paid the equivalent in naira to his Nigerian account. I wasn't close to any of the engineers, but I had no problems going into the factory. Most of the factory workers knew me.

On that day, I drove to the factory after my morning clinic. Thankfully, the gateman recognised me and let me in without asking any questions. I had been to the factory before and knew the names of two of the engineers. I had met them before. One came to see one of my colleagues in the hospital, and I met the other when he stood at the roadside chatting to Mr Ilesanmi. I remembered the name of the second one and hoped he would remember me, since Mr Ilesanmi had introduced me to him as his brother. Even if he didn't remember me, I would mention Mr Ilesanmi to him.

"I would like to see Mr Darling, please," I said to the receptionist.

"Is he expecting you, sir?" the young receptionist asked.

"No, but tell him it's the doctor," I said.

"Okay, sir," the girl said, as she rose from her chair to inform Mr James Darling of my presence.

She returned to inform me that Mr Darling was happy to see me.

"Good day, Doctor. How nice to see you." He beamed a warm smile and directed me to one of the seats.

"Good day, Mr Darling." I shook his hand and took my seat.

Without wasting time, I told him exactly why I had come to see him. I needed him to help me send a cheque in British pounds sterling for my deposit. I would give him the naira equivalent.

"Is that all?" he asked.

"Yes," I confirmed.

"That is not a problem. Let me have the details. I will get my wife to send the cheque," he reassured me.

It was as though James Darling had just taken off a tonne of weight from my heart. What had kept me up several nights was no longer an issue. That sorted, all I needed was to obtain the letter of recommendation from the Federal Ministry of Education and Central Bank approval for foreign exchange. I didn't have to have the government approval, since I was going to be self-sponsored. Neither must I have Central Bank approval since I had the option of transferring money through the black market, like my friends had suggested. And I didn't have to have a visa to travel to the UK. Nigerians needed no visa to enter the UK. These sounded like easy options, but I wanted to do things properly, so I resolved to pursue the official route. I trusted that God would provide all the help that I needed.

After reading the information provided by the Edinburgh Surgical College, I spotted a course that I thought wasn't on the programme of the Nigerian Medical College. There was no provision for the fellowship in accident surgery. But I needed an official confirmation in writing. So I decided to write to all the six Nigerian universities. All I needed was a letter from one of them, stating that the proposed course was not available.

Within two weeks, I got the replies from three of the universities. Both Ibadan and Lagos referred me to the prospectus of the Nigerian and West African Medical Colleges. Nsuka sent an acknowledgement of my inquiry, but that wasn't what I wanted. That wouldn't take me anywhere. The breakthrough came a week later. The letter that I wanted arrived from Ahmadu Bellow University.

Thank you for your inquiry. We do not offer a course for the fellowship in Accident and Emergency Surgery… the letter stated. It went further to state, *Such fellowship may be available abroad.*

That was it, written exactly how I had wanted it. But I still needed a letter from the Federal Ministry of Education. And I knew nobody there. I spoke with the few people that I knew, but no one knew any big person at the ministry. Then Uncle Olola referred me to one of his former classmates, who worked as a senior officer at the ministry. When I visited him, I regretted the appointment. Two of his undergraduate daughters were with him in his office on that day. I informed him that I had been accepted onto the Edinburgh postgraduate training in Surgery and needed a letter of support from the Federal Ministry of Education.

"Why are you running away from the country?" he asked.

"I am not running away, sir," I replied. "I am only going for the fellowship. I will come back on completion."

"The government has said that no one should be allowed to go abroad for any course, except for courses that are not available in the country," he said.

"I am aware of the rule, sir," I said. "My proposed course is not available in the country."

"Are you telling me that medical course is not available in Nigeria?" His eyes widened. Then he turned to one of his daughters. "Don't they do medicine in your university?" And he asked the other girl the same question.

"I am already a qualified doctor," I made him aware, in case he didn't know. "I have even done my National Service. I now work as a medical officer in Okitipupa," I said.

"Go and finish your course. Don't run away," he said. "Or do you think it is easier abroad?"

I made up my mind that this was a waste of time. This man was either ignorant, which would be surprising, or pretending to be ignorant so as not to help me. I wouldn't have been offended if he had been honest and told me that he was unwilling, or had no power to render the help that I had requested. Instead, he turned me into an object of ridicule before his teenage daughters.

"Thank you very much for your time," I said as I rose to take my leave. "I don't think you can help me."

I left Mr Oluwole's office and didn't know what to think. My mind was completely blank. It was as if I was in the middle of the sea. The engine of my boat had packed up. The waves rocked my boat here and there, as it drifted to no particular destination. I walked up and down the multi-storey building, with no purpose in my mind and no destination in my vision. The time was around two in the afternoon. Soon the offices would close. I needed to talk to someone, but who would I talk to? I got in the lift to join five other people.

"What floor?" the woman closest to the buttons asked.

"Eight, please," I replied. I didn't know why I said eight. I knew nobody on that floor. As a matter of fact, I knew nobody on any floor. That was what came to my mouth.

I got out of the lift on the eighth floor like I had done all day, going from floor to floor. I was about to go back into the lift to avoid the embarrassment of a security officer asking me where I was going. Then I saw a woman, probably in her early forties, marching in front of a group of fifteen people or so, as they trooped behind her, holding envelopes and pleading. I wondered who this woman was. She must have been an important person in the ministry. I waited until they had all followed her into her office. Then I strolled to the front of her door. Mrs Rita Obi, Senior Executive Officer, Scholarships and Overseas Grants. This must have been the person who could give the letter of approval that I desperately needed. But I hadn't made an appointment. There were already fifteen people waiting to see her. I had no chance, I thought. I sat on the bench, waiting for a window of opportunity.

As I sat there, I watched people coming out, one by one, from Mrs Obi's office. Some of them were smiling and some were indifferent. But most of them cried as they left her office. I wanted to ask them if that was Mrs Obi, the officer in charge of overseas education. But I decided not to. I didn't want to have any bias. I would talk to her myself.

I said a short prayer. It was simple and direct. "Oh God, make her one of your angels, so I may soar on her wings."

Just then, Mrs Obi's door opened. I thought that the person who emerged was one of the hopefuls who had followed her into the office.

"Are you waiting to see madam?" the messenger asked, with a deep

Eastern Ibo accent.

"Yes, I have been waiting since," I replied, praying that he didn't ask me my name. If I had booked to see her, my name should be on the appointment diary, and the messenger would simply turn me away as my name was not there. But he didn't do that.

"Her office is the last on the left," he said. "There's no one with her right now. Just knock and enter."

Mrs Obi was on the phone when I entered. She nodded me into an empty chair in front of her massive desk. My mind pounded. I needed to play this game well. If I got it wrong, that would be it. She didn't seem to mind me listening to her conversation, and she kept waving to me and apologising repeatedly.

"Hello, sorry for keeping you waiting," she said, after hanging up.

"Don't mention it, Ma," I said.

I introduced myself as a medical doctor and added, "I have gained admission into Edinburgh University to undergo specialist training in surgery."

"I would love to help you. You look like a decent gentleman," she said. "Trouble is, the Federal Government has placed an embargo on overseas scholarships and grants, except for courses that are not available in the country."

"The course I am going for is not available in the country," I said. "But I am sponsoring myself. All I need is a letter of support from your kind self."

I showed her the letter that I got from ABU.

"You have done your homework," she remarked, after reading the letter. "You are the kind of person that I like to help, but it's too late to do anything today. Come back tomorrow and I'll do the letter."

I didn't know whether to kiss her, hug or squeeze her. I simply held her hand, as I fought back the tears of joy.

"Thank you, Mrs Obi. Thank you very much, Ma. May God bless you," I said, from the deepest part of my heart.

It was the longest night I had had. I lay in my bed, checking the time repeatedly. I couldn't wait for the morning to come. This woman that I didn't even know blew my mind. People had to book appointments for several weeks before they could see this powerful officer. There I went, without booking and without any go-between. Yet she treated me with a great deal of compassion and respect.

"God, you certainly are in control," I said to myself. "And I sincerely thank you for all you have done."

I arrived at the ministry of education the following morning, just as work began at seven-thirty. Mrs Obi hadn't arrived. I sat on the bench in front of her office and asked the messenger, but he had no idea where Mrs Obi was or why she hadn't arrived. He told me that she normally came early to work. "Maybe she was held up in the traffic," he suggested.

The time had gone past twelve noon and still no one knew her whereabouts. My body was fighting anxiety and disappointment. I had trusted her. I never thought she could disappointment me. She seemed like a genuinely nice person. What would she gain by promising what she couldn't do? Nothing at all, I rationalised. There must be something important that had delayed her. So I decided to sit tight and wait for her. I would only give up if she hadn't arrived when they were locking up for the day.

I hadn't had a meal or drink all day, but I wasn't prepared to go and look for food. I had to catch her when she arrived.

The messenger came out of the office a number of times. He seemed to be in a rush whenever he passed by on an errand. At first, he ignored my presence. He reassured me once or twice that Mrs Obi would still come, but as the day drew closer to an end, he no longer talked about Mrs Obi. I wondered if he had known that she was not coming to work, but why would he try to avoid me? Why would nobody talk to me?

At exactly three o'clock, Mrs Obi emerged from the lift, looking tired, with only a small amount of make-up on. I stood up to greet her, with my heart racing. I had thought that she would ignore me, but she didn't. Instead, she walked straight to me.

"I am sorry, Doctor," she said, and urged me to follow her into her office.

Mrs Obi informed me that a car had knocked down her daughter that morning on her way to school. She took her to Igbobi Orthopaedic Hospital. The doctors were nice to her, and they were kind to her daughter. As she watched the doctors tend to her daughter, she remembered that she had kept a doctor waiting for her at her office. She had to try, by all means, to get to the office that day. And she was committed more than ever to helping me.

"Oh, I am sorry about your daughter," I said. "I wish her a full recovery."

She gave money to the messenger and sent him to buy pies and a chilled bottle of Coca Cola for me. I wondered how she knew that I hadn't eaten all day. I guessed they must have told her that I had waited all day in the front of her office. Nevertheless, there was no doubt in my mind that Mrs Obi was genuine and kind.

Most of the staff had left, so Mrs Obi typed the letter herself. After signing it, she handed it to me and wished me good luck in the UK. And so, I had climbed the hurdle at the Federal Ministry of Education. Mrs Obi was God-sent.

Back in my car, I prayed from the bottom of my heart for God to bless her. She had provided help where I never expected. And I prayed that all the doctors that had helped her daughter would continue to help her.

The Bank's Approval

All the things pertaining to foreign exchange had to go through the Central Bank of Nigeria. That was the unchangeable rule. And I had known that right from the start. But an individual couldn't go directly to the Central Bank. The application had to go through the Commercial Bank. I learnt from previous inquiry that it would take a minimum of four weeks to process foreign exchange. The course would be starting in under a week. That posed a great challenge. How could I get all the paperwork done within the time constraint? I wondered. It seemed impossible, but I wouldn't give up. I would never give up. God had allowed me to get that far. He had brought the likes of Mrs Obi into my path. I trusted He would send His angelic men and women to provide the help that I needed.

I got back to Okitipupa around eleven at night. Throughout my trip from Lagos, there was a thought that kept coming into my mind. The husband of the woman that I did caesarean section on at Akure was a bank manager. I wondered if he would be able to help. But that was four years previously. I wasn't sure if he would still remember me. In any case, I had lost his business card. There was no way I could find him. So I tried to brush that option aside, as I thought that wouldn't work. I recalled that the woman's mother-in-law told me she had a restaurant on Adesida Road, not far from the Cooperative Bank. But that was a long street, and there were many restaurants in the street. I decided to go to Akure the following day.

I arrived at Akure just before lunch. I needed to see Eben Adetoro, one of my friends. He was an accountant at the Cooperative Bank. A cool-headed gentleman, Eben was reliable. He grew up and worked in Akure. I believed he would be able to make contacts that would lead to tracking down the woman's restaurant. I had no doubt she would recognise me.

Eben had left for lunch when I arrived at the Cooperative Bank, so I waited in my car to catch him on his way back before he went into the bank. A tap on my windscreen startled me. I hadn't expected Eben to be back that soon. He told me that he had been out to do something at the post office. He still had twenty minutes left on his break.

Eben took me to a restaurant three streets from the bank. As we entered, he recognised almost everyone there. I concluded that it wasn't only a popular restaurant but the favourite for the bank's staff. When I told Eben why I visited, he advised me that since I had account with his bank, it wasn't a problem, having the application submitted that day, but it would also need to go to Ibadan, from where it would be sent to their headquarters in Lagos. They would then send it to the Central Bank for the final approval. He informed me that the son of the lady who owned the restaurant was the regional currency manager. He was the manager in charge of foreign exchange. And he was the person who would approve my application. After our meal, one of the staff directed us to a detached bungalow further up the street. The gateman opened the gate to let us in after Eben introduced us as 'doctor and bank manager'.

"Doctor," she shouted with excitement, "how nice to see you."

"Good afternoon, Ma," I greeted. "It's a pleasure to meet you."

I thought I had seen the woman before, but I couldn't remember where. As a doctor, it was not unusual to meet patients and their relatives wherever I went. So I presumed she must be one of them.

"Thank God they have brought you back to Akure," she said. "They always transfer the good ones."

I didn't realise that she was the mother-in-law of the woman that I had performed the caesarean section on until she reminded me.

"See the photograph of your son," she said, pointing at a toddler playing with a toy. And when I took another look at the woman, the picture of that woman who knelt down in tears on that Saturday was so vivid.

"I am glad that your grandson is growing well," I said. "How is his mother?" I asked.

The woman informed me that the boy's mother had since had a baby girl. She was expecting them that weekend.

Meanwhile, Eben watched us, wondering how the woman knew so much about me. He had brought me to see her so she could link me with her son to help me with my papers. But the woman and I knew each other. He wondered why I hadn't realised that the woman's son was the very man whose help I needed most.

The woman saved me from explaining to Eben, which might sound like singing one's own praises, something that I didn't like. She gave him the full account of the event on that day. I reminded Eben of that Saturday four years previously, when I arrived late at my cousin's girlfriend's birthday party, where I was expected to be the DJ. Eben recalled that I had had to do an emergency operation, but I hadn't given out the details.

Eben went on to tell her that I had got an admission to go abroad for further studies. He wondered if the woman would be kind enough to talk to her son to help with the necessary papers.

"Tola will do anything for you, Doctor," the woman reassured me. "They are coming on Saturday. I will tell him about you."

"Thank you, Mama," I said. And I really meant it.

The woman gave me Mr Tola Babalola's address. She reassured me that she would tell him to expect me on Monday.

I went back to the bank with Eben. He was already twenty minutes late from his lunch, and customers had queued to see him. I offered to wait until he had seen them or come back the following day, but he insisted that I completed the initial application forms, as Mr Babalola would need them completed at my branch before his approval. With his help, I completed them, and he promised that he would send them by courier to arrive at Ibadan early enough for my meeting with Mr Babalola.

I arrived at the Cooperative Bank, Ibadan, around nine o'clock in the morning. Mr Babalola had left a message with the receptionist. So when I introduced myself to her, she ushered me to his office.

"How nice to see you, Doctor!" Mr Babalola greeted me with a warm handshake.

"It's nice to see you, too," I returned his greeting. "How's the family?"

"Segun is a big boy, now," he said, holding a four-inch by six-inch, framed photograph. "He now has a sister, too."

"They are beautiful," I remarked.

Mr Babalola thanked me again for saving his wife and their son's lives. He told me that he had tried several times to see me. His mother informed him that I had been transferred from Akure, and she didn't know my whereabouts. I explained to him that I left Akure for my NYSC.

My documents from Akure arrived in Ibadan that morning. As a matter of fact, Mr Babalola had processed everything. All that remained was my signature. He assured me that the files would be batched for Lagos that afternoon.

The Final Laps

I was now two days into the course, and I still had to have the Central Bank Approval of my foreign exchange before applying for the visa. I couldn't book my flight since I couldn't predict how long it would take or even the day that I would complete everything. One of the requirements for that approval was that I must have two guarantors. Both guarantors must each either be on level sixteen government-salary scale or have income equivalent to at least that level. These requirements effectively made it impossible for someone like me to obtain foreign exchange for overseas education. No member of my wider family that I knew was on level sixteen. I would be able to get one guarantor among my senior medical colleagues, but the second guarantor would certainly prove hard to find.

Dr Abitoye had been my mentor when I was a house officer. I had kept in touch with him throughout. His intervention in helping me to register my private clinic in Kwale saved me from the snare of Dr Odeda. He, himself, had a big private hospital, and I believed he would be a suitable guarantor if he was agreeable. He was about to travel when I arrived. As a matter of fact, the gateman was unbolting the gate. When the doctor saw me, he ordered the driver to park. He was apparently going away for two weeks. After greeting him, I apologised for coming at that time. He knew, of course, that I was planning to go abroad. In fact, he had provided me with a non-confidential reference. So he thought I had come to bid him goodbye. He didn't seem to be in a rush. Still, I thought I should tell him straightaway the reason for my visit.

"Is that all?" he asked with a smile.

"Yes, sir," I replied.

"That's not a problem," he reassured me, and beckoned me to follow him back into the house.

Dr Abitoye completed and signed my form as the first guarantor. He also gave me a copy of his current certificate of tax clearance.

I left Dr Abitoye and drove straight back to Okitipupa. The only person that readily came to mind was Uncle Olola. Though I was unsure of the extent of his wealth, I believed that the income from his business would be sufficient for him to be suitable as my second guarantor. I assured uncle that being my guarantor would cost him nothing. He knew, of course, that I had enough money to sponsor myself. I even showed him my latest bank statement just so he might be convinced that I was self-sponsoring and he wouldn't incur any liability whatsoever.

"No problems," he said, "but come tomorrow, as I can't do anything right now."

I visited uncle early in the morning the following day. His wife informed me that he had gone for a meeting. He would be back later that morning. I asked if he had left any message or paper for me. His wife told me that he hadn't. That was a big disappointment and gave me a great deal of concern. I was already late for my course, and every minute counted. But I had no other choice than to come back.

I returned to my uncle at exactly two that afternoon. He still hadn't come back. So I waited. I had planned to travel to Lagos that day to submit my papers to the Central Bank. Uncle arrived at three in the afternoon. He knew, of course, that I had waited all day for him. And I had informed him before that I was getting late for the course. Still, he didn't seem to be bothered and went straight into the room, behaving as if he had forgotten what I had come for. Thirty minutes later, he came out to meet me on the corridor.

"Uncle, I have come about the issue of guarantor that I told you about yesterday," I reminded him.

"Oh yes," he said, "concerning your going abroad, isn't it?"

"Yes, Uncle," I replied.

He went in again and came back with a piece of paper. "Take," he said, as he handed me the paper. "That is what you need, isn't it?" he asked.

I stared at the A4 paper and thought my head would explode. My stomach was in a rage. I felt sick as I read my uncle's tax clearance:

Occupation: Petty Trader

Tax: 150 Naira

That was his declared income. And it wasn't even a current certificate. When I told him that I needed a current one, he told me that it didn't matter. But I knew, of course, that it mattered. With that declared income, he would be the most unsuitable person to be my guarantor. I concluded that Uncle wasn't happy to be my guarantor. I took my leave after thanking him for his help.

I left Uncle, completely dazed. I didn't know who else to turn to. No one that I knew. But I would not give up. I prayed all night. I wasn't expecting God to come down from heaven, but I trusted that He would send someone, one of his angels, to supply all the help that I needed.

The night seemed as if it would never end. As I watched the early morning sun, it hit me like a bullet, the realisation that all my efforts would end up in vain. I concluded that my prayers had not been answered. Maybe it was never meant to be, I reasoned. I was physically exhausted and emotionally drained. I couldn't think straight anymore. The enthusiasm that I once had was no more. I began to feel that I shouldn't have left Kwale. I was a coward. After all, I had big people who could protect me. The DPO was my friend. He could have handled the bandits that came to me that night.

I wanted to take the day off to ponder over everything, but staying alone at home wasn't going to make it easy. I couldn't think. I didn't know what to think.

"Come, get up and brace yourself," I said to myself. "Your God, who has begun it, will carry it to completion."

So I braced myself and went to work. I didn't know it showed on my face, but many people remarked that I looked tired and unwell. I thought I could pretend all was well and didn't want to discuss what I was going through with anyone. And, of course, there was no one I could discuss it with. No one that I could trust.

After finishing seeing my last patient, my anxiety returned. I took a piece of paper and listed people that could possibly help if I contacted them: Senior Loyola, now a manager, could help, but I wasn't sure of his salary scale, and I wouldn't want him to feel bad if he couldn't. Mr Babalola was a senior bank manager, but I had no idea about bankers' salary scales. Although he had encouraged me to inform him if I needed any help, I was reluctant to request his assistance as my guarantor. Dr Abitoye could introduce me to some other big people, but he had travelled. My last option was the Ondo State Chief Medical Officer. But he could discourage me from leaving the service since they needed more doctors, particularly in the less popular areas, such as Okitipupa. He might promise me state sponsorship, which might never materialise if someone else became the Chief Medical Officer.

I was in the middle of my mental turmoil when a knock on my door startled me. I had seen my last patient and wasn't expecting any more that morning. A young man in a complete white lace Agbada walked into the room, smiling gracefully.

"Good morning, Doctor," he greeted, still smiling.

"Good morning," I greeted, and smiled back.

"Larry," he said, "Deji's brother."

Larry Oguns was the younger brother of Deji, my friend and former junior in UGS. He was also a friend and classmate of my cousin, Fidelis. He had become a successful businessman. Although he had put on a bit of weight, he was still looking handsome and still remained humble.

He told me that he had been trying to catch me. He wanted to invite me to have a meal with his family. I thought it wouldn't be nice to turn him down. But as I had kept my plan away from people, I didn't want to tell him that I wouldn't have the time to visit.

"Doctor, you don't look right," he observed. "Is everything alright?"

"Not really," I replied. I had to confess. No need to hide it. I was desperate. I never knew who could provide the help that I needed. "I have gained admission for specialist training in Edinburgh, but I can't find anyone to be my guarantor," I informed him.

"Is that all?" he asked.

"Yes," I replied, "and the course has started."

"That's not a problem," he said, with a reassuring smile. "I will be your guarantor."

I felt like a million-tonne stone had just been lifted from my chest. My eyes sparkled, and my whole body woke up to the breath of hope that Larry had just breathed into me. I left my car in the hospital and went in his immaculately clean, white Peugeot 505. Within fifteen minutes, we were at Larry's house, a two-storey mansion in the prestigious part of the town. I settled down to Larry's vegetable soup and pounded yam. And for the moment, I forgot about the course and the guarantor problem, as I devoured the mountain of pounded yam in front of me and washed it down with a bottle of chilled Gulder.

Larry didn't have a current tax clearance, so he drove to Ondo that afternoon to obtain one. As his declared income was below what the Central Bank required, he had to pay thousands of naira to the tax office to obtain an acceptable tax clearance.

The Central Bank

I had passed in front of the Central Bank before, but I had never entered. Although it was a busy street, the security officers kept people away. No one was allowed to loiter around the bank. I didn't know anyone working at the bank, so I got a letter from my uncle to his former mate, Mr. Ezekiel Mabinu, a manager there. The receptionist directed me to the lift to take me to the ninth floor. Mr Mabinu was expecting me. My uncle had spoken with him and requested his help, but his look of surprise made me wonder if he knew the exact reason for my visit. So I went through everything. I told him that I had all the documents that the Central Bank would need for my foreign exchange approval.

"Go and submit them," he instructed.

I told him that all the documents were waiting at the Cooperative Bank Lagos. But my course had already begun. I needed his help so things could be expedited, in order for me not to miss my place on the course.

"I have a meeting shortly," he said, after gazing at his wristwatch. "Just submit your papers. Come back to see me next week."

"But … Oh, that's alright. Thank you, sir," I said. I wanted to say, "But the course has already begun." There was no point pleading. He knew, of course, since I had previously informed him.

Next week. No day. No time. Just next week. That would be the second week into my course. I concluded that this man wasn't prepared to help me, and I couldn't wait that long. I didn't want to be taken up to the mountain summit and then thrown into the valley. That would break and crush me.

I left Mr Mabinu's office disappointed but not beaten. "He couldn't help, or he wouldn't help, but that was alright," I said to myself as I waited for the lift. Soon the lift arrived. Unlike previously, when the lift was packed full, when I was coming up, it was empty this time. Alone, I cried out to God. "Please God, send your angel to me once again to complete your plan for me." After praying this prayer, a surge of confidence and energy overwhelmed me that I couldn't explain. I felt as though the lift was full, but there was no one else but me.

I left the bank with no plans in my mind. As the security officers wouldn't let me stay around, I decided to walk up and down the street, hoping that I would meet someone who might help me. I didn't know why I thought that way, but I felt happier doing that than going back home.

I was on my seventh round of walking when I bumped into my old pal. Banjo Akeke was a year my senior in UGS. We met again at Ibadan in my preclinical years, where we were both Zikites. I didn't realise that Banjo worked at the Central Bank. He told me that he went for his postgraduate studies in the US after graduating from Ibadan, and had since been working as a senior officer in the IT section of the bank.

Banjo took me to the Senior Staff canteen. I told him about my difficulty in getting my papers through and the fact that I was already almost a week late for my course. He told me that if I followed Mr Mabinu's plan, I would never leave the country. Of course, I already knew that. It could easily take up to two weeks for my papers to reach the Central Bank from the commercial bank. If I was lucky, my approval could take more than four weeks to come through. Banjo promised to personally collect my documents from the Cooperative Bank that afternoon, and would push my papers through all the necessary stages at the Central Bank. After exchanging our addresses, I left for home. He promised to contact me as soon as everything had been finalised.

Two days later, on Thursday evening, Banjo branched at my house in Ebute Metta with my Central Bank Approval for four years. I had decided to remain in Lagos until I knew one way or another. This was fantastic news. I was at the British High Commission just before eight o'clock on Friday morning. The queue had started to build up, but I had submitted my application before then, just waiting to be called in for interview.

"I have confirmed with the Edinburgh Postgraduate Board for Medical Education," the immigration officer informed me. "Though the course has begun, they reckoned that you could still make it. Congratulations and good luck in your course."

I had a six-month visa stamped on my passport. Everything was set. All I needed was my flight.

I got back to Okitipupa around eight in the evening on Friday. My father had brought three patients to see me, so I could repair their hernias. They had gone through my father, hoping he would use his influence not only to do their operations quicker, but also so I might charge them less. The men tried to persuade me to just do the operation and leave my nurses to look after their wounds. I advised them that I would be leaving on Monday night, so it was practically impossible to do the operations. I told them that I was only going for a conference, and would be back in a few weeks' time. I felt bad that I hadn't until then even informed my parents of my intention to go to the UK. I had kept it from them and close family members and friends. I didn't want to cause any panic. And since I wasn't sure of the outcome of my travelling applications, I had thought it better to feel the consequences of disappointment alone. Now, with my departure booked for Monday night, I could only inform very few people.

The news about my travelling gave my parents mixed feelings. They were glad that I had the opportunity to go to the UK for further medical training. If I had told them about it earlier, it would have called for a big celebration and a fanfare send-off ceremony. A large crowd would probably follow me to the airport, but I would have found this embarrassing. The other feeling was that of nostalgia. They knew about many parents whose sons and daughters had gone abroad and never came back.

Chapter Thirteen
LIFE IN THE UK

Only those who will risk going too far
can possibly find out how far one can go.
T. S. Elliot

Mike and I planned to travel together. I had included his application in my batch, so his application was approved with mine. I didn't have much packing to do: only one large suitcase and a few clothes. My books took most of the space in the box. I took every medical book with me. I didn't want to spend money on books when I got to Edinburgh. As I sat in the British Caledonia Airways jumbo jet, I imagined what Edinburgh would look like. From what I had read in books such as *Kidnapped*, I imagined Edinburgh was a beautiful city with tall buildings. I imagined people living as good neighbours. I had read a few other novels that made me imagine that Scotland was a beautiful country with friendly people.

We arrived in the autumn. Prior to leaving Nigeria, colleagues who had been to London had warned me that Scotland was cold. They had advised me to buy a thick jumper before leaving Lagos. I told them not to worry, I could handle the cold. So I wore a green, short-sleeve suit, that we referred to in Nigeria as a French suit, with a pair of green shoes to match. Mike was wiser. He had travelled more than me. Having visited his brother in Canada, he knew what to expect. So he took a jumper with him.

We arrived at Edinburgh around two o'clock in the afternoon.

"You are welcome to Scotland," the immigration officer said, as he handed my passport back to me. "All the best on your course."

As I passed through the hundreds of people waiting in the arrivals hall, the sun shone through the glass windows. I said to myself, "I thought they said Scotland was cold!" But I should have guessed that it must be cold. Unlike in London, where most people wore T-shirts and light jumpers, I could see not one person wearing T-shirts in Edinburgh, even inside the airport. People wore thick jumpers and heavy winter coats.

If I had any doubt about the Scottish weather, all my doubts disappeared as the sliding door at Edinburgh Airport slid to let me into the real Scottish weather. My skin was bumpy like that of a goose whose feathers had been plucked. I felt as though the airport door had let me into the middle of the North Sea.

The university had given us a list of B&Bs, and we needed to find our way to the Ivy Cottage. We had no idea how to get there and how much the fare was.

"It's going to cost you a lot to take a taxi from the airport," a gentleman advised us. "I am taking the bus to the city. The bus will pass through the B&B. I will tell the bus driver to stop when we get there."

That was Mr Alex Obina, a Nigerian PhD student. I hadn't realised that he was on the same plane from Nigeria. Alex informed us that he was at Heriot-Watt University, Edinburgh and offered to pay our bus fares. He got off at the university, but reminded the bus driver to drop us close to the Ivy Cottage.

We came with one hundred naira travellers allowance, which fetched us one hundred and nine pounds. This was all we had. We knew, of course, that we wouldn't get far with this amount of money. So Mike and I shared a room to reduce the cost. After settling down, we decided to locate the Edinburgh Royal College of Surgeons in order to plan how to get there in the morning, including what bus number and whether it was walking distance. We soon found out that it would take us about half an hour to trek the distance and decided to walk to save money. We needed a good winter coat, jumper and hat, but we could only afford a second-hand one. I bought a heavy woolly coat at the Heart Foundation Charity shop for one pound. I also bought a woolly hat for twenty pence.

On our way back from the college, we saw a takeaway place where they sold a whole roasted chicken for forty pence. I couldn't resist the temptation. I bought one whole chicken and a portion of chips. Back home, we had to book for chickens and eggs. One would often have to book in advance for a crate of eggs. Even if some of the eggs had cracked, we would still pay for them. Unlike back home, where chickens and eggs were rationed, they were plentiful in Edinburgh, and you could buy as many as you liked. I devoured the whole chicken without mercy, but in the night, I was in and out of the toilet with severe diarrhoea from eating too much chicken.

They were into the second week when I joined the surgical trainees at the Edinburgh Royal College of Surgeons. The class was a mixture of trainees from different backgrounds. Most of them had passed the PLAB and were already working in the hospital. As for me, although I needed the money, I decided to concentrate on passing my Part One FRCS before attempting the PLAB to enable me to work. I learnt from colleagues that the Part One FRCS was a tough examination. Some of my colleagues had made several attempts and had failed. I didn't want that to happen to me. Certainly, I wouldn't want to go back home without my surgical qualification. So I planned to give it my full attention.

The first lesson on my first day of the course was physiology. Professor Samson Wright gave a lecture on reflex action. The topic wasn't new to me, but I had never seen it demonstrated in such an unprecedented way. And to watch a professor of physiology, and the author of the famous Sampson Wright *Applied Physiology*, lay down on the floor just so we might fully understand how our body responded to an unexpected event, blew my mind.

After the first physiology lecture, we had a break. I was coming from the toilet when Professor Wright appeared from the other end of the long corridor. I felt like running back into the toilet, but he beckoned on me. I froze when I stood in front of one of the greatest teachers of physiology. His book, *Applied Physiology*, was the most popular physiology book in medical schools all over the world. I felt privileged to be taught by him.

He recognised that I had just joined the course and introduced himself simply as Sam. "Call me, Sam," he urged me when I called him Prof. It was a culture clash for me. In my culture, it was prohibited to call an elderly person by his or her name. And in the university, you wouldn't be standing in front of a professor and calling him by his name. I recalled when I was an undergraduate, even the mention of some certain professor's name would cause you to tremble.

I followed Professor Wright to his office, as he directed, which was like the inside of a book of physiology. The office, just a little smaller than the lecture theatre, was a book itself. No part of the wall was bare of papers and drawings.

"My office is never locked," he informed me. "If you need any information, you will find it here." I wasn't surprised that he was a great author. "And, of course, Sam is always here," he said. He advised me that the FRCS was a tough examination and that it was much better to take the Part One examination straight after the course, since all that I had learnt would still be fresh in my memory.

"Edinburgh is a vibrant city, and the nights are full of fun. But you must ignore the social distractions and face what you've come for," he advised.

He then handed me a folder with the handouts that he had given out to my colleagues the previous week.

I felt the way I had when my father advised me, back in those days, when I was going to university for the first time. Of course, I needed no one to advise me. I already knew that I must focus on my studies, but I did genuinely appreciate this fatherly advice.

Three weeks into my life in Edinburgh, I ran dry of cash. Though I had approval for money transfer from Nigeria, my money hadn't arrived. It was a Friday morning, and the landlord would collect her weekly rent that evening. I had enough money to pay for that week, but that was all I had left. There was no money to pay for subsequent rent. I had to do something before the end of the week, or else the landlord would throw me out in the street. I approached the university and requested a loan to help with my subsistence, pending the arrival of my money. But despite showing them my foreign exchange papers, they turned me down.

"We can't do that," they said, "as we've had bad experiences with students from your country."

They advised that it was better for me to take a week off and go to Nigeria to ensure the transfer of the money. Alternatively, I could instruct my guarantors to help me out. I even showed my bank statements to them. Still, they turned down my request.

Things looked desperate. Is that it then? I will be going back home after just three weeks in Scotland? Is that the end of my dream?

As I left the registrar's office, I saw the Bank of Scotland, the university branch. Should I talk to the manager? Maybe if I showed him my Central Bank documents, he could give me a small loan to sustain me until my money arrived. He might even open an account for me so that the money could go directly into that account.

I joined the queue of customers waiting for enquiries, but when I was third in the queue, I decided to drop the idea. It wouldn't work, I thought.

Now out of the bank, as I turned to start my walk back to the college, I saw a young man walking ahead of me. From behind, he looked like someone that I knew. He was quite a distance from me and seemed to be in a hurry. Back home, I could shout or beckon someone to stop him, but that would be viewed as a social nuisance in the British culture. In just three weeks, I had learnt a lot about the British culture. I learnt that the British were reserved, and they valued their privacy. They queued and waited for their turn, and they didn't like a noisy environment. So I thought it wouldn't be a good idea to call out to the man walking ahead of me.

As I took double steps to catch up with him, he stopped and looked back. I couldn't tell what made him look back, but he did, and this brought back the smiles that had left my face.

"Great Zikites!" he shouted.

"Great!!!" I shouted back in the characteristic way that the Nnamdi Azikiwe Hall students greeted each other in my undergraduate days. Tunji Ogunjobi was unmistakable. He read veterinary medicine. My good friend in my Prelim year, we hadn't seen each other since we graduated. What a place to meet, and at such a time like this. I had needed someone to talk to, and God had provided. This was an answered prayer.

Tunji informed me that he had just completed his postgraduate course. I told him my problem and that I would use my return ticket to go back to Nigeria. I would then return once I successfully processed my foreign exchange.

"Does that mean you are giving up?" Tunji narrowed his eye.

"You could say that." I scratched my head.

"Where is your Zikite's spirit?" he asked. "A Zikite doesn't give up. He fights to get what he wants."

True. Tunji was right. That was a principle that every Zikite understood. If you had a survival spirit in you, Zik Hall would help you to keep it alive. And if you didn't have it when you came into Zik Hall, you would be forced to develop it. Other halls viewed Zikites as

257

troublemakers, but in reality, the hall gave the residents the opportunity to develop life skills: how to survive the daily problems that life throws at you.

"Great Zikites!" I greeted him again and gyrated like we used to do.

Tunji informed me that he was going back to Nigeria that night. He regretted that he had only just handed in his key. He was on British Council Scholarship, and still had three months left on his tenancy. He could have let me squat in his room pending the arrival of my money, but as he had signed off his tenancy and returned the keys, he could no longer take back the room.

"But I have a good Nigerian friend," Tunji suggested. "I will introduce you to him and hope that he will be able to help."

Tunji took me to Yemi Aderinoye. He and his wife, Funmi, and their toddler son, Damola, lived in a one-bedroom apartment. This wonderful couple didn't have to think twice. They received me with a great deal of enthusiasm. Yemi advised that his wife was still nursing their baby. He wished me to understand that she might not be able to provide all my needs. I assured him that all I needed was somewhere to lay my head. I didn't need food or anything more – just the barest survival needs. That was all I needed.

That evening, Yemi drove me to my B&B, and I checked out after paying the week's due. I suggested sleeping in their sitting room, since the only extra room was their son's room, but they wouldn't let me. Instead, they moved their son to share their bedroom with them. And so I had a room that I didn't pay for, and I was kept warm without paying a bill. I later learnt that Funmi was a younger sister to one of my classmates in medical school.

That Sunday, I joined the Aderinoye family to fellowship in Charlotte Baptist Church. That day, the preacher preached about sin. He told the story of Adam and Eve in the Garden of Eden. This Bible story was well-known to me. We even staged a drama about it in the primary school. He reminded the congregation that the sin that Adam and Eve committed separated human beings from God.

"Sin has put a barrier between man and God," he said. "Not one of us could boast that we had not sinned against God. For all have sinned and fallen short of the glory of God," he quoted from a bible passage,

Romans 3:23 (NIV). "But God demonstrates his own love for us in this: While we were still sinners, Christ died for us." Romans 5:8 (NIV). "Christ has taken down the barrier through his resurrection," he continued. "Christ came to Earth from his holy heavenly temple. He suffered for our sins and died so that we may have life and have it abundantly. And to whoever follows him he gives everlasting life."

Bible stories were not new to me. I could recite so many verses and had attended many Christian meetings and crusades. When I was in the university, I attended the Chapel of Resurrection, and Christian friends had tried on several occasions to make me follow the way of the cross. I even had friends send me Christian books, tracts and daily readings such as, *Our Daily Bread* and *Purer than Gold*. None of these changed my love for the things of the world. But on this day, as the preacher continued, something happened to me, something I had never experienced. Tears streamed down my cheeks. I couldn't contain them. My heart raced and my muscles twitched. I felt something whispering to me, "This is your moment. Don't reject the Messiah like you have done so many things. Throw away your shyness and follow the one who has forgiven your sin."

And when the preacher asked for people who had accepted Jesus as their Lord and personal Saviour, I raised my hand high and boldly and publicly gave my life to the one who is my Redeemer and my Saviour.

Knowing Christ is a personal encounter and a personal decision, and my life was transformed. I became born again in the Spirit. I became a new creature. And I had peace like I had never experienced.

That night I couldn't sleep. I kept reciting Romans 5:8. That was true about my life. I had no doubt in my mind that God loved me, for even in my filth and disobedience, He answered my prayers and provided help when I needed them. What a love! I thought my head was going to explode. I couldn't contain the excitement. I promised to worship Him all the days of my life.

Yemi introduced me to other Christian friends. We formed a house group and had weekly meetings at the Aderinoyes. Dr Alastair Reid and his wife, Jane, attended. The couple were GP trainees. This couple helped me when I realised that I had come to Edinburgh with a box full of books that were of no use to me, as they were many editions out of date. My surgical textbook, Bailey and Love, was ten years old. Alastair and Jane gave me current editions of the recommended books, so I didn't have to buy them. I only needed to buy one or two books that they didn't have.

Three weeks after living with the Aderinoyes, my money arrived. I could now rent my own apartment. I had enough money for my rent, complete payment for my course and examinations and my subsistence.

Yemi and my other friends started house hunting for me. That Friday, they finally found an apartment in Newington. It was a studio apartment in the sub-ground level. Gary King, the landlord, was a senior technician at the anatomy laboratory. He was excited to have a surgical trainee as his tenant.

"If you need anything, let me know," he said.

"Skeleton and cadaver?" I requested.

"That's not a problem," Gary reassured me.

My new residence was further away from the College of Surgeons than either Yemi's house or the Ivy Cottage bed and breakfast. So I had to leave home earlier, in order not to be late for lectures. Although bus services were regular, I decided to trek the three miles to save on transport.

One day, after a long night of snow, for which I hadn't prepared myself. I trekked to the college in my James Brown-type platform club shoes that I brought with me from Nigeria. As I walked fast to get to the college in time, I slipped and landed flat on my back. I felt embarrassed, but the people didn't make a meal of it. They were used to falling or seeing people fall in the snow. Nobody laughed. Nobody bothered, everyone minding their own business, all trying to do what they had to do even in the harsh weather. I learnt a life lesson from this event: Get on with it even if harsh wind blows against you. You've got to soldier on since you're not alone. Other people are fighting their battles too. That's just life.

Gary brought a complete human skeleton as he had promised. He also provided me with a key to the laboratory, with liberty to enter whenever I liked.

Jacqui King, Gary's wife, was a nice person. She helped with tidying up the apartment and ensuring that it was kept warm and I had warm water.

Prior to this, I visited the library to study. But the house was off the main street and quiet, and I no longer needed to go. I had everything I needed: no disturbance, warmth, hot water, books and a full human skeleton.

I passed the Part I FRCS at the end of the course. The next step in my training was to seek placement for my clinical experience in preparation for the final FRCS. But I still had to pass the PLAB, without which I wouldn't get on the GMC register. With the surgical examination out of the way, I could concentrate on my preparation for this. I met a few other foreign doctors preparing for the PLAB in the library. Whilst some of them inspired me, most brought fears into me. I heard all sorts of stories about the PLAB, particularly from those who had made several unsuccessful attempts. I met a particular doctor who had been barred for two years from retaking the examination, after failing it three times. That was the rule. You weren't allowed to make further attempts at the examination after three attempts. You would have to wait for two years before trying again. He was open and honest. He told me that he had attended courses. He had made good notes and had many questions-and-answers books. But despite his efforts, he kept failing the English component of the examination. Krishnan wouldn't be eligible to resit the PLAB until a year's time. He was gracious to lend me all his study materials.

Krishnan and I met regularly at the library. As he wasn't ready to take the PLAB, he made himself available to mark my answers and to conduct vivas for me. One Monday morning, I was just about to leave home for the library when my phone rang.

"We have a cancellation at the London centre next Wednesday. Would you like to take that slot?" the examination officer from the GMC asked me.

"Yes, please," I replied.

I hadn't thought before answering. I had been pestering them incessantly since I received my date, which was four months away in Edinburgh. I had asked to have my examination date brought forward. I had told them that not having my registration was causing a delay to my training. I even told them that I was prepared to sit at any centre. So when this woman phoned, I didn't give my brain any chance to process that information. After she hung up, it was as if my brain was asleep and had just woken up.

"Next Wednesday! Just over one week! Hmmm!" I sighed. "But it's doable."

"That's alright," Krishnan said, when I broke the news to him. "There's never the right time. Everything depends on the day. Go for it," he encouraged.

"Yes, I will," I reassured him, and really meant it.

Krishnan introduced me to four of his friends. The five of them, including one who had gone to Dublin to take the Part I of the Irish FRCS, shared a top-floor apartment close to the library. Krishnan's friends were also preparing for the PLAB. But I was the only one with an imminent examination date. So everyone played his part, giving me study materials, their attention and times, and the much-needed encouragement. It was as though I had known them for years. And so, I embarked on the marathon preparation, spending a lot of time with Krishnan and his friends.

I left Edinburgh by the National Express night ride. I needed to find a B&B that wasn't too far from the examination centre, but I knew nowhere in London. I came out of the Victoria bus station and didn't know whether to turn to the right or to the left. As I was about to go back into the station to ask for directions, I heard someone asked with a distinctive Eastern Ibo accent, "You seem to be lost. Can I help you?"

He introduced himself as Charles Igwe. I told him that I had come to London to sit the PLAB examination and was trying to find an affordable B&B close to the centre. I couldn't believe it when he told me that he too had come for the PLAB examination.

Like most Nigerians, when they meet each other, we started to chat as though we had known each other before. Charles informed me that this was going to be his second attempt. He lived in London with his cousin who worked as a senior house officer in one of the London hospitals. He reassured me that his cousin wouldn't mind me staying with them. And it would provide an opportunity for us to study together.

The PLAB result came out the following Saturday. Although I thought that I had done well enough to pass the examination, my confidence disappeared like the air in a ruptured balloon as Jerkil handed the envelope to me. My heart missed a beat as my eyes caught the GMC logo on the left top corner, and the return address on its back. Jerkil must have suspected that it was my examination result. She knew, of course, that I had been in London for the examination the previous week. As a nurse, she knew about the PLAB, and I had previously expressed to her and her husband how crucial passing the exam was to me. She took her leave after a nervous cough.

I left the envelope on my bed with no courage to open it. Yet I was curious to know the outcome. I wished I had someone to help me out, someone to take the shock of failure. I picked up the envelope once again, tore a tiny bit of its corner and peeped to see if there was any clue of passing. One of the contents was yellow. From talking to colleagues, I had learnt that if you passed, you would receive a yellow form to complete to apply for a Limited Registration. I wanted to go upstairs to ask Jerkil to open it for me. Then I thought that was ridiculous. It was my cross. I must carry it myself. There were only two possibilities, like two sides of a coin: pass or fail. Even if I failed, that wouldn't be the end of life. I would still be able to make further attempts. So with two determined fingers, I tore the envelope. Out of all of the sentences on the A4 sheet, my eyes caught only one word – *Successful*. That was the most important word. I had passed the dreaded PLAB.

I thanked God from the deepest part of my heart and flew upstairs to share the fantastic news with the Kings. That afternoon, I bought a wristwatch from the sales, a nice jumper, four new shirts and ties, and a new pair of shoes in preparation for my hospital job.

Chapter Fourteen
LIFE AFTER THE PLAB

Don't wait for someone to take you under their wing.
Find a good wing and climb up underneath it.
Frank C. Bucaro

I had no idea how to get a surgical job, so I went to seek advice from the college. They advised me that jobs were advertised weekly in the *British Medical Journal* (BMJ.) I would need to apply with my CV and provide two referees. As I hadn't joined the British Medical Association, I had no copy of the BMJ, so I spoke with Krishnan, who advised that there were copies in the library. I showed him my CV, and he told me that I hadn't done it the British way. He also advised that they would need local referees, and not the ones that I had brought from Nigeria.

"That is going to be difficult," I told him, "since I have never worked in this country."

"Unfortunately, that's the system," he said. "You have to do that to stand any chance of getting a job."

I had no idea who would be willing to provide my reference. Perhaps Gary could provide a character reference. But would they accept a reference provided by a lab technician for a surgical job? Even if he wasn't suitable, perhaps he could introduce me to someone who would help, based on his recommendation. I remembered him telling me when I first moved in that a consultant surgeon lived close by, and he was their family friend. I wondered if he could seek his help. These were the thoughts going through my head as I left Krishnan. But when I got back to my apartment, I didn't have the courage to ask Gary, as I feared he would turn me down.

I went to church the following Sunday, as usual. After service, as I waited in the foyer for Yemi and Funmi to pick Damola up from the children's room, I decided to look at the various plaques and photos on the walls. One particular plaque caught my attention. So l walked to take a closer look at it. It bore the names of all the people who had gone to be missionaries in many parts of the world. I rubbed my finger over one that had been in Nigeria and shouted with excitement as I pointed to my friend. "Even Nigeria," I said.

"Allan is still here," an old lady said from behind me. "I'll take you to him."

We tore through the crowd in the foyer, back into the inside of the church. Professor Allan Norman was talking to the pastor. He sensed that we were coming his way, so he beckoned us. I waited with the old lady to give him time to finish his discussion with the pastor.

"You are my fellow countryman," Professor Norman said, as he shook my hand.

"Nice to meet you, Prof," I said, wondering why he called me his fellow countryman.

He explained to me that his father was a missionary in Kano, Northern Nigeria, where he was born. After his A Levels, he came back to Scotland and gained admission into Edinburgh University to study medicine. After completing his specialist training, he returned to Nigeria where he joined the teaching hospital. Unfortunately, he and his family had to flee Nigeria during the political crisis that led to the civil war in the 1960s. Mrs Norman joined in. A beautiful woman, probably in her late fifties, with a graceful smile, she nodded as her husband recalled their experiences when Western Nigeria was on fire. Professor Norman was attending a meeting in the UK, leaving his wife and children in Nigeria, when the crisis broke out. His family was among those that the British government evacuated when the crisis broke out.

The Normans took me to have dinner with them. As we drove to their house, Professor Norman asked me in what subject I was doing my postgraduate course. He had thought that, being Yemi's friend, I was also doing my PhD like him. I told him that I had come for my surgical training. I had passed the Part I FRCS and the PLAB, but I didn't know what to do to get a job to enable me to gain the necessary experience for my final FRCS.

"I will see what I can do," he said. "I'll call you tomorrow."

"Thanks, sir," I said.

I spent the whole of that Sunday with the Normans. He told me stories and showed me memorable photographs: those with him and Prime Minister Tafawa Balewa, President Nnamdi Azikiwe and when the University of Ibadan was still a College of the University of London. One particular photo fascinated me. He stood in the middle of Dugbe Market pricing fish.

"That's one of the things I missed in Nigeria," he remarked, when he saw me staring at the black and white photo.

Professor Norman called as promised just after ten o'clock on Monday morning. He would like me to see Miss Sutherland, head of Plastic Surgery, the following day at two o'clock in the afternoon. If I had any problems, I should let him know. And after wishing me well for the future, he hung up.

Bangor Hospital was situated in St Lawrence, on the outskirts of Edinburgh. I wasn't aware of the shuttle bus between the Edinburgh Royal Infirmary and Bangor Hospital, so I took a bus from the bus station. The bus dropped me at the gate of the hospital, and I had to trek the one-mile distance into the hospital. The hospital showed its unique character as a former military camp. It was in blocks of bungalows, spread over several acres of land, interspersed by green fields and small paths and walks. A village of its own, it was a prestigious hospital, boasting excellence in plastic surgery.

I had thought that I had come for an interview, so I wore a complete suit and held a briefcase containing my certificates from primary school to university, my NYSC certificate, Part I FRCS result, PLAB result, two open references from Nigeria and my passport.

Miss Sutherland waited for me in her office. A middle-aged woman with the look of a caring mother, she stood up and welcomed me with a hospitable smile. I was shaking even though she was smiling. After offering me a cup of coffee, she settled back at her desk.

"Professor Norman has said good things about you," she informed me.

I didn't know what to say. I simply nodded, just as a cue that I was listening.

"I myself know that Ibadan products are excellent doctors," she said. "And if Professor Norman has recommended you, then the job is yours."

"Thank you, Ma," I said.

She directed me to the medical personnel office. The hospital paid my fee for Limited Registration with the GMC and my subscription to the Scottish Medical Defence Union. They also gave me a salary advance. After confirming that everything was in order, the medical personnel officer directed me to the sewing room to have me measured for my white coat.

I didn't have much to do on my first day, as it was meant to be mostly administrative to complete all the employment forms, sign the contract, introduce myself to hospital staff and familiarise myself with the environment. I thought it best to shadow the house officers and senior house officers to see how they did things.

But there was one area of the hospital prohibited to me: the burns unit, which was separate from the main block. I had had swabs taken from my nostrils, armpits and groins for screening for methicillin resistant staphylococcus aureus (MRSA), and the result was expected to be out in seventy-two hours. I wouldn't be allowed to enter until I was confirmed not to be a carrier of this highly infective and difficult to treat bacteria. These germs could colonise over nine percent of the community. Most carriers harbour the MRSA in their nostrils, where they pose a significant risk, particularly in areas such as the burns unit. They could cause devastating infections on burns or reconstructive procedures. Every plastic and reconstructive unit ensured that none of their staff had the germs. In the Bangor plastic unit, it was routine to screen every new employee and all clinical staff three monthly. Any employee found to be a carrier would need to be treated and confirmed to be decolonised before they would be allowed back into the operating theatre and the burns unit.

I went around all the wards and found the nursing staff to be friendly. They offered me a cup of coffee on each ward. Many things were new to me, but everyone was eager to show me how to operate the medical equipment that I was not familiar with. They also showed me the staff accommodation. This consisted of single rooms with shared toilets, bathrooms and kitchens, within the same block as the doctors' mess. Although accommodation was free, almost all the doctors and nurses lived in the city, as it was lonely, especially on weekends. As I still had some six months or so on my rent contract, I decided not to take up the accommodation in the hospital. I only stayed there when on call. My city accommodation was best suited for going to church, taking part in home groups, as well as shopping.

We were two senior house officers. Ramona, my colleague, had been working in the department for nearly two years. Although not planning to be a career plastic surgeon, she had decided not to change job, as it was convenient for her. We did one-in-two on call with colleague cover, which meant that if one of us was unable to work or on annual leave, the other doctor would take the call. Essentially, he would be on call every day and every night, with no rest between the calls.

The job in the burns unit was intensive. As the main burns unit in the West Lothian area, we had at least one patient with major burns injuries every night.

The duty plastic surgeon would set up good venous access, and in the event of inaccessible peripheral veins, he would have to do a venous cut down. He also needed to set up a central line and take blood from the radial artery for arterial blood gases. In some cases, the patient would be taken to theatre at night for escharotomy, an operation performed to treat full-thickness (third-degree) circumferential burns. In full-thickness burns, both the epidermis and the dermis are destroyed, along with sensory nerves in the dermis. The tough leathery tissue remaining after a full-thickness burn is termed *eschar*. Eschar is dehydrated and tight tissue that has lost its elasticity. It can lead to impaired circulation in tissues beyond the burnt area. An escharotomy can be performed to prevent or treat this impairment of circulation. Antibiotics must be given per clock time. Thus, the doctor would give intravenous benzyl penicillin every six hours.

We also dealt with facial and limb traumas. We had so many cases of nasal and maxillo-facial injuries. We took many of these cases to theatre in the middle of the night to straighten a bent nose bridge with septal haematoma or nasal passage blockage. We also carried out tendon repairs and neurovascular reconstructions on patients with hands and feet injuries. Some of these procedures took a minimum of three hours. And with the intensive burns unit care, there was no chance of having a nap when on call.

We started each day with a ward round at seven-thirty. Hot breakfast was provided whilst we reviewed case notes with the nurses and the doctors on call the previous night. We then went around to see the patients on the wards and lastly, those in the burns unit. Everyone was expected to participate and contribute to discussions. I had very supportive registrars and senior registrars, who ensured that I received good hands-on experience. At first, I had difficulty in understanding some patients with deep Scottish accent. The same applied to patients and staff, who struggled sometimes with my deep Yoruba accent. But things changed pretty soon, and there were fewer 'Pardon?' 'Sorry?' 'What does that mean?' and 'Say that again'.

The post in Plastic Surgery gave me a great deal of enthusiasm. It was a good start for my surgical training and future career as a surgeon. Firstly, it was exactly what the Federal Ministry of Education had approved for me: Trauma and Reconstructive Surgery, and I loved it. Secondly, it provided a great opportunity to see new things and learn new skills.

The excitement and the great interest in my training blinded me to the fact that my SHO colleague, Ramona, was taking advantage of my readiness to say yes whenever she asked for a cover or a swap of our on-calls. Nurses had remarked several times, saying, "All these changes make a mess of the rota." Ramona would ask for cover because she needed to travel urgently to Heathrow Airport to welcome her fiancé. Then at other times, she would claim that she needed to go again, as the flight disappointed last time. Other times, she would say that she needed to go to Kenya for her wedding. I couldn't recall how many times she said she was going to get married or the wedding had been cancelled. She seemed to be avoiding busy times. As a result of her inconsiderate requests, I ended up doing the on-calls on Christmas Eve, Christmas Day, New Year Eve and the New Year. I was exhausted. It showed on my face. Many people, including even the patients, commented that I looked pale. But I didn't mind. I was single and alone. I reasoned that, as a matter of fact, I was better off working than having a lonely Christmas and New Year. I thought I should help my colleague, irrespective of the inconveniences that I experienced.

One day, the Monday after the New Year celebration, the medical personnel officer called me. She informed me that Ramona had put in a request to take the following weekend off. They had told her that she couldn't, since that would mean I would be working three busy weekends in a row.

"But that's up to you," she said.

No sooner had she hung up than Ramona arrived.

"My fiancé's family is arriving this weekend. Can you cover for me?" she asked in the front of everyone at the nurses' station.

"Sorry, I can't," I replied.

"Okay, then," she said, with no expression of emotion, and left the ward.

This was the first time that I had said no to a request, and I felt bad that I refused to help her.

"Good for you," the sister said. "She is such a lazy brat. No wonder she hasn't passed her exam. Look at you. You have passed your exam even before you started. But she has been trying for the past two years."

I didn't know that Ramona hadn't passed her exam. I knew, of course, that she wasn't a JJC like me, but I never thought that she had been on the job for two years. She often told me that she should have been put on the registrar's rota and not the SHO's. And sometimes, she gave me instructions as though she were my registrar, marching all over the place like she was the boss. No wonder the nursing staff didn't like her. But I felt bad that I had turned down her request. I drew my face and dropped my head.

"Hmmm!" I sighed.

"There is something called assertiveness, you know, Doctor," the sister said. "You don't have to always say yes, you know. People will always take you for a ride."

"But I find it hard to turn down a request," I said.

"Well, you better learn to be assertive," she advised. "It is a necessary life skill."

Sister Stewart advised me like a mother. And she was right. People had made me do things to please them, ignoring how it might impact on me. Sister's remarks ruminated in my thoughts for a long time, as I reminisced instances when people had played on sentiments to gain something from me. Sometimes, they blackmailed my emotions to get what they wanted. I had to learn to be assertive. That was a necessary life skill, as the sister had advised.

As the months rolled on, I found that I needed to do more than I was allowed to do. I needed a job that would provide the opportunity to do more operating. I should be a pre-fellowship registrar and not an SHO, since I had obtained my Part I FRCS. I wanted to discuss my feelings with Miss Sutherland, but I didn't know if she would be disappointed. She might even think I was ungrateful. So I decided to soldier on, hoping that the opportunity would arise when I would be able to tell someone what was going on in my head. And that opportunity came one day, when I was on call with the senior registrar. Mr Richard Ferguson had taken interest in me since I joined. He often talked about his experience in Uganda, where he did his one-year elective. That night, we carried out a four-hour neurovascular reconstruction and tendon repair on a factory worker who had slashed his wrist on a chainsaw.

"So, what are your plans?" Mr Ferguson asked, as we relaxed over our cups of coffee at the end of the operation. "You are on government's sponsorship, aren't you?"

"I planned to be a trauma surgeon," I said. "I didn't come on government sponsorship, so I had to arrange my own training posts."

Mr Ferguson advised me that since I had passed the Part I FRCS, the next step was for me to get into a good surgical rotation, to enable me fulfil the requirements for the final FRCS. It was not of any use for me to spend all my time as SHO in Plastic Surgery. I only needed to do six months in that specialty at that level. I would be wasting my time hanging onto that post. Furthermore, there were few training posts in Plastic Surgery in Scotland. So he advised me to apply for jobs in England, as there were a lot more opportunities. He reassured me that it wouldn't be too hard for me to find a good job.

I had thought that I should be a specialist surgeon within four years; yes, four years, at the end of which I would return home to use my skills to help my people. This was my hope and my prayer. But my meeting with Mr Ferguson had changed my perspectives. Now I knew that having the FRCS alone would not make me the specialist I had hoped for. "The fellowship is the passport for your specialist training," as the senior registrar had advised. So I prepared myself for the challenges of looking for training posts wherever I could find them.

Chapter Fifteen
OUT OF SCOTLAND

Everything you want is out there waiting for you to ask.
Everything you want also wants you.
But you have to take action to get it.
Jack Canfield

I heeded Mr Ferguson's advice. After the call, and once I had had some rest after work, I put together my curriculum vitae and brought it to show him when we were on call together again, three days later. It was handwritten, one-page information on A4 Paper. All that I wrote were my name, gender, date of birth, qualifications, schools and university attended, completion of my National Service and the hospitals that I had worked, all written in blue ink with my best, fanciful, cursive style of penmanship. I handed it to Mr Ferguson, smiling with pride.

"Rubbish!" he said, with his Highlander accent. "This won't take you anywhere. You will never get a job with this."

I raised my eyebrows. I had thought he liked me and I could call him my friend. Why was he suddenly being so critical? I wondered.

"That is not how to write a CV," he said. "And it's got to be typed and well-presented."

I gave an affirmative nod.

Mr Ferguson sensed that I had written the CV the best way I knew. He knew, of course, that I always tried to do things to the best of my ability. But this time, my best was not good enough. He offered to rewrite the CV and would bring it after the weekend.

We started the day with an early morning grand round, as usual. Mr Ferguson didn't talk to me about my CV or my job plans. So I decided not to say anything about it, as I didn't want to put any pressure on him. I thought he probably hadn't put the CV together. But I had to inform the hospital within four weeks if I wanted them to extend my contract. From my previous discussion with Miss Sutherland, she had told me that they would see if they would be able to get me into the Edinburgh surgical rotation. But nothing was guaranteed, and I learnt that the Edinburgh rotation was very competitive. So I agreed with Mr Ferguson that my best opportunities rested on my move to England.

I was in the middle of updating all the case notes before going off for the day, when Mr Ferguson breezed into the ward.

"Oh, you are here," he said, as he handed me a large envelope.

"Thank you very much," I said, without opening it, as I knew that it was my CV. I raised my eyebrows, as I hadn't expected it to be that bulky. But I decided not to open it until I finished my ward work.

I couldn't wait till I got home before opening the envelope. I was on the backseat on the Bangor-Infirmary shuttle bus, so I had no inhibition. I opened my mouth wide as I opened the heavy A4 envelope. Mr Ferguson's edited copy of my CV made the one that I had produced look like a primary school pupil's scribbles. Not only did Mr Ferguson write my CV, but he also made twenty photo copies.

As soon as I got home, I checked the classified section of the BMJ, where I found twelve adverts for training posts in General Surgery. I applied to eight of these jobs and put my applications in the post before the post office closed for the day.

I received my first letter of shortlisting the following week, inviting me to attend an interview in two weeks' time. The news excited Mr Ferguson. He spent over two hours with me after work, the day before the interview and taught me interview techniques, covering everything from making sure that I arrived in good time to common medical interview questions and how to answer them. I must dress smartly, sit confidently and make good eye contact. I must be honest with the answers that I gave. He then wished me good luck.

I was one of seven candidates shortlisted for the interview for the post of SHO in General Surgery at Bishop Auckland General Hospital, County Durham. It had just snowed on that day, but it wasn't too cold, and the sun was shining. The interview was scheduled for two o'clock in the afternoon. I arrived in Bishop Auckland at just past ten o'clock in the morning, so I decided to go by bus rather than take a taxi, since I still had plenty of time. A young man joined me as I waited for the bus. The man, probably a little younger than me, with blonde hair and Harry Potter-type glasses, sat beside me.

"Hello," he greeted.

"Hello," I replied.

That was all we said to each other. He was reading a newspaper. I remained in my own world, reciting all the answers that Mr Ferguson had taught me by heart. I pictured myself walking smartly into the interview room, curtseying to the panel and smiling confidently. I reminded myself of the answers to questions like 'Tell us about yourself,' 'What particular highlights in your CV would you like to talk about?' 'Why do you need this job?' and other questions that I had discussed with Mr Ferguson.

"Are you here for the interview?" He broke the silence.

"Yes, I replied," without asking him what interview, where or when.

"Very good," he said.

"Which interview?" I asked, after regaining my senses. I needed to know. And I wondered if he was also there for the interview.

"The surgical SHO interview," he replied.

"How did you know that?" I wondered.

"I just guessed since you look like someone going for an interview. And I am aware of the interview taking place this afternoon," he replied. "My friend is also going for the interview."

"Good to know that," I said.

The journey to the hospital took just over twenty minutes. I could have walked it if I had realised that the bus station wasn't too far from the hospital.

The man didn't ask my name, and I didn't ask his. Just before the bus stopped, he told me that he had just rotated from General Surgery to Orthopaedics. There would be five interviewers. I must study my CV properly, because they would ask me to take them through my CV. They would ask me to pick one aspect of my CV that highlighted my strengths and one aspect that highlighted my weaknesses.

"Just be yourself," he said. "All the best."

"Thanks," I said, and shook his hands.

We both went our ways – he, towards the doctors' residence and I towards the main entrance. After the man had left, I regretted that I hadn't taken his name and contact details. He seemed to be a nice person, and I would have liked to keep in touch with him even if I didn't get the job.

I needed to hang around somewhere since I still had over three hours to the interview. The administrative officer directed me to the library. She also gave me a note to the canteen so I could have a free lunch.

The interview was conducted in one of the large rooms at the administrative building. I was the first candidate to arrive. I took a seat in the waiting room, as the other six candidates arrived one by one. I was the last patient to be called into the interview room. Those who had been called in before me had shown no clue on their faces how the interview went. They all came out smiling. No one asked the other what they asked them.

"Good luck!" they all wished me as the officer called me in.

Five interviewers sat behind a long table, as the man on the bus had told me. They gave me a warm welcome, and after showing me to my chair, they encouraged me to relax.

The interview began with this question: "Tell us about yourself."

I took them through my general education and my undergraduate life. I discussed my career up to date, the reason for my coming to the UK and my career aspirations. I had recited these answers, so I didn't have to think long. Then the second question followed in which the most senior surgeon asked about my strengths and weaknesses. Finally, the last surgeon asked me to highlight anything in my CV that made me feel special and demonstrated my true character. I had also practised the answer since the man on the bus had advised me. I thanked the panel at the end of the interview, and left the room to join the other interviewees to await the outcome.

Twenty minutes later, they called candidate number four in again. After five minutes, he emerged smiling, and I knew that the rest of us were deemed unsuccessful. I picked up my briefcase and was about to leave, like the other unsuccessful candidates, when the officer came out again. This time she called me in. The chairperson informed me that they liked me and were pleased to offer me the job. I hadn't realised that there were two posts until then. I felt on top of the world and didn't think twice to confirm my acceptance of the offer.

As I was about to come out of the main door of the administrative block, I saw the man that I met on the bus again, waiting.

"Congratulations!" he said. "I knew you would get it."

How did he know that I would get the job? And why did he decide to stand in the cold, waiting for me? I wanted to ask him, but in the end, I felt that it didn't matter. I got the job. That was what mattered. And that was all I needed. So I simply replied, "Thank you, hope to see you when I start in February."

After shaking each other's hands, we bade goodbye and went our separate ways.

Chapter Sixteen
BISHOP AUCKLAND

God provides the wind, but man must raise the sails.
Saint Augustine

Prior to starting my new job, I decided to spend my three-week holiday in Nigeria. I had not seen my parents since I left. I had no doubt that they would be looking forward to my return since I had told them when I was leaving that I was only going for a few months. I needed to reassure them that everything was going well, and explain to them what my training entailed and how long left for me to do. I also needed to catch up with my friends and update them with my progress.

My parents were excited to see me. My father saved me from having to explain to him the reason for telling him that I was only going to spend a few months knowing that I was going to spend years and not months. One of his friends whose son was in the US had been gone for many years. So after I had been away for more than three months he had thought that I, too, would be abroad for many years. Nevertheless, my parents and family were glad to see me.

I spent a weekend with my uncle in Ibadan. On my return to Lagos, I decided to take a bus from Ojota to Ebute Metta. When we got to Fadeyi, the bus stopped and the conductor announced that they had changed the plan. The bus was no more passing through Oyingbo, and advised the passengers going to Oyingbo to disembark. So, like the other passengers I left the bus. At first, I wanted to take a taxi, but decided to wait for another bus. Looking across the road, I saw a girl about to enter a taxi. I blinked twice and instantly, I shouted, "Theresa!" I hadn't expected that the girl heard my call from all the noise on Lagos-Ikorodu Road. But she did. That was the girl that I thought I had lost forever. She, too, had come to Lagos, and as she confessed, she had not stopped thinking about me since we went our ways just before I left the country.

It always amazes me how God does His things. Our relationship broke down due to my own fault. I had not expected Theresa to be back in my life. I tried everything I could to find her but I couldn't. But God brought her back into my life in a spectacular way. Had the bus driver not changed his route I would not have found her. It is said, every disappointment is a blessing in disguise. This is true, and I believe, what we call disappointment is God's appointment. God can turn a bad situation to good. We got engaged and planned to have our wedding in the UK.

We were three SHOs. The other candidate, who was appointed at the same time, whom I now knew as Waseem Salem, a married doctor from Malaysia, was one of the SHOs. He looked reserved and intelligent with his heavy-framed glasses. He radiated confidence and was always smiling. I had no doubt in my mind that he was a good person and I would get on well with him. The third SHO, Rebecca Dixon, was a female trainee on the Newcastle rotation. Unlike Waseem and me, she was much younger and hadn't done much surgery. But she was enthusiastic and showed a great keenness to learn. We had two registrars and one senior SHO with registrar responsibilities. Each registrar with his SHO and HO were allocated to a consultant firm.

I was attached to Mr Roberts with a major interest in urology. A bearded surgeon who paid a great attention to detail, he was extremely supportive to his juniors. He rarely smiled, making him look unfriendly, but in reality, he was a kind and down-to-earth surgeon and a great teacher. My registrar, Mr Simon Naaeder, was a Ghanaian. He was much older than the other registrars. I liked him a lot, not because he was from the same part of the world as me, but he was an excellent surgeon. He was in his final year of training, and he was treated like a consultant. Another advantage for me was that, having the same background as him, he knew exactly my needs, ensuring that I had a lot of operative experience.

Prior to leaving Nigeria, I had had experience in common surgical procedures. I had carried out operations such as appendicectomies, laparotomies, bowel resections and anastomoses, inguinal hernia repairs and removals of lumps and bumps. Simon advised me that in order to learn how to do things properly, I had to pretend that I had never done them before. Unless I adopted that strategy, my brain would refuse to accept and process new information, and I would continue to do things in my former ways and become untrainable. Mr Roberts had worked in Ghana before, and he was an external examiner in one of Ghanaian medical colleges. Although he hadn't worked in Nigeria before, he informed me that he trained with many respectable Nigerian surgeons that I knew. So working with my consultant and my Ghanaian registrar, I couldn't ask for anything more. I felt so relaxed but disciplined, as it provided me with an excellent learning environment.

During my time at the small hospital, which was never particularly busy, I was provided with a two-bedroom flat that I shared with Rathood Bathul, a doctor from Malagasy. He was a trainee in internal medicine. Rathood was a great cook. He taught me that the best way to cook rice was to cook it on a low heat and keep the pot covered. Rathood, Waseem and I often drove to Sunderland to buy fresh fish. We would gather in his house after his wife had prepared the meal.

The staff club was situated close to the Accident and Emergency department, and we often stayed there, listening to music or playing games, when we were on call. Being close to Newcastle and Durham gave us the opportunity to have a good social life. We also had a hospital football team in which I was a midfielder. In one of our several matches, we drew with the town team. So despite being a small town, I was never short of things to do.

I was enjoying this placement, but, of course, that was soon to change. During one of my on-calls, I admitted a twenty-eight-year-old woman with severe abdominal pain and vomiting. After assessing her, I made a diagnosis of acute appendicitis. My registrar reassessed her and agreed with my diagnosis. He authorised me to take her to theatre that night to remove her appendix. When I opened her up, I found the appendix was not inflamed, but a cyst on her right ovary had twisted. I removed the twisted cyst. I also removed the appendix to prevent future appendicitis. The patient made a good recovery from the operation. Mr Roberts saw the woman on the fifth post-operative day on his end of the week ward rounds, as was his practice.

"You had a small cyst on your right ovary, which was bleeding, what we call haemorrhagic cyst," he explained to the woman. "The surgeon has fixed it, and you are doing great," he said. "Oh, by the way, he also took your appendix. So no chance for appendicitis in the future," he added.

"Thank you very much," she said. "I feel great."

Mr Roberts discharged her with the plan to review her at the outpatient department in six weeks' time. I, too, was pleased with the outcome of the operation. She thanked me once more, as we moved to the next patient.

Three weeks later on a Saturday morning, I received a letter from a solicitor. I had had a busy day and night on Friday, so I didn't get the chance to check my mail. I simply left it on my table, hoping to read it in the morning. I had a late breakfast, as I woke up late. Most of the letters were rubbish: drug representatives advising new medications and devices, magazines and invitations. The only important letter was the particular one in a white envelope with a first-class stamp on it. I had made a large portion of scrambled eggs, bran flakes and a jug of strong Yorkshire tea. And as I gobbled the sandwiched fried egg in moderately toasted, sliced, brown bread, I read my letters one by one, with my music booming.

You have removed my client's ovaries without her consent. You have rendered a young promising woman menopausal. She will be suing you for medical negligence, the letter from the solicitors stated.

Of course, I remembered the woman. She was the only person that I had operated on in that situation. My appetite disappeared like vapour. I blinked several times, as I struggled to focus on the one-page letter from the patient's solicitors. I felt like my world had collapsed on my head. My heart raced as I read the letter again. Someone once warned me, when I told him that I was going to Great Britain for my surgical training, that the people sued their doctors when they made a mistake. But I didn't think I had done anything wrong. If I hadn't done the right thing, Mr Roberts would have pointed it out and corrected me. And of course, my registrar knew about the case and my plan of management. I had done what I did the way most British surgeons would have done it. I couldn't believe that a woman whose life I had saved with an uncomplicated operation, had decided to sue me. Back home, if I did such an operation, the patient would thank me and give me gifts. I felt saddened and unvalued. Could I have done things differently? I wondered.

I couldn't cope on my own, the way I felt. I needed to talk to someone before my head exploded. The first person that came to my mind was Simon, my registrar. Trouble was, he rarely stayed at home on weekends. He tended to go away with his family. And as expected, there was no answer when I knocked at his door. I returned to my room, disappointed and dejected, resigned to my fate and destiny.

I wanted the weekend to pass, but it snailed on, seemingly unending. At last, time moved me to the anticipated Monday. It was cold, wet and windy, but it was a day I had desperately looked forward to. I must catch Mr Roberts before he started his ward round. Having worked for him for over four months, I knew his routine exactly. He would first go to his office, where he would do some paperwork on a cup of coffee. He would then have a short meeting with his secretary when she arrived, before joining the rest of us on the ward. Simon would normally do a case note ward round before the consultant round. We would sort out all the nurses' queries and ensure that all test results were made available for the consultant. I had left my room earlier than usual to ensure that I caught Mr Roberts. I waited in front of his office, and within twenty minutes, he arrived, carrying his briefcase in his left hand and an umbrella in his right hand.

"Good morning, Mr Roberts," I greeted.

"Morning," he said. "Is everything alright?" he asked. "You look like you've just escaped a lion's chase."

"I am in big trouble," I spat. I felt like I had a ticking bomb in my head, ready to explode.

"Oh, come in with me." He patted me on the shoulder as he pushed his office door. "Now tell me what is it that makes you look like you're in the boxing ring with the great Muhammad Ali?" he urged me, as he directed me to a chair by his desk.

"I received this on Saturday," I said, as I handed him the solicitor's letter.

Mr Roberts adjusted his glasses as he settled to read the letter. He put on a sarcastic smile after he has finished reading it and placed the letter on the table.

"Rubbish!" he said, and got up.

I scratched my head and waited for him to say more, as he plugged in the kettle and switched it on.

"Are you the consultant?" he asked, when he returned to his seat.

"No," I replied.

"Did you remove her ovaries?" he asked.

"No," I replied.

"Did she sign a consent form?" he asked.

Just then there was a knock on the door. That was Simon. He had come to check on Mr Roberts, as they had expected him to come to the ward.

"Good morning," Simon greeted.

"Morning," Mr Roberts returned the greeting. "See this?" he said, as he handed the letter to Simon.

"What?" Simon screamed. "I can't believe this," he said. Then he ran his finger under a line that read: *My client has been condemned to premature menopause.*

"How ridiculous!" Simon laughed.

I, too, couldn't help laughing. I had not seen the funny side of the letter until then. I had focused my attention on the intent to sue me. The lawyer must be absolutely lacking in medical knowledge or ill-informed. Even if the woman had had both her ovaries removed, she would not be menopausal that soon. At least, I wouldn't expect her to start having symptoms so soon. No wonder, Mr Roberts trivialised it.

"Right, leave it in my hands," Mr Roberts reassured me.

At that time, his secretary had arrived, and he dictated a letter for her secretary to type. It was a short letter. He informed the solicitors that we had not removed his client's ovary. She had had a cyst on her ovary, which had burst and was bleeding. Only the cyst was removed. Her ovaries remained intact. Histology had confirmed a ruptured theca lutein cyst, which was bleeding. He advised that if the client was unwell, the sensible thing for her to do was to first see her GP for a check-up and advice, and not rush to a solicitor. The solicitor should inform us if they still wanted to pursue the case, so we could inform the Medical Defence Union.

Two weeks later, I was in the outpatient department. Mr Roberts breezed into my consulting room. He threw an A4 letter in front of me.

"Something for you," he said, smiling.

I picked up the quarter-of-a-page letter and raised a questioning fold on my brow. My frown disappeared as my eyes settled on the letter heading. It gave me a déjà vu effect, as the letter heading registered its familiarity in my brain. That was the patient's solicitor. What is it this time? I wondered. Then I read: "My client has decided not to proceed. We have therefore closed the case."

"Hmmm!" I heaved a sigh of relief.

"There you go," Mr Roberts said and went back to his consulting room.

Two weeks later, I had just had my lunch. I decided to go to Mr Roberts' office to do some discharge summaries and other things.

"I was about to bleep you," Mr Roberts' secretary said as I stepped into the office.

"Oh!" I raised a questioning eyebrow.

"Yes, your friend is coming to see Mr Roberts this afternoon. He asked me to inform you so you could be present."

"My friend?" I wondered.

"Michelle Bould, the girl who wanted to sue you," she smiled.

"But," I scratched my nose. "I thought Mr Roberts said it was all over."

"Yes, it's all over, but she has some explaining to do. Mr Roberts wants to find out why she has taken action."

"I see," I sighed.

Michelle Bould arrived half an hour later. The secretary phoned Mr Roberts, informing him of Michelle's arrival. Mr Roberts asked his secretary to send me in first. He explained to me that he had sent for the patient, as he believed somebody must have instigated her action. Hopefully, he would get to the bottom of it, and she would offer an apology.

"She must apologise to you," Mr Roberts' secretary said.

"Me?" I wondered.

"You, of course," she confirmed. "She hasn't treated you with respect, has she?"

"It doesn't matter to me," I replied. "I'm glad it's all over."

Shortly afterwards, Mr Roberts' secretary ushered her into the office. She came with her mother. Her face glowed, and she trembled as Mr

Roberts directed her and her mother to their seats. Her eyes caught mine briefly. She grinned shyly. I grinned back. There was no need for formal introductions. Michelle knew all of us, and Mr Roberts' secretary had already told Michelle's mother who we were.

I didn't know what to think of Michelle. I was angry and disappointed, but I tried not to let it show on my face. I wouldn't say anything unless Mr Roberts asked me or Michelle or her mother. One thing that I hoped would gladden my heart was if we could get to the bottom of the issue – to know why Michelle, who had thanked us every day whilst on the ward for saving her life and giving her a neat scar, had decided to turn against me with a threat of legal action.

Mr Roberts welcomed them and urged them to relax and not to feel intimidated and expressed his concerns about the decision that Michelle had made. Of course, she had dropped the case, but he felt it was prudent to find out what really happened and if there was any lesson to be learnt from it.

Michelle informed Mr Roberts that on that day, when she was discharged, Mr Roberts informed her that they had removed something from her ovary. She had no idea what that thing was, and she didn't know what to expect. She wanted to ask, but she didn't have the courage. After the doctors had left the ward, a nurse came to her. She asked if she understood what the doctors had said. She told the nurse that she didn't. She explained that they said that they had removed her ovaries and asked the nurse what would happen to her now. The nurse told her that since she no longer had her ovaries, she would go into menopause. And when she asked her the symptoms of menopause, she told her that it would cause her to have hot flushes, sweat and itch around her scar.

When she got home, she started feeling hot and her wound itched. She had headaches, and she couldn't sleep. She felt that the doctors had lied to her. When she mentioned it to one of her mates, she called it negligence and advised her to see a solicitor. That was why she contacted the solicitors. Michelle apologised, and she truly meant it. She handed a bag and said, "Please have this as a token of my appreciation."

It was the biggest bottle of Scotch whisky I had ever seen.

"This is yours," Mr Roberts said to me. "You deserve it."

"No, Mr Roberts," I protested.

"You're the right person to have it," Mr Roberts insisted. "You certainly deserve it."

Michelle, her mother and Mr Roberts' secretary nodded encouragingly.

This was a learning experience for me. I had focused on Michelle's action, and her seemingly ingratitude had clouded my insight. I had focused on the anger and disappointment, but after this meeting, I had learnt an important ingredient to any relationship – communication. It is the key to any successful relationship, whether in marriage, work or even a football team. To win as a team, you must have a good communication and cooperation with your team mates. The role of communication is particularly great in a doctor-patient relationship. This understanding remained an ingredient throughout my medical career. And when Mr Roberts asked me, "What have you learnt from this incident?" I didn't have to think long to reply. "The importance of good communication."

At the end of my posting in Bishop Auckland, I had completed the minimum requirement in General Surgery for part two of my surgical fellowship. I still needed Accident and Emergency experience and further specialty training, so I turned down the offer to stay on. I also turned down the offer of a six-month posting in Accident and Emergency. I wanted a Trauma posting, which encompassed Orthopaedics, rather than a stand-alone Accident and Emergency. I didn't want to be up all night attending to drunken teenagers or babies with coughs and colds. Those were not part of my surgical training. I would be better off channelling my time and energy to what was relevant. I had learnt that in life you don't have to accept what you don't want. It's better to reject an unwanted offer. That would be an opportunity for someone else to grab and for me to look for an open door elsewhere. Even though I loved Bishop Auckland, and I had made friends, I knew I had to move on. So I updated my CV, and with the help of Mr Roberts' secretary, I had several copies ready for the all-important job hunt.

Within a week of posting my applications, I had four shortlists and invitations for interviews. I declined two of the invitations, as the rotation included a posting that I had done before, and I didn't need to repeat it for the sake of my qualifying examinations. One of the interviews was in Devon, in a hospital more than six hours' drive from County Durham.

Despite its distance, I found it to be the most relevant rotation, as it included Orthopaedics and Trauma, not just Accident and Emergency. So I decided to go for it, with the determination to accept the job if I was successful at the interview.

"Best part of the country," Mr Roberts said, when I informed him about the interview. "Go for it, son," he encouraged.

With Mr Roberts' approval and encouragement, I put my hope and energy into the upcoming interview at the Devon hospital. Although I liked the potential job in Devon, I tried not to let it stress me. I still had five more interviews waiting, some of which were even nearby. So I attended relaxed, hoping to get the job, but I wasn't having palpitations over it.

It was on a hot sunny afternoon. Just as Mr Roberts had said, it was a beautiful place, and the people were friendly. I wanted to be in this place. The seaside brought nostalgia: memories of my early life. And from the 'I don't care' feelings, I now became desperate to get the job, and somehow, I believed the job was meant for me, and I would get it. So whilst the other six candidates were waiting anxiously, I sneaked into the toilet, dropped to my knees and prayed.

"God, I need this job. Make it mine if it is your plan."

They were all very experienced doctors. Most of them had orthopaedic experience. One particular candidate had done three years in Orthopaedics, and we were all resigned to him getting the job. How could I, with no orthopaedic experience, get the job? No chance, I thought. But I had prayed about it, so, with confidence, I marched into the interview room when they called candidate number seven. Although I had waited a long time to be summoned, I didn't have to wait half as long to be called back into the room and informed that I had got the job.

Chapter Seventeen
LIFE IN NORTH DEVON

Do not let what you cannot do interfere with what you can do.
John Wooden

By the end of my posting in North Devon Hospital, I would have completed my requirements to sit the final surgical examination, the FRCS. I was now married and expecting our first baby.

Unlike in my previous jobs, I now had to establish a good work-job balance. I had a busy job, but I recognised the fact that my pregnant wife also deserved to have my attention.

The baby was due close to the date of my examination. With the arrival of the baby, I knew I wouldn't have enough time to study. We hadn't made close friends, and I would have to give as much time as possible to help my wife attend to the baby. So I started my preparations early in the job.

The posting was just right for me. It provided not only experience in general surgery, but also in vascular surgery, urology, gastroenterology, trauma and orthopaedics. My registrar was absolutely brilliant. An Egyptian of about my age, Martin Loka had bagged the fellowships of the English, Edinburgh, Glasgow and Irish Colleges of Surgeons. Yet he was humble about his achievements. Unlike other registrars, he wasn't insistent on being called 'Mr' instead of 'Dr', something that would upset other surgeons. He not only had a brain for surgery, but gifted hands to complement it. Martin was a God-sent surgeon to my life. He was worthy of my emulation.

"Listen, don't let anyone frighten you about the FRCS Examination," he advised me, when I told him about all the things that people had told me. "I will show you my own approach to the exams," he further advised. "Maybe it will work for you; it worked for me."

I smiled, thinking if he had passed the examinations of all the colleges of surgeons, his approach must be right. And I was determined to open my eyes, tune my ears to the right frequency and charge my body with all the strength, while my brain processed Mr Loka's approaches to passing the FRCS.

I met Eloka Menakaya, who was a registrar in Obstetrics and Gynaecology at the North Devon Hospital. I didn't know him in Nigeria, but we had a lot of common interests and common history, so it didn't take us long to become close friends. Although married, his family hadn't joined him, so we spent time together, when not on call, watching football, going to the cinema or playing table tennis at the staff club.

The hospital was situated on an elevation about three miles on the outskirts of town, and I was the only licensed driver. Although there were bus services between the hospital and the town centre, I often had to drive my heavily pregnant wife to town whenever she needed to buy things. She later made friends with other doctors' wives. Much later, Eloka's wife, with their two-year-old son, joined. Having Nkiru Menakaya with her son around was a good thing. My wife had someone who understood her culture. Her son saw our son as a younger brother. Both families jelled together. My wife and Eloka's wife often went for shopping together, and I was no longer concerned about leaving my wife with the baby behind when on call. I also had more spare time for private studies in preparation for my examination.

We attended the local Baptist Church. The moderate size church, situated in a conspicuous location near the town centre, was a convenient place to worship, and we met and made friends with so many Christians there. We were particularly close to the Smith family. Jonathan and Beverly Smith lived in a four-bedroom house in a quiet part of Barnstaple. They had a son and two teenage daughters. We often had Sunday dinners with them, and we were in the same cell group that met every Wednesday evening. An ex-oil engineer, Jonathan had worked in Southern Nigeria, and we had a lot of shared history. Though naturally a quiet man, he was always excited, and always had something nice to say about Nigeria. He made me proud of my country of birth whenever we talked about Africa.

Bev was a teacher. She had a great interest in art and interior design, and she was a great cook, sharing the same interests as my wife. The church was full of God's presence, and I always looked forward to the Sunday services. My family and the Menakayas always went to church together, and one gave the other a lift to church when either Eloka or I was on call on Sunday. In church, Bev always took away our son to give my wife some breathing space to worship without the burden of tending to a baby. Our son rarely needed his nappy changing in the church, and he was always pleasant. So many mothers were eager to have him with them, and we were happy for them to pass him from hand to hand. The presence of these wonderful people made what would have been an isolated life so inclusive, warm and beautiful. We will never forget them in our life journey.

The on-call rotas were organised on a team basis.

Consequently, I was always on call with Martin. We strictly followed the traditional approach to care. That way, the most junior member of the medical team, that is, the house officer, saw the patient first. I then did my own assessment and drew up management plans before the registrar reviewed the patient. That gave my registrar the opportunity to ask me questions, the FRCS-style. He conducted vivas and clinicals as though I was in the examination room, and he encouraged me to take things that way.

At first, I found it embarrassing to make mistakes in the presence of my junior colleagues and patients, but Martin practised in such a professional way that it never bothered me anymore, and making mistakes was never viewed by them as a failure. I remained respectable.

The consultant was aware that I was in the final stage of my training, and he too ensured that I not only had hands-on experience, but also drilled me whenever the opportunity arose on the wards, outpatient departments, Accident and Emergency, and the operating theatres.

My fixed-term contract came to an end when our baby was two months old. Although I was eligible to sit the final FRCS exam, I decided to wait until my next job.

Applying for jobs was no longer a problem. I had mastered how to write a British-style CV, and I now had a number of willing referees. So in the last six weeks of my posting, I circulated a good number of my CVs for both registrar and SHO posts.

I was shortlisted for many posts. I attended an interview in Lancashire, but I was turned down on the basis that I was too experienced for an SHO job. I attended another interview in Leicester and was advised that I wasn't experienced enough. I attended several other interviews with mixed feedback: either too experienced, not experienced enough or unlucky. I didn't know what to do. When I brought this up with Martin, he advised me not to panic.

"As you become more experienced, jobs become more difficult," he said. "Just keep on pushing and don't change what you are. You will find the job meant for you."

I sent out another batch of CVs. I had a six-week-old baby at this point, and it seemed there was no hope of a job after the current one. I was desperate, but I was finally shortlisted for an interview in the South Wales surgical registrar rotation. It was my dream job, as it met all my expectations. And I believed I was suitable for it. I woke up in the night prior to the interview. As I turned in bed, I looked at my wife, who was fast asleep after the daunting task of breastfeeding and nappy changes. I watched my baby sleeping peacefully in his cot. It dawned on me then that I would soon be out of job. I sneaked out of the room into the spare room. Then I dropped to my knees and cried to God. I told Him how desperate I was, not only to complete my surgical training but, of course, to provide for my young family.

It was a dry and sunny day in July. I was the first candidate to arrive at the South Wales interview. At first, it seemed like I was the only candidate. Then fifteen minutes before the interview, other candidates turned up one by one, to fill the vacant four seats. They all seemed to know one another, apart from one female doctor, who took her seat next to me, after exchanging greetings with me. As the interviewers walked through the reception into the interview room, their body language showed the obvious familiarity with the other candidates. But I didn't allow that to bother me.

It was my first interview for a registrar post. All my previous interviews had been for the SHO posts. So I wasn't expecting things to be easy. I had practiced interview techniques with my registrar and consultant, and I vowed to give it my best shot.

I was the first candidate to be called. The atmosphere was friendly, with each interviewer nodding and smiling, as they highlighted interesting bullet points in my CV. I was relaxed. I had been asked almost all the questions before in previous interviews and at the mock interviews that my registrar had given me, and I came out of the interview room smiling, in the hope that I had got the job. But with five more candidates remaining, it was a long wait for me. At last, the last candidate had his turn. But soon after he came out, he was called back into the room. Having had so many interviews, I had learnt that the candidate who got called back after an interview was the one that got the job. My eyes welled up in utter disappointment. At first, I wanted to leave straightaway in anger, but I wanted to know why I was unsuccessful, so I could learn from it. Then they called in another candidate who also came out smiling, as he was successful. Until then, I hadn't realised that there was more than one post. Then they called the third candidate in. He too was given a job, and he emerged with victorious smiles. Finally, they called me in.

"You are a very strong contender, but the interview has been very competitive," the chairman said. "Unfortunately, we are unable to offer you the registrar post, but there is an SHO post coming up," he informed me. "We are happy to offer that to you without the need for another interview."

This was a big shock to me. I had not anticipated this level of discrimination in such a civilised country. Of course, I wasn't expecting to get every job that I applied for, but how else could I explain my rejection when a job was offered to someone less qualified than me? Wouldn't it have been fair if the SHO post was offered to the least experienced candidate? I had no choice but to accept the SHO post since I could not afford to be out of job with me now having my family.

"Thank you," I said.

They all put on questioning smiles. I guessed they wondered what I meant. How could I thank them when they had just rejected me for a job that I was one of the most, if not the most, qualified candidates for? From talking to candidates whilst we were waiting, I found out that only one candidate had about ten months of surgical experience. I had two years' experience in the UK, and at least four back home. And having passed the part I of the surgical fellowship, I was qualified for a registrar post. Nevertheless, I accepted the SHO post.

"Don't you worry that it's an SHO post," the professor advised. "We will ensure that you have no less experience than the registrars."

I left the interview room after confirming my acceptance of the offer, determined to make the best of it.

Chapter Eighteen
SURGICAL TRAINEE IN WALES

*If you believe in what you are doing, then let nothing hold you up
in your work.
Much of the best work of the world has been done against
seeming impossibilities.
The thing is to get the work done.*
Dale Carnegie

The first lap of my rotation was in Newport, where married accommodation was made ready for us – a two-bedroom flat among the blocks of flats on the hospital grounds, a stone's throw from the academic building. Typical hospital staff residence, it consisted of blocks of flats put together. Unlike the hospital in Barnstaple, Gwent Hospital was located within walking distance to the town centre. This was one of the exciting things about our relocation. My wife could go shopping without relying on me to drive.

Changing jobs and moving from town to town wasn't much of a problem for me when it was just my wife and me. Now married with a few-weeks-old baby, we had a lot of stuff to pack. We filled our Ford Fiesta to the brim, so much so that we had to put our baby in his cot on the load, strapped securely to the collapsed rear seat.

As I drove the over-packed coupe on the winding, narrow Barnstaple-Exeter road with the wind buzzing, I had to be fully alert, with all my reflexes sharpened. On arrival, after off-loading the car, I decided to clean it whilst my wife arranged the kitchen as she preferred. As I looked across the road, I couldn't believe what I saw. My old friend, Akonam Onuzo, emerged from the library, holding a book and a folder. We flew to each other and hugged. I hadn't seen him since the medical school days. Hugging him reminded me of the last time we hugged, but then it was a hug and the believer's prayer, when he made unsuccessful attempts to persuade me to accept the Lord into my life. I say 'unsuccessful' because although I agreed to accept the Lord and attended the Chapel of Resurrection, I wasn't prepared to change my lifestyle. I rejected the Lord as my personal Saviour, preferring the palm wine drinkers' gyration, student politics and Saturday nights clubbing. So Akonam and I drifted apart, and we were never close to each other again till we left the medical school. And now, we were back as friends in the new world as believers. His wife, Maruwa, had been my classmate in medical school. We both started as prelim students in Ibadan.

The Onuzos lived in a similar apartment, two blocks from ours. I was glad that Maruwa and my wife got on well. Akonam loved *Moinmoin*, and my wife was a specialist in making it. She often made a large quantity for him, which he stored in his freezer. Maruwa loved our son. My wife often left him with her. This was a good thing, as it gave her time to herself.

The Onuzos introduced us to the local Pentecostal Church. The medium-sized church was a fifteen-minute drive from our residence. Here, we made new friends. It was good to be in the community of these good people. We met a particular delightful family from Antigua. Ben and Denise Johnsons loved us. And within weeks, it was as if we had known one another for years. Denise often babysat for our son when my wife and I were at work or had a night out.

My job was exactly as Professor Bryan had promised me. My registrar, Tony Cummins was one of those appointed at the interview that I attended. He was a tall man with an athletic figure with a strong Welsh accent. He knew, of course, that I was interviewed for the same job and that often caused him a great deal of discomfort and he lacked confidence whenever we operated together. I tried to make him relax by talking less when assisting him, but rather than benefit from my experience he often preferred having the house officer to assist him. Although I was on the SHO on-call rota, I did more than the SHOs. Unlike my previous job, we were not strictly on call as a team. So sometimes, I was with other consultants and different junior doctors. Unlike Tony, most of the registrars recognised my experience and often accepted my offer of assistance when they had difficult cases. But, like Tony, some of them felt too big to ask for my assistance. They would call the consultant in the middle of the night in panic. I shook my head when the consultant flicked out an appendix with his finger after the registrar called to tell him that he couldn't find it. With time, other consultants realised that I was more experienced than many of the registrars, and they allowed me to do more procedures on my own.

I eventually applied to attempt the final surgical examination. Working in the professorial unit, and having had several tutorials with my former registrar, Mr Loka, I felt I was ready and applied for study leave to sit it in London. One Thursday, I had just seen my last patient in the outpatient clinic. I was about to leave when my phone rang. At first, I ignored it, thinking the call must have been meant for the receptionist from patients wanting to book their appointments. I knew it wasn't from my wife. She wouldn't call me at work. Besides, she would normally call me through the switchboard, and the number on the phone wasn't our house number. After persistent ringing, I picked it up.

"I just want to let you know that your study leave has not been approved," the medical personnel officer informed me.

"But I have already paid for the exam," I said.

"Well, you should have first checked that your study leave was approved before paying," she said without any empathy.

"I have prepared for this exam," I told her, "and as I said, I have paid for it."

"If all the doctors were on study leave, who would be left to run the service?" she asked.

The personnel manager informed me that all the six registrars had applied for study leave, and they had all been granted. Therefore, there was no way she could approve mine. When she hung up, I felt dizzy. I didn't know what to do. I resigned myself to the fact that perhaps it wasn't the right time for me, but I couldn't understand why my study leave should be turned down when we were all taking the same examination, and I was responsible for my own finances. And as far as I knew, I applied for study leave earlier than all of them.

I got home that afternoon, completely dejected. When I broke the news to my wife, she patted me on my back and encouraged me that there would be a breakthrough. Our son was asleep then. We knelt down in the sitting room and prayed to God for help.

"Have you told your consultant about it?" my wife asked me after our prayer.

"No," I replied.

"Why not?" she narrowed her eyes.

"I don't know," I replied. "I guess they are all the same. They all treat people of our kind like we are nothing. No need to tell him since I know what he will say."

The injustice at the interview was still fresh in my mind. Had I been appointed as a registrar the personnel manager would not have treated me the way she had done. Surely, my consultant was aware of the way they had discriminated against me. So, I reasoned he, too, would have racial bias even though since I joined his team, he had shown me nothing but love and respect.

"How can you be so sure?" she asked.

I scratched my head.

"Was he not the one who told you that you were a fellowship material?" she wondered.

I nodded.

"I think the professor genuinely likes you. I don't think he is one of those who don't like our kind," she encouraged. "He may be able to put pressure on the personnel officer to grant your study leave."

"And if he doesn't?"

"Come back and play with your son," she said candidly.

I went to the library to collect some papers that I had asked the librarian to search for me. As I trekked to the library, I reflected on what my wife had said. She was right. Professor Bryan took a great deal of interest in me. He regretted that I hadn't got the registrar position, and since I joined his firm, he often remarked that I was better than most of the registrars. This was humbling, and I had no doubt that he was honest. I had previously informed him that I was planning to sit the fellowship examination, and he had encouraged me to do so as soon as possible. So I made up my mind to let him know about the situation.

Monday was our all-day theatre day. Normally, the consultant wouldn't turn up early in the morning. He would put the less complex procedures that needed no consultant input at the beginning of the list. I started the list with my registrar, as usual. But the theatre was as quiet as a graveyard. Normally, I sang and whistled whilst operating. All the theatre staff enjoyed being in the theatre with me. Even Professor Bryan himself liked that. But when the professor arrived, there was no singing or whistling. I had just finished a case. I sat in the coffee room, waiting for the next one to be anaesthetised. I was still sat in the coffee room when Professor Bryan arrived. He wondered why I was sitting on my own.

"What is the matter with my African friend?" he asked. "Has your wife dumped you? What's making you look like someone waiting for his sentencing?"

"I have already received my sentence," I said.

"That sounds serious," he said with concern. "Shall we talk about it?"

Professor Bryan beckoned, and I followed him to his office. He directed me to one of the seats, and after pouring a cup of coffee for me and himself, he sat in the low chair close to me.

"Right, who has upset you?" he asked.

"They have advised me to postpone my exam to allow the registrars to do theirs first," I said, as a matter of fact.

"Who told you that?" His eyes widened.

I told the professor the conversation that I had had with the personnel officer. And as they haven't approved my study leave, I planned to postpone the exam.

"She told me that all the registrars are taking the exam and she has approved their study leave," I informed him. "And she advised that there would be no doctor to run the service if she approved mine."

"Rubbish!" he exclaimed. "You are more ready for the exam than any of them."

Professor Bryan rang the personnel officer.

"In that case, he will use his annual leave. I have approved that for him. If you don't have enough doctors to run the service, then you've got to find locums," Professor Bryan said, after a heated argument.

"Thank you, Prof. Thank you very much. I promise I will not disappoint you," I reassured him.

Professor Bryan brought back my hope. It was like light had returned to my life. I gulped down my coffee and returned to the theatre. I was back to my usual self, singing, whistling and entertaining my theatre colleagues, to make the otherwise stressful theatre atmosphere less stressful.

That was just over two months before the exam, and with Professor Bryan's approval of my annual leave, no one could stop me. The exam was certain, the date for the exam was unchangeable, and so I resumed my preparation in earnest. Living close to the library was beneficial. I did a lot of my study there whenever my wife was out with our baby or when other mothers visited. I tried to spend as much time as possible with my wife and our baby. Fortunately, the baby was good at night. He never gave us any problems, always a pleasant baby. So I could do my reading then. My wife was supportive towards my exam. She often helped me with mock vivas. She did this by reading out the questions that I had written on sheets of paper. She wasn't a doctor, so she didn't know if I gave the right answers. But as an intelligent person whom I highly regarded, she monitored my confidence, body language and timekeeping. She could also spot when she thought the answer I gave was either vague or incorrect from the way I had presented it. And she often took away our baby to enable me concentrate on my reading. She wasn't always successful at this, as our son often toddled to the study and climbed on my lap as I studied. He saw me as his playmate, and I tried to spend as much time as possible with him.

Three weeks to the exam, my enthusiasm disappeared, and I completely lost my confidence. I had been studying for nearly two years and had looked forward to the great day. I had thought that I should pass the exam at the first sitting. Senior colleagues had felt that way. Even my professor expected me to sail through. Still, I no longer believed in myself. In life, one tends to see the difficulty rather than the goal. Negativity often appeals to our emotions more than positivity, and this was how I was feeling. I couldn't read. I stopped the mock vivas. Nothing made sense to me anymore. My wife tried all she could to encourage me, but I fixed my thoughts on the negative advice and remarks that I had received from colleagues in the past. I had been told that the college had a predetermined number of passes. Local graduates had easy rides. They were made to take the passes. The few remaining passes were shared among the foreign graduates. One particular colleague had warned me not to waste my money applying to the English college.

"You have no chance," he had said, "as they don't like people of our kind."

These were the negative thoughts that agitated my mind all the time, depriving me of my sleep, and took my substance and confidence away.

I forgot to encourage myself with the achievements of the likes of Mr Loka, my former registrar, who had passed the fellowship exams of all the royal colleges. He was an African like me. My former Ghanaian registrar was an English fellow. My professor often referred to me as a registrar material and expected me to pass the exam. Yet, the negative thoughts pushed these motivational remarks and instances into the remotest part of my mind. I lost my appetite, I lost sleep, and I began to see playing with our son as a burden. My head pounded. In the morning of the Friday before the exam, I felt like I could no longer cope with the way I felt. I told my wife that I was going to cancel the examination. It was too late to postpone it.

"Why?" my wife asked with empathy.

"Well, as you know, I have not been studying lately." I gave an excuse. "I don't think I have any chance of passing."

"And what happens if you fail the exam?" she asked.

"Well, I will lose my money," I replied. "I guess I can try other colleges."

"Are you listening to yourself?" She stood up and faced me. "You will lose your money if you fail!"

"Yes," I confirmed.

"Will you have your money back if you fail to show up for the exam?" she asked.

"No," I replied.

"So you will lose your money if you fail. But they won't refund you if you cancel. So either way, you will lose your money."

I scratched my head.

"And what will you say to Professor Bryan?" she asked.

"Don't know," I murmured.

After clearing her throat, she continued, "Oh, he would pat you on the back and tell you he is proud of you, wouldn't he? And your colleagues and I would congratulate you, wouldn't we? And the personnel officer will be vindicated that she thought you wouldn't pass the exam. And that was why she didn't approve your study leave."

What my wife said hit me like a bullet. She could be blunt sometimes. I knew she always said it as it was. She wouldn't say something just because that was what you wanted to hear. I knew, of course, that I could trust her advice. After all, she was the closest person to my heart, and she wanted the best for me. Still, I made a final attempt to justify my intention.

"You see, if I fail the exam, it will knock down my confidence and affect my future attempts," I argued.

"In other words, you are afraid of failure."

"No. I'm not," I said.

"It is pride then, isn't it? Arrogance?" She stared into my eyes. "Oh, I see, you don't want to lose your place as the most brilliant person on planet earth!"

"Don't be ridiculous," I said. "It's nothing of the kind. It's just that I have not studied in the past few weeks."

"But you had studied until then," she encouraged.

The room went silent. I knew my wife had made good points. She had won the argument. I could see her point, and she was right.

"Remember, you told me that one of your consultants sat the exam six times," she reminded me.

I nodded.

"So, if your consultant sat the exam six times and became an eminent professor of surgery, what does it matter if you sit the exam once, twice, thrice, four times, five times, six times or even twelve times?" she reasoned. "My dear, the number of attempts you make doesn't matter, as long as you pass."

After the discussion, we had our morning devotion. Our son was up by then and had toddled to me, climbing onto his usual place of comfort – my lap. He always kept quiet during prayers, but he said the loudest 'Amen' at the end.

We shared the biblical story of Caleb and fellow Israelites as recorded in Numbers chapter thirteen. Moses sent twelve men, including Caleb and Joshua, to explore the land of Canaan, the land that God had promised to give to the Israelites. After exploring the land for forty days, the men returned. They reported to Moses and their fellow Israelites that the land was bountiful, but they wouldn't be able to acquire it because the people living there were too strong. "But the people living there are powerful, and their towns are large and fortified. We even saw giants there, the descendants of Anak!" Numbers 13: 28 NLT. Caleb was optimistic. "Let's go at once to take the land," he said. "We can certainly conquer it!" Numbers 13: 30. Other Israelites focused on the obstacles but Caleb focused on the solution.

We linked this story to that of David and Goliath as recorded in the first book of Samuel, chapter seventeen. Goliath was a giant Philistine. No one could match his physical strength among the Israelites, even when he despised the Almighty God. A young shepherd named David stood up to Goliath, and by the grace of God, he slew him.

"Well, think about what we have discussed. Whatever is your decision, I am here to support you," my wife said as she left for the kitchen to prepare our breakfast.

We had just finished our breakfast when the phone rang. I wondered if it was the personnel officer wanting to inform me that I should cancel my annual leave. She had already told me that Professor Bryan had granted my leave in spite of her protesting that all the middle-grade doctors had taken their study leaves. Yet she had pestered me a number of times to take my annual leave when the other doctors returned from their examination. And when I had reminded her that I, too, was taking the same examination, she had replied, "Wait till you are a registrar." I had tried to explain the requirements for the fellowship examination, but I couldn't get through to her. I couldn't face another conversation with her, so I asked my wife to answer, as I thought I might say something that I would regret.

"Austin," she said, with a smile, as she handed me the handset.

Austin Amaechi was two years ahead of me in medical school. We met again in Edinburgh. I was about to leave Scotland when he arrived. We had kept in contact since then. He was working at Carmarthen in South Wales. He had previously informed me that he, too, had registered to take the exam.

"I was wondering if we could travel together to London on Sunday," Austin requested.

"Yes, of course," I replied without any hesitation.

After hanging up, it struck me that I hadn't thought of the fact that I was having second thoughts about the examination. Now, the thought of my friend coming lifted my spirit. My headache disappeared. I felt as though my powerhouse had been infused. My thinking became clearer. I was back in my exam mood.

When my wife returned and saw me smiling again, she encouraged me. "You will be fine."

Although I was in a better frame of mind and exam mood, I felt that there was no way I could cover every exam topic. Of course, I had read so many of the subjects and books several times, performed many of the common operations, assisted at those that I hadn't undertaken on my own and rotated through all the major surgical specialties. Nevertheless, I admitted that it was a tough exam with a high failure rate, and I hadn't studied in the previous few weeks. That challenged my confidence. I knew I couldn't cover everything that I had earmarked to revise. So, I embarked on a study strategy that I dubbed 'qualitative study'. I revised common surgical conditions: everything about them, including the symptoms and signs, clinical assessment, investigative modalities, surgical principles and management. I cast my mind back to those patients that were on the surgical wards: what their conditions were and the procedures that they had undergone. I reflected over patients who had suffered complications, and how those complications had been dealt with. I recalled that we had a patient with spinal tuberculosis in my previous job and one with sickle cell crisis during my posting in Trauma and Orthopaedics. I realised that these cases were rare in the UK. However, I decided to study the role of surgery in these tropical conditions, among the few rare conditions that I studied.

Austin arrived as planned. He parked his car beside ours on our drive, and we travelled to London together. There were many candidates for the exam on the coach, so there was no embarrassment as we all discussed in our own groups, like primary school pupils. It was off-peak time, so passengers who couldn't stand our noisy coach moved into other coaches. Austin and I sat together. We did our own mock vivas. Austin was working in Orthopaedics. I last did Orthopaedics more than eighteen months previously, so I wanted to refresh my knowledge. I asked him to take me through the operative techniques of hip and knee replacements.

We also discussed controversial issues in Orthopaedics.

Austin and I checked into the same hotel and were able to have a few more revision sessions. The more we studied, the more it made me feel like I didn't know enough. Doing more revision made me anxious, and my tension headache returned. Eventually, I decided to take a stroll to take my mind off the exam the following day. I didn't know much of London, and there were lots of things to see, not all of them good. Whilst I was standing at Euston station, two guys were fighting. No one separated them. They fought for over twenty minutes until one of them collapsed after a kick to his abdomen. A passer-by called for the ambulance, and the man, who had possibly sustained a major blunt injury to his abdomen, was rushed to the hospital. The incident reawakened my brain to the reason that I was in London, and I was back in exam mood.

"Now, tell me how you would manage a patient who has sustained a blunt trauma to his abdomen," I asked myself.

I returned to the hotel and asked Austin to conduct mock vivas for me. We covered the management of abdominal injuries generally, and specifically, the management of blunt trauma to solid and hollow organs. After having a meal at the nearby KFC, I had my shower. My headache had subsided. And I decided to have an early night.

For several weeks, that was the longest I had slept. I felt as though I had already done the exam. There was no shaking and sweating, like I had experienced in the previous few weeks. I had no headache, and I was thinking clearly.

The following morning, I knelt and prayed this prayer:

"God, it is my wish to pass this exam. But it will be to your glory for me to pass. So if it is your will, let me be counted among the successful candidates today."

I was among the afternoon candidates. We were all assembled in a large hall. Even to the last minute, people were still swotting and discussing. We were prohibited from talking to the candidates who had already had their turn. Even so, I knew from medical school experience that asking about what cases people had or the questions that they asked them was dangerous. Even if you had the same case, the examiner wouldn't necessarily ask you the same questions. So I went in with an open mind.

My first case was orthopaedic – an old woman with severe osteoarthritis of her hip. When the professor asked, "Take me through the procedure of a total hip replacement," I almost laughed, as I couldn't believe that was what he would ask me.

He nodded as I poured out everything in my brain. Then he asked, "Are you training to be an orthopaedic surgeon?"

I replied that I wasn't.

"Very good," he said.

After this case, I felt that God was really in control. And as I got through the other cases, I was convinced that it wasn't me doing it; it was God.

The last examiner, who looked very much like a military officer, asked me about the role of surgery in tuberculosis and sickle cell disease. I thought I was in the middle of a dream. But it was real. I was in the middle of the fellowship exam of the prestigious Royal College of Surgeons of England.

The officer who was assigning us to the patients held his head as he allocated the next patient to me. I couldn't explain why he did so.

"Good luck with this patient," he said and hurried away.

I pulled the curtain to reveal a woman in her thirties, who broke down in tears as I appeared. My feet were stuck to the floor. I went blank. I had no idea what to do.

"Don't panic, my son." A voice quickened my heart. I looked around, but there was no one. Only a confused me and a crying patient. "Take out your handkerchief. Go to her and wipe her tears," the voice continued. "She will tell you what to do."

I had read in the Bible that God had spoken to people. Prophets had brought God's messages to people. Men and women of God had seen visions. But I had never heard the voice of God. He had never spoken to me. I must be hallucinating, I thought – auditory hallucination. The voice came on again, this time louder. I felt a cloud move across my face, and I took the steps of faith and confidence.

I took out my laundered, immaculate handkerchief from my breast pocket and gently sat next to her. As I dried her tears with the handkerchief, I asked in a low voice, "I guess you don't like my look." I don't know why I said so, but that was all I could say to her.

"Oh no, I don't dislike you," she said. "Why would I hate coloured people? My husband is a black man like you."

I smiled and allowed her to talk.

"It's all drama," she informed me. "I had to pretend to be a difficult patient. That was what they told me to do – to make it hard for you. And you have done very well because you are genuinely sympathetic and caring."

A seemingly uncooperative and difficult patient became a smiling and helpful patient. I took a full history from her, made the diagnosis and formulated management plans. It was like watching a movie, one that troubled your heart at the beginning but caused you a massive sigh at the end.

The examiners returned after the bell. I went through the case, like reading a textbook.

"Did you obtain this history from the patient?" the examiner asked, with a deep Irish accent.

"Yes, Prof," I replied.

"Tell us her smoking history," the professor said.

"She used to smoke forty cigarettes a day," I informed him. "She has done so since her teenage years and only stopped two weeks ago."

The examiners asked several other questions. I informed them of the diagnosis and discussed the management plans, which they considered to be appropriate. As we moved to the next station, I looked back and winked a 'thank you' to this helpful patient.

Finally, the professor asked me about Anderson-Hyne pyeloplasty, the operation for treating pelvi-ureteric junction obstruction. This is a condition where there is a narrowing of the junction of the kidney with the ureter. I had recently performed one with Professor Bryan assisting me. Everything was still fresh in my memory. The examiner nodded as I took him through the procedure step by step. We discussed the controversies regarding stenting, the use of it and whether to put a drain or not. He asked if I had read a recent South American publication about the problems with the use of stents. Of course, I had read the paper. And I gave a scholastic digest of the paper. The professor agreed with my critique of the paper, and we both concluded that the data was too small, and their findings were not persuasive enough to cause a change in the current practice. And so, I concluded my exam session. Everything that they asked was all that I had read and practised.

I was the last candidate before break. I was in the corridor, still undecided whether to go out and come back or hang around for the result.

"Go and have a drink," the professor said, with a gentle pat on my shoulder, as he emerged from the exam hall.

I didn't know what to make of this gesture. Did he mean to informally hint that I had passed? Did he mean I had finished now and should chill out irrespective of the outcome? Or was he just a nice person who would do that to any candidate whether they did well or not? Judging by his gentle, reassuring pat on my shoulder, I felt it was a good news gesture, though I resisted giving myself a false sense of reassurance. Better to think the worst, and when the best came, it would be better celebrated.

I looked around the college and acknowledged the pioneers of surgery whose photographs occupied strategic places on the walls. I stood by the statue of John Hunter and promised myself to pose with it in my graduation gown if I passed.

I couldn't stand the anxiety, as there were still many candidates to have their exams, but I decided to chill out, not to drink, as there was nothing yet to celebrate.

All the candidates had had their exams when I returned. The college lobby was packed full, and I joined the rest of the candidates. It was as if we were waiting to be sentenced. Some people chatted away their anxiety. Others remained in nooks and corners of the college. The toilet was kept busy with people suddenly developing urinary urgency and frequency. After a brief chat to Austin, I took a quiet position close to the door. Austin had told me that he didn't think the exam went well for him, but I tried to encourage him that no one could be too confident.

The examiners were having a post-examination meeting in which they would confirm those that had satisfied them in the exam. The examination secretary finally emerged from the meeting room at about five-thirty in the evening. An eerie silence engulfed the whole place. After clearing her throat, she started calling the exam numbers of successful candidates. If the number she called was after yours, then it meant you had been unsuccessful. I watched as people whose numbers hadn't been called grab their bags and leave through the revolving college door. I didn't hear my number, so I picked up my briefcase and prepared to leave. But before the revolving door, that had rolled eminent surgeons in and out of the four-century-old college, rotated me out, I heard my name. The secretary had called my number, but I hadn't heard her from where I was. That must have been because the hall had become noisy or perhaps because my brain had shut down my ears not to receive bad news. But when the secretary called my name, all my senses returned. My ears heard it, my brain gave it clear and prompt processing, all my facial muscles worked at their best, my vocal cords pitched my answer of "Yes!" and my legs propelled me to join the successful candidates in the boardroom, to have the prestigious champagne with the president of the college and the board of examiners.

Only eleven candidates were successful on that day.

As I shook hands with the president, I felt like I was in another world, paradise perhaps. The examiner who examined me last, a bearded Irish professor, the one who had patted me on the back earlier on, walked straight to me.

"Congratulations," he said. "You were brilliant on your discussion of that operation. I enjoyed it."

"Thank you, Prof," I said. I didn't know what else to say.

"Where are you working at present?" he asked, after a sip at his champagne.

"Newport," I replied, "with Professor Bryan."

"Oh, you're working with one of the best surgeons in the world. I'm sure he will be proud of you."

"Thank you, sir," I said.

We had further discussions about general issues and my future career. Then Professor McGill took his leave to chat to other fellows.

And so, I returned home as a fellow of the Royal College of Surgeons of England. My life became transformed in one day. No more headaches. No more aches and pains. No more flutter in my heart. I thanked God for the people that he had put in place for my good cause and for a wife who had supported and encouraged me.

Professor Bryan was up in the sky when I informed him about my result. I was the only one that passed out of the seven trainees, including six registrars from our rotation. Within hours, the news had spread around the hospital like a wildfire, and I received several congratulatory telephone calls. Even the personnel officer called to congratulate me. And she apologised for refusing my study leave. I walked shoulder high whilst keeping my head low.

As I continued my post at the hospital as a newly qualified fellow, I knew that certain changes needed to be made. Central to this was the fact that I was not happy to operate with my registrar. He was a nice and easy-going person, but he lacked experience, and I felt that being his surgical assistant was not benefitting me. It didn't provide me the opportunity to learn new surgical skills. Additionally, he had failed the very exam that I had passed, and this threatened his confidence. But I couldn't tell my consultant that I needed my independent operating list. This impasse came to the boil one day, when my consultant went on a conference in Dublin. He didn't cancel his operating session. He had made the list, hoping that my registrar would be capable of doing the procedures with my assistance. I arrived in the theatre and changed into my theatre clothes. Tony was on the phone. He hadn't changed, and they hadn't sent for the patient. That was unusual. I grabbed a cup of coffee and waited in the room for him.

"Have you seen the list?" he asked me as he breezed into the room, looking like he had confronted a prowling lion.

"Yes," I replied. "Is there a problem?"

He scratched his head and stared into space.

"He shouldn't have put the simple mastectomy on the list, knowing that he wouldn't be here to do it," he lamented. He scratched his head again. "I've never done one on my own," he confessed.

"That shouldn't be a problem," I said to him. "I will give you a hand."

"Are you suggesting that you are going to *teach* me how to do a mastectomy?" He raised his voice.

"Far from that," I replied. "I am going to assist you."

"No, that won't work," he protested.

"Why not?" I asked.

"What if something happens?" He brushed the panic sweat from his forehead.

"Nothing will happen," I reassured him. "And if anything happens, Mr Jones is on call. Besides, Mr Thomas is next door, so we are safe."

In actual fact, it wasn't the fact that there was a mastectomy on the list that caused my registrar's agitation. It was his ego that overwhelmed him. He couldn't stand the fact that his SHO would be the main surgeon. He couldn't accept the fact that I had passed the fellowship exam that he had failed. Staff and colleagues had started to address me as 'Mr' whilst they called him 'Dr'. But I hadn't bragged or put on a big head. I still respected him as my registrar, and I called him 'Mr Cummins' when I referred to him on the ward, outpatients and other places.

It had past nine thirty, and they hadn't sent for the mastectomy. I suggested that we did the simple mastectomy last. "Maybe the boss would be joining us later," I said to Tony. And he agreed. He was about to order a change of the list as I had suggested, when the anaesthetist called him to the phone. The consultant told him that he should let me do the mastectomy whilst he did the other procedures. He told him that he had expected me, not him, to do the mastectomy. That was why he had written both our names on top of the operating list. Tony felt humiliated, and it took him so long to change into his theatre garments. He looked pale with a vacant stare. I felt sorry for him, and asked once or twice if he would go for a cup of tea whilst the HO assisted me, but he insisted on staying. The operations went well, and despite the delay, we finished the list in good time.

Professor Bryan returned from his one-week conference. He called me into his office, where he had spoken with me when I was denied study leave for my exam.

"Thank you for saving the day when I was away," he said, and really meant it.

"There's nothing to thank me for," I said. "It was a privilege to do the cases."

I had never seen anyone so humble. I couldn't imagine an eminent professor thanking his junior doctor for doing the operations that he had assigned to him. Most senior doctors wouldn't show any appreciation. Instead, they would look for what to criticise, just so they might show they were the boss. But I wasn't surprised about the degree of Professor Bryan's humility. He had confessed to me that he sat the fellowship exam three times before he passed. Few senior doctors would be so honest, like parents who never told their children that they had failed exams before. Professor Bryan was my professional father. And he reminded me of my own father, who often said sorry to me when he felt that he had upset me. I grew up with humility. I was glad that I had the opportunity to work with Professor Bryan, and I promised myself to be humble like him in my profession and in my life outside of the profession. Professor Bryan promised to give me an independent list after that, which was something that I had always wished for. I didn't want to be a surgeon with academic accolades and no operative experience. I didn't want to be a textbook surgeon, but one who would be busy in the theatre saving lives.

Passing the English fellowship exam on the first sitting transformed my life. I had tremendous respect among both junior and senior colleagues. Most registrars liked me to be on call with them, as they knew that I wouldn't wake them up in the middle of the night for pretty little things. And Professor Bryan gave me my own list as he promised, in a twin theatre with him. He made the registrar, whom he said 'needed to learn', assist him. The house officer or a medical student assisted me. Sometimes, the nurse assisted. And so, for the rest of my post-fellowship period, I had my daily operating lists, consisting of various cases selected by Professor Bryan. If he had a major procedure or any case that he thought I would learn from, I wouldn't have a list, but join in with the registrar to assist him.

Working in South Wales, and with an excellent trainer, gave me tremendous experience, and by the end of my posting, I was confident to deal with most surgical procedures at registrar level.

I had hoped that three years of post-fellowship training would provide me adequate experience for a consultant post when I returned home. In preparation for our return, I spent every free time including bank holidays and most weekends doing locums to make extra money. I started acquiring surgical equipment. We bought household gadgets in pairs including washing machines, dryers, dishwashers, microwaves and televisions. We were looking forward to going back home. A Locum work that I undertook in Bournemouth changed everything. I met a Nigerian professor who had come to the same hospital to do a Locum as a Senior House Officer. His story about the situation in my dear country moved me to the core. He told me about the deplorable way the government had treated doctors in Nigeria. He could not handle the situation any longer, and had decided to leave the country to do any job to sustain his family. He further informed me that he had got a job in the Middle East, and would be starting after the Locum. "You are lucky to be here," he said. "Do whatever you have to do to make a career here. If you have to tie their shoe laces for them, do, because going home is not an option," he advised.

What the professor told me brought tears into my eyes. I had not planned to settle in the UK. I wanted to return to practise as a trained surgeon and help my deprived people. But what do you do when your country doesn't value you? We had already had an indefinite stay on our passports, but even with our immigration status, I hadn't given up the plan to return home, with the hope that things would change before I completed my three-year post-fellowship registrar training.

After the two-week Locum I returned to my family. I discussed what the professor had told me with my wife, and we both agreed that perhaps it was not the best time to go home. We were eligible to applying for British citizenship, and within six weeks our application was granted. And so, we became British citizens although we hadn't ruled out returning home.

Months later I came across many Nigerian doctors and nurses who had fled Nigeria. Some of my highly regarded friends and senior colleagues who were on the Nigerian and West African fellowship programmes had abandoned their training in search of better lives in Europe, America and Australia. And most of those who had gone back home after completing their training were back, but were now finding it difficult to get back into the system. All these people told me horrific stories about life back home. And so I made up my mind to settle down in the UK. I was committed more than ever to work hard, do approved training jobs and become a consultant surgeon in the UK. I knew it wouldn't be easy, but I trusted the Lord to make it possible.

Chapter Nineteen
GREATER MANCHESTER

It's not the situation,
but whether we react (negative)
or respond (positive) to the situation that's important.
Zig Ziglar

I didn't think I would be successful at the registrar interview in Oldham Hospital. Not because I thought I wasn't good enough. Of course, I was confident, and without self-gratification, I believed I was up to the task. But I had had many unsuccessful interviews, and I had prepared myself for the usual after-interview feedback: "Oh, you are so unlucky!" And I was glad that unlike previous interviews, I was appointed out of eight candidates. My consultant, Mr Hani Lah, the most senior surgeon and head of department, was on holiday when I started. His colleagues willingly supervised and supported me in his absence.

I was three weeks into the job when Mr Lah came back from holiday. In his absence, I had had the opportunity to work with the other consultants. And they had been pleased with my performance. One day, when I was on call with one of the consultants, he advised me to be careful with Mr Lah. "He could make things difficult for you," he said. "But you are a good man."

My first meeting with Mr Lah was in the outpatient department. I had wanted to catch him in his office before going to the clinic, but his secretary advised that it was always difficult to predict what he would do at any particular time. He could decide to go straight to the clinic and he would be upset if I wasn't there to start. I followed her advice and headed for the outpatient department.

"Mr Lah wants you, Doctor," a nurse auxiliary said to me, just as I was about to call in my next patient.

"Oh, I didn't realise that he had arrived," I said.

"He has just arrived," she said and smiled wryly. "He has come early today." And that was more than thirty minutes into the morning clinic.

"Good morning, Mr Lah," I greeted him, as I gently closed the door to his consulting room behind me. "I am your new registrar."

"They have told me," he said in an unwelcoming tone. I didn't know if it was because he didn't like me or because he felt let down by his colleagues. But that wasn't my problem. They had appointed me, and I had vowed to work hard and do my best.

"So, tell me about your experience."

"I am a fellow of the Royal College of Surgeons," I began. "I have done—"

"The exam is cheap nowadays," he interjected.

"It's become more expensive," I said. "They keep increasing the fee every year."

"You don't get it, do you?" he asked, and smiled wryly.

I narrowed a questioning eye.

"I mean, they've made it easy to pass. They just hand the coveted fellowship to every Tom, Dick and Harry. Never mind," he said.

"I am not sure many fellows share that view," I said.

"I see," he said. And without looking up, he looked through the mountain of case notes in front of him. He singled out ten notes and put them to one side. And without saying a word, he pushed the rest to the outpatient sister.

As I left my consultant's room, I knew that I was going to have a tough time with him. He had his opinion about me and had shown me no respect. But I hoped that with time he would realise that my fellowship wasn't handed to me. It was merited. Mr Lah only saw ten patients and left. I saw the remaining forty patients with the SHO.

That afternoon, I had my first theatre session with Mr Lah. I was used to having my own operating list, but I didn't mind the fact that Mr Lah didn't make a separate list for me. Of course, I was happy to learn new techniques. I was happy to give him a hand to ease his operations. But I found it a waste of time that all I was supposed to do was hold the retractor and cut the stitches, even for simple hernia repair or excision of bumps and lumps.

Mr Lah did everything possible to humiliate me in the presence of everyone, as he openly accused me of not knowing how to handle tissues, not tying knots properly, even that I didn't know how to dress a wound. I tried not to let these bother me and trusted that I would be able to cope with whatever life threw at me, resolving not to challenge his ideas. I was only meant to work with him for six months, after which time I would rotate to another firm.

One day, after spending most of the time in the morning on a difficult gallbladder operation, we overran. The outpatient session would be starting at two in the afternoon. Even if we missed our lunch, there was no way we wouldn't be late if we did all the cases on the operation list.

"Theatre three is free now, Mr Lah. Would you like me to move some of the cases there for the registrar?" the senior theatre sister suggested.

"I will free my SHO to help with the cases if you like," the consultant anaesthetist offered.

"I can't give my list to *him*," Mr Lah said.

"You cannot give your list to your registrar?" the consultant anaesthetist wondered.

Mr Lah nodded.

"Why?" the consultant anaesthetist asked.

Mr Lah ignored the question. He continued with the operation with the SHO assisting him, as he had done for most of the morning, except for the gallbladder operation, where I joined in at his request.

"Which of the cases would you like me to cancel?" the sister asked.

Mr Lah ignored the sister, just as he had the anaesthetist. It was past one o'clock. I was supposed to be at Outpatients at two o'clock. I wasn't doing anything useful in the theatre, and I didn't see any sense in hanging around doing nothing.

"Can I go and start the clinic?" I asked Mr Lah.

"You've got a list to do," he replied, "and the sooner you start, the sooner you'll finish."

And so the sister opened theatre three for me. I was on my last case when Mr Lah breezed into my theatre.

"That's not how to remove a sebaceous cyst," he said.

I hadn't put the cyst in the pathology pot, so I placed it on my palm and showed it to him.

"It is completely removed, and the wound has been nicely stitched," I said. "Will you show me how *you* remove a sebaceous cyst next time?"

"Hmmm!" he sighed and left the room.

"You'll be alright." The sister placed a reassuring hand on my shoulder. "Everyone in the hospital is singing your praises, except him. I have watched you operating, and I know that you are a good surgeon."

"Thank you, Sister," I said. "I really appreciate that."

Mr Lah had long left the theatre. I hurried to the outpatient department to start the clinic with no time to have my lunch. The outpatient clinic was full beyond its capacity, and patients spilled over onto the corridor. At first, I wanted to go straight to my consulting room. On second thought, I decided to check Mr Lah's room in case there were any particular patients that he would like to see himself. I had learnt that my consultant was one of those unpredictable characters. One minute he said one thing, but he would say or do the opposite if the situation arose again. I had tried to tread carefully since I joined, but I could do nothing to please him.

Mr Lah's room was full, as usual. It was always like a meeting place. There were two medical students, one house officer, one senior house officer, one student nurse, two staff nurses, the outpatient sister, two auxiliary nurses and his secretary.

I gently tapped on the door and closed it behind me. Mr Lah checked his watch. And after clearing his throat, he asked the outpatient sister, "When does the clinic start?"

"Two," she replied.

It seemed out of context for Mr Lah to ask the sister the clinic time. They had worked together for many years. So, why would he now ask her? These thoughts were going through my head when he said to me, "We all keep to time here."

I couldn't believe Mr Lah talking about timekeeping, when he was always late to clinics, theatres, ward rounds and even meetings. He had put aside everything else and rushed to the clinic so he could get there before me, knowing that I would be held back in the theatre doing the cases that would have been otherwise cancelled. I wondered what he planned to gain out of this. I had saved the day. I had even forfeited my lunch to ensure that I got to the outpatient department in good time. Still, that wasn't good enough for Mr Lah. He seemed to have a mission: to destroy my credibility, to prove to his consultant colleagues that they were wrong to appoint me in his absence. His strategy was to find a reason to sack me and promote his favourite SHO to registrar.

"I am sorry," I said.

It is a common saying in my village that if you want to catch a monkey, pretend to be a monkey. So I decided to pretend that I didn't know he was being unfair. I resolved to do everything to the best of my ability. It was reassuring to know that people loved and respected me. So it was up to Mr Lah how he treated me.

"Look at all the patients outside there. They are all waiting to be seen. And you are here telling me sorry," he said.

"Can I go and start, sir?" I asked.

Without saying a word, he shifted a large pile of case notes to the sister.

I smiled. As I was about to take my leave, he asked, "Doctor, have you had your lunch?"

"I came straight from the theatre," I replied. "But, that's alright, sir."

"I'll get the girls to fetch you sandwiches," the sister said. "You can't be expected to work with an empty stomach."

"Thanks, sister," I said, "but I am alright."

"Thank you, sir," I said to Mr Lah. "Can I go now?"

He nodded.

As always, Mr Lah singled out about ten case notes and pushed the rest to me. I took my leave and pushed the trolley into my consulting room. Sister came with a tuna and sweetcorn sandwich and a can of coke soon after I left Mr Lah's room, as she had promised. I offered to pay for it, but she refused to take the money.

"You are doing your best, and the patients and staff love and respect you," she remarked. She scratched her head. "I just can't get my head around why Mr Lah is treating you like this."

I didn't know what to make of her actions and her statement. I found it hard to trust the sister. But whatever her motives, she certainly was a caring person.

"I must get to the bottom of this," she said. "I must find out why he has been treating you with disrespect and is so unappreciative of all you have been doing. His former registrar wasn't half as good as you. Yet he never treated him like this despite all the complications and complaints."

"Don't worry about that, Sister," I said. "But, thank you for the sandwich. That's very kind of you."

I appreciated the sister's kind gesture. I didn't realise how much I needed to eat until I finished the sandwich. She was God-sent. I felt strong again. I finished the clinic at nearly six o'clock. As usual, Mr Lah had disappeared with the SHO long before the clinic finished. Sister made another cup of tea and left me to dictate my notes. The other nurses went to tidy up the rooms and ensure all the notes were arranged in the trolley for the secretary to collect in the morning.

I was about to leave when sister and one of the staff nurses returned.

"Sit down, Doctor," the sister said, smiling. "I have important information for you."

"Oh!" my heart raced as I sat down with my back straight on the chair. "Okay, I am all ears," I said.

"Mr Lah had wanted to give your job to his SHO," Sister informed me, after clearing her throat. "His SHO is not even a mister like you. So he was angry when he came back to find out that the job had been offered to you and not his SHO."

I had already heard the rumour, so there must have been some truth in it, but I didn't show that I had heard about it before.

"Why would he take his anger with his colleagues out on me?" I wondered.

"It's simple," she leaned forward. "To give you a colour that is not yours."

I narrowed my eyes.

"You don't get that, do you?" she smiled wryly.

I shrugged.

"He wants to make you look like a bad doctor to frustrate you and make you resign. He has done that before. I remember, he frustrated a South African surgeon a few years ago. The poor chap couldn't stand his antics. He resigned only a few weeks into the job. And did you know what the big man did?"

I shook my head.

"He appointed a registrar without his colleague's approval," she said. "He never conducted any interview. He simply handed the job on a golden plate to him," she continued, after clearing her throat. "The registrar was full of himself. He paraded himself all over the hospital. You would think he was a consultant."

"And he kept renewing his contract," the staff nurse added.

"Oh yes," the sister added, "the registrar must have been in the post for about four years. I think he's now working in Saudi Arabia."

"Hmmm!" I sighed.

I was glad to have this information, but I still couldn't figure out why they chose to tell me, and I didn't know whether to believe them. I wondered if it was all made up. Maybe it was a trap that Mr Lah had set for me. I had to allow my brain to do the thinking and not my heart.

"You probably wonder why we are telling you all this stuff," Sister said. "You remember, I told you earlier that I would get to the bottom of it?"

I nodded.

"I don't like the way he has been treating you," she said. "You are a decent, respectful person. And you know your stuff. I feel like he hasn't treated you with decency. I hate it when people behave like that."

"It doesn't bother me," I said. "I get on with the job, do my best and let posterity judge."

"Life is not like that sometimes," she said. "If you make yourself a doormat, people will step on you and use you to clean their dirty feet."

"True," I nodded.

"I don't take nonsense from anyone," she said, "and he knows."

"You see, when Sister sent me to fetch your sandwich, he said she had sent me on an unofficial errand, when I should be doing an official job," the staff nurse said.

"And I asked him why he would treat a hardworking doctor like that," the sister said. "It was then he let the cat out of the bag. Of course, he was too full of himself to realise the implications of what he had said."

Now I realised why Mr Lah hadn't been nice to me. But I resolved that I wouldn't resign. I would continue to work hard and do everything to the best of my ability. At the end of six months, I would rotate to another consultant, so I would take all the insults that he threw at me. But, if he crossed the red line, I would use the sister and the staff nurse as my witnesses.

Mr Lah's attitude remained unchanged throughout my six-month posting with him, but time eventually passed, and the posting was over. I then joined Mr Duthie, a fantastic Aberdeenian surgeon. A man in his late fifties, he had seen and done it all. There was no operation he wouldn't let his registrar do, but he was there, providing guidance and inspiring confidence.

Thursday was our main operating day. At the end of each week, he would ask me to look at the waiting list and tell him which of the operations I would like to do. And unless there was a mitigating reason, he would put the patient on my list.

Mr Duthie changed my perspectives about the job and brought sparkle to my surgical career. This transformation in my work life translated into a happy social and home life. I had kept my wife out of the situation at work when I was with Mr Lah, and it was after I moved to Mr Duthie's firm that I could talk about Mr Lah on reflection. But I didn't hate him for the way he had treated me. In life, good things look better when you have had bad things. A loaf of bread in the hand of a beggar feels like a barn full of yams. Working with Mr Lah not only toughened me, but also taught me one of life's skills: to not allow any situation to beat or break me.

One Monday morning, I received a notification from the accommodation manager. The rent had gone up. That was the third increment in six months. I was discussing this with his secretary, when Mr Duthie came into the office.

"Why are you paying rent?" Mr Duthie asked.

I didn't get that. Of course, I had to pay rent. It wasn't a rent-free accommodation. And he knew that. So I couldn't understand why he should ask me that question.

"I mean, why are you throwing away your money on rent when you can pay the same, if not less, on a mortgage?"

"I can't," I replied, "since my job here isn't permanent."

"So what?" he narrowed his eye. "You can sell your house, make some profit and buy another property in your new place. You could make it a base and settle your family whilst you go about your training. You could even rent it out if you had to go with your family. And if you decide to return to your home country, you could rent it out as an investment."

What Mr Duthie had told me sank into the deepest part of my

cognition. No one had ever given me such a comprehensive and meaningful piece of advice. Everything made sense.

When I got home, I brought up the issue with my wife. Since our arrival in Oldham, we had made new friends. We attended a lively church, we had had our second child, and my wife had registered for her postgraduate study at Manchester University. Unlike where we had lived before, Manchester had a large population of Nigerians, and there were many shops selling Afro-Caribbean foodstuff. We both agreed that the best option for us was to buy a property.

It was no problem getting mortgage approval, and very soon we booked an appointment to view a property – a three-bedroom, semi-detached house at the outskirts of Manchester. My wife and I, with our toddler son and our a few-weeks-old daughter in the pram, stood by the door as I pressed the bell. We were about to take our leave, after I had pressed the bell ten times, when a middle-aged man with a bushy beard and big tummy unlocked the door. Our frown of disappointment melted into smiles of excitement when the man opened the door with his wife behind him. But what he said wiped off our smiles in a flash.

"We are not selling our house," he said.

"But the estate agent told us your house was still on the market," I reminded him.

"Sorry, we don't sell to people of your kind," he said. "You will be odd in this community." He slammed the door.

"Why is the man so horrible?" our two-year-old son asked.

"Oh, I think we are too late. The house is gone," I replied.

How could I explain to a two-year-old child that even though he had a doctor father and a lawyer mother, still we were not fit to live in certain parts of the country because of our colour?

Although I had had several interviews, where the only feedback, after denying me of opportunities, was "Sorry you are so unlucky", I had never had it so direct. I felt like I was a destitute. But I tried not to show it to my family. Instead, I simply told my wife that it wasn't meant to be.

"All things work out for good," I encouraged her. "God will provide something better than this." And God did provide something better. The following day, the estate agent phoned my wife to inform her of a similar house on the next street to the one that we had attempted to view. At first, we felt there was no point going to view it, thinking that we would be treated the same way, given that the house was in the same area.

"The sellers are different," the estate agent advised. "They're serious about selling their house. And they are open to negotiation."

And so, we visited the seller to view the property.

"This is it," my wife concluded, after viewing the house. "I love everything about this house," she said. And that was it. My wife had approved it. I was happy she liked it, as I, myself, liked it. We put in an offer, ten thousand pounds lower than the asking price, and the sellers accepted our offer. And so, we purchased our first property, a three-bedroom, semi-detached house with gardens in the front, side and back. Ideal for bringing up our children, it was only a stone's throw from the park.

Having our first house gave us an experience that I couldn't describe, and I had never seen my wife so happy. We were proud to join the community of home owners and to have a place we could call our own, where we could plant beautiful flowers in the garden and the children could run around freely.

My surgical experience also grew tremendously. I wasn't only confident in opening and closing the abdomen, both electively and in emergency, but also opening the chest to do an oesophagectomy. I also had the opportunity to build on my urological experience, and by the end of my posting in Oldham, I had developed steady hands in transurethral resection of the prostate. I had undertaken the largest part of a cystectomy and ileal conduit.

Apart from Mr Lah, who messed me up in the first six months, I worked for surgeons who had offered me the opportunity to broaden and improve my surgical skills. Even Mr Lah contributed to the development of certain philosophical approach to life: to treat every situation that I find myself in as a learning opportunity. Mr Lah was a difficult person. But I learnt from this experience that not every fight is worth the time and energy. Many things in life are not worth sacrificing your sleep for.

Following Mr Duthie's advice, I settled my family in Oldham, whilst I sought opportunities for further surgical training all over the country. But as my seniority advanced, the opportunities became harder. Beginning my job-hunting spree towards the end of my contract, I applied to so many jobs, but I either didn't get shortlisted for interviews or received the "Oh, you are so unlucky" feedback that I had now got used to. One such application was to Wakefield. I had applied two months previously, but I wasn't shortlisted. As it was the same job for which I wasn't shortlisted when I previously applied, I decided to phone the medical personnel officer. The personnel officer informed me that it was indeed the same job. The person that they had offered the job to had resigned two weeks in to take up his preferred job in London. When I mentioned my name to her, she said, "Oh I remember that name!" I couldn't tell what made her remember 'that name'. I couldn't imagine that she would remember the name of an applicant who wasn't even shortlisted. But then I got the message when she urged me, "Send your CV. Maybe you'll be lucky this time."

After speaking with the personnel officer, I put a copy of my CV in the post, hoping that I would indeed be 'lucky this time', as she had said.

That afternoon, I received a phone call from St Thomas's Hospital, inviting me for an interview for a different job. I hadn't thought that I would be shortlisted, having not heard from them for nearly four weeks. The confirmatory letter arrived the following day. I was excited by the prospect of training in this prestigious London hospital. I attended the interview the following week and didn't wait for the result, as I had to catch my train back to Oldham. I had no mobile phone, so the news was passed to my wife that I got the job, and I should call back to confirm my acceptance.

When I applied for the job in St Thomas's, I didn't ask myself the question that I should have asked: Where will this lead me? Working for an author and internationally renowned authority in urology would pave my way to obtaining the coveted Diploma in Urology, and would almost certainly pave my way to becoming a consultant urologist. But that wasn't where my interest lay. I was confused and couldn't think straight. My wife had never liked the idea of living in London. I myself didn't like the London lifestyle. But I had to balance that against the opportunity to work in a prestigious hospital, and the prospect of becoming a consultant urologist. I was supposed to call the personnel officer as per the message she left with my wife. We both decided to take the matter to the Lord in prayer, and let His will be done. And so, after prayer, we let the matter rest for the night.

I called the personnel officer the following morning. I didn't know how to inform her that I was rejecting the offer. She made it easy for me when she asked: "Are there any questions you would like to ask me?"

Something that I hadn't thought about came into my mind. "What about accommodation?" I asked.

"Oh, we don't have accommodation for our staff," she replied. "But there are properties around that you can rent."

I breathed heavily as she told me the average rent for a one-room apartment, which was more than our monthly mortgage repayment for our three-bedroom house. The mortgage on an equivalent property like ours was almost three times. I thanked them for offering me the job, but I had to turn it down. The officer couldn't believe that I was turning down a job that people were dying to have. But I had to do it. I felt a sense of relief, though with a bit of guilt, as I hung up. I had no job offer, but I trusted that I had made the right decision.

That week, after turning down the offer, I received three invitation letters, including one from Wakefield. The Wakefield interview came first. With two more interviews at hand, I attended the interview at Wakefield with a 'nothing to lose' attitude. I was well-prepared but not stressed. My heart was for the Wakefield job, and I had made up my mind that if they offered it to me, I would accept it.

The interview started at eight-thirty in the morning. I had never attended an interview so early. There was construction work going on on the M62, so I left home around five o'clock in the morning in order not to be late. As I parked my car, another car reversed and parked next to mine.

"Are you here for the registrar interview?" the African doctor in a white coat asked, with a smile.

"Yes," I gave a simple answer.

"Come with me. Let's have breakfast together," he offered.

Although I didn't really know this man, I thought he was a genuinely nice person. And, of course, arriving just after seven-thirty, I was too early for the interview.

He introduced himself as Omer, a Sudanese, and he was a surgical registrar. That was God-sent. I needed as much information as possible about the set-up in the surgical department, and I couldn't have asked for anyone more suitable than a registrar, who had been on the job for about twelve months. Omer advised that the post was of senior registrar status, and they would be looking to appoint someone with that level of experience. They would ask me how much I knew about the hospital, and what would make them offer the job to me rather than any other candidate. He also added that they would ask me about my future aspirations. I should tell them that I looked forward to pursuing my career to ultimately become a consultant. The consultants liked an ambitious forward-looking candidate. Omer told me so much about the hospital and the department of surgery that I felt like I was already part of the team. After talking a bit about life back home in Africa, he saw me off to the administrative office, where the interview was to take place.

"Oh, by the way, if you were to write your own reference, what would be your highlights?" he asked. "Think about that. All the best."

Omer disappeared into the big hospital, whilst I went into the toilet to freshen up and reflect on all we had discussed, before joining the other candidates.

We were six candidates for the interview. Although I was the first to arrive, I was the last to have my turn. Each interview took thirty minutes. It was a good thing that I had had breakfast with Omer. Whenever a candidate emerged from the room with a smile, my heart beat fast. I tried not to get worked up as I had hoped. But I couldn't help it. I paced the waiting room and visited the toilet several times to stop my brain sending panic signals to the organs of fright and flight. I needed to stop the shakes and sweat. At last, after waiting nearly three hours, the personnel officer called me in. I was surprised that she called my name with a great degree of accuracy and fluency. At most interviews, they would ask me, "How is your name pronounced?" In some cases, they would simply tell me, "I can't pronounce this."

She smiled and led me into the large interview room.

"Sorry, you've had to wait so long," the chairman said as I entered.

The other four panel members nodded.

"Take your seat and make yourself comfortable," he directed.

"Thanks," I said.

I felt humbled. How could they apologise to me when I was the one who needed a job and a training opportunity? But that indeed increased my desire to work in Wakefield. Even if not all of them, certainly the head of surgery was a nice person.

I sat straight in the chair, crossed my legs and looked straight with a smile that told them I was ready to take their questions.

"Tell us about yourself," the chairman said, after introducing all the members of the interview panel.

This was an expected opening question in any interview. But despite that, I always found it difficult to tell people about myself. How much did they want to know? How far did they want me to go? And where did they want me to stop? Of course, they all had copies of my CV. Going over the information about myself as detailed in my CV would be boring. And I thought it would be an insult to them, as it would suggest that they hadn't read it. I needed to sell myself, as a desirable but not expensive commodity. I must not appear to be a perfect human being and a 'know it all' doctor. Neither must I portray myself as a useless piece of dough unsuitable for baking. So, I decided to highlight aspects of my professional experience and personality that would give them my true picture. I highlighted the incident as a house officer, where I acted in the best interests of the young woman and her unborn baby despite the threats from my boss. My experience as a youth corper, where I single-handedly ran the mobile clinic, earned me a great deal of respect from the community and a golden handshake from the governor. I deliberately ignored my spectacular performance in the fellowship examination, as I sensed that didn't matter much. Rather, I put it in a different way. I informed them that passing the exam early in my career provided me the opportunity to focus on operative experience and writing papers. Other members asked questions. These were all the questions that Omer had discussed with me earlier that morning, and I had no problems discussing them. I was so relaxed. As I discussed them, I had a mental picture of my time with Omer earlier on. And finally, the last member asked, "If you were to write your own reference, what bullet points would you put in it?" I had a brief mental block. I couldn't believe that this question would come up. That was Omer's last tip, and it was now the last question. I took a deep breath and allowed my brain to process the information and organise my response as follows:

A caring person, who believes in the ethical principle of primum non nocere.

An innovative and forward-looking person.

A surgeon who is keen to learn, but also eager to share his knowledge to improve others.

A reliable and trustworthy person with probity.

A team player, who is always willing to make things work.

An experienced surgeon, who recognises the limit of his experience and calls for help when needed. A person who believes that learning does not end, and it goes on throughout his career.

"Yes!" the interviewer exclaimed, as others nodded. "That's an impressive reference. But we will see what your referees say about you."

"Thank you," I said as I took my leave to join the other candidates and await the panel's decision.

I didn't know what to make of the interview. I believed I had given it my best shot and hoped that was good enough for them. Judging by their attitude to me, I thought they liked me or at least, they were impressed by my credence. But of course, nothing was predictable. I had prepared myself for the usual 'You are so unlucky' feedback. I made a cup of coffee for myself and sat in one corner in reflection with a couple of digestive biscuits.

I had barely finished one biscuit when the personnel officer emerged from the door. I had assumed that I was unsuccessful when she called another candidate in, but she told the rest of us not to depart yet. The candidate returned to the waiting room and informed us that he didn't get the job. She called the second candidate, but that too was unsuccessful. After she called the third candidate, who was also unsuccessful, I realised that Wakefield had an unusual way of informing the candidates of the outcome. Normally after an interview, the successful candidate would be called in first. Only the candidates who wanted feedback would be called back into the room. In Wakefield it was different. Candidates were called back into the room according to how they were called in the first time. The fifth candidate was called in; she also did not get the job. As I waited to be called in, I thought perhaps they had decided not to appoint any candidate.

At last, the personnel officer called my name. As she led me back into the room, she whispered to me, "Congratulations!"

"We are all delighted to offer you the job," the head of department informed me. He stood up, shook hands with me, and the rest of the panel rose one by one and shook my hand, saying, "Congratulations!"

I thanked them and confirmed my acceptance of the offer. The consultants then left me with the personnel officer to complete the paperwork. As I walked to the personnel office, the officer informed me, "They all thought you were brilliant."

"That was very kind of them," I replied.

As we were about to enter her office she asked, with a smile, "Do you know the problem you have now?"

I shook my head.

"They all want to have you," she said.

"I am all theirs," I said.

Chapter Twenty
Wakefield

Success is not measured by what you accomplish
but by the opposition you have encountered,
and the courage with which you have maintained
the struggle against overwhelming odds.
Orison Swett Marden

I decided to commute daily to my new post, so I didn't have to move my family, and the hospital provided rent-free, single-person accommodation within walking distance of the hospital for when I was on call, couldn't drive home during bad weather or if I was too tired to go home after work. Omer was also living in single-person accommodation. He had lived in married accommodation until his wife got a job in Blackburn. They decided to buy a house there, and so he went home on weekends. He was delighted that I got the job, and I was grateful for his tips. Although I sometimes struggled with his accent, he was chatty and knowledgeable. He was also conversant with African politics and football, so we had a lot to talk about when we weren't busy.

I started the first part of my rotation in vascular surgery. This was an exciting way to start the job, as it was one aspect of General Surgery in which I felt the need for more hands-on experience. Mr Gerrard, the middle-aged vascular surgeon, was not just large in build, but he was larger than life, and he created terror all over the hospital. Even his consultant colleagues wouldn't dare confront him. His demeanour was protective to the junior members of his firm. However, it reduced my liberty to make independent decisions as a senior registrar.

One day, I had a call from the intensive care unit. The patient was a victim of a road traffic accident. The eighteen-year-old man had suffered a severe head injury, among other multiple injuries. He was on a life-support machine. The intensivist had suspected intra-abdominal trauma, so he instructed the nurse to page me. On arrival on the ITU, I demanded that the registrar make a formal referral before I could see the patient. This was the rule that was handed to me by my predecessor, Mr Ali Akbar. Mr Akbar had been Mr Gerrard's registrar for many years, until they no longer renewed his contract, despite Mr Gerrard's insistence. In the end, they promised to employ him as an associate specialist. He was awaiting his formal appointment. Meanwhile, he remained in the hospital accommodation. He had no regular duties, and was only there to help out as a locum when required. Ali was everywhere all the time. He watched over me like a hawk, following me everywhere. He even did his own ward rounds after I had done mine, and he would phone Mr Gerrard, following which he would make changes to my directives. The nurses didn't like this situation, but invariably, they would carry out his instructions rather than mine. Even in the theatre, he would displace me from my supposed position as first assistant and reduce me to second assistant.

I agreed with the intensive care doctors that the teenager had a major intra-abdominal trauma. And he needed a laparotomy. I rang Mr Akbar to seek his advice, as Mr Gerrard wasn't contactable. I knew he always knew how to contact the boss. I also knew, of course, that even if I didn't inform Ali, he would know through his informants. So, I thought it was reasonable to contact Ali to inform him.

"I advise you not to take instructions from a nurse," Ali warned me. "You know that Mr Gerrard doesn't like that. Ask the registrar to put it in writing. Meanwhile, I will try and contact him for you."

"The patient is seriously unwell," I informed Ali. "I think he has ruptured his spleen."

"Don't worry," Ali said. "I will contact him and get back to you."

I sat down in the nurses' station, pretending to read the patient's notes, as my brain wrestled with my heart to make the right decision. If I took the patient to theatre without informing Mr Gerrard, he would shout at me. But that was all he would and could do. He couldn't sack me. I had to balance that against possible difficulties in the theatre. But that would be taken care of. I trusted that any consultant in the hospital would rise to my call should I need assistance, so that wasn't a problem. But if I didn't intervene and the patient died, it would haunt me for the rest of my career, if I still had one. I also reckoned that Ali could come to the ITU and pretend that he was the one who had made the decision to take the patient to theatre, after he had spoken with Mr Gerrard. He would tell him that I didn't recognise a critically ill surgical patient. He had done that before in the case of an elderly patient with a perforated duodenal ulcer on a Saturday when I was on call. I had prepared the patient for theatre, and whilst I waited for them to finish a case of ruptured ectopic pregnancy, I thought I should take the opportunity to go for lunch. Ali took the patient to theatre before my arrival, without informing me. He told me that he thought I was too busy. But what he told Mr Gerrard was different. He told him that I delayed the patient's laparotomy, so he had to intervene.

Whilst all these thoughts were going on in my head, I felt a gentle tap on my shoulder.

"If I were you, I would get on with the laparotomy, my boy," Mr Towers, consultant neurosurgeon advised me.

Mr Towers was held in a high esteem. He was a little older than Mr Gerrard, and I knew that Mr Gerrard respected him a lot. Even if Mr Gerrard decided to reprimand me, he could defend me; he was the one, after all, who referred the patient to me. Just as he finished talking to me, the nurse ran to us.

"His BP's dropped again," she reported.

I was glad that a senior surgeon felt the way I had felt. The patient needed an emergency operation without which he would die, and I was competent to do the operation. That was the litmus test. Would the majority of surgeons, with same competency level as me, take a patient like this to the theatre without their consultant's approval? I believed Mr Towers had helped me to answer that. "If I were you..." he had said. So that was the right decision. And I stood by my decision to intervene and not wait for Mr Gerrard.

I took the patient to theatre for an emergency laparotomy. As suspected, he had a ruptured spleen. He also had a tear in his liver. I had removed the spleen and stopped the bleeding, when Ali breezed into the theatre.

"Mr Gerrard asked me to give you a hand, so I might show you how he does a splenectomy," he informed me.

"Oh, thank you," I said, "but I think that's too late now. Maybe you can show me next time."

I didn't want to say anything nasty, there was no need for that, but he clearly got the message as he receded and breezed out of the theatre, the way he breezed into it.

"You are a senior registrar, aren't you?" the consultant anaesthetist asked.

"Of course, yes," I replied.

"How come you allow him to control you?" he asked.

"Because Mr Gerrard always passes instruction through him," I replied.

"Are you sure Mr Gerrard really said that?" the anaesthetist narrowed his eyes.

"I don't know," I replied, "but that's what Ali told me."

"You believe him?" he asked.

"I don't know what to believe anymore," I replied.

"You know what they say?"

"What?" I coughed.

"A doormat cannot place itself on the door floor," he said. "Someone has to put it there. And once on the floor, it is there for everyone to step on and clean their feet on it." He coughed and after clearing his throat, added, "No one can make you inferior without your permission."

"True," I said. "My mother has said that before. She often added another version. 'If you turn yourself into a dustbin, people will put their rubbish in you.'"

We all laughed. I had always enjoyed operating with Dr Gold. Since the first day, when we did an elective aneurysm repair, and I told him that I had worked in Scotland, we had become friends. Despite being a consultant, he would be the first to greet and often embarrassed me with his 'Thanks, sir' or 'Boss'.

The lacerations on the liver were on its surface and didn't require stitching. Bleeding from these injuries stopped after packing them with pieces of *surgicel*. There was also a small tear in the diaphragm, which I stitched up. I checked the rest of the abdomen and confirmed that there were no other injuries. I was closing the abdomen when Mr Gerrard arrived.

"Mr Towers told me you were looking for me," he shouted from the door.

"Yes, Mr Gerrard," I replied briefly.

"Why were you looking for me?" he asked.

It was obvious, I thought. And of course, Mr Towers would have informed him about this patient. Otherwise, how would he have known that I was in theatre? Also, Ali had informed him. I didn't want to say 'That's obvious' or 'Don't be daft'. Instead, I made it casual and gave a simple reply, "Oh, I just wanted to inform you about this patient before taking him to theatre."

"Bloody hell!" he yelled. "My registrar doesn't chase me about the city. I appointed you as my registrar because you are experienced. You are a senior registrar, for God's sake. Get on with it."

"Mr Akbar advised me that you would like your registrar to discuss all patients with you before taking them to theatre," I said.

"Did I say that myself?" he asked me.

"No," I replied. "But…"

Dr Gold coughed, and I got the message. There was no need arguing with Mr Gerrard. Either he was feeling guilty for not being contactable or he had realised that Mr Akbar had been feeding him with the wrong information. One thing was clear; I was in charge, and from then on, I would not let Ali push me around.

"I am sorry," I said.

"Jolly good," he said. "So what have you found?" he asked.

I told him about the injuries on the liver, the ruptured spleen and the tear on the diaphragm.

"I have done a splenectomy and repaired the diaphragm. The liver lacerations are superficial. They only required haemostatic packing," I reported.

"Have you checked everywhere and no other injuries?" he asked.

"Yes, Mr Gerrard," I replied.

"The pelvis, the peritoneal recesses, the pancreas, the bowels, the root of the mesentery and the major vessels?" he asked.

"Yes, Mr Gerrard, I have checked and ensured that everything else was intact," I reassured him.

"Very good. Thank you very much. I am proud of you," he said, and closed the door behind him.

My head swelled. I couldn't believe this good gesture coming from the man that I had thought didn't like me. This incident changed my perspectives about Mr Gerrard. He was a genuine person. His large build intimidated everyone, but I had no doubt in my mind that his heart was as big, if not bigger than his body.

Mr Gerrard spent more time outside than inside the hospital, so I was in charge of the day-to-day running of the department. Some patients even thought I was Mr Gerrard, since they saw very little of him. And I saw very little of Ali as he slowly disappeared from the scene, and he no longer interfered in my affairs.

Mr Gerrard had left the ITU when I visited later after the operation. The patient had returned from theatre, remained stable, and his observations were satisfactory. I knew that Mr Gerrard tended to write his instructions in patients' case notes rather than by word, so I checked in case he had left me instructions since he had been. He wrote in his characteristic monosyllabic way, and my eyes widened as I read:

"The decision to intervene was brilliant, and the surgical procedures were precise."

And then my eyes caught the bamboo tree scribbles, his signature, and a red tick of endorsement beside my own signature at the end of the operation note. I blinked several times as I tried to settle my eyes on Mr Gerrard's scribbles. They were scribbles of his trust and belief in me. As I closed the notes and rose to leave the ITU, Sister breezed into the nurses' station.

"What have you done?" she asked me.

I looked around and raised a questioning ridge on my forehead, wondering what she meant.

"I mean, what have you done to Mr Gerrard?" she asked.

"Sorry, I don't know what you mean," I said.

"He is a completely changed man," she informed me. "He was here, singing your praises, something he has never done before. I have never heard him praise his registrar before …" She scratched her head. "Or anyone for that matter, if I'm honest," she added.

"Hmmm!" I sighed.

I was just about to leave when Mr Towers breezed into the ITU. Mr Towers was one of those people who smiled all the time. No matter how tough things were, nothing would make his smiles go.

"Just the man I was looking for," he said. "Come with me."

I followed Mr Towers to the ITU corridor, wondering what he had in mind.

"I'm glad you saved that boy's life."

"Thank you for your fatherly advice," I said, after clearing my throat, and I really meant it.

"I spoke with Tom whilst you were in the theatre," he informed me. "I told him how wonderful you were. He never knew. None of us knew that the boy is the son of a parliamentarian. Can you imagine what would have happened if you hadn't intervened?"

"I have to thank you, sir," I said. "You gave me the strength that I needed at that time."

Mr Towers stopped walking. Strangely, the normally busy corridor was empty, as though the hospital had closed down. He looked straight into my eyes and said to me, "One thing I have learnt in life is that if you think good and do good, there will always be someone to do good to you. So don't stop doing good that you know how."

I nodded. He reminded me of my father. That was how he used to advise me in my childhood days. In those days, when I accompanied him to fish and hunt at night, he told me so many inspirational stories. He gave me words of wisdom. I recalled one of the things he used to say: "If you do good, good will follow you. And in the time of your need, God will send his angels to you." All through my childhood, and most of my early adulthood, I had sought these angels. I had imagined how they looked – winged creatures in white robes. As I matured, I soon realised that my angels wore no white robes. And they had no wings. They were the wonderful people whom God had used for my good cause.

I thanked Mr Towers for his advice and promised him, just as I had promised my father, that I wouldn't depart from the path of goodness. I would always tell the truth and do good, even if people disagreed with me. And in my profession, I would do all that I did in the best interests of my patients.

The patient that I had operated on made a good recovery. He was transferred to the general ward under the care of Mr Gerrard, where I continued to look after him. Everything changed after that. Mr Gerrard ceased to criticise me openly, even when he disagreed with me. If he disagreed with a particular area of my management, for instance, he would gently tell me on the way to another ward: "If it was me, I would leave a drain or an NG tube, but the patient is doing alright without it. Maybe you were right." We disagreed on a number of surgical techniques and principles – he believed in making large incisions, even when that was unnecessary, and I believed in minimally invasive surgery, limiting the size of my incision to the minimum required – but I could understand why he made large incisions. His hands were massive, and he needed large incisions to accommodate them. We also disagreed on suturing techniques. With my background in plastic surgery, I paid great attention to the quality of my scars, so I used the subcuticular wound closure. He hated that technique, and I wondered if that was because he had not mastered such techniques, and he felt too big to start learning again. One other area of disagreement was in our speeds of operation. He was extremely slow, but I admired his thoroughness, and I understood that. He hated to have complications, which was the reason he gave his registrars very little to do. He wouldn't cut any tissue unless he was sure that he had separated it from other structures.

"Nature has put planes between structures, and if you go between the planes there will be less bleeding," he often told me.

Mr Gerrard wouldn't close a wound until even the slightest ooze had stopped. Even though his operations were incredibly long, I learnt a vital principle from him: to be a safe surgeon.

As Mr Gerrard took a back seat and left me to run his firm, I did daily ward rounds and put patients on operation lists. Even consultants from other departments preferred to refer patients to me or discuss their care with me rather than my consultant. This was great, and it gave me the confidence and the responsibilities that befitted my level of training. But I didn't let that get into my head. I constantly reminded myself that I wasn't a consultant. And I had to draw my own limit, even if my consultant did not, lest I get myself into trouble. I was a registrar, even if I was senior and experienced.

Months after the ITU incident, I rotated to Mr Graham, the most senior surgeon and head of department. I had looked forward to working in his firm. Working with Mr Gerrard had provided the opportunity to gain valuable experience in vascular surgery, but my interests were more on breast and endocrine surgery, as well as gastrointestinal surgery. I had more experience in these aspects of surgery, and it was my opportunity to work with the consultant who knew and had seen it all.

Mr Graham was a complete contrast to Mr Gerrard. He let his registrar do any operation, but he was readily available and approachable. In life, sometimes what you need is someone there to pat you on the shoulder and tell you 'well done', and to tell you a better way of doing things in a non-judgmental manner. Mr Graham was certainly that person, and I was glad he came into my life.

I learnt, for the first time, the importance of record keeping. My term was nearing its end, and I needed to update my records of operative procedures that I had carried out. Hitherto, I had printouts from the theatre register, which often meant that I sat in the theatre all day to scan through the register for my name. This was daunting, as the A3, hardback register contained information about all the surgeons. One day, after the day list, I decided to stay behind to write up my list. I hadn't realised that Mr Graham was still in theatre.

"What are you up to?" he asked, as he stood in front of me.

"I am writing up the number of operations that I have performed independently, those that I have assisted at and those that I have been assisted with," I replied.

"How are you sure you'll catch all your data from the register?" he asked.

"I assume that they must have correct information in the register."

"Says who?" he smiled wryly. "Come with me."

I followed Mr Graham into his office. The large office, situated at the end of the rows of the consultants' corridor, couldn't have been more strategically located. On one side of the massive office were rows of filing cabinets, arranged in an orderly manner. The one at the extreme corner had a slightly faded label: *June 1964*. That was the folder containing the operations that Mr Graham performed in his first month as a consultant surgeon. After going through the first few months, I walked back to the cabinets in the front. Those were the recent operations. It required discipline and a great deal of commitment to file these thousands of operations so meticulously.

Then he hobbled to another side of the room, an adjoining recess to the side with the filing cabinet, and pulled out a large cabinet with rollers. Whereas the other cabinets were unlocked, this one had a coded lock. He pulled out one of the folders and yanked it on the table. As I read the bold writing, *RECURRENT BASSINI REPAIRS*, I wondered why he had pulled out the folder.

"That is a list of my recurrent hernias," he reported.

I didn't see anything special about recurrent hernias. It was a common belief, and most general surgeons accepted the fact, that no matter how well you repaired hernias, some would recur.

The first thing that came to my mind was that I could write so many papers with all these materials.

He pushed that back and pulled out another. This was partitioned into three columns: *RECURRENT BREAST CANCERS AFTER MASTECTOMY, RECURRENCE AFTER WIDE EXCISION, BREAST CANCER DEATHS.*

I opened my mouth wide as he pulled one folder after another, each containing useful information. There were folders for anastomotic leakage, burst abdomens, bowel cancer related deaths, common bile duct injuries, post-thyroidectomy haemorrhages and many more. I nodded my respect and admiration as I scanned through each folder.

"I'm glad that you are keeping a record of your operations," he said, after slotting back the last folder. "But it is not enough knowing just the number of operations you have performed. It is more important to know your complications. This will enable you to audit your work and learn from your mistakes."

That was exactly what he had shown me, and I made a conscious determination that if I didn't learn anything more under Mr Graham, I had learnt the art of discipline, good record-keeping, probity, self-auditing and continued learning.

Chapter Twenty-One
MOVING ON

A constant struggle, a ceaseless battle to bring success from
inhospitable surroundings,
is the price of all great achievements.
Orison Swett Marden

The job at Wakefield was originally meant to be a numbered registrar post progressing to senior registrar. That was what they offered to the original candidate, who had turned down the job, preferring the job in London. However, when I reapplied, they made the job a stand-alone position with no opportunity to move to the next stage, as was originally designed. Mr Graham was disappointed by the changes that the teaching hospital programme authority had made, so he arranged for me to see the programme director.

I had sent my CV prior to the meeting, which had been scheduled for four o'clock on a Monday afternoon. I arrived at Professor Rainer's office half an hour before the meeting. His secretary, a beautiful lady with a strong Yorkshire accent, informed me that she didn't know his whereabouts, but she was certain that he was aware of the meeting, so I took a seat in her office to await his arrival.

I also had a copy of my CV in my briefcase. Of course, I knew everything on my CV by heart, but I browsed through several times whilst awaiting his arrival. As a surgeon, I knew, of course, that you couldn't predict the length of a surgical procedure – a minor operation could turn into a major one if a complication arose – so I didn't fidget when the professor hadn't arrived at four o'clock, as scheduled. At five, his secretary asked if I would like her to reschedule the meeting. At first, I thought perhaps she should. But on a second thought, I decided to wait for as long as possible. The afternoon was already wasted anyway, and I had intended to go home from the meeting, since Mr Graham had allowed me to take the afternoon off. So I would wait until the secretary started to lock up.

At a quarter past five, I was resigned to the fact that Professor Rainer had forgotten about the meeting, and I accepted his secretary's earlier suggestion to reschedule. The secretary was looking at his booking diary when the door was pushed open, as though someone had broken in with a bulldozer. The middle-aged professor marched into the room, breathing like a hippopotamus. His suit looked like he borrowed if from a toddler. He stood straight in front of his secretary, deliberately ignoring my presence.

"Mr ... erm ... the registrar from Wakefield, has waited for you all afternoon," his secretary informed him, struggling to pronounce my name. Normally, when someone struggled to pronounce my surname during a conversation, I would insinuate. But I had been with the secretary for over three hours. I had introduced myself to her, and she wrote down my name when I arrived, so if she had been interested in pronouncing an unusual name, she could have learnt it.

"You don't have to hang around," he said to his secretary.

I coughed, trying to attract his attention. I knew, of course, that he knew I was in the office. I stood up when he stepped into the office. It beat my imagination that he could flagrantly ignore my courtesy to him.

"The registrar has been waiting since—" she reminded him.

"Of course, I know," he said. "I will see him on my own, if you don't mind."

"Okay, I will catch up with you tomorrow," she said, as she prepared to close for the day.

"Now then, come with me." Professor Rainer led me into his office.

I stood in front of his desk, waiting for him to tell me to take my seat.

"What's that your name?" he asked, whilst I was still on my feet.

I told him my name and advised that he could simply call me Joe, if he so preferred.

"Your consultant has said nice things about you," he remarked, without looking up. He hadn't made eye contact with me, except briefly, when he asked my name. He pulled out one drawer and pushed it back, then shuffled the piles of files on his cluttered desk here and there. I sensed he was looking for the copy of my CV that I had sent to him prior to our meeting.

"Are you looking for this?" I asked, as I handed him a copy of my CV.

He scanned through the fifteen-page CV, like a child turning the pages of a book that he couldn't read.

"Impressive!" he remarked. "So, what did you want out of this meeting?" he asked.

I wondered why he had asked me this question. Mr Graham had discussed my needs with him. If he had read my CV and the accompanying letter, he would have known my needs. And he knew, of course, that my post was linked to the teaching hospital in its original form.

"I have come to seek your advice and guidance regarding how to progress my training," I said, all the while still standing.

"I don't give out jobs. You need to apply for jobs and hope for good luck," he said.

"As you know, Prof, my job was advertised as 'Registrar to progress to Senior Registrar'. My Wakefield phase is coming to an end, and I am supposed to rotate to your department as Senior Registrar."

He blinked several times. "They made the decision to give you the job," he said. "The job is now a stand-alone job, no longer linked to my job."

"What about the number?" I asked, calmly.

"What number?" he asked.

"My training number," I said, "the number assigned to the post."

"Sit down," he directed. "Now, then, are you British?" he asked. He obviously hadn't read my CV. Otherwise, he would have noted *Nationality: British* on my personal profile.

"Yes," I replied.

"Are you married?" he asked.

"Yes," I replied.

"Is your wife your type of British?" he asked.

"My type of British?" I narrowed my eyes.

"I mean someone like you." He smiled wryly.

"Oh, I see. Yes, she is," I replied.

"Are there no beautiful proper British nurses in your hospital?" he asked. "If you want to become a consultant, divorce your wife and marry one of them. Then you'll become a consultant."

"What about the training number, sir?" I asked again, deliberately ignoring his remarks. I had not come there to challenge his beliefs.

"What training number?" he yelled.

"The number attached to my post," I replied. "I'm told it's a numbered post."

"Oh, that number has been suspended and will be reassigned in the next wave of rotation," he said.

"Can I at least do it as a locum?" I requested. "I would only need one more year of senior registrar experience."

"Well, I have told you what you need to do," he concluded.

"Oh, I see," I said. "Thank you very much for your advice."

"Jolly good," he said.

He didn't need to tell me to leave. I got the message and called it a day. And it was a clear message. This senior surgeon had no problem with my experience and knowledge, as he had acknowledged. However, based on his statements and the fact that the job was changed from what it previously was since they could not find a white doctor, I had to believe that I was denied the opportunity to progress because of my colour and country of origin even though I had naturalised. This was not the first time that I had experienced discrimination, and it seemed so sad. I knew I could not fight the system, and I simply decided to move on and look for opportunities elsewhere.

Chapter Twenty-Two
HOPE REKINDLED

In everyone's life, at some time, our inner fire goes out.
It is then burst into flames by an encounter with another human being.
We should all be thankful for those people who rekindle the inner spirit.
Albert Schweitzer

My meeting with Professor Rainer completely knocked the life out of me. I had had people say or do nasty things to me because I was different to them. People had taunted me, asking me where I hid my tail. I recalled a child touching my skin whilst in supermarket queue, wondering if I had just come out of the coal mine. I had even had someone ask me how comfortable it was living in treetops. And I had people telling me, in the front of other people, that my name was unusual, or asking, "Where's that name from?" just to make me feel, and make people see me as, an alien. Although I felt humiliated, I didn't get angry. As a matter of fact, I understood and pitied them for their ignorance. But for someone as high profile as Professor Rainer to treat a professional colleague the way he had beat my imagination. According to him, my CV was impressive and my consultant had said good things about me. Still, he wouldn't release my training number to me.

My interview with Professor Rainer gave me nightmares for several months, but I tried not to tell anyone exactly what was said. When my wife asked, I simply told her, "It's not my luck yet. But I trust God to provide a way out."

I hadn't said anything to Mr Graham. One mind told me to be honest, but if I told him, I wondered what the consequences would be. And who would be caught in the middle when the big people were at war? No one but myself – the grass that the elephants trampled on when they fought. That was what my brain was thinking, but my heart had a different thought – to tell Mr Graham about my disappointment but keep the details away and let posterity judge. I decided to follow my heart.

Mr Graham made other contacts for me, and I went up and down the country to meet the big people in surgery, but the outcome was the same. Of course, most of them showed their sympathy. Some offered words of encouragement, but none of them could make things happen. Finally, I decided I had had enough and stopped applying for jobs. Perhaps the time had come for me to go back home. I even started making plans. That was at a time when the NHS was undergoing major changes. The first waves of Trusts had just taken off. Cottage hospitals were folding up. Hospitals merged to become Trusts, and many of them put their equipment up for sale. I bought not only surgical, but all imaginable equipment that would be useful back home. Our garage had no room for anything else.

As I didn't have a job at the end of my contract, Mr Graham recommended me for the renewal of my contract. This took away the pressure.

My wife had only one more year to finish her postgraduate study, so a one-year extension was just right for us. After that, we planned to go back to Nigeria.

One Saturday, about six weeks after my interview with Professor Rainer, I was on call. Friday night was very busy, and I operated all night. I had just retreated to my room, hoping to have a nap before the Saturday morning post-take ward round, when my bleep went off. The SHO informed me of a newly admitted patient with a bleeding stomach ulcer. I took her to theatre for a laparotomy. I operated, successfully stopped the bleeding, and when I reviewed her the following day, her condition was stable.

"Thank you for saving my life, Doctor," the fifty-eight-year-old woman said, sitting up in bed, after clearing her throat.

"Nothing to thank me for," I said. "I'm glad you are doing well."

"You must be from Ibadan," she said, as she adjusted herself in bed.

I raised a questioning brow, wondering how she knew that, and reached for her notes. As I opened the first page, my eyes settled on *Next of Kin: Professor S. Ade*. I blinked several times as it hit me like a bullet that the woman I had just operated on was the wife of my former trainer, an eminent and respectable professor of surgery, herself a consultant physician.

"I am sorry that I did your operation," I said. "In the dire situation that you were in, I hadn't realised who you were. I should have got my consultant to do it."

"Don't be silly," she reassured me. "You saved my life, and my recovery is going well."

"I am honoured," I said.

Mrs Ade informed me that her husband had already been and would be visiting again the following day. She would ask the staff to bleep me when he visited, so I could see him.

I was about to leave for another ward when Mr Graham breezed in.

"How's the bleeder that you did yesterday?" he asked.

"She is doing okay," I replied and took him to Mrs Ade.

"Very good." He patted me on the shoulder, after reviewing her and her notes. He then explained to her, as I had done, that she had a bleeding ulcer. "The senior registrar has fixed it. You should be out of the hospital within a week."

Mrs Ade nodded a thank you.

I was proud of myself and the privilege and professional liberty that I enjoyed under Mr Graham. He always made me appreciate and believe in myself. But that was how he was with everyone. He never looked down on anyone. Even the cleaner didn't go unappreciated.

"That woman is my professor's wife," I said to Mr Graham, as we stepped out of the ward.

"What do you mean by that?" Mr Graham asked, with a wide stare.

I informed him that Professor Ade was an eminent and respectable professor of surgery in Nigeria, with high international repute. I was going to start my surgical training under him, but I chose to come to the UK instead.

"I would never have imagined that I would operate on my professor's wife thousands of miles away," I confessed. "I am sorry that I didn't let you know, so you could perform the operation yourself."

"What's wrong with you performing the operation?" He stood in front of me, raising his eyebrows, resting his hands on my shoulders, as he stared into my eyes. "Listen, my son," he said, "you should be proud of yourself. You know what?" He tapped my shoulders. "You see, many things happen that we cannot understand. Perhaps your professor's wife's bleeding ulcer has brought an opportunity for you to see him – an opportunity to do some catching up. On the other hand, you might have been a blessing to his wife. What if she had come under those inexperienced registrars?"

I scratched my head, like a child in front of his father, offering him words of wisdom.

"And you know what?" he asked, removing his hands from my shoulders.

I shook my head.

"If I needed such an operation, I would smile under your knife," he said candidly.

My head swelled. I couldn't say a word. I simply stared at this senior doctor that I respected greatly. It was a humbling experience and a humbling remark from a surgeon who had seen, known and done it all.

Mr Graham was a great man and I was honoured to know him. He said so many things that showed me his true character: his beliefs, ideas and philosophy. "Nature harbours no vacuum," he had said. "The famous scientific fact is true even in our everyday life." He advised that both bad and good events in our life have their own purposes. Sometimes, opportunity can arise from a bad event. And it is an opportunity to learn, so you will enjoy when good times come. Nothing good comes with ease. Even bad people come into one's life to make one appreciate good people.

The following Sunday, as his wife had said, Professor Ade visited the hospital. Unlike Friday and Saturday, Sunday wasn't busy, so I had plenty of time to spend with him. As soon as we took our seats in one quiet corner at the hospital canteen, I saw that he hadn't changed. Apart from a small quantity of grey hair on his head and a couple of senile streaks on his face, he looked like he did ten years before, when I last saw him. As we talked, he informed me that there was a dispute between the junior doctors and the Nigerian Government. The Nigerian Government, as typical of the military dictatorship, had made a knee-jerk response. They brought in draconian rules and brought misery to the doctors. Some senior doctors openly criticised the government in its handling of the crisis and offered suggestions on how to resolve it.

344

"Rather than take on our suggestions, the government alleged that we supported the junior doctors. As a consequence, they sacked some senior doctors."

Prof told me that the government sent armed soldiers to his residence, and he was given twenty-four hours to move out. The government refused to pay salaries. He couldn't provide support for his daughter who was an undergraduate student in the UK. So his wife decided to come to the UK to do locum work whilst he took up a job in the Middle East.

I fought tears welling up in my eyes as I listened to Professor Ade's account of the situation in Nigeria after I had left. He was one of the few pre-independence professors. These were doctors who had the opportunity to have a better life in Europe and America but chose to go back to Africa to help build the post-independence healthcare delivery. And they gave all that they knew to raise future generations of doctors. I was privileged to have been taught by Professor Ade. I recalled how he spent his time between the wards, theatre, outpatient, library and lecture theatres. Unlike many of his colleagues, he would never shout at or intimidate you, but would gather us together like a father and feed us with the medical skills and knowledge to make us good doctors. He did very little, if any, private practice, and so didn't build his own house and didn't have a prestigious car. Instead, he put one hundred percent of his life into teaching the medical art. To hear that someone of his calibre could be sent away with one sweep of the broom brought tears into my eyes. I had lived long enough in the UK to know that the government always tried to bring the health professionals with them before making major policy changes. They would negotiate and be guided by them. Sadly, in Nigeria and many other African countries, the situation was different. Instead of listening to the professional leaders and negotiating with the professionals, they would send armed policemen to torture and imprison them.

"I am sorry that I didn't get my consultant to operate on your wife," I said. "I should have called my consultant, but I only realised after the operation."

"She couldn't have had a better surgeon," he said. "And I thank you so much for your prompt intervention and successful outcome."

I cracked my fingers. "It was a privilege, sir," I said.

Then looking straight into my eyes, he informed me, "Your consultant spoke very highly about you. You made us proud."

"My consultant?" I squeezed my eyes, wondering how he knew Mr Graham.

"Oh yes, he came to see me earlier on," he informed me, "and we had a chat. He seemed to be a nice man."

"Indeed," I said. "And I am lucky to work with him."

"So, what are your plans?" Professor Ade asked.

I scratched my head.

"I mean your plan for the future," he clarified.

"I had hoped to progress my training to reach the top," I replied. "But that's proven impossible. So we plan to go back to Nigeria when my wife finishes her postgraduate study next year."

"Why is it impossible with all the accolades that your consultant has accorded you?"

I cleared my throat, took a deep breath and informed him about the difficulties in getting a job.

"I have been rejected for every job I have applied for," I said. "The turning point was when the training director told me to go and divorce my wife for a local girl to have my training number."

"So you want to give up your ambition because someone has told you that you can't make it?" Professor asked, after taking a deep breath.

I nodded. "And I believed, because everything made sense to me. I've applied everywhere. It's the same answer everywhere. 'Oh, you are so unlucky' or 'It's been a highly competitive interview.' That's all I get. That's all they tell me wherever I go."

"Hmmm!" he sighed. "How many hospitals are there in England?" he asked.

"Thousands, I imagine," I replied.

"How many are there in Scotland?" he asked again.

"A thousand, maybe less," I replied.

"And in Wales and Northern Ireland?" he asked.

"Probably hundreds," I replied.

"And how many of these have you applied to?" he asked.

I scratched my head. "Twenty or a little more," I replied.

"You see, home is always best, and we all love to go back home. No doubt, someone like you will be an asset to our dear country. But what do you do when your country rejects you? Look at me now. Should I at this stage be looking for work abroad after over forty years of service?"

He shook his head. "Listen, my son, right now home is not an option," he said, after a long pause. "Cast your net wider so you can catch more fish. Send your CVs to the hospitals. When all the hospitals have turned you down, that's the time to pack in the gloves and make your way home."

He also advised me to look for a research post and to keep on writing papers. I mustn't let anyone steer me away from my goal. He recognised that things were hard here, but it was worse at home, so I should climb as far as possible on the professional ladder. The higher I went, the better for me, even if I decided to return home in the future.

I couldn't believe this advice, coming from the professor. I recalled that when I wanted to leave for the UK, he advised me to continue on the Nigerian/West African fellowship. But I insisted on travelling. For him to now encourage me to remain in the UK, intrigued me, but I had no doubt that he had offered genuine and honest advice, and I resolved to follow it and to press on irrespective of people's efforts to discourage me.

As advised by Professor Ade, I initially printed thirty copies of my CV and sent applications to job adverts. Within two weeks, I had four shortlists, the first one of which was a research post in South Wales. This job appealed to my interest, as it was relevant to gastrointestinal surgery, which was my area of interest then. Also, going back to research in hospitals where I had previously worked was exciting. I knew most places in South Wales and I had made so many friends, so I was excited when I got shortlisted. Fortunately, it was the first interview, but the only research post. The rest were clinical registrar posts. I had envisaged a highly competitive interview, and it was indeed so, but I was successful among six candidates. This was an answered prayer and I accepted the offer.

Chapter Twenty-Three
RESEARCH POST

Patience and perseverance have a magical effect before
which difficulties disappear and obstacles vanish.
John Quincy Adams

The decision to undertake a two-year, full-time research post was challenging. My family had settled in Oldham, and my wife was in the middle of her postgraduate study, so we decided not to relocate as a family. Rather, I should go alone.

I rented a flat in the staff residence and was paid basic registrar salary with a significant reduction in my take-home pay.

My study centred on the development and calibration of a device for non-invasive method of monitoring gastric pH. Endoscopic based, I had to collect gastric samples from consenting patients. In addition to gastric acid analysis, I also conducted an epidemiological survey, looking at the prevalence of *Helicobacter pylori* in South Wales. Undertaking this research was a boost to my competencies in endoscopic and minimally invasive surgery. It afforded me the opportunity to extend my endoscopic skills to the management of bleeding varices and peptic ulcers, as well as endoscopic management of common bile duct stones.

The clinical aspect of my research involved three hours of endoscopy in the mornings three days a week. The rest of the week involved laboratory and academic work. With so many free hours at my disposal, I decided it was the right time to undertake the degree course in Law that I had always wanted to do. I hated to see people cheated and maltreated. I wanted to not only treat people's diseases and prevent death, but I also wanted to defend the vulnerable. So I applied to study Law and I received an offer.

At this time, the M5 motorway was under works to widen it, so the journey from Cardiff to Oldham took me at least seven hours. Added to that, my salary was much smaller than previously, and I had to do locums to boost my income, so I only came home every three weeks. On those weekends when I didn't do locum work, I would arrive home late on Saturday. As I turned my car into our drive, the first faces I would see were the smiling faces of my kids shining through the window as they raced up and down like a loyal dog on the arrival of its owner. The affectionate kiss from my wife, and my arms around our kids, reminded me of how much I missed my family. I had to leave Oldham for Newport around three on Monday morning to beat the traffic to get to work by eight o'clock.

It was a difficult time for the family, but my wife was terrific, juggling between looking after the kids and her postgraduate study. Like many junior doctors' wives in my training days, she had to learn to do everything on her own, whilst their husbands went up and down the country in pursuit of their training posts.

We purchased a second car, an old Renault 5 GT, for £1,200, but, if anything, it made life more difficult, with only enough lifespan for a short-distance drive. The radiator would always dry up after driving a short distance, so we made sure there were Jerrycans of water in the boot. It broke down regularly, and I had to rely on my friends in Oldham to help with taking the children to and from school when I was away. And they often helped with simple mechanical issues. One of the prayers the children used to say during the family's prayer time was simply for the car to start in the morning.

One Monday, I left home later than usual, since I didn't have to start work early that week, and relieved my wife of the trouble of taking the children to school. After dropping off our son, I drove to the other end of the city to drop our daughter at her nursery. As I drove, she asked me with a voice louder than the car music, "Dad, are you really going again?"

I turned down the music.

"Yes, my little princess," I replied, as I fought back my tears.

"But why? Why, Dad?" she sobbed.

"Don't worry. I'll soon be back and will get you a large pack of Bounty, the taste of paradise," I reassured her.

"Oh! I think I have headache tummy," she said, with a tone of disappointment. And she was sick in the car.

We drove back home. After cleaning her up and the car, I reassured her that it was necessary for me to work away from home. I reminded her of other children that she knew whose dad or mum worked somewhere far from home. Her smiles returned then, and she was back to her bubbly self, singing and chatty. She was only a little late, but her teacher was understanding. The incident showed to me how much my family missed me. It wasn't easy for my wife. No doubt, she missed me so much, but she supported me in the pursuit of my surgical career with absolute dedication.

The years seemed to go really fast. The kids got used to my absence most of the weeks, but I made sure that the short time I spent with them was quality time. Eventually, I completed my research and also completed my Law Degree.

I was aware of three senior registrar posts coming up shortly, so I decided to hang around doing locum work. I thought I had a good chance of getting one of them, but when I discussed my intention with my consultant, he took a long look at me and asked, "How many Nigerians can we help?"

I stared at him. I couldn't believe what came out of his mouth. I recalled the discussion that I had with him when I started my research. He advised that undertaking the research would improve my chances, and he would do everything he could to help progress my career. I wasn't expecting him to hand me a job like a plate of rice, but I hadn't expected that question from him.

I wanted to answer his question with a question: "How many Nigerians have you helped?" But that would be immature. You don't touch a hot iron or else you get your finger burnt. I needed his reference and support. I couldn't confront him. In life, some people will stick their necks out for you. They will go the distance with you. Some people neither like nor dislike you. What they do depends on the circumstances. If you are doing well, they will help you, but in times of your struggles, they will leave you on your own. There are other people. These are people who hate you with all their guts. Such people will never help you, and they indeed will do things to your detriment.

They shortlisted me for the first senior registrar post, and I was on top of the moon. I had completed my research, got some publications, and I had backed up all this with a wealth of experience, so I believed I had ticked all the boxes.

Four candidates attended for the interview. Apart from me, only one other candidate was local. I knew all the members of the interview panel, so I felt at home, and the interview went well. I had given it my best shot, but it wasn't meant to be. The local graduate got the job.

"You are a strong candidate," the chairman fed back to me at the end of the interview. "The interview was highly competitive. You are so unlucky."

"Thank you for the feedback," I nodded.

That wasn't new to me. I had received such feedback numerous times: a polite way of telling me, 'Sorry, you don't deserve our job.'

I smiled and thanked them once again.

"Never mind," the chairman added, "there are two more posts coming up soon." He crossed his fingers.

I smiled and took my leave.

Six weeks later, I again faced the interview panel for the second training post. It was the same panel. I knew all of them. And they knew me too. My CV hadn't changed. Nothing about me had changed. As I sat in front of the seven-man panel, I closed my mind to my experience at the previous interview. I had been given another opportunity to prove myself.

The questions were the same, the fake smiles were no different, and the acknowledgement of my many years of clinical work, research and publications were all highlighted. But in the end, these didn't qualify me for a place on the career ladder. I was the only candidate from the deanery, but the post went to a British graduate from Liverpool. As before, they called me in for feedback, and I thought they were going to tell me something different, something I had done wrong that cost me my success at the interview, but that wasn't the case. It was the same feedback that I had received countless times. As the chairman began, "What can I say?" I almost said, "You are so unlucky…" I could recite it in my sleep.

And as anticipated, "You are so unlucky…" he said, after clearing his throat.

I could read the guilt on the faces of some members of the panel.

Even the chairman stuttered as he fed back to me. And then after regaining his composure, he said, as before, "Another one is coming up soon. Keep trying."

I blinked several times. I couldn't hide my disappointment.

"Thank you for giving me the opportunity to attend yet again," I said and took my leave.

I sat in my room and held my head in my hands. I couldn't think of what more I needed to do to improve my chances. I had done more than both candidates who got the jobs. There was nothing wrong with my interview technique. I knew all the members of the interview panel, and they all knew my career plan, since I had met with them and had informal discussions on a one-to-one basis. I just couldn't think straight. I didn't want to call my wife in my state of mind. I knew she would be by the phone eager to hear of the outcome of the interview, and I knew she would offer me sympathy and words of encouragement, but I had no doubt that she would be upset and perhaps cry in bed on her own at night. So I had to find the best way to break the news.

I was just dozing off when my phone rang. I became mute as I heard my wife's voice.

"We have been waiting for you to call. How did the interview go?"

"Not good, I am afraid. I was unlucky again," I said. "I am sorry, I wanted to wait for the kids to go to bed before phoning."

"For the kids to go to bed?" she almost tore my eardrum.

Of course, she knew that wasn't right. I always called before the kids went to bed, and I prayed for them on the phone, so she sensed my state of mind.

"Erm, I just thought I should keep it from them," I said, after clearing my throat.

"Of course, they knew that you were going for an interview. Remember, we prayed about it last night?"

Of course, they knew about it. No one kept anything to himself or herself in our family. We were open, and we shared our joy and disappointment. We celebrated when we needed to, and we shed tears together.

"Just couldn't think straight," I confessed. "I am sorry."

"Of course, I understand," my wife reassured me. "And the kids understand that you are trying your best."

That was a soothing balm to my aching heart. My wife's sweet and kind words had been my strength, following the numerous disappointments that I had experienced in the pursuit of my goal. And to know that my kids appreciated my efforts was the strength and encouragement that I desperately needed.

I was booked as a locum in Swansea that weekend, but I was desperate to be with my family, so I cancelled. As I had finished my research, the use of my time was at my control, and I didn't have to rush back in the early hours of Monday. I also tried to find locum work closer to home, but I remained in Wales in the hope that I might get the last training post yet to be advertised.

That Saturday, it was one of my friend's son's birthday party, and the family had invited us to join them. My friend informed me that he had secured a training post in Bradford. This was the kind of news I had needed. It rekindled my hope, and I was determined more than ever to soldier on, hoping that one day, someone somewhere would look beyond my appearance and see me as a surgeon who was determined to do his best for his patients irrespective of their origin, beliefs, gender or colour of skin.

The third post was advertised two months after the last interview. I wasn't sure they would shortlist me, since I thought I had become an embarrassment for them. But if I didn't apply, I would have no chance of getting the job. And I couldn't blame anyone for that. After all, that was the reason I had stayed behind, now almost five months after my research. There was nothing to lose.

So, after updating my CV with an additional, new publication, I submitted my application. None of the remaining registrars was ready to progress to the senior registrar stage. Even the most senior of them still had one more year, and he hadn't done research. So I reasoned that, all things being normal, I was best suited for the post. But all things were not normal. The game of life is not fair.

The interview took place on a sunny afternoon. Five candidates were shortlisted. I was the first candidate to arrive in the waiting room. Three other candidates arrived shortly after. The last candidate arrived wearing a white shirt with a tie, but no suit. At first, I thought he had come to help out at the interview. That was Phil Baker, one of our registrars. Phil was a fourth-year medical student when I first joined the department as an SHO. He told me then that he wanted to be a surgeon, so I always took him with me whenever I was on call. At this time, whilst we were in the doctors' mess, I got a needle and thread from the theatre and taught him how to tie surgical knots and advised him to practise on it. The following week, when I was on call, he assisted me with an appendicectomy, and I allowed him to close the skin wound.

Phil took his seat among the rest of us, with a folded sheet of paper in his hand.

"Are you for the interview too, Phil?" I couldn't help asking.

"Yeah," he replied, with a casual voice, "but I don't think I have any chance, with someone like you around. At least it'll be an experience for me."

"I don't think anyone is guaranteed for the job. We can only try," I said. "Anyway, good luck."

"I need it," Phil said.

Phil was the first person to be called in. He was back in the waiting room in less than ten minutes. I thought it was a joke, but it wasn't. He had had his interview. He informed me that he was going back to the vascular clinic, and he would return for the result. The other three candidates went before me, each interview lasting twenty-five minutes. Then it was my turn. And like the previous two interviews, I had no problems with the all-too-familiar questions. Everything seemed perfect, so I thought. I took my leave to join the other candidates to await the result.

Phil returned to join us nearly two hours after he had his interview. He was now wearing a complete suit. He paced the room, breathing heavily as he made occasional eye contact with me. Within minutes of his arrival, the medical staffing officer emerged from the interview room.

"Mr Phil Baker," she called, glaring with a smile of reassurance as she led him into the interview room.

We didn't have to be told. He was the successful candidate. Some candidates hissed. Others sighed and others shook their heads as they picked up their briefcases and took their leave. As for me, I froze like a carcass buried in the Antarctic, not because of fear, but a technical knockout by disappointment.

Phil emerged from the interview room and walked straight over to me.

"I am sorry," he said and shook his head.

"Never mind," I said to him. "I am sure the best candidate has got the job."

"I don't think so," he confessed.

But there was nothing I could do about that. He was luckier than I was. Or should I say, he was the lucky one, and I was the unlucky one.

No sooner had Phil left than the medical personnel officer called me in. She forced a smile as she ushered me in for feedback.

It was a different chairman this time. Although I knew Professor Lleweny, I wouldn't say that I knew him very well. I only knew him as a vascular surgeon. I knew the rest of the panel. They were the same people who had interviewed me both previous times. But the language was the same, and the feedback was no different. It didn't surprise me when the chairman said, like a rehearsal of a verse in Shakespeare's book: "You are so unlucky. It was a highly competitive interview. You are so unlucky."

"Unlucky?" I smiled wryly. "I didn't know that the senior registrar interview was a game of luck." I narrowed my eyes. "When I attended the first interview, I was told I was unlucky. The same feedback went for the second post. And now, I am unlucky again for the last and only post." I lost it, and I needed to really open my heart. It would help me to come to terms with the great injustice. So I continued as they looked on. "If you had advised me to take another fellowship exam, I would have had no problem with that. If you had told me I had not written enough papers, I would have tried to write more." I scratched my head as they looked on. "My problem is, no amount of bleach would give me good luck," I spat. "Thank you for everything," I said and avoided their curious eyes as I took my leave.

I lost my mind. I simply wandered through the main hospital corridor, desperate to talk to someone. I bumped into Jenny, Professor Bryan's former secretary. She was pushing the trolley of case notes from the clinic. An experienced secretary and a devout Christian, Jenny was someone I could trust, and I was pleased that she showed up at that moment in time.

"How did it go?" she asked.

"Phil got the job," I replied.

"I knew that would happen," she said.

I raised an eyebrow.

"I warned Professor Lleweny about this injustice. It's a sin," she said.

Jenny told me that she was in the vascular clinic when the whole thing was planned. Professor Lleweny arrived, carrying a large folder of applications under his arm. He advised his registrar, Phil, to apply. Phil reminded him that he still needed one more year of registrar experience, but the professor urged him to apply nevertheless. "There are no local candidates," he had told him. "This is your opportunity. And if you don't apply, you will make our African friend lucky. We will have to give the job to him."

"Hmmm?"

"You know what intrigued me most?" she asked.

I shook my head.

Jenny told me that the closing date had passed when Phil applied. Despite that, they still shortlisted him. "I don't think Phil himself expected that he would be on the shortlist let alone get the job," she said.

"Oh well, that's his luck," I said. "I guess I was unlucky, as they said."

Talking to Jenny Davies was like drinking a large glass of ice-cold water in the middle of the dessert. Though I was still aggrieved, I got my thinking back. And as I walked back to my flat, I couldn't take my mind off the injustice that I had suffered. I don't believe in quitting, but I believe that sometimes in life, we may be facing the wrong direction. And sometimes we look for treasure where it isn't buried. So I concluded that perhaps it was time for me to change the course of my voyage, and try my luck somewhere else. Maybe the angel that was holding the next baton of my race was waiting for me somewhere else. I had already booked to do some locum work in the hospital, so I planned to return to base in Greater Manchester after completing it.

That Friday, I was about to get into my car when my phone rang. At first, I ignored it. I wouldn't normally return to my room to answer a phone once I was set to go somewhere. Some phone calls could delay you and cause you to be late for your appointment. But I have also learnt in life that some phone calls may be your saviour. It may be someone warning you about a risk or danger on your journey. It might even be a last-minute call to cancel your appointment. So I raced back to my room to answer the call.

"I don't know how to say this." The medical personnel officer's voice was unmistakable. "You know that job," she reported, carefully choosing her words, after clearing her throat. "Mr Baker cannot be appointed into the post straightaway."

"Oh, I see," I said. I blinked several times, thinking that they had now reasoned that I was the most qualified person for the job.

"Oh God, I don't know how to say this," she continued. She coughed and after clearing her throat, said, "The college has advised that Phil would ideally need to do one more year or at least six months before taking up the job." And then after taking a deep breath, she asked, "Would you like to locum for six months to hold the post for him, whilst he completes his registrar rotation?"

"If I heard you clearly, you want me to locum, so he can fulfil the requirements to become a senior registrar. In other words, I'm not lucky enough to be appointed to the post that a lucky candidate has been offered, but I am only good for it as a locum."

"Don't look at it that way," she said. "You see, Professor Lleweny is only trying to help you. If you can do six months, then you have six months less of your senior registrar requirement to become eligible for a consultant post."

"I see," I said. "Please tell Prof that I thank him for the offer, but I am sorry that I cannot accept it."

"Okay then, all the best," she said and hung up.

I knew, of course, that it might have been possible to locum for twelve months, given that that was what Phil needed to do as registrar before progressing to senior registrar. But I needed my own dignity. Besides, I wouldn't be happy on the job, knowing that a great injustice had been done.

I was supposed to locum for them the following day. I wasn't happy to do it, so I went to the personnel department, handed over my bleep and cancelled the shifts. I had already packed most of my personal effects. I packed the rest, including the stuff I had in the fridge, after which I went to the accounts office to settle my rent. I had no job on the horizon, but I trusted God to provide something somewhere.

Chapter Twenty-Four
A LEAP OF FAITH

Have I not commanded you? Be strong and courageous.
Do not be afraid, do not be discouraged,
for the Lord your God will be with you wherever you go.
Joshua 1:9

That week, my wife attended an interview, and we had hoped that it would help our financial situation if she got it. It would mean that I wouldn't have to go about doing locum jobs everywhere. My wife was well-qualified and best suited for the job, and we had high hopes, but it wasn't meant to be. The job was offered to someone else, despite our prayers. A few days after the interview, my wife received a phone call. They unashamedly confessed that the person they had appointed to the job had no experience to work on her own as the job demanded. They invited her to come and do voluntary work so she could help to train the appointee.

The resemblance of my wife's situation and my own event beat my imagination. How could human beings behave like that? It was bad enough to deny us the positions, but this was like rubbing pepper on our burnt skin. I wouldn't have raised any concerns if we weren't qualified for the jobs – I didn't expect to get every job that I applied for, and if the best candidate got the job, there was nothing wrong with that, no matter how painful – but to deny you of a position that you were best suited for and offer it to a less-qualified candidate, and then invite you to hold the post for the candidate or do the same job unpaid, to train the less-qualified candidate, was an unimaginable injustice.

But we knew we couldn't fight the system. It wouldn't get us anywhere. In such situations as this, we had to leave posterity to judge. And that was what we did.

That weekend, an old friend of mine, Felix Onuku, visited us. I informed him of all that I had been through. I also showed him the surgical equipment that I had purchased and stored in the garage, with the hope of going back home. He advised that things were bad for doctors back home. He informed me that he had, in fact, left the medical profession and become a businessman. He imported medical equipment into Nigeria, and there was a good market for them.

As he said, "They sell like hot cakes." He advised that the equipment would fetch me millions of naira. "You have many millions of naira wasting in your garage," he told me. I thought Felix had come at the right time, as I needed to send money home for my parents and for the completion of my building project that I embarked on before leaving home. Felix knew my mother. He had visited us in Lagos countless times, so I trusted him.

Within days, he arranged shipment of the equipment to Nigeria, after which he left for Germany.

I phoned my mother about six weeks later. She was in good spirits.

"Please thank your friend, Felix," she said. "He visited and gave me one thousand naira."

"Is that all?" I asked.

"Yes," she replied. "He was really kind."

My mother informed me that Felix had promised to come back to see her again. So I decided not to tell her about the equipment business, thinking that perhaps he had not sold them, hoping that he would return to her when he had.

I waited several weeks for Felix to return to my mother as he had promised, but he never did.

I started job hunting in earnest when I arrived back home. I recalled the advice that Professor Ade gave three years previously: to cast my net beyond the shore to increase my chances of a big catch. I applied to as many jobs as were advertised: senior registrar and registrar. Although I had so many shortlists, the outcomes were the same. It seemed as though all the interviewers were taught to give the same feedback. Virtually all of them told me that I had a good CV and track records, good interview technique and good references. And then they ended their feedback by the usual, "But you are so unlucky."

I was shortlisted for a training post in Birmingham. I visited the hospital a number of times and had informal chats with the consultants.

The head of gastrointestinal surgery took me around the department. He even introduced me to the staff in the endoscopy department by my first name, informing them, "Hopefully, he will be joining us soon." He told me that he had read my paper on ERCP, and the innovation that I had discussed fascinated him. He looked forward to learning from me. I felt on top of the world to hear this from one of the top surgeons in gastrointestinal surgery.

I phoned my wife and told her, "I may have made a breakthrough."

She sighed and asked, "Can you trust him?"

"He seemed to be a genuine and trustworthy person," I replied.

"I don't want to sound pessimistic," she cautioned, "but you have come across seemingly genuine people who have let you down."

She was right. My wife had always been more cautious when dealing with people. Whenever she felt uneasy about a particular person or situation, I often found in retrospect that she was right. But this time, I followed my heart and ignored her reservations. With the hope that I would get the job, I trusted him with detailed information about our device and how I made it happen.

"Very innovative," he said. "We need someone like you to join our department."

I was one of the five candidates shortlisted for the interview. The administrative officer ushered me into the large interview room to face a panel of eight interviewers. I was the first candidate to be interviewed. It started with the chairman urging me to tell the panel about myself. That was not a big issue. I had heard that so many times that I didn't have to think before taking them through my CV. Everything seemed to go smoothly with each interviewer asking me the usual questions that I had answered countless times. Then it was the turn of Mr Dodds, the consultant whom I had visited several times, expressing a great interest in me and all that I had done, the one my wife had cautioned me about.

"What is happening in Africa?" he asked through his bushy moustache.

I folded my forehead, wondering what he meant.

"I mean, what is happening in Nigeria?" he narrowed his eye.

"I am sorry, I have not listened to the news today," I replied, thinking there had been a military coup, violence or disaster.

"I have seen your CV. And of course, you have visited the department," he said. "Don't you think that if highly skilled doctors like yourself could go back to Africa, you would help to train the doctors and stop them coming to clog the system?"

I had to quickly process the question and allow the rational part of my brain to take over, or else I would say something terrible. I adjusted myself in my seat and braced up. Then with a stare that, no doubt, made his heart flutter, I took a deep breath and ensured that my voice did not shake.

"Thank you for your observations and the question," I replied. "But with due respect, sir, will you ask the Scottish guy out there or the Irish lady why they did not go back to their countries to stop their fellow men and women coming to clog the system? Will you?" My frustration brought out the monster in me. I couldn't control my emotion.

"They are British, so they can't clog the system," he replied.

"And I am British, too," I said.

"But I am—" he said.

"That is alright," the chairman interrupted to diffuse the situation that was heading towards a nasty end. He then turned to the other interviewers. "Have you any more questions?" he asked.

"No more questions," they replied one at a time.

"Thank you," the chairman said to me. "You may take your leave."

I knew there was no way I would get the job, so there was no point raising my hopes. And I needed no feedback from them either. I smiled as I walked through the waiting room, trying not to give other candidates a clue about how my interview went.

As I drove back home, I couldn't get my head around the conduct of the interview. Why had this consultant, whom I had trusted, treated me the way he had? What changed the dynamics of the interview? Was he trying to deliberately annoy me to test my resilience? Had I overreacted? All these and a million questions rattled my brain. I knew, of course, I would never know the answer. And I left it to posterity.

A week later, my consultant informed me that he had received a feedback letter from Birmingham. They alleged that I couldn't take simple jokes and I was argumentative. These were damaging assertions, and I felt angry.

"How could anyone call a racist remark a simple joke?" I clenched my fist. I didn't want to be that blunt, but I couldn't help it in my state of mind. "I met Mr Richard Dodds three times before the interview. We joked and laughed. If he had thrown such questions in during those times, I wouldn't have felt offended. But to ask me at a senior registrar interview, oh no, that was too much to take."

"Hmmm!" he sighed. "He might not mean it the way you had thought." He paused to gauge my countenance. "Have you wondered whether he said all those things to give you an opportunity, for example, to persuade the team to look at you with sympathy? In other words, an opportunity to convince them that going back to Africa was not an option?"

What my consultant said made sense. He could have asked those questions to help me. Maybe I should have shown maturity by answering in a non-confrontational manner. I could perhaps have replied by sincerely acknowledging the problem. I could then provide reasons why it wasn't safe to go back home. I had spent a larger part of my life in this country and had undertaken virtually all my surgical training here. I wanted to give back to the country that had accepted me as I was and adopted me as its citizen.

"I know you are not argumentative, and you have a good sense of humour," he reassured me. "I will write back to Richard and explain the situation." He put his arm over my shoulders like a father to a son and said, "If I were you, I would put that behind me."

I phoned Mr Dodds and arranged a meeting with him. At first, I thought he would decline, but he said he had tried unsuccessfully to contact me. That was why he wrote to my consultant. He would be delighted to see me.

I met Mr Dodds in his office. He had just finished operating. There was no smile on his face.

"What happened?" he asked, his eyes almost popped out from their sockets.

My throat tightened. How could he ask me what happened? I should have been the one to ask him that. And he was the one who should answer.

"You had a job on a plate in front of you, but you blew it," he informed me. "Completely lost it!" He shook his head.

"But I didn't know that," I said, still staring at him.

"I am sorry that I made you feel the way you did," he regretted. "Maybe I had put it to you in an insensitive way. But I was only trying to help you."

"I am sorry that I reacted the way I did," I said, now softened. "I have been through a lot."

I told him what I had experienced at many interviews and what people had said to me. I narrated my experiences at interviews and the great injustice that I had suffered. These incidents had dented my trust in people. It made me think that they didn't like people of my colour. They didn't like foreigners, thinking they had come to take their jobs and their places. Even when they smiled at me, I saw their smiles as frowns.

"Hmmm!" he sighed. "I can understand how you feel, but I want you to realise that there are still some nice people in the world. I also want you to know that some people are put in place to straighten a crooked path. Try to give people the benefit of the doubt," he advised.

"Thank you," I said, and really meant it.

"Believe in yourself," Mr Dodds advised. "You've worked so hard. Your time will come. If there's anything I can do for you, don't hesitate to contact me."

My meeting with Mr Dodds changed my mindset. Of course, in life you will come across people who don't like how you look or where you come from. You will meet nice and not-so-nice people. When you are in the rain, not everyone will offer you an umbrella. When you are hungry, not everyone will offer you a loaf of bread, and when you cry out in pain, not everyone will offer you a shoulder. There are people who can give their eyes to you and those who hate your guts. But the world is big enough for all of us. You can't stop them feeling the way they feel about you. But how you react to their feelings is your own prerogative.

After the Birmingham interview, I had no further invitations for job interviews, and life was tough for the family. I was everywhere doing all sorts of locum jobs to make ends meet. I even did house-officer locums, and I often did nights – so many nights in Accident and Emergency. During such shifts there was no chance of sleeping.

One day, after one of those marathon night shifts, I was absolutely exhausted. It was my last night shift for the week, having worked nonstop for six consecutive nights. I didn't realise how exhausted I was until I had a head-on collision with a bus in a sleepy moment at the wheel. I was only an hair breath from death.

The bus driver got out of the bus and found me wedged behind the steering wheel. My bonnet was a write-off and my windscreen had shattered. The driver's door of my Ford Orion had been crushed; I couldn't open it from inside.

"Are you alright?" the bus driver asked me, concerned.

Everyone on the bus was concerned. Even the passers-by stopped, all fearing for my life or that I was badly hurt.

"I am fine," I replied. Despite my car being a total write-off, I hadn't the slightest scratch.

The bus driver pulled the car door and helped me out of the wreckage. Having ensured that I was unhurt, he walked around my car and inspected his own bus. Then he faced me and asked, "Can you buy a bus?"

My heart sank. I blinked several times.

"Oh, my God," I replied. "If you sell me and everything I have, it wouldn't be enough to buy one tyre let alone a whole bus."

The bus driver rubbed his hand on the broken indicator light and the slight dent on the bumper of his bus. And he turned back to me.

"Your car's badly damaged," he observed. "Don't worry. I'm glad you're not hurt. You, go and fix your car. And get yourself checked."

Three men stepped off the bus and joined us to push the car to the roadside. I couldn't explain why the bus driver had been so good. Even when the police arrived, he told them that we had settled things between ourselves.

Everyone who passed by wondered if the driver of the car survived. They marvelled when I informed them that I was the driver.

As the AA towed my car away from the accident site, I couldn't cease to thank God for his mercy. But the incident had given me a fright, and I began to reconsider my decision about locum work. Of course, I had a family to support, but as a doctor, my options were limited. If I didn't have a regular income, my best bet was to do such work until I found a regular job. I had considered going to the US or Canada, but I wasn't prepared to start all over again, considering how far I had gone in my training. I had heard that surgeons were highly paid in the Gulf States. Perhaps if I could work in the Middle East for two or three years, I could make a good income and go back to Nigeria, hoping that things would improve. But if after working in the Middle East things hadn't changed in Nigeria, I would have to return to the UK. And it would be even more difficult, if not impossible, to return to the career ladder.

I discussed the options with my wife. We had a long debate far into the night. She reasoned that the accident could have happened even if I had a permanent job. It could happen at leisure. I should simply thank God and be more careful. I completely agreed with her. And with regard to the discrimination that I had suffered, she asked, "Isn't it worse back home?"

Of course, she was right. At least, in the UK, the main issue was colour discrimination, and to a certain extent, whether you were a foreign graduate. Back home, the issues were much more complex: your tribe, religion, gender, political affiliation, having wealthy parents and bribery all interplay to define your destiny. You might even be denied of a post for shear fear of rivalry or vendetta.

I was up most of the night weighing all the options. In life, many things happen that don't make sense, but when we look back, they turn out to be a blessing in disguise. Something told me that I wasn't far from reaching my goal. I remembered the prayer that I prayed when I was planning to leave Nigeria. I asked God to make it possible for me to travel only if it was His will. I had also learnt that when life is tough, that's when one needs to try the hardest. After struggling for so long, I eventually dosed off. I dreamt that I became a consultant surgeon. I was even a departmental head, and I had a meeting with other senior surgeons. It was so real that I wished I had continued my life in the dreamland, where everything is possible. But how could that be possible? How could I become a consultant when no one was willing to offer me an opportunity? How could I rise to the top in a community where my background gave me a bad luck? I thought I had fulfilled all the requirements, at least on paper. I had ticked all the boxes except the luck box. I left it in the hands of God to tick this essential box for me, and I trusted that He would make it happen in His own time.

As I meditated, I remembered the story of Abraham. He waited on the Lord, and God gave him his precious Isaac. I remembered the Israelites who would have heard 'You are unlucky' for centuries, like I had heard as a foreigner. And the story of Hannah also came to my mind. She prayed to God for many years before the Lord blessed her womb. Waiting on the Lord has values. It is a test of my faith and trust in God.

"I will not give up," I resolved.

I woke up in the morning with a surge of energy. I had to make it in this country. Home was not an option. Surely, God had brought me out of my country of birth for a purpose. Packing up and giving up my ambition would amount to not trusting God enough.

I made copies of my CV. I scanned through the heap of the BMJ on the floor, looking for job adverts that hadn't closed. That day, I sent off ten applications. I applied for not only senior registrar posts, but also registrar and long-term locums.

I was eventually offered a six-month registrar locum position in Liverpool. I was loading my car when my phone rang. It was the chief of surgery from Doncaster. I had thought that I hadn't been shortlisted for the registrar post, as it was nearly three weeks since I sent my application. Normally, it was the personnel officer who would phone shortlisted candidates. It flabbergasted me that the head of department personally phoned me.

"I have seen your CV. Would you like to come for an interview next week, Wednesday afternoon?" he asked.

At first, I hesitated. Of course, it was good news to get back onto a training post, a glimpse maybe, and it was better than going up and down locuming. But I hesitated because I had already accepted the locum post in Liverpool. For the senior consultant to make a personal effort to contact me, he must have held me in high esteem, but I had been knocked down many times by people that I trusted. They had the precious key to unlock the door of opportunity, but they only dangled it in my face, so I decided to test my chances. I informed him that I had been offered a long-term locum position in Liverpool. As a matter of fact, I was getting ready to travel at just that moment. If I cancelled, I would have no job. With no hesitation, he urged me to cancel and come for the interview.

Seven candidates attended the interview. Unlike previous

interviews, I wasn't anxious. That wasn't because I was sure of getting the job. I had learnt from experience that, as far as job interviews were concerned, nothing was guaranteed. One powerful consultant could put words in for a candidate and change the dynamics. So I went in with a relaxed but professional manner.

I was the first candidate to have my interview. Everyone was polite to me. And when I answered questions, all the interviewers gave nods of encouragement. It was all smiles. I felt like I had met everyone before. At the end of my interview, the head of department told me not to wait and that he would phone me.

"But don't go to Liverpool," he teased.

"No, I won't," I said and thanked him and the panel as I took my leave.

It was past seven in the evening when he called. I had thought that he wasn't going to call me. But thankfully, he informed me that I had got the job. As I had cancelled my Liverpool position, he wondered if I could start that weekend. That seemed a good idea and I agreed to his suggestion. The following day, I received a call from Omer Alli my old Sudanese friend. We were both registrars in Wakefield. He left to take up a consultant job in Abu Dhabi. I hadn't realised that he had returned to the UK. He was working as a registrar in Doncaster. He was the person who helped me when I had the interview for the Wakefield job that I eventually got. He warned me that the consultant I was going to work for was nasty. His previous registrar resigned in the first week. He advised he would frustrate me and it was better for me to look for another job. I thanked him for the advice and told him that I would think about it. After he hung up, I gave it some thought. A rose is a beautiful flower. If you focus on its thorns, you will miss its beautiful colours. He was a nasty consultant, as he had told me, but by the grace of God, I could change him. He had shown his interest in me, and I committed the job to the hands of God, trusting that all things would work out for good.

I started the job on Saturday, leaving home at four o'clock in the morning to arrive early, as there were roadworks on the motorways. I had done some locum work in the Accident and Emergency in Doncaster before, so I knew a fair bit of the hospital. I knew where to find a white coat. Piles of them were stacked in one corner in the Accident and

Emergency department.

Mr David Frankman had asked me to meet him on the ward at one o'clock in the afternoon for a ward round, but I decided to go earlier to familiarise myself with the patients and ward staff, as well as my SHO and HO.

The ward sister immediately took me to one of the patients. The sixty-five-year-old had been admitted with a flare-up of his ulcerative colitis. Following a week course of steroids, he had a colonoscopy and had become increasingly ill. The registrar who was on call the previous night had prescribed morphine for the night nurse to administer as needed.

As I examined him, he was struggling to take in deep breaths due to severe abdominal pain. His abdomen looked like that of a woman with an overdue twin pregnancy. I gently placed my hand on his abdomen, and it was tender with board-like rigidity. And when I listened with my stethoscope, there were no bowel sounds. I had no doubt that he had generalised peritonitis. I had seen it before: a case of acute toxic dilatation with bowel perforation following colonoscopy. I organised the theatre and anaesthetist and informed Mr Frankman.

"How could that happen?" he asked.

"It must have happened after his colonoscopy," I replied. I didn't understand why he asked that question. It wasn't uncommon to have a perforation from severe acute toxic dilatation, particularly if the patient had had a colonoscopy.

"I know that," he said. "I mean, why did no one recognise that? And why did no one inform me?"

"I don't know," I replied.

"I don't believe you," he snarled.

"Well, with due respect, sir, if you don't believe me, I think you have to come as soon as possible, because he is in pretty bad condition."

"So what are you doing about it?" he asked, after a long pause.

"I have arranged theatre and anaesthetist. His last bloods were satisfactory, and he is well hydrated, so he is in a stable condition for laparotomy," I informed him.

"Right, take him to theatre, and I will join you," he said finally and hung up.

"Wow! You stood up to Mr Frankman," the sister remarked. "I've been on this job for twenty years. No registrar has ever challenged him."

"No worries," I said with a smile and made my way to the theatre.

As suspected, the patient had faecal peritonitis. His paper-thin colon had several holes on it. No part of his large bowel was suitable for preservation.

Mr Frankman arrived an hour into the operation.

"What's the score?" he thundered from the theatre door.

I informed him that the situation was exactly as I had thought. "I have done a total colectomy. I am just about to fashion an ileostomy and we are done," I explained.

"No, you couldn't have done that within an hour," he remarked. And then he marched to the theatre corner. He took the bowel out of the bucket and spread it on the floor. He nodded and worked back to the operating table.

"Brilliant." He then patted me on the shoulder. "Make sure that the ileostomy is at least two centimetres and well-sprouted," he added and left the theatre.

I hadn't realised that Mr Frankman's office was situated opposite his ward. As I was about to enter the ward with my SHO, he called me into his office. He made me a cup of coffee, opened a large pack of biscuits and put several pieces on a gold-rimmed plate.

"David was right," he informed me.

I raised a questioning brow, wondering who David was.

"Yes, my friend David Harris. Brilliant student and excellent surgeon," he remarked.

That was the consultant that I had worked for in Devon earlier in my career. True, he was excellent. Mr Harris and I got on very well, and I learnt a lot under him. Mr Frankman informed me that he and Mr Harris had been friends since childhood. They attended the same primary and secondary schools. They were both classmates in medical school at Cambridge. And they did most of their surgical training in the same hospitals.

"When I saw in your CV that you had worked for my good friend, I called him and he told me excellent things about you," he confessed. "Of course, your references were fantastic, but I trusted the informal words from my friend. I said to myself, 'If he's good enough for David, he's good enough for me.'" Apparently, he had made up his mind to give me the job before the interview, which was just a formality. He also told me that he did his elective in Lagos University Teaching Hospital, and he shared good memories of his time in Nigeria.

My head swelled as this senior surgeon showered me with praise on my first day under him. He also knew some of the other surgeons that I had worked with. We had so much to talk about. We joked about the unreliable NEPA (Nigerian Electricity Power Authority) and his experiences taking the bus in Lagos. It was fantastic. I felt like I had known this man all my life. And as we talked and laughed, my heart thanked God for His help. I believe that some things we call problems are not. They are simply part of God's jigsaws of miracles. Some problems in life are not caused by the devil. They are simply a means to fulfil God's miracles. I had thought negatively about starting my job on call, but having to undertake a challenging procedure for a consultant that no registrar had ever challenged couldn't have been anything other than part of God's plan for my life.

The news of my management of the man with the perforated bowel spread through the hospital like wildfire. Wherever Mr Frankman went, he would tell people about his 'fantastic registrar', and didn't hesitate to give me my own list, something I was told, he had never done with his former registrars.

As I settled into the job, I got to know more people and made friends. Mr Frankman's consultant colleagues respected me greatly and were all happy to have me on their on call team. I also spent a lot of time with my junior colleagues. I enjoyed teaching.

As I did weekly commuting, I only went home on Fridays when not on weekend call. So I was in Doncaster during the week. During that time, I spent time on the wards, teaching medical students, helping the HOs and SHOs to find difficult veins and interpreting blood results and X-Rays. They all loved it, and Mr Frankman was highly impressed, as he received good feedback about his department from the medical school.

My post also included urology, working with Mr Andy Tyler. He was much younger than Mr Frankman, and I didn't need to prove myself to him. As far as he was concerned, if Mr Frankman had said it, he required no more evidence. He gave me two urology lists. I undertook an average of six TURP's (Transurethral Resection of Prostate) a week. I broadened my experience in urological procedures, including simple and radical nephrectomies, a minimum of twenty cystoscopies per week, Transurethral Resection of Bladder Tumours, Cystectomy and ileal conduit, vesico-vaginal fistula repairs and bladder neck suspension for stress incontinence. As Mr Frankman once remarked, I had gained enough experience for a consultant urologist position, if I wanted to be one.

A few weeks into the job, my wife was expecting. The pregnancy was complicated. She was in and out of hospital. I couldn't leave her on her own, so I decided to commute daily. I didn't inform Mr Frankman, but he sensed that my heart was greatly troubled. I was normally the first doctor to get to the ward. By the time the rest of the team arrived, I would have everything ready for the consultant ward round, so it would be smooth and stress-free for everyone. But since I started commuting daily, I couldn't do those things. Consequently, the consultant's ward rounds were no longer what they used to be. The consultant asked questions that no one could answer, something that I would have known if I had come earlier to get the results of all the investigations ready.

On this particular day, Mr Frankman zoomed out of the ward in anger without completing his ward round. The ward sister informed me that that was his character, and that he had only changed when I joined.

"We thought you'd changed him. No wonder nobody wants to be his registrar," she remarked, as she pushed the trolley back to the nurses' station.

I couldn't let it go. If Mr Frankman had changed because of my presence in his team, then he had changed now because I had made myself absent or, should I say, less present. That was because I now had less time with the patients. Even the end-of-the-day ward round that I used to do was no more, since I had to get off early to get home before the traffic became busy.

I had to inform Mr Frankman about my problem. He had asked me several times what was bothering me, but I had told him everything was alright. Now I realised that I couldn't let him down like this. He believed in me. That was the real me. It wasn't a pretence, but my very self. So I decided to talk to him.

Mr Frankman was sorting through a pile of case notes in his office when I arrived. He briefly looked up and then got back to what he was doing. When you don't know why someone is angry, it's always best to find out, lest you make the wrong judgment and react the wrong way.

I waited at the door. There were two possible reactions: either let me in and we can talk or shout me out of the office and make me resign, like the sister had informed me on the ward.

"Why are you standing there looking like you're awaiting a death sentence?" he asked. "Come in my Yoruba friend," he urged, smiling.

My heart melted that he still teased me the way he did on my first day. I knew then that whatever were his grievances, they were not directed specifically at me. He still called me his friend, and that meant a lot to me. Since the day he told me that he had spent some of his training days in Lagos, we had related to each other like pals, even though he was much older than me, and he was my boss, a highly regarded surgeon, the chief surgeon. But that didn't stop us saying silly things in the theatre. He had picked up some Pidgin English in Lagos, and he was proud to speak in that vernacular language at every opportunity. He said things like, "Yeye Man," "Which one you dey?" "E don do," "Na Shakara!" "You dey look for wahala." Often, when we finished a procedure, he would switch off the lights and announce, "NEPA don go!" And when he switched it back on, he would say, "NEPA don come back." And all the people would laugh. They had never felt so relaxed with Mr Frankman. And I was glad that my presence had made a difference.

I apologised to Mr Frankman for the fall in standards and informed him that I had started commuting daily from Manchester. Before I could explain to him what made me decide to commute, he was on the phone to the medical personnel officer. He ordered her to relocate me into more decent accommodation.

"He cannot continue living with the nurses. You must find him better accommodation," he said to her. After receiving her assurance that she would relocate me into one of the flats in the married quarters, he hung up and turned to me.

"All done," he said. "So there's no need for you to commute daily."

I then confessed the real reason for my change of plan. He had to know. I knew he genuinely cared about me, and he had my best interests at his heart. When I told him about the problems we were having with my wife's pregnancy, he was genuinely concerned. He encouraged me to give my wife as much support as possible.

I commuted for several more weeks until my wife got stronger. The traffic on the M62 East had eased with the completion of the western wing of the motorway, and I was able to get to work early like I used to do and leave late. So I resumed my usual early-to-start and late-to-finish habit. I also moved into the new accommodation that Mr Frankman had secured for me. It was self-contained and more private than the one in the nurses' building. I had a big fridge and freezer, so I brought cooked food from home at the beginning of the week, which would last the whole week. Also, with Mr Frankman's approval, I went home in the middle of the week and on Friday if I was on weekend call.

The job in Doncaster was extremely busy, and with my wife's situation, it was difficult to do locum work. Consequently, our financial situation got worse, and it got harder to meet domestic financial obligations. Our children's school threatened to eject our children as we were three terms behind in their fees. We had used up our overdraft facilities, and our banks had rejected our loan applications. The only solution I could see was take my annual leave and work as a locum during that time.

I had decided to give my annual leave application to Mr Frankman for his signature after theatre. I wasn't sure he would approve my leave at a short notice, as they would need to appoint a locum in my absence. But Mr Frankman had been so nice and understanding. Whenever my wife was admitted to hospital, he would give me permission to leave work without any force. And those days didn't count towards my leave entitlement. They were the days that he used his position to veto without any questions. He had been so kind that I couldn't give the form to him. If he refused to sign it, that would really hurt me, and it would seriously affect our relationship. I slumped in one of the chairs in the surgeons' room with a troubled heart.

"My Yoruba friend!" Mr Frankman startled me.

"Oh!" I rubbed my hand across my face and blinked several times. I felt as though I had slept for several hours. Yet I had only had a snooze, as my problems had crushed my heart and drained out all the strength in me.

"Tell me what's happening?" he asked. "You look like you haven't slept for a whole week. Has your wife left you?" he asked, trying to soften me, as he pulled a chair close to me.

I had been with Mr Frankman for over six months. I had learnt to trust him. He had shown a genuine interest in me, and I knew that he always listened to me. I had to open up. They say that some people can read other people's minds, but the mind is not a book that you can open and read. And even if it were a book, you might need to understand what you read. So the only way to know Mr Frankman's mind was to show him my own.

"I need to take the whole of my annual leave as soon as possible," I said.

"That is not going to be a problem," he said. "But why so desperate?" he asked with concern.

I explained to Mr Frankman how I got into the financial mess that I was in. I told him that I was able to stay above the troubled waters by doing locum work, but I had stopped so I could give a hundred percent attention to my job. "My children's private school education will cease if I can't settle at least one term fee when they resume after the Christmas holiday. And my mortgage is in arrears. Oh God." My eyes welled up with tears.

Mr Frankman stared at me and shook his head.

"You are a nice person," he remarked. "And you are honest. You demonstrated this quality from that day that I phoned you, through the interview and to this day."

My head swelled as this senior surgeon that everyone feared sat by my side and listened to my plight, with a fatherly empathy.

"Hmmm!" he sighed. "You don't need to spend your annual leave doing locum work."

I gave him a questioning look.

"You know how to do a vasectomy, don't you?" he asked.

"Yes," I replied. "I've done loads."

"Good," he said. "I'll ask Jenny to sort something out for you."

"Thank you, sir. Thank you very much. You are my saviour," I said, and really meant it.

And so, Mr Frankman changed my all-day Friday list to a vasectomy list. This operation was separately paid for and, in those days, most were done by the consultants. Passing his vasectomy lists to me gave me a great opportunity to make extra income, doing a minimum of thirty vasectomies a week. By the time my children resumed after Christmas, I had settled my debt with their school. I cleared my overdrafts and brought my mortgage up to date. I also changed my wife's car to a newer, more reliable one. My wife's health had improved. The pregnancy was progressing well, and through the help of our friends in Manchester, she was able to cope better on her own.

Chapter Twenty-Five
End of the Road?

*What appears to be the end of the road may simply be a bend in
the road.*
Robert H. Schuller

The job in Doncaster was a one-year fixed contract, so as my time drew
to an end, I intensified my efforts to find another job. Mr Frankman also
did everything within his power to progress my career. Still, it got harder.
At first, I got many job interviews, but they soon dried up.

One Friday afternoon, I made many copies of my CV. I wanted to
send them off before going home for the weekend. Whilst stapling them
in the doctors' mess, I received a bleep from the ward staff to come and
review a patient urgently. I couldn't take the large pack of CVs with me
to the ward, so I left it on the central table in the doctors' mess and raced
to the ward. After seeing the patient, I sat at the nurses' station having a
cup of tea and biscuits. Mr James Cooper, the senior registrar joined us.
He had just received a letter of invitation to an interview for a consultant
post. He wanted to travel that weekend, so he could have time to look
round and meet as many people as possible. Unfortunately, he was on
call that weekend, so he was looking for someone to cover for him. He
hadn't informed me earlier since he knew that I had been on call the
previous weekend, but the other registrar had turned him down at the last
minute. After confirming with my wife that she was happy for me to do
the second weekend on a row, I agreed to cover.

The following week, James gave me the good news that he got the
job. He was appreciative of my help, and I congratulated him on his
successful interview.

"Oh, I accidentally saw your CV," James confessed.

"My CV?" I raised my eyebrows, wondering where he had seen it.

James told me that he had mistakenly looked at my pile of CVs in
the doctors' mess, thinking it was something else. Then, out of curiosity,

he couldn't resist reading through.

"Quite an impressive CV," he remarked.

"Hmmm!" I sighed. "Not impressive enough to get me a senior registrar job," I said.

"That should get you even a consultant job. It's better than most people's I know, and they're consultants," he said.

"Well, I guess that's life," I said.

"So what are you going to do now? Your job finishes next month. Is that right?" he asked.

"Yes, end of May," I confirmed. "Then back to the locum market, I guess."

I hinted James about my interview encounters. He was close to tears when I told him about the incident at my last interview, and he tried to encourage me by telling me of his own experience. He attended an interview in London, and someone told him he wasn't speaking proper English, just because of his Aberdeenian accent. "You see, these things happen everywhere and to everyone. You just have to put it behind you and wait for your time to come."

"But my time seems to have expired. I think I have reached the end of the road," I said with frustration.

"Have you considered taking up a staff grade job?" he asked. "It's not ideal for someone like you, but it's better than doing locum work up and down the country. It's a permanent contract and you can settle down with your family."

"I have, as a matter of fact, considered that option. I know a few of my friends who have taken up staff-grade positions, and they seem to be enjoying it. My problem is, I think it's the end of the road: the end of the pursuit of my goal, which is to become a consultant surgeon."

"I don't think it will stop you reaching your goal," James encouraged me. "It doesn't stop you writing papers, learning new skills and applying for senior registrar or even consultant posts. Staff grades are valuable members of the team, a cheaper way to get the work done by experienced doctors."

What James said made sense. I hadn't thought of the many positive things about a staff-grade post. I knew of two people who were staff grades and later became consultants. It was certainly a better alternative to locum work. And going back to Nigeria was certainly not an option.

"I think I will give it a try," I said, "and see what happens."

"Once again, thank you for the cover," he said.

"And thank you for spying on my CV," I said.

And we both laughed.

I went home that weekend. My wife thought the idea of a staff grade was good. At least we would all be together. It would also enable us to make permanent investment plans. But she urged me to look at the drawbacks to the plan.

"How would you feel if someone you had trained came back later to become your boss?" she asked.

"Well, I will deal with that as it comes," I replied. "Hopefully, that wouldn't happen before I left the post."

"But you can't stop them appointing whosoever they want," she cautioned.

"Of course, I know that," I said. "But I also believe that God will provide something better before then."

"Let's keep the faith," she encouraged.

What my wife said made sense, so we prayed about it and allowed God to give a clear direction.

That night, I had a dream in which I was working as a consultant. I had had a dream like that before, but unlike in previous ones, I had to do an examination. I brushed it aside as wishful thinking: those thoughts, wishes and aspirations that lock themselves in various corners of the brain and manifest as dreams.

I narrated the story to my wife, but she disagreed with my interpretation.

"Rather than being a manifestation of your thoughts," she believed, "it is God's own revelation of his plan for you. And He will bring it to pass at his own appointed time."

I returned to Doncaster on Monday morning as usual. As I rushed to the doctors' mess to grab some toast before going to the ward, I bumped into James.

"Have you seen this week's BMJ?" he asked.

"No," I replied. "Will check after work."

"Chesterfield is looking for an experienced staff surgeon. I have mentioned you to the consultants. I think you have a good chance of getting the job. So send in your application as soon as possible."

"Thanks, James," I said, and really meant it.

I was shortlisted for the staff-grade post in Chesterfield, but the interview day clashed with another one in Blackburn. I also had two other interviews coming up the week after. I had more shortlisting for staff-grade posts than I had ever had for other grades.

After an informal visit to Chesterfield, and chatting to the consultants and other members of the surgical team, I fell in love with Chesterfield. I presented the desire of my heart before God, and asked Him to make my wish come true if that was His will.

The process was conducted in a different manner to registrar interviews, with more emphasis on experience. Seven candidates were shortlisted, but one didn't turn up. I believed that all the other candidates were experienced too, and some of them could even be more experienced than me, so I brought my other assets into the discussion – research experience, publications, teaching and non-medical qualifications – to portray my versatility.

I was offered the job.

It made my head swell up when the chairman announced, "We are very honoured and delighted to offer you the post of staff grade in surgery."

Chapter Twenty-Six
DERBYSHIRE

You can learn new things at any time in your life if you're willing
to be a beginner.
If you actually learn to like being a beginner, the whole world
opens up to you.
Barbara Sher

Chesterfield was a commutable distance from Oldham, but I wanted the family to relocate. After all, that was my main reason for taking a staff-grade job. The hospital had given me a robust relocation package, which included free married accommodation pending the sale of our property in Oldham, transportation of the family from Oldham to Chesterfield, and financial help towards carpets and furniture in our new house, so we all looked forward to moving, but I still had to find a school for our children. They had started in a private school, and it was our desire that they continued to receive private education.

We phoned a friend living in Chesterfield for information about local private schools. He and his wife informed us that there was only one, at which their children attended. But they advised us not to bother to apply, saying that the school was oversubscribed. We asked for the name of the school so we could contact them, but they didn't tell us, insisting that there was no point contacting them since they were certain that there was no place for new entrants. The children's excitement died when we informed them that only I would go to Chesterfield since we couldn't find a school for them.

"Does that mean you will be travelling every day again?" our son asked, with his eyes welling up.

"Oh!" Our daughter pulled on the hem of my jacket.

"What shall we do now?" I asked my wife, with regret.

"We will find a solution," my wife reassured me.

I took the children to the park to keep their minds off the

disappointment. When we came back, my wife was all smiles. "God is good all the time," she said. "All the time, God is good."

Whilst I was out with the children, she had called the accommodation manager at the hospital. She gave her the name and the telephone number of the private school that our friends had refused to give us. My wife phoned the school and pleaded with the headmistress that without a suitable school, the family wouldn't be able to relocate. That would mean that I would decline the offer. The headmistress told my wife that she could accommodate our daughter, although that would mean one person more than the recommended number in the classroom. But with regard to our son, the only way she could accommodate him was to split his form into two classes. That was indeed a blessing in disguise, since they had been thinking about doing that for some time. And so, with places secured for our children at St Joseph's Convent School, the family moved into a semi-detached house in the staff residence.

My first day in the hospital was my endoscopy list. My consultant was on holiday, but he had made a list for me. So after signing my contract and collecting my bleep and white coat, I made my way to the endoscopy suite.

"I can't let you do the list," Sally Bulley, the endoscopy sister said, her mouth sprouted, making her look like the Devil, as she showed me to the door.

"I beg your pardon?"

"I won't stand here and see you damage the endoscopes or even worse, kill a patient," she snarled.

"Is this a joke?" I asked, smiling wryly.

"I don't joke with my words," she replied. "I meant everything I said."

"I see," I said, and made my way to the clinical director's office. He was about to go to the outpatient department when I arrived. I informed him of my encounter with the endoscopy sister.

"I'm sorry you had to start that way," he said. "I'll go with you."

Sister Bulley wasn't around when the clinical director arrived. By that time, all ten patients on the list had arrived. Some of them had waited for over an hour.

"We employed you to do the job," the clinical director said. "Now get on with the job and let me see if she has the audacity to stop you." And turning to the nurse, he instructed, "Now send the first patient in." As he was about to leave, he ordered, "Tell Sister Bulley that I need to see her ASAP."

Sister Bulley returned an hour later. I was doing a colonoscopy, having already done nine gastroscopies.

"What!" She startled me as she stepped into the room.

"Sam is a liar," she roared. "I will tell it to his ugly face."

I frowned over to her.

"Yes, Sam Oluchi, the Nigerian doctor; he told me you couldn't do endoscopy," she confessed and shook her head.

"Sam said that?" I smiled. "I see."

"Yes, he said it," she maintained, "but the girls have told me how fantastic you are. And you have proven it. Even the patients are singing your praises. I'm sorry for the way I have treated you."

"No worries," I said.

I followed Sister Bulley to the coffee room, as I really wanted to hear more about what she and Sam had said about me. I wanted to find out what made them discuss me. It would also give me the opportunity to tell her and the girls a little bit about myself. They needed to know that I was an experienced endoscopist.

Sister Bulley told me that when Mr Smart was going on holiday, he sent the endoscopy list in my name. As she was pinning the list to the board, Sam came in.

"I had been told, when I had asked him how to pronounce your name, that you were a Nigerian," she said. "So when Sam came, I asked him if he knew you." She went on to tell me that Sam told her he didn't know much about me. And when she asked him if I was good at endoscopy, he told her that he didn't know. I expressed my disappointment to Sister Bulley. Firstly, I told her that Sam was a close friend of mine, and I was surprised that he told her that.

"I did two-year endoscopic research, and Sam knew about it. How could he say that he didn't know if I could do endoscopy?" I wondered.

"Well, it tells you the kind of person Sam is," she said. "But I will certainly take it up with him."

I left the endoscopy suite with a troubled heart. How could someone I called my friend, someone I trusted, give such a negative recommendation about me? It made me wonder what would have happened if I had informed him about my intention to apply for the Staff Grade post in his hospital. He probably would have either discouraged me or given negative recommendations to the consultants.

As I was going to the ward I bumped onto Sam. He was coming out of the theatre. I related what Sister Bulley had said to him. He brushed it aside, as he said, "I didn't say it like that. I just didn't want them to give you so much work on your first day."

I wondered where else he had talked about me: theatre, ward, outpatient, so that they wouldn't give me things to do on my first day. But I left it to posterity. I left it for people to make their judgment about me, as I carried on with my job.

Mr Tony Smart resumed work after his two-week holiday. A tall handsome man who looked younger than his age, I had met him twice: firstly, at a pre-interview, informal meeting, and secondly, at the interview. He was an embodiment of humility. He treated me like his equal, and I felt uncomfortable about that, since I was his junior colleague. Even when he introduced me to patients, he referred to me as 'my colleague'.

Throughout this posting, I had the opportunity to develop my career further in breast and endocrine surgery, as well as maintaining my competence in General Surgery. Mr Smart involved me in all the activities in his unit and made me feel valued. I felt like I was already a consultant. He also organised training for me in modern aspects of breast disease management. I attended regular teachings and updates, and learnt new techniques.

As I settled into the hospital, my children settled in their new school. My wife was heavily pregnant at this time, and I had hoped that we would have our baby in our new house. But we were yet to find a buyer for our house in Oldham.

Living in the hospital accommodation had an obvious advantage. I didn't have to drive to work, and I could have lunch with my wife. And when she was resting in bed, it was convenient to check on her regularly. It was also easy to arrange taxis to take the children to and from school.

But the house was too small for us as a family, and we couldn't wait to move into our own house.

That Christmas, we planned to spend the festivities with friends, and we hadn't had the chance to check our property in Oldham for a few weeks. A phone call from our neighbour, however, turned our Boxing Day into a nightmare. A pipe had burst from the week-long snow. We raced over there, and when we opened our front door, we discovered that our house had flooded. Our carpet was irreversibly damaged and the furniture was unrecognisable. We had no chance of selling our house in that state. Only a miracle would make it possible to find a buyer. And that miracle came the following day. The estate agent informed us that there was an interested buyer who would like to view our house. Notwithstanding the deplorable state of our house, they placed an offer. That same day, we found our ideal property. We too placed an offer. And as we accepted the offer for our house, so did the sellers of the house in Chesterfield.

God's miracle didn't end in just the sale of our house. Our insurance company was happy to cover us for the damaged carpet and furniture. They did this by offering us a lump sum towards our new house.

Chapter Twenty-Seven
A MOVING GOALPOST

Rise above the storm and you will find the sunshine.
Mario Fernandez

Four years into my staff-grade post, the consultants recommended me for the post of associate specialist to partner Mr Smart in delivering care in breast surgery. Mr Smart, instead, sought the creation of a second consultant post. With the creation and provision for this post, he saw an opportunity for me to become a consultant. They therefore stopped the plan for appointing me as an associate specialist. They would, however, need the college and the GMC approval for my appointment as a permanent consultant, so I was appointed as a locum consultant with a renewable one-year contract.

But whilst in my locum consultant post, the rule changed. The government brought out Articles 11 and 14. Like other sub-consultant doctors, I would have to undergo further training and pass another fellowship examination before I could take up a substantive consultant post. The consultant post, that was within arm's length, was now no more reachable. The goalpost had been moved again.

Mr Smart and the hospital fought unsuccessfully on my behalf to exempt me from these new rules. I was already a trained surgeon, with fellowships of two colleges. And I was already in a consultant position, albeit as locum. What more training did I need? And what was the need for another fellowship examination?

The National Association of Sub-consultant doctors (Staff Grade and Associate Specialist) and the BMA also challenged the changes. I was the secretary of the Chesterfield branch of the group, and we had several national meetings, lobbying the MPs. I wrote a direct petition to the Prime Minister. He wrote back to me, thanking me for my letter, and promised that the government would look into it. After several months of negotiation, the government directed that doctors in the sub-consultant grade would be required to apply to the newly created Specialty Assessment Board. The board was saddled with the responsibility of assessing the doctors and determining the required training for the award of a Certificate of Completion of Specialist Training (CCST).

The Assessment Board recommended one-year further training, another fellowship examination and award of a CCST before I would be eligible to take up a substantive consultant post. But the government didn't provide training posts. Each person would have to find his own job. The training and its completion also had to take place within a prescribed time scale. In effect, this was the same situation as before, when I was going up and down the country to find jobs. The only difference was that there was less chance of the 'You are unlucky' factor, since the government had provided each deanery with extra funds to implement the changes.

Mr Smart worked so hard on my behalf behind the scene, making phone calls and meeting influential people, but the Specialty Assessment Board maintained their decision. I was disappointed at this outcome. But I was also grateful to God for creating an open door for me. I thought the door of opportunity had been locked for ever. I was even more appreciative when I later learnt that some of my sub-consultant colleagues were instructed to undertake three-year training, whilst others had their applications totally rejected.

The board recommended that I did the training in my area of interest. This was a blessing in disguise. I chose to undergo training in oncoplastic breast surgery. This would fulfil my ambition to train in reconstructive surgery, the primary aim of coming to this country. It would also satisfy my interest in surgical oncology. I accepted the verdict, and trusted God to provide an appropriate training post.

Through the relentless efforts of Mr Smart, and by the grace of God, I secured my one-year fixed training contract in oncoplastic breast surgery. At first, I had very little enthusiasm, as I had gone from the level of a trainer to a trainee. But my father used to say that if a farmer focused on the blisters on his palms, he would never harvest. So I put away my negative drives and focused on the prize: the attainment of my goal.

One of my trainers was Patrick Krant, a brilliant South African consultant breast surgeon. A quiet but no-nonsense person, he was supportive to me. We had met several times at breast meetings and training sessions when I was a staff-grade and a locum consultant. He recognised my experience and showed me a great deal of respect. I enjoyed academic meetings whenever Mr Krant was there. He would tear research findings to pieces with his analytical acumen. I learnt from him a critical way of statistical analysis.

The year went faster than I had envisioned, and I learnt various oncoplastic techniques in breast surgery. I also continued in General Surgery, picking up new techniques, as well as sharing my experience in endoscopic and laparoscopic procedures. I knew, of course, the recommendation and prescriptive requirements by the Specialty Assessment Board: to undergo a twelve-month Higher Surgical Training and pass the specialty examination. There was no leeway. Both the training and passing of the examination must be accomplished within twelve months. I was eligible to sit the examination within three months of completion of the post, but I had no money to pay for it. My income had gone down, and my family was again suffering financial strain. One day, just under a week until the closing date for the examination, Mr Krant asked me when I would be sitting the examination. I told him that I had planned to sit the forthcoming one but would have to defer it as I had no money to pay for it.

"That's not going to be a problem," he said. "I'll lend you the money."

I couldn't thank him enough.

I sat the examination and was successful.

Chapter Twenty-Eight
AT LAST

We've removed the ceiling above our dreams.
There are no more impossible dreams.
Jesse Jackson

Having undertaken the prescribed further twelve months of higher surgical training and passed the Specialty Fellowship Examination, I obtained my Certificate of Completion of Specialist Training. My registration changed on the GMC register, and I was now eligible to be appointed to a substantive consultant post. I couldn't return to my previous post in Chesterfield, as it had been taken, but I knew that obtaining a consultant appointment was only a matter of time.

I took up a locum consultant post as soon as I completed my training. I didn't want to rush into a job that I would regret. Unlike a junior job, a consultant contract is permanent. So I had to be certain that I liked the job and the place before applying.

Whenever I attended breast meetings, I had many consultants approach and chat to me about the possibility of joining their departments. One particular hospital requested we visited them. They offered my family and me luxurious hotel accommodation for a weekend, so we could spend time and look round. It was truly a beautiful part of the country, but there were no private schools close by. Moreover, we would be too remote from our friends. And so, regrettably, I had to turn down the offer. I couldn't believe that I, who had been begging for posts for several years, had now become someone who could pick and choose. All of a sudden, my life had been transformed.

Many things happen in life that we can never understand. When God opens the door, no one can lock it. And so with glorious keys of opportunity in my hand, I trusted God to show me the particular door destined for the keys as I kept my eyes and ears open.

Whilst on my locum consultant post, I operated a one-stop colorectal clinic. So when the GP referred a patient with rectal bleeding, I would assess him with a flexible sigmoidoscopy at the same outpatient attendance. As rectal bleeding could be a symptom of colorectal cancer, I ensured that I read all the referral letters and decided which patients were suitable for my junior.

One Friday afternoon, there were ten patients booked to my clinic. The case notes of nine patients were on my desk. I had assumed that the patient whose case notes were missing had failed to turn up, so I had planned to offer her another appointment.

Later, when I thought I had seen everyone that needed to be seen, I was just finishing dictating the last clinic letter when I had a knock on my door. My SHO entered holding a case note.

"Please, will you see this patient?" she asked. "I think she needs a sigmoidoscopy."

"How did you come by her notes?" I asked.

"Sister passed them to me," she replied. "I thought you'd seen her letter."

I checked her name with the computer printout on my desk; it was the patient whose case notes I hadn't been able to find, the one that I thought had failed to attend.

"Sister did what?" I tried to control my anger and sent for the sister to come into my consulting room. She had to give me a good reason to deviate from my usual practice.

Sister breezed into my room with an emotionless face. I couldn't tell if she knew about my query. If she did, she must have played the game of pretence very well.

"Sister, will you please explain to me why you singled out this patient's note and made her see the SHO without my approval?" I asked, with a measured level of tone.

"The patient didn't want to see you," she replied, "so I passed her to the SHO."

"What you are telling me is that the patient didn't want to see me, so you passed her to the most junior member of the team?" I narrowed my eyes.

"It's patient's choice," she said. "And I can't see what is wrong with that."

"Whose clinic is this clinic?" I asked.

"Yours, of course," she replied and scratched her head.

"Which consultant's name is on the GP's referral letter?" I asked.

"It's your name," she replied.

"And who would be doing the sigmoidoscopy?" I asked, trying to control my twitching muscles.

"You, of course," she replied.

"Sister Francis, you know the system very well. You know how I run my clinic," I said. "Whilst I recognise a patient's right of choice, I also believe that the patient has the right to be well informed by the staff to enable her make the right choice."

"Well, I couldn't do anything about that I'm afraid." She was unrepentant.

I ignored Sister Francis for the time being and followed my SHO to her consulting room, where the patient was waiting.

"I want to see the consultant, not you," the seventy-two-year old woman protested as I pulled the blind.

"I am the consultant your GP has referred you to," I said, smiling.

"No, it couldn't be you," she said. "I thought the young lady was the consultant. But if she's not, I would like to book with a consultant, sir."

"By all means," I said and left the room.

After documenting everything, I left the consulting room, hoping to take up the issue with the hospital executives.

Four weeks after the event at the outpatient clinic, I was on call for the weekend. I arrived on Saturday morning to undertake a weekend ward round, and the on-call registrar couldn't go around with me as she was busy on one of the wards. So I went with the SHO and HO. I had wondered what was holding up the registrar, so after I had reviewed all the patients that they had admitted in the night, I made my way to Ward 21. I soon discovered that the registrar had been put on hold by the switchboard, as she tried frantically to contact one of the consultants whose patient had caused her some concern. She had tried to arrange a radiological investigation, but the radiologist had deemed it inappropriate. Upon seeing me, she hung up and reported the case of a seventy-two-year old woman who had a bowel resection more than a week previously. She hadn't opened her bowels. The staff had reported to the registrar that the patient was in a lot of pain. Despite several doses of morphine, her pain remained severe. She now had a swollen and generally tender abdomen with absent bowel sounds. The registrar informed me that she had requested barium studies as she suspected anastomotic dehiscence, but the radiologist had turned down the request and urged her to discuss it with her consultant. At first, I wanted to ask her why she hadn't discussed the case with me rather than chasing up the consultant who wasn't on call. But, on second thought, I ignored that. I directed her to take me to the patient.

The patient lay in bed trying hard to take in deep breaths. Even before I placed my hand on her abdomen, I had no doubt; she had peritonitis. And when I gently pressed her abdomen, she screamed and resisted further pressure. Despite being distended, her abdomen was rigid and bowel sounds were absent. The unequivocal diagnosis was faecal peritonitis, a life-threatening complication. I advised the registrar that the patient needed to go to theatre as soon as possible for laparotomy.

I hadn't realised that this was the patient who had refused to see me four weeks previously since she didn't think I was a consultant. But as I looked through her notes, I saw my entries. I shook my head. I needed to make a decision. The registrar must have guessed what was going through my head. She had read the notes and seen what I had written.

"That was the reason I hadn't informed you about her," she confessed.

"Never mind," I said to her, as I took the patient's case notes and marched back to her bed.

I informed her that she had suffered a serious complication. The joining on her bowel had come apart. She needed to undergo emergency surgery to put it right.

The woman nodded.

"Can you remember me?" I asked.

"Oh, yes, you were the junior doctor that came to the room when the consultant wasn't in the clinic," she recalled.

"Don't be silly, Mrs Daniels," the ward sister cautioned her. "He is a consultant."

"Oh!" Mrs Daniels said. "We don't see many people like him as consultants."

"Well, Mrs Daniels, unfortunately I am the consultant on call this weekend," I informed her. "They have tried unsuccessfully to contact your consultant." After clearing my throat, I continued, "We have three options: We could try and see if we could transfer you to another hospital, hoping to find an approved consultant to do the operation, but I can't guarantee that we will find one that doesn't look like me. And even if we find one, he may advise that you are too sick to be transferred. Another option is to continue to search for your consultant. But I must warn you that every minute counts in peritonitis. The third option is for me to take you to theatre to deal with the complication to save your life."

She didn't have to think twice to condescend. "Please, save my life," she pleaded.

I took the patient to theatre after she had signed her consent form. As suspected, the joining had come apart with both ends of the bowel more than two inches apart. Her abdomen was totally soiled. I cleaned her up and fashioned a colostomy. Her condition was stable throughout the weekend in the intensive care unit.

I bumped onto Mr Fraser in the corridor the following Monday. He was coming from the Intensive Care Unit.

"Your patient is doing well," he said, and took off before I could discuss her with him.

I couldn't explain why Mr Fraser had behaved that way. He didn't have to thank me. As a surgeon I knew, of course, that no surgeon could boast that he had never had a complication. And as it so happened, these complications tended to come at a time when you weren't on call, leaving your colleagues to sort things out. No one earned the pride of sorting out a colleague's complication. We are all in the same family – the family of surgeons, working together in the best interests of the patient. I was unsure if Mr Fraser had behaved that way out of shame or pride, but I found his behaviour to be discourteous. Whatever his motive, I decided to not let that bother me.

When I visited the patient, I noticed that they had changed her consultant. Instead of Mr Fraser, they had put my name on top of her bed. The ICU staff informed me that they did that on the instruction of Mr Fraser. He didn't want to have anything to do with her. He must have thought that she wouldn't make it. But she did. And she was discharged home, fully independent.

I had hoped to take up the job when my locum post was made substantive, but with the behaviour of the likes of Mr Fraser, I turned down the offer, preferring to continue in a locum capacity. I didn't think I would survive in that hospital. It didn't appeal to my heart. I prayed about it and waited on the Lord to give me a clear direction.

I was at the Nottingham International Breast Cancer Conference when Dr Liz Seaman, consultant radiologist and director of breast screening, approached me. I had met her before, and we were in the same group at a workshop in one of the previous meetings. She told me that their breast surgeon would soon be retiring. They needed a surgeon with fresh ideas to help establish specialist breast services. This sounded interesting. It was the type of position that I liked. But I told her to give me time to think about it. I took her number and promised to call.

The following day, I received a phone call from the medical director of Barnsley Hospital. He invited me for a chat. I had two interviews coming up the following week.

"Where have you hidden yourself?" the medical director asked me. "We have searched everywhere for someone like you."

"I am greatly honoured," I said. "Thank you."

The medical director took me around the hospital. I also had the opportunity to meet my prospective surgical colleagues. As I toured the moderate-size, district general hospital, my heart felt at ease. My first impression was the friendly staff. Almost everyone we met gave their best smiles and greeted us. Everyone made me feel as if I was already part of them.

"So what do you think?" the medical director asked me at the end of my tour.

"I think I would like to join the team of happy people," I replied.

"That's what we like to hear," he said, smiling.

Of course, I would have loved to join them, but I was on a six-month locum consultant post. I would need to resign from the post before starting in Barnsley. So the plan was for me to start as a locum, pending the formal advertisement of the job, which they were required by law to do.

I had no problem resigning my locum post. As a matter of fact, the medical director had already informed them of my decision to join them in Barnsley.

My locum role was in gastrointestinal surgery, which of course I had vast experience in, but my desire and major area of interest was in breast oncoplasty. My employers understood and they were happy to release me the following week.

As I accepted the job in Barnsley, I remembered the biblical story of Joseph. The Jewish captive was locked up in Egyptian prison, but they couldn't lock his talent away. No one could prevent him from fulfilling his destiny. At God's appointed time, Joseph's talent was revealed to Pharaoh, and he rose from the position of a slave to that of a master. People had tried to hide my talent like a candle under the bushels, but God provided a glorious candlestick and placed it on a high table for all to see. I thanked God from the bottom of my heart for His faithfulness.

After a month in the job, it was formally advertised, and I had the privilege of writing my own job description.

Within one month in the hospital, I had patients and staff singing my praises. My breast care nurses were fantastic. I brought dynamism and enthusiasm to the breast multidisciplinary team, and my nurses received training in pre-operative and post-operative management of patients undergoing mastectomy and immediate reconstruction. I also trained them in recognition and aspiration of seroma after breast surgery. So the breast services were transformed just within a month. The management team and colleagues appreciated the innovative endeavours that I brought, and I was glad that they confirmed my substantive post with the successful outcome of my interview.

Having had my post confirmed, I settled down to work towards my vision for breast services in Barnsley. And I couldn't have come at a better time. The hospital had a plan for expansion and modernisation. Expansion of the breast services was part of the plan. It was agreed to build an ultramodern, dedicated breast department as part of the multi-million-pound project. With my leadership, we came up with a design that was within budget, with radiologist and pathologist input for a one-stop, triple-assessment clinic.

Our outcome data in mortality and breast-screening uptake rate were above local and national average, and our mastectomy rate was comparatively low. I also trained in the use of a handheld ultrasound scanner. This was a valuable asset.

Being able to offer breast reconstruction was my greatest source of satisfaction as a consultant breast surgeon. No cancer is good. No one wants to be diagnosed with cancer, and it is so emotive. It gladdened me to see women, whom I had treated, return looking like their breasts hadn't been removed. With ultramodern radiological equipment and experienced radiologists able to offer accurate marking of cancers that couldn't be felt, we were able to offer our patients breast conservation procedures.

In addition to my clinical work, I chaired the breast cancer multidisciplinary team. I became the lead surgeon in breast surgery, the chairman of breast cancer steering group, and I was appointed the Royal College of Surgeons College tutor and honorary senior lecturer at the University of Sheffield. I was a higher surgical trainer, passing my experiences and surgical principles to future generations.

But with fame comes responsibility. The demand for care under me rose exponentially. Patients came from neighbouring trusts, all wanting to have me manage their cancers. Those who had the financial means chose to consult me privately, just to ensure that I was personally involved in their care. Such was the case of a twenty-two-year old, newly married woman. She found a lump in her breast whilst on her honeymoon. Her doctor reassured her it was a fibroadenoma, a non-cancerous growth, and referred her to her local hospital, where they reassured her. Her friend, however, who had been my house officer, then training to be a GP, directed her to me. Despite her young age, it was clear to me that the lump was cancerous, and imaging and histology confirmed the cancer. The woman had a strong family genealogy, her mother and grandmother died of breast cancer. One of her aunts, who was still alive, also had the disease.

Eventually, the volume of work became too much for me alone to cope with. We had colleagues from Sheffield helping out, but I still struggled to cope. At last, we appointed a second consultant. Miss Arista Cannon was brilliant on paper. Her CV was mind-blowing and her presentation at the interview was captivating. It all seemed too good to be true and made me wonder why a surgeon with such brilliant credentials waited until her fifties before her first substantive consultant appointment. But judging by my own experiences, I gave her the benefit of the doubt.

No sooner had Miss Cannon joined than she began to show her real self. Her first decision was to direct the appointments' clerks that all GP referrals should be sent to her. This was never discussed with me or any of the breast secretaries. I had wondered why my cancer cases had gone down, so I audited our referrals. It was then that the appointment clerks confirmed the instructions that Miss Cannon had given. She had been directing cancer cases to herself and non-cancerous ones to me. When I asked her, she told me it was to relieve me of too much work. But, as a matter of fact, it was for her own selfish interest. By having many patients waiting for surgery, some of them would decide to see her privately to expedite their surgery.

In her first month, the breast care nurses reported their concerns. Three reconstruction patients under her care had serious complications. I discussed these concerns with her and suggested that we had one joint list for reconstructive procedures. This would enable us to share experiences. My plan was to provide her the opportunity to learn.

"Are you suggesting that I don't know how to operate?" she asked.

"No," I replied. "I only thought we could learn from each other. People have known me for many years. And if we have a complication, they will be less likely to complain. And even if they do, it will be a collective responsibility."

Miss Cannon declined my advice. She continued to undertake the procedures, causing complications on a weekly basis. These concerned me, and I again raised my concerns with her. I even suggested that I would support her in her training needs, but she declined my offer once again, claiming that she had worked with eminent breast surgeons. She didn't have any training needs.

One day, I was in my office. I had no clinical commitment that afternoon, which was set aside for support programme activities (SPA). I had a phone call from the breast unit. One of Miss Cannon's patients had come to see her, as she had problems with her reconstructed breast. She had her operation three weeks previously and had been coming to see her thrice a week. Miss Cannon had advised her not to see anyone else, as she was the only person who would know what to do. Whenever she attended, Miss Cannon would do the change of dressing herself. Normally, the patient would phone her directly before coming to the breast unit. On this day, she had called her several times, but she didn't answer. So as the patient was concerned, she made her way to the breast unit for someone to have a look.

I could smell the foul odour as I stepped into the main corridor of the breast unit. It needed no professional to recognise a necrotic tissue. The flap had totally necrosed. The implant showed through the necrotic, overlying skin.

I called Miss Cannon several times and left messages for her to return my call so we could discuss the patient. But she ignored me. I had to act in the best interests of the patient, and so I organised for the patient to be taken to theatre to tidy things up for her.

Miss Cannon came to work the following day and was angry that 'someone' had operated on her patient. Even when they informed her that I tried to rescue the situation, she blatantly ignored me.

The situation got out of hand as the patient involved the press. The story was published in the local and national newspapers. Even with the media publicity, she still maintained that the way she had performed the procedure was the standard way, something that even a registrar wouldn't do. Following the publicity, many more patients came out. Those were the patients that had had complicated procedures and bad outcomes. She had kept them away from other members of the team as a cover-up for her failures.

My heart was heavy. It hurt me badly. All the efforts that we had put in for many years were brought into disrepute by just one person's uncaring attitude.

Whilst I was busy trying to sort out the mess that my colleague had caused in the department, I received a message that my mother was critically ill. I sought the favour of God. And the Lord intervened. I received an email from my wonderful friend, Dr Wole Kukoyi. He confirmed my mother's illness. He told me not to panic and that he had admitted her into his hospital. When I thanked him, he replied, "I know you would do even more for me if it was you." That is who Wole is – an embodiment of humility and a kind-hearted, God-fearing person.

My mother spent three months in Wole's hospital, without any financial burden on me, and by the grace of God, made a full recovery. By the time that I travelled to Nigeria, she had been discharged. I was glad to be with my mother once again and I thanked God for her recovery. Not many friends could have been so gracious. I felt honoured and privileged. This was the teenage boy with whom I did my preliminary medicine in Ibadan. We did everything together as medical students and maintained our friendship up till this day. He hasn't changed from when I first met him, except that his heart is now even bigger, as he continues to do good. Having Wole to see to the welfare of my parents took the pressure off me and enabled me to focus on my work. I am eternally grateful to God. I pray that God continues to show special favour to him and his family.

When I returned from my visit to Nigeria, the situation with my colleague's conduct had become the headline in most of the popular papers. But with the timely intervention of the hospital authority and the GMC, she was relieved of her post, and we heaved a sigh of relief.

Around that time, I was selected to make a presentation at a conference in Hamburg. It was an honour. It was also an opportunity to visit the beautiful city. My wife accompanied me to the week-long conference. I presented my data on breast conservation surgery and the outcomes of immediate reconstruction in a district hospital setting. After my presentation, I stood by my poster among other poster presentations.

"I knew you would make it," Professor Rainer said. "You made us proud."

I hadn't seen him since my meeting with him, when he advised me to go and divorce my wife and marry an English girl. That that same person could congratulate me with such enthusiasm beat my imagination.

"Yes, I have made it," I said, "and I am glad about it."

He smiled and left my station. I bumped into him a few more times and he grinned at me. I was proud of myself and thankful to God. A few years previously, he was a tin-God. But now, we were equals, rubbing shoulders, each of us forming opinions and defending them. I held no grudges against him or anyone for that matter. But I had no doubt that his conscience must have reminded him of that day when he thought little of me.

The Hamburg conference and my encounter with Professor Rainer will never leave my memory. I felt good, and was sincerely grateful to God. Sometimes in life, you don't need to fight people who wrong you. Let them live with their guilt for ever.

As I sat in my office, I tried to put all these things behind me. It had taken me a long time to reach my goal, but my journey has provided me several opportunities to understand God's character. God works in a way that we don't understand. His way is perfect and He does things when He chooses. I have learnt to put my trust in Him, knowing that no matter what I go through, it's all for my good. As his Word says, "And we know that all things work together for good to them that love God, to them who are called according to his purpose." Romans 8:28 (KJV). These powerful words of faith have been my source of inspiration in my times of despair and seemingly disappointing moments. And in those moments, I rest assured that God's sure "goodness and mercy will follow me all the days of my life …"

God's faithfulness extends beyond my professional realms. This was the case on one of our wedding anniversary trips to Venice. We missed our connection at Amsterdam, owing to flight delay. We checked into a hotel to make a fresh connection later in the morning. The time was around one o'clock. We were desperately hungry. We had no euros, but their machine wasn't working, so we couldn't pay by our credit or debit card. As we contemplated what to do, a young man appeared behind us. He offered to pay for our meal and even ordered drinks and another pack to take away. What intrigued me was that this man didn't buy a meal for himself. He left as soon as he paid for ours. Later, we tried the phone number that he had given us, but that number didn't exist.

On the same trip to Venice, we returned late in the night after a shopping trip to Milan. We hadn't realised that the water boats stopped services at ten in the night. We arrived at the bus terminus in Venice after the services had stopped. We needed transport to take us to our hotel in Lido, an island about forty minutes from the bus terminus. It was a cold and wet winter night. As the water boats had stopped their runs, we stood at the station, stranded, hungry and cold. We tried to check into another hotel just for the night, but there was no vacancy anywhere. Left on our own, with no hope of finding shelter for the night, my wife and I cried in desperation to God for a miracle. And that miracle came just before midnight. A woman, probably in her twenties surfaced from nowhere.

"Are you waiting for transport?" she asked, in English with a great degree of fluency.

"Yes," we replied simultaneously, "but it looks like we are not going to find one this time of the night."

"The boats have closed," she informed us. "Services close at ten."

"What shall we do now?" we asked. "Do you know where we can find a hotel with vacancies?"

"No need for that," she said. "Don't despair; a boat will come your way in the next few minutes."

Ten minutes later, a boat showed up. The woman waved at the driver and he stopped. After speaking with him in Italian, the driver beckoned us to embark. I had thought that the woman was stranded like us, but after we embarked, she simply waved us off and disappeared into the heart of Venice. The boat driver told us that he had closed for the day, and he was on his way to park his boat. He wouldn't normally take that route, and he didn't know why he chose to. This couldn't be anything but divine intervention. He didn't take any fare from us. God answers even little prayers if you care to trust Him.

Back in my office after my holiday, I am having a fresh cup of coffee after a four-hour mastectomy and immediate reconstruction. My eyes settle on the heap of *Thank You* cards on the cabinet. These are from men and women whose lives I have saved and whom I have relieved their pains and given hope. And then I stare at the framed photograph of my parents on the window, which gave me nostalgia. Despite my success, I have some regrets. I wished I was back home using the skills that I have acquired to help my suffering people. And I wished I could be with my parents in their old age. Nevertheless, I have every reason to thank God. I had set a goal and have travelled on hard and bumpy road in pursuit of this goal. The journey was long, but by the grace of God, I got there in the end.

As I take another sip at my coffee, my mind travels back to the woman with advanced breast cancer who came to see me in the Mobile Clinic whilst working in Kwale decades ago. How I wished I had this level of expertise then. I sympathise with millions of people in my native land who are suffering. But I have no regrets, for if I do, I am not being grateful to God and to the country that has given me a happy home and the opportunity to show my talents and fulfil God's plans for my life. God decided to take me out of my country of birth to fulfil my destiny, for which I am grateful.

I feel fulfilled and accomplished. That village boy who was looked down upon as a hopeless child has now risen to stardom. Although I still live in a village it is not like my home village in which I ran up and down in tattered clothes and bare feet. It is a village where I share a good life with the elites of the society.

My life is a story of success, and as I reflect, it confirms what my parents have planted in my mind: Nothing is impossible. Obstacles will always come your way, and some people will try to stop or change you. With perseverance, prayer and belief in yourself, you will succeed. There is still a lot that has happened in my life, breakthroughs that I have had and so many people that God has brought into my life to make me fully accomplished. I cannot mention all the individuals, not because they have contributed less, but there is no scope in this book to mention everyone. And as I put a full stop to this writing, I couldn't but give God the glory. My journey has not ended, but here is a convenient place to stop.

The End